Y0-DLE-066

THE
ASCENDED MASTERS
ON SOUL MATES AND TWIN FLAMES

Shiva, Parvati and their son Skanda

THE ASCENDED MASTERS

Initiation by the Great White Brotherhood

ON SOUL MATES AND TWIN FLAMES

BOOK I

PEARLS OF WISDOM
TEACHINGS OF THE ASCENDED MASTERS
Mark L. Prophet • Elizabeth Clare Prophet
VOLUME TWENTY-EIGHT • 1985

SUMMIT UNIVERSITY ◆ PRESS®

The Ascended Masters
on Soul Mates and Twin Flames
Initiation by the Great White Brotherhood

Pearls of Wisdom 1985
Volume Twenty-Eight   Book One

Published by
The Summit Lighthouse®
for Church Universal and Triumphant®

Copyright © 1981, 1983, 1985, 1986, 1988
by Church Universal and Triumphant, Inc. All rights reserved.

No part of this book may be reproduced
in any form or by any electronic or mechanical means
including information storage and retrieval systems
without permission in writing from the publisher, except
by a reviewer who may quote brief passages in a review.
For information, write or call Summit University Press,
Box A, Livingston, MT 59047-1390. Telephone: (406) 222-8300.

Pearls of Wisdom, The Summit Lighthouse, Church Universal
and Triumphant, Summit University Press, and ꙮ are registered
trademarks of Church Universal and Triumphant, Inc.
All rights to their use are reserved.

LIBRARY OF CONGRESS CATALOG CARD NUMBER: 87-62297

INTERNATIONAL STANDARD BOOK NUMBER: 0-916766-85-3

Printed in the United States of America

Summit University Press®
First Printing

The Divine Lovers

The attributes of God's Power, Wisdom and Love appear archetypically in the Twin Flames of the Father/Mother God. Hinduism has uniquely conceptualized the Divine Personalities of the Trinity and given them specific names: Brahma and Sarasvati, Vishnu and Lakshmi, Shiva and Parvati. Let us contemplate the Truth and Beauty of God defined by these Divine Lovers.

In this relationship of the Divine Absolutes, the Father Principle is thesis, the Mother Principle is antithesis and their synthesis produces the Christ Consciousness with which they endow the sons and daughters of God. The Masculine, or Spirit, aspect of this Divine Polarity, being inactive in the manifest creation, requires the activating force, the Feminine aspect who is *Shakti,* to release the God potential from Spirit to Matter.

The term *Matter,* derived from the Latin *Mater* 'mother' connotes the world of *mater*ialization, or *Mater realization.* The Matter Cosmos is, then, the womb of creation wherein the Divine Mother actuates physical *phenomenon* born out of the seed (the so-called spiritual *noumenon)* of Spirit. And Spirit's Cosmos—the origin of all Immutable Ideas which become clothed with material form—is sustained by the Divine Father through the Law of Causation.

Thus the Divine Lovers who represent the Trinity hold the entire Spirit/Matter Cosmos and all the evolutions of God in the antahkarana* of their Power, Wisdom and Love. And when the twin flames of their sons and daughters return to the Great Central Sun, they celebrate the Holy Communion of Alpha and Omega—the ultimate reunion in the Trinity of their God Parents whereby the creative reason for Being is fully realized. In the ritual of the soul's ascension to the heart of the I AM

---

*antahkarana [Sanskrit 'internal sense organ']: the web of Life; the net of light spanning Spirit and Matter, connecting and sensitizing the whole of creation within itself and to the heart of God.

THAT I AM in the white fire core of Being, the issue of God, as twin flames made in the image and likeness of the Divine Us *(Elohim)*, are become God in the same triune manifestation out of whose Flame they were created in the Beginning.

For twin flames spiraling to the Sun by the law of cycles, the first of a thousand times ten thousand steps is to know the Divine Lovers, our God Parents, as they appear to us in each of the offices of the Trinity. Wherefore they have endowed us with the Threefold Flame in our hearts, the divine spark, that we might realize their God Consciousness and Divine Personality.

This Flame has three plumes—the blue, yellow, and pink—and resembles a fleur-de-lis. As we get to know our Father/Mother God who appear to us in this triune way in order to unveil the mysteries of their glorious Power, Wisdom and Love, let us remember that we may become all that we see and know and love of our Creator *because* this Threefold Flame—this flaming Trinity of our hearts—bestows upon us the full potential for Godhood. For in this Tri-Unity we behold the redundancy of the Divine Image that is reflected in our twin flames. And by the geometry of this Tri-Angle of our God Identity, things equal to the same thing are equal to each other: We *are* One in and as the Father/Mother God!

The first plume, the blue, denotes the attribute of Power. The Divine Lovers fulfilling its plus/minus interchange are Brahma and Sarasvati, who exemplify the masculine and feminine embodiment of the Cosmic Force. Brahma as Father-figure, the First Person of the Trinity, is the Immense Being—the Creator, Supreme Ruler, Lawgiver, Sustainer, and Source of All Knowledge. He is Godly omnipotence incarnate.

Sarasvati represents eloquence, the Mother who articulates the Wisdom of the Law. She is Mother/Teacher to those who love the Law as God's will revealed by Brahma. Thus she is Shakti, the All-Power of volition, the will and motivation to be the Law *in action,* the Source, the river and the riverbed, that sets the worlds in motion. Out of her belly flows universal knowledge as abundant appreciation for the Law of the Creator self-contained in every particle of the creation. The whirling of electrons, atoms and universes untold are the workings of her Universal Mind.

All hail, Brahma and Sarasvati, the All-Knowing Mind of God!

The Divine Lovers

The God-pair in polarity who comprise the Law of the One on the second plume, the yellow, in the attribute of Wisdom are Vishnu and Lakshmi. As is the case in all three pairs, each encompasses all of the qualities attributed to the other, which they lovingly share and divinely surrender in the whirling sphere, the T'ai Chi, of their Oneness. Thus, in heaven the plus and the minus equals One individed Whole.

In the shining splendor of the Sun, Vishnu, the immortal Son, the Second Person of the Trinity, stands as the embodiment of Cosmic Christ Wisdom whose essence is duration, the enduring quality of omniscience, the continuity of the consciousness of God. He is cohesiveness personified, bonding by Wisdom's Love the cosmic forces conceived in the All-Knowing Mind. His way is liberation by Self-knowledge in the Highest God Self.

Vishnu, whose more famous incarnations have been Rama and Krishna (always manifesting the qualities of Hari*), is the all-pervading Protector—protecting the Son in manifestation by God-awareness of both Self and anti-Self. He wields the sword of the Word for the annihilation by Wisdom's fire of the forces of the anti-Self that would steal the Light of that True Self before it is self-realized in the issue of God. This personification of the Godhead is the Preserver of the divine design conceived in Wisdom's flame out of Power's lawful Presence. Vishnu is the Restorer of the universe by Wisdom's all-healing Light, by the Science of Mind that is the true Power of illumination's alchemy of Love.

Lakshmi, Vishnu's consort, is eternally identifiable as the polarity of all that he is. She is Wisdom unveiled in blessings of prosperity, the precipitation of abundance by the science of *Prakriti*† and *Purusha*‡ and the control of the four cosmic forces. She bears a cornucopia of good fortune by the 'eye-magic' of the all-seeing eye of her Beloved. She teaches the mastery of karmic cycles on the cosmic clock, and multiplicity and beauty out of the Law of the One. Herself the Beautiful Mother, she mirrors the image of Wisdom's God as health and holiness to her children.

Hail to the Word Incarnate of Vishnu/Lakshmi!

---

*Hari is a name for Vishnu, sometimes rendered "the Remover of Sorrow"; thought to be derived from *hri* 'to take away or remove evil or sin'. †*Prakriti:* [prüh-kruh-tee] Sanskrit; Hindu term meaning the original or natural form or condition of anything; cause or original source of the material world; matter, Nature.
‡*Purusha:* [pů-roosh] Sanskrit; man, soul or spirit; the animating principle in man; the Spirit as passive, as distinct from *Prakriti*, the active, or creative, force.

So, too, the Holy Spirit, the Third Person of the Trinity, comes alive in the charming personages of Shiva and his Shakti. Each one a sphere of wholeness yet simultaneously a half of the other, they are divine complements of the third plume, the pink, denoting the attribute of Love. They stand as living proof before all twin flames in Love that the opposite of Divine Love is not hatred but the balance, whether of masculine or feminine charge, of compassion—of kindness chastening with firmness, giving and receiving gratitude as active and passive modes of appreciation of the same verb, "to love."

The dual nature of Shiva, the Lord of Love, himself the Destroyer/Deliverer, is complemented by his consort who in manifold form is both demon slayer and child saver. As Parvati, benign "daughter of the mountain," she is the beneficent, gentle Mother and Wife. Her union with Shiva is a prototype of the ideal marriage. A beautiful, gracious woman, she is often depicted in domestic scenes with Shiva or seated beside him in discourse. Shiva and Parvati sometimes appear with their son Skanda, also known as Karttikeya, who is identified in the *Chandogya Upanishad* with the sage god Sanat Kumara (see frontispiece).

Shiva and Shakti are the omnipresence of Love in action. As such they take many forms, moving as 'cloven tongues of fire' to the side of their children assailed by sinister forces of Death and Hell. Shiva is known for his whirling cosmic dance that dispels by fohatic keys the ignorance and ignominy of all forces of anti-Love.

Durga is another manifestation of Shiva's consort, fierce defender of her children, terrible and menacing to her enemies—the "Goddess Beyond Reach." Kali, a third metamorphosis of Shiva's feminine nature, represents the supreme night of the Mother that swallows up the grid of karma and the time/space worlds that contain it. She complements Shiva's Power in the destruction, by Love, of the energy veil (illusion). She is the Mother who lays down her life for the Cause of her consort and her children. Her dread appearance is the symbol of her boundless Power.

Glory to Shiva and Parvati, God Parents of Sanat Kumara!

The path of fiery Love, which is God's all-consuming sacred fire, consumes even the forces of Anti-Power, Anti-Wisdom and Anti-Love, the Absolute Evil of reprobate angels against the Godhead. For Divine Love is more than Love—it is Power and Wisdom self-contained all in One—and then some. And herein lies Love's mystery. Love is more than effect or lesser causation, it is First Cause and the point of Light beyond all light and darkness. Love is all Love excelling beyond Love's visible expressions and interchanges. Love is the unbeatable cosmic force!

And Lord Shiva is just that diamond hardness, that indomitable ruby ray everywhere anywhere you need him to defend the sacred fire of twin flames. Because he is the Holy Spirit, Shiva is the most active and most loved member of the Trinity. For his fiery discipline, his all-forgivingness, and simply his adorableness, Shiva is the cherished Friend of the chela in distress who need only shout the distress call, Shiva! Shiva! Shiva! to discover how the Shiva/Shakti of a cosmos will come to the rescue.

Thus, by the Threefold Flame connection, the true Love of the Divine Lovers in its very magic can still be known by twin flames dwelling in the twilight zone of adulterated love. For the Love of our Father/Mother God is always pure and does not contain within itself any self-polluting, self-mutilating force such as fear of failure, fear of Truth, fear of Life. Nor the fear to be Power, Wisdom and Love in action—the Shakti in the Matter Cosmos of Brahma, Vishnu, Shiva, the World Mother, the Three in One!

No interplays or power plays of human psychology can mar our Trinity of Love but these can and do mar human love in incubation waiting, tending the flocks of consciousness until the angel of the LORD should trouble the waters of the mind and raise a single drop to the Sun whereby the whole fabric of human love surrenders in the embrace of the Divine.

True Love is always understanding, yet not necessarily always understood. It speaks with the Shepherd's voice of authority, never the petty tyrant; it chastens, peeling away by its caressing flames the layers of self-deception. The love of our God Parents, expressed in Wisdom's rod, alone can bind the tyrant ego of child-man and set free the captive soul.

From Christ's heart of true Love, then, the words "Father, forgive them, for they know not what they do" are easily uttered.

Love has no imitators, for God alone is Love.

Contents

On Soul Mates and Twin Flames   Following Page

In Search of the Power of Moses
Reclaiming Our Spiritual Heritage
The Illumination of the Scriptures .... *xviii*

Love, Marriage and Beyond 132

Soul Mates and Twin Flames
The Quest for Wholeness 228

Love Wins Out
In This Lifetime... or the Next
The Story of Jeanette MacDonald and Nelson Eddy ... 324

Pearl Number	Date Dictated		Pearl Date	Page Number

New Year's Light of the World
"I AM the Light of the World... You Are the Light of the World"
December 27, 1984 – January 1, 1985
Camelot, Los Angeles, California

I

1   Keep the Trust!
     Beloved Mother Mary .... January 6   1
     (December 27, 1984)

II

2   The Judgment of Peshu Alga
     Beloved Archangel Michael .... January 13   13
     (December 29, 1984)

III

3   The Process and the Procession of Liberty
     Beloved Arcturus .... January 20   27
     (December 30, 1984)

IV

4   The Sign of Excalibur
     Beloved Lanello .... January 27   37
     (December 31, 1984)

V

5   Qualifying World Teachers to Dispense
the Illumination of the New Age
Beloved Archangel Jophiel .... February 3   45
(December 31, 1984)

We Work While We Have the Light!
Beloved Archangel Uriel 54
(December 31, 1984)

VI

6   Gentle Hearts and Gentle Candles
New Year's Eve Address by the Lord of the World
Release of the Thoughtform for the Year 1985
Beloved Gautama Buddha .... February 10   57
(December 31, 1984)

The Turning Point of Life on Earth:
A Dispensation of the Solar Logoi
Beloved Sanat Kumara 60
(December 31, 1984)

VII

7   New Love
Beloved Vesta .... February 17   67
(January 1, 1985)

---

8   The Battle of Armageddon
in the Classrooms of America
Beloved God and Goddess Meru ... February 24   71
(January 6, 1985)

9   Remember the Ancient Encounter
On Discipleship under Lord Maitreya
Beloved Kuthumi................... March 3   81
(January 27, 1985)

Celestial Order of the Child
Mark L. Prophet......................... 100

10   The Summoning: Straight Talk and a Sword
from the Hierarch of Banff
Beloved Archangel Michael .... March 10   101
(February 3, 1985)

11 Chela—Christed One—Guru
    Offices on the Path of the Individualization
    of the God Flame
    Beloved El Morya....................March 17   123
    (February 3, 1985)

12 Send-off of the Messenger's Stump to the Nations:
    We Seek a Change of World Consciousness
    Beloved Saint Germain ....March 24   133
    (February 10, 1985)

13 The Lord's Promise of Deliverance
    A Sermon to the People of the Philippines
    by Elizabeth Clare Prophet
    The Beloved Messenger ....March 31   149
    (March 3, 1985)

14 The Lord's Prophecy unto the Philippines
    Beloved Saint Germain................April 7   155
    (March 3, 1985)

15 Saint Patrick's Day Address
    by Elizabeth Clare Prophet
    The Beloved Messenger ....April 14   167
    (March 17, 1985)

16 I Call the Living Saints
    Beloved Saint Patrick ....April 21 203
    (March 17, 1985)

17 Palm Sunday 1985
    The Mission of a Living Flame
    The Triumphal Entry of the Buddha of the Ruby Ray
    Beloved Zarathustra...................April 28 215
    (March 31, 1985)

Easter Conclave at Camelot
"Come, leave your nets—I will make you fishers of men."
April 3 – 7, 1985
Camelot, Los Angeles, California

I

18 Love's Fulfillment of the Law
    in Christ—His Messengers,
    His Apostles, His Disciples and His Community
    John the Beloved.....................May 5   229
    (April 4, 1985)

Contents

II

19 Archangel Michael's Rosary
   For Armageddon
   The Beloved Messenger .... May 12   243
   (April 5, 1985)

III

20 We Shall Have the Victory!
   They Shall Not Pass, in the Name of Almighty God!
   Beloved Archangel Michael .... May 19   265
   (April 5, 1985)

IV

21 Profile of the Woman Initiate
   The Hour of the Raising of the Feminine Ray
   Beloved Lady Master Venus .... May 26   271
   (April 5, 1985)

V

22 Called of God
   Seraphic Purging of Sons and Daughters
   before the Living Flame of God
   Beloved Justinius .... June 2   283
   (April 6, 1985)

VI

23 The Lord's Day
   Jesus' Message for the Revolutionaries of the Spirit
   Beloved Jesus Christ .... June 9   295
   (April 7, 1985)

VII

24 The Sun behind the Sun
   God-Government and the Dedication to Truth
   Beloved Surya .... June 16   309
   (April 7, 1985)

Index of Scripture 325

Index 330

Contacting his amanuensis Mark L. Prophet in Washington, D.C., the Ascended Master El Morya, Chief of the Darjeeling Council of the Great White Brotherhood, founded The Summit Lighthouse in August 1958 for the purpose of publishing the teachings of the Ascended Masters. The anointed Messengers Mark and Elizabeth Prophet were trained by their Guru El Morya to receive the Word of the LORD in the form of both spoken and written dictations from the Ascended Masters. Since 1958, the personal instruction of the Masters to their chelas in every nation has been published in weekly letters called Pearls of Wisdom. Before his ascension on February 26, 1973, Mark L. Prophet transferred the mantle of the mission to Elizabeth Clare Prophet, who continues to set forth the mysteries of the Holy Grail in current Pearls of Wisdom, Keepers of the Flame Lessons, and at Summit University. These activities, headquartered at the New Age community at the Royal Teton Ranch in Montana, are sponsored by the Brotherhood as the foundation of the culture and religion of Aquarius. For information on other volumes of Pearls of Wisdom published since 1958 and numerous books and audio- and videocassettes distributed by The Summit Lighthouse, write for a free catalog.

The Ascended Master El Morya
Chief of the Darjeeling Council of the Great White Brotherhood

The Messenger Mark L. Prophet

The Messenger Elizabeth Clare Prophet

Then shall the kingdom of heaven be likened unto ten virgins, which took their lamps, and went forth to meet the bridegroom.

And five of them were wise, and five were foolish.

They that were foolish took their lamps, and took no oil with them: But the wise took oil in their vessels with their lamps.

While the bridegroom tarried, they all slumbered and slept.

And at midnight there was a cry made, Behold, the bridegroom cometh; go ye out to meet him.

Then all those virgins arose, and trimmed their lamps. And the foolish said unto the wise, Give us of your oil; for our lamps are gone out.

But the wise answered, saying, Not so; lest there be not enough for us and you: but go ye rather to them that sell, and buy for yourselves.

And while they went to buy, the bridegroom came; and they that were ready went in with him to the marriage: and the door was shut.

Afterward came also the other virgins, saying, Lord, Lord, open to us. But he answered and said, Verily I say unto you, I know you not.

Watch therefore, for ye know neither the day nor the hour wherein the Son of man cometh.

Jesus

IN SEARCH OF
THE POWER OF MOSES

RECLAIMING OUR SPIRITUAL HERITAGE

The Illumination of the Scriptures
by Elizabeth Clare Prophet

How to contact the Presence of God which appeared to Moses in the burning bush to help yourself, your loved ones, your nation and world.

I want to tell you about our ancient spiritual heritage—one discovered by the greatest revolutionaries of all time, East and West, who brought together and focused the ancient scriptures on a certain purpose and calling. But somehow in today's world, we have lost the threads that tie it all together.

We see challenges in every nation, in all strata of human events. Most of us feel helpless to make any change whatsoever. Our hearts are burdened by the oppressions of people in many nations, under many, many sorts of tyranny.

I see those who come to the place where their concern for loved ones and for the nations is great enough to impel them to seek God, to find him, to want to know the science that unlocks the Light. The Light is the means whereby we may truly banish war from the earth, whereby we will no longer have need for nuclear weapons or be beset with the manipulations of our economy, our supply, and our very bodies by the pollutions that are put upon us.

We need divine solutions to human problems and these solutions I would like to share with you.

The healing of the nations begins with the healing of ourselves. We must draw forth from the Great Central Sun—the highest concentration of Spirit in our universe, the Great Source of light and energy—that eternal Light with which we were anointed from the beginning.

We can trace our spiritual lineage back to Moses, God's messenger to the children of Israel, who was the witness of an extraordinary manifestation of God's Presence.

Let us discover who is that I AM THAT I AM, that Presence of God, and how each of us can release that Light from our hearts for immediate action in this city and nation to the highest interests of all people. From the base of the pyramid of life to its apex, we find that the blessing of God resolves all human problems.

Now Moses was in the mountain Horeb, the mountain of God, tending his father-in-law's sheep, as it is recorded in Exodus, chapter three.

"And the angel of the LORD appeared unto him in a flame of fire out of the midst of a bush." Out of the very midst of a bush, an ordinary bush, a sacred fire is burning, "and he looked, and, behold, the bush burned with fire, and the bush was not consumed."

I am the bush, you are the bush, and the great symbology and teaching of our God is this: it is that that which is common may become extraordinary by the descent of the sacred fire of God. God has placed the divine spark within you; it is tiny. It must be fanned with devotion, with meditation, with love for him.

And the voice of God called Moses for the liberation of the people. That same voice that called to Moses calls to you and me, each one of us, individually today: "Let my people go!" We cannot ignore it. Though we would pursue a life of pleasure and all kinds of personal interests, the voice comes back and back again. It is the voice of the I AM THAT I AM.

And so what happens? "God called unto him out of the midst of the bush, and said, Moses, Moses." He was calling to his soul. He was quickening the ancient memory of Moses who had come from God to save a mighty people.

So your divinity, your higher consciousness, calls to you by name. And Moses said, responding to that Presence, "Here am I."

"And the LORD said, I have surely seen the affliction of my people which are in Egypt, and have heard their cry by reason of their taskmasters; for I know their sorrows."

God is saying that to us today as clearly as he said it to Moses. We are afflicted by our own enslavement to materialism, to the burdens of plague and famine and terminal illnesses. And God knows our sorrows. And he is here to heal us of all our diseases

Kunsthistorisches Museum, Vienna

and to heal the planetary body if we will discover this key which he gave Moses for us.

God says, "I am come down to deliver them out of the hand of the Egyptians, and to bring them up out of that land unto a good land and a large," to bring them up out of the consciousness they have fallen into of accepting the binding action of their oppressors. I will raise them in consciousness, I will deliver them, I will show them the way through my Presence, "unto a land flowing with milk and honey."

And God says, "Come now therefore, and I will send thee unto Pharaoh, that thou mayest bring forth my people the children of Israel out of Egypt. And Moses said unto God, Who am I, that I should go unto Pharaoh, and that I should bring forth the children of Israel out of Egypt?"

Do we not say that today? "Who am I?" We are not the important people. We are not the powerful people. Who are we to offer ourselves as the instrument of the solution to global problems?

You are the manifestation of God, and God in you is worthy of accomplishing his works. And if you will it so—because it is your free will that is the catalyst— you can become the instrument.

The individual is the one who can manifest the divine solution. God is one individual (the individed Reality) in the bush that is burning. Moses is the individual (the individed expression of that One). And together they change the course of history. You can change the course of history of your individual life, your families, your children. And when you accomplish that, you can change your community and your nation.

"And Moses said unto God, Behold, when I come unto the children of Israel, and shall say unto them, The God of your fathers hath sent me unto you; and they shall say to me, What is his name? what shall I say unto them?"

Moses knew they wouldn't believe him if he couldn't tell them his name. "And God said unto Moses, I AM THAT I AM: and he said, Thus shalt thou say unto the children of Israel, I AM hath sent me unto you."

This is your key. You must discover the way to be sent by your I AM Presence, the Presence of God with you. The name is I AM THAT I AM. It is a most profound revelation and it is one that has not been used or taught to the people. That I AM Presence is the power to be. It is the verb to be, and when it is repeated twice, it means the I AM who is in Spirit is the I AM who is manifest where I AM in Matter.

"And God said unto Moses ...this is my name for ever, and this is my memorial unto all generations."

The memorial to all generations—it is the memory, it is the keepsake, it is the key, it is the name of the LORD that is given to us whereby we unlock the power of that Presence.

We are the sons and daughters of God; no matter what our physical ancestry, we claim that spiritual descendancy, we claim that

Your Divine Self

Light as our heritage and our origin. We, too, have inalienable spiritual rights, even as we have claimed our human rights. And one of those rights is the right to the Presence of God with us, the right to his I AM name, and the right to use that name to release the same power which was released to Moses for the deliverance of the people of God.

When you see the word *Lord* in the Old Testament—and the o-r-d have small capital letters—you know that that four-letter word LORD stands for I AM THAT I AM, Yahweh, in the Hebrew, YOD HE VAU HE, four Hebrew letters. Unto the Jews it is the name sacred which is not pronounced, therefore in its stead they say LORD. But the people have forgotten that LORD means I AM THAT I AM.

The I AM THAT I AM who appeared to Moses—that Almighty God—has the power to and does manifest himself individually to us, each one of us. So we can say that each one of us has the Presence of God with us. We have all believed that forever. And yet we do not say that that means there are gods many.

There is only one God. And this Presence of the Father is duplicated wherever he has created his offspring.

When God created your soul and sent you forth from his heart, He gave you the gift of himself—the replica, the manifestation of his Presence and of his eternal Sun—so that through that promise, that oneness, that feeling of God with you, you might find your way back home.

And the name I AM THAT I AM is not merely a name, but it is the personal Presence of God with you which it is your heritage to invoke.

The chart on the previous page is a pictorial representation of your being. The upper figure in the chart represents the I AM THAT I AM which spake to Moses. It is the Presence of the Father surrounded by these spheres of light, which we call electronic rings of light. They are pulsating from the center outward.

It is that which surrounded the angel with a rainbow upon his head recorded in Revelation 10. It is the sign of the Presence of the LORD. And the seven spheres within spheres represent the potential of God which you can draw down to yourself as you are represented as the lower figure in the chart.

The Presence even resembles a Tree of Life or a burning bush. As the lower figure, you are called to be the temple of the living God and you *can* be that temple here and now and God can dwell with and in his people.

You are intended to glow from that Tree of Life. In the very center you can see the crystal cord coming down. John saw it as the River of Life. And so we have the River of Life flowing through us. That is what beats our heart. That is what puts all systems "go" when we are born—the mighty action of this Presence.

Now the middle figure in the

chart, the Great Mediator, who stands between the I AM Presence and the lower figure, is the Person of Christ. Who is this Christ? It is Christ Jesus and it is the Universal Christ. Jesus said of this Christ, "This is my body [my Universal Body of Light] which is broken for you." So this figure of Christ is the manifestation of Christ with us as the mediator between ourselves and the Father, the I AM Presence.

Now, God says, Draw nigh to me and I will draw nigh to thee. Through meditation, through prayer, through dynamic decrees, through love and service to life, to our fellowman, to our families, we can increase our awareness of God and draw this I AM Presence and Holy Christ Self to us.

God has given to me dynamic decrees for this age which will draw his Presence closer to us. The "Heart, Head, and Hand" decrees are very simple and powerful decrees. The first one is for the invoking of violet fire. This fire is the agency of the Holy Spirit whereby God keeps his promises when He says, In that day, "I will remember their sin no more."

You can see the violet fire surrounding the lower figure in the chart which represents you. This fire is the action of the Holy Spirit. Moses said, "Our God is a consuming fire." No sin is too great for this universal solvent. And as we give our violet flame decrees, God consumes our sins, and we draw down the Presence of God to us, and God draws nigh unto us as surely as he came to Moses.

So I invite you to give this call to the Father and the Son, and visualize this violet flame blazing within your heart as you say:

Violet Fire
Heart
>Violet Fire, thou Love divine,
>Blaze within this heart of mine!
>Thou art Mercy forever true,
>Keep me always in tune
>>with you. (3x)

Head
>I AM Light, thou Christ in me,
>Set my mind forever free;
>Violet Fire, forever shine
>Deep within this mind of mine.
>
>God who gives my daily bread,
>With Violet Fire fill my head
>Till thy radiance heavenlike
>Makes my mind a mind of
>>Light. (3x)

Hand
>I AM the hand of God in action,
>Gaining Victory every day;
>My pure soul's great
>>satisfaction
>Is to walk the Middle Way. (3x)

The next step is to call down the light of God with the Tube of Light decree.

In reverence and honor to the I AM THAT I AM who spoke to Moses and said, "Put off thy shoes from off thy feet, for the place whereon thou standest is holy ground," we always stand to give the Tube of Light. And I invite you to stand because you can visualize yourself draped in this Tube of Light.

God prophesied to Israel, "I will be unto her a wall round about and the fire in the midst." This is the Tube of Light—the wall around you that seals and protects you from the mass consciousness, from thoughts of jealousy or envy, from all kinds of conditions of disease in the planet. It is a spiritual protection which we all need. And so, we face the LORD God in the morning, visualize the light descending in a pillar nine feet in diameter, and we say:

Tube of Light

Beloved I AM Presence bright,
Round me seal your Tube of Light
From Ascended Master flame
Called forth now in God's own
 name.
Let it keep my temple free
From all discord sent to me.

I AM calling forth Violet Fire
To blaze and transmute all desire,
Keeping on in Freedom's name
Till I AM one with the Violet
 Flame. (3x)

The more you decree, the greater momentum you will have, and the more light your I AM Presence will release to you. As you give these and other decrees* daily, God will increase his Presence with you enabling you to take command of your life. You can individually increase the Presence of God within you to take command of your life and become a greater force for the good of your community, nation, and planet.

So the salvation of the nation begins with the individual. That is the great tradition of the ancient prophets of Israel that is consummated in the life of Jesus Christ, for he is the supreme individualization of that Universal Word. And his example is the path we must emulate—not remaining forever as sinners, but becoming one with that Christ and putting on the garment of our birthright and claiming our divine inheritance.

---
*For more about decrees, read *The Science of the Spoken Word*, by Mark and Elizabeth Prophet.

Keep the Trust!

My beloved, the hour is strenuous, as it always is just prior to the birth of the Child, as every mother and father knows. And so, my beloved, understand that what we did in that hour is now being done through you. This is the hour and the day and the year and the moment of eternity when the age must give birth to the Universal Avatar of itself.

As we wrestled with forces determined to snuff out the life of our Child, so do you also. May you listen and learn from the Masters and the Mother what are these hideous, hydra-headed beasts that move against your children, your families, your community.

It is the hour designated for Christ to be born throughout the earth and in every heart. Now watch how great is that resistance in the areas of the comfortability of the carnal mind. Now understand: as we two and other holy ones held a circle of fire for Jesus, for the God-man sent to be the pillar and the Light of nations, so you are here—a larger community and more vast, with a dawning awareness of what it means to hold back not one but many planetary Herods who would (if they could) destroy all of the newborn children to be certain that they destroy the One. They think that in the abortion of flesh and blood they can stop the oncoming Light. But the encounter is with Maitreya and Buddha. The encounter is with Sanat Kumara and your own Christ Self.

Beloved ones, our tutoring of your hearts is to show you the necessity of the oneness of the flame of community. It is to show you that there is nothing more important in all of earth than the protection of the birth of this consciousness by the communion—the assimilation of the Word of the Ascended Masters' teachings.

Copyright © 1985 Church Universal and Triumphant, Inc.

A fire is kindled at the altar. It is transmitted to you not for you alone but for you to run with as torchbearers in the streets and in the night to proclaim that Word which you have become. You must drink in the sacred fire and then preach it to the nations.

Will the fire of the altar be stillborn? Will you take the teaching or the book or the tape recordings of our Word and admire the cover, thumb the pages, and think, "What a great book!" but fail to realize that this is my Body, this is my Blood; this is my Self—[as a representative of] the Universal Mother— this is my Son? If you do not eat it up, if you do not understand that the bitterness in the belly of our Word is the demand for change and resolution, if you do not understand that if the first rings of seraphim surrounding the Central Sun did not transmit those electronic fire-rings to the worlds, the ideations of the Mind of God would be stillborn, then how will you run with the fire of the altar?

Thus, it is not yours to consider whether or not friend or foe or stranger is ready. The readiness is predetermined by the authorization of the release from the Lords of Karma. Heaven cannot wait. Heaven says this day: The encounter with Maitreya must be! Let the Word go forth! Let the message of Jesus' travels to India be known.[1] And let the reason thereof be known—that there is an ancient hierarchy to which all pay obeisance and from whose fount all deliver a mighty Word of the ages from the Ancient of Days.

Beloved hearts, it is the statement of El Morya: Let the chips fall where they may![2] You must stand as the first rings and the firstfruits of the message. To sit in a corner and read it and place it on the shelf, to leave it there for private meditation and private spiritual development is not the purpose of our release.

You are torchbearers and runners in the night—Keepers of the Flame! Have you forgot or taken so lightly the Word of Sanat Kumara and of God the Father through the prophets and the Christed ones? The command to preach the Word to the nations is upon you. Will you forget so great a salvation? Will you lay aside the garment of your office and therefore forfeit the inheritance?

Blessed hearts, the Pearls of Wisdom not read are stillborn. And the one who does not assimilate the Word cannot deliver it. The sending of the Messenger has as its purpose the transformation of thy life. It is *thy* Christhood which counts for all, not that of the Messenger. If the Messenger's Christhood be therefore sustained, will this save the planet? It may, but then this is not the divine plan of the age. This is the igniting of a fire and the passing of a torch!

And so, the Messengers decrease as thou must increase.[3] So, the Messengers ascend as thou must descend yet into the depths of hell to rescue the lightbearers. We have kindled a fire. *Where* are the burning branches? *Where* is the brand of fire? *Where* are those who deliver it and set afire the nations?

Blessed hearts, knock on the door of my heart and apply to stump with the message worldwide. But, then, you have, of course, your neighbors and friends. You also have those who have created a circle of self-styled enemies. How could they do so? Only because the fiery hearts have not burned through with love to compel them—by the grandest desiring of the soul—to impart the beauty of Christ.

We say, therefore, as the conclusion of the Darjeeling Council in this hour of winter solstice, that the flaming ones must become aflame. No longer shall we wait at the gate for the fires to start. We compel and command that you *must* drink of this Blood and eat of this Body, else you will have no Life in you.[4] And you cannot live upon the Life of one or two or a thousand Christs. For only thine own will suffice for the victory.

I commend you to fasting and to the digestion of the Word, for only thus can thy life be a fulfillment of all of the promises. Truly you have not lived until you have become and then transmitted the Word.

I say to all of you, let your threefold flames be the means to ignite those in whom that flame has gone out. Let us hold hands in one grand circle of fire. Let us know ourselves as the electrode. And as this oneness and this circle of Light is formed, beloved hearts, *where* is the Christ? Who *is* the Christ?

The Christ is the One, the circle of Infinity formed. Can any lay claim to it and say, "Lo, here, lo, there"?[5] All in the oneness of the circle must be the transformers and transmitters of Light. Will you be the one light in the chain of the Christmas lights that causes all the rest to go out because you short-circuit the rest?

Beloved hearts, Light carries responsibility. Wisdom carries responsibility. And having a Messenger to deliver the Word from our bands is an immense responsibility. To whom much is given, much more is expected. Let us, then, be roused from comfortability and from self-arrangement and self-avoidance of the encounter with Maitreya and Christ.

Be willing to be in pain once a day because you have forsaken something that was unreal, yet something you wanted—something to which you were attached. Let every day know the release and the liberation of thy heart from sympathy with the unreal ones and with thy self, who does deceive itself into thinking it has need of so much consolation from the godless.

Let thy comfort be from God, and let it be sealed there.

O blessed ones, we forge a new age, and the city we build is a heavenly one and a center of healing Light. For this you must sacrifice the old self. Make your resolutions sure. Write your letters to the Karmic Board. And let us see now the fiery brands become the quickening sparks.

Gentle hearts, know and understand that the testing of this individual Christhood does demand the assimilation of all of our Light. It does demand that the right hand of myself through you quench the fiery darts of the wicked who would destroy by their hatred and incendiary intent—malintent—the noblest efforts of our lightbearers.

Morya stands with me, as we are devoted to the diamond heart in each one of you. Can there be any greater evidence than in the calamity at Livingston[6] that the encampment of the LORD's hosts requires *physical* counterparts who understand the meaning of the manifestation of the Inner Retreat and that it is the Place Prepared for the remnant, for those who will hold up the standard, the true standard of Israel, that all might come to understand that "I AM" standard?

O beloved ones, I pray on bended knee to the hosts of the LORD that they might deliver unto you worldwide the perception of the necessity to gather for the protection of cosmic purpose, that the ascended ones might have the platform for the ascension and that this teaching might swallow up bigotry and fanaticism ere the fallen ones consider they have the upper hand. Let, then, the presence of the Universal One in each and every one of you inspire you to new dedication to take the shortcut route to centeredness in the heart of Christ. Let all these things and desirings and doubts and fears and procrastination be put behind you in this hour. This is my message.

Christ is waiting to be born in Afghanistan, in Russia, in Ethiopia, in South Africa, in Nicaragua. How shall it be done? I tell you, it is by the mirror of the consciousness of God which we mirror from that retreat and send through the currents of the earth, the fire of the rock, the mighty river of the Yellowstone, and the subterranean chambers and movements in the rock.

Blessed ones, let the earth be filled with the sacred fire. And

Keep the Trust!

let those who have perceived the cosmic moment and the age from the beginning rouse themselves from that slumber of boredom and the lie that since nothing has happened of any great consequence, why should we bestir ourselves? Well, things of great consequence have happened over these decades. And each new onslaught against the children of the Light first produces shock waves and horrification, and then it, too, becomes the norm as people, weary in the fight, tire then of challenging evil.

I tell you, *the challenge of evil is your reason for being!* And I, your Mother, come to remind you of this fact and to underscore that you may no longer avoid the Teacher and the Teaching! You have come to the Ark of the Covenant, and the Shekinah glory drenches your hearts. If you so neglect this Light, I warn you, you will not have the wherewithal to face what is coming in your own life as karma, in the planet as karma. For it is truly the acceleration of the Dark Cycle and our preparations are necessary.

Let the humble of heart who are mighty in spirit, who are intelligent, who are the professionals, understand that the basics of life must be mastered. Thus, the judgment that begins in the base of the pyramid is a judgment of teaching and instruction that physical life must be preserved in order that the Light might penetrate and that Death and Hell might be conquered. Did you think it was created to move on forever? I tell you nay, not so, but in this hour and age to be devoured by Light.

Let the children of the Sun understand what it means to give birth to the planetary Christ consciousness. Let each and every one of you now become the Mother and have the responsibility of the Mother and hold this Christ in your arms from the cradle to Gethsemane to Golgotha. And, as Christ is placed in your arms, taken down from the cross, know that it is your life once again infused in him that gives him the new day and the resurrection and the opportunity to walk the earth as the resurrected one to restore divine purpose.

Blessed hearts, in some areas I weep by way of showing my sorrow. But here I must come and say I am ashamed that you have not understood the meaning of the sacrifice of all who have gone before and that you dally in self-analysis when the great God Self within and without beckons you to a world victory! I am ashamed that you have not implemented the Word and become all that you are. I am ashamed that you have not read the writing upon the wall of life and reckoned with the intensity of the darkness and its determination to put out the Light of this community.

I speak to every Keeper of the Flame worldwide who has succumbed to the temptation of every other purpose save that which we have designated as the primal one: the building of this retreat for your own spiritual survival. As the very hairs of your heads are numbered, so the very hours of thy life yet fall through the hourglass. Every hour of postponement is the shortening of the opportunity for your fulfillment of your personal goals, of becoming masters and walking the earth to demonstrate the Law as world teachers. I commend you to the contact with God that will light your whole being and consume all darkness and deliver you in the reality of your Christhood.

Thus, while some toil, while some give all, others yet play and fantasize in their fanciful doings that have naught to do with the single-minded purpose of the building of the temple of man and the oneness of community.

Where are the fifty righteous men to save the city of the Industrial Park? Where are those who stand guard that the nefarious ones who have sworn to destroy that place might not enter? The ring of fire must be established. The land that is hallowed must be guarded. And you must make a statement of courage and conviction that there is no other desire, no other plan of import save this one. You have sacrificed with your life, your supply, your gifts, yet you have stayed back to warm yourselves in your particular situations. And thus the few, spread so thin, have not been the match for those who come in the night to destroy the manger. If the manger is not there, where shall Christ be born?

I tell you, beloved hearts, another opportunity or place or time shall not be given. *This is it.* This is the one and the One Sent. Make haste, then, for never has there been so beautiful a place so cherished by angels, so determined of elemental life to become the open door between the octaves of earth and the etheric plane as this one.

Fear not the cold or the isolation or the mountains. Fear not the separation. Will you be like the children of Israel who murmured and complained, having left the fleshpots of Egypt—murmured and complained all the way to the Promised Land, which could have been gained in short order but was postponed forty years for their backbiting and complaining and criticism of Moses?

Blessed hearts, as we have said before and as my Son has pleaded, you know not what is taking place on earth. You know not the larger conspiracies of which this one burning in Livingston is only the tip of the iceberg. You know not the fear of the dark ones and how it impels them to terrorism and destruction. Thus, let us renew our courses. Let us appreciate what is given. Let us assimilate the Word and preach it and guard it and guard its citadel, to which Lanello himself did give his life. And therefore, this being done, that the world also be saved.

It is the numbers of decreers and Keepers of the Flame who shall establish the Great Central Sun Magnet there, who shall come, who shall lay their life and fortunes and honor on the altar to precipitate these plans, this hospital, this protection, this Word—who, having so come and formed the Magnet of the Central Sun, will then have the means to transmit the power for the saving of each and every nation as we send our Messenger to the nations to carry that Light. How shall she go to the nations, one by one, when she herself must go to the Inner Retreat to guard it because you have not come?

You see, precious hearts, it is the physical presence of the Guru *and* the chelas who must anchor *God* in the mighty figure-eight flow, as Above so below. The physical body of the Messenger must carry the flame of the Inner Retreat to the nations, yet who will kindle the flame and keep it that it might be carried? Who will be the torch of the Goddess of Liberty, and Liberty herself, at the Royal Teton Ranch? There must be a fountain that is physical in order for the Mother to bring the fountain to the earth.

Let us see, then, how there must be the turning of the worlds of individual Keepers of the Flame, even as the Elohim came for the turning of planet Earth and by their coming did establish the call and the retreat and your answer.

Blessed hearts, as it has been taught to you, so I say it: Every condition at large in the world scene, unless defeated and overcome where it is, will by and by encroach upon family, community, and child and, unless stopped by the circle of Light, come all the way to the Inner Retreat. These conditions must be defeated by the Holy Spirit long before they find their way to the holy mountain of God. Thus, let them be blinded by the Light of the mountain instead of finding darkness and an absence of the watchman of the night. For they will always penetrate where they are allowed.

Thus, may the lesson be plain. Whereas our Messengers have spoken, now we speak. Let the hearts and the supply come as a mighty river of a vote of confidence in the Great White Brotherhood. Let the buildings be rebuilded. Let the tent, the tabernacle, let the farms and the presses, let the schools and the workshops be established.

We do not have eternity. And I will tell you from the Messenger's heart, as the daily phone calls and the letters in the mail report this one and another terminally ill, facing now the abyss and the challenge of another life out of the body—disease is multiplying in the earth and it, too, must be turned back by a pillar of fire so intense that the Light devours it and sets aside the place for healing. Death multiplies and stalks, and even the lightbearers are beset because the body bulb of community must be brighter! It must be cohesive, it must be a Central Sun that shines; and then its rays emitted penetrate the bodies and consume the disease and death and penetration.

Let the waterfall of Light flow. Let nothing be able to move against it, against the stream so powerful. Let the chelas understand the keeping of the flame of the nations from the Heart of the Inner Retreat. Events have a way of carrying a message and speaking on their own. May you read the sign and run and discover your own vulnerability to your tarrying in the cups of concupiscence or of delay or of whatever illusion has invaded thy house to the devouring of thy soul.

Fear not, then, that which does kill the body, but that which does devour the soul in hell.[7] Fear the cancer of the soul, far more deadly than the cancer of the body—which itself is a sign that the soul must rise and throw off its own affliction.

The time is short for thy own proving of the Word. Christ must be born in the nations, else they collapse. Let the message of healing and all that is abundantly given be spread abroad. And let it be done swiftly.

In the name of my Son, I have spoken to you, beloved hearts. Now I penetrate with the sacred fire breath and with the eye of Omega. I penetrate the soul and the mind for the quickening intelligence that points the way and does not err.

Come, my children. I am big with Child. This Child must be born. Where are the wise men and women of Aquarius who will follow the star to the Place Prepared and keep the flame for this birth?

The Light is all. Only stand and still stand and thou shalt behold the reward of the wicked. But thou must stand physically to drive back an enemy one-pointed in the destruction of this Church. They shall not pass when the right hand of the physical chelas is raised in commemoration of Gautama, Jesus, my own heart, and all saints.

They shall not pass! They have no power. Let the devouring Light of Shiva now consume them in their own misery and

Keep the Trust! 9

malintent. This is my fiat. You must make it your own and the light of your chakras must ascend; and the requirement for the wise virgins guarding the light of the chakras in the temple has never been greater.

Death hath no power over those who keep the flame of Life. There is a requirement if the promises are to be fulfilled. In the name of Morya, Archangel Michael, and Mark, I say:

Keep the faith. *Keep* the trust. *Keep* the hope. And go to that place. Guard it for me and my work through you.

"The Summit Lighthouse Sheds Its Radiance O'er All the World to Manifest as Pearls of Wisdom." This dictation by Mother Mary was delivered through the Messenger Elizabeth Clare Prophet on Thursday, December 27, 1984, during the 6-day *New Year's Light of the World Conference,* at Camelot. (1) See *The Lost Years of Jesus* by Elizabeth Clare Prophet, newly released from Summit University Press. Paperback, $12.95 ($14.08 postpaid USA). To help you share *The Lost Years* with loved ones, the publisher is offering a special 20 percent discount when you buy five or more copies. Five copies, with discount, $51.80 ($54.90 postpaid USA); each additional copy, $10.36 ($10.71 postpaid USA). (2) "Let it be made clear at the beginning that all who read the words of the Ascended Masters and all who hear our word are not necessarily counted as chelas of our will. Let it be quite clear that there are requirements. As the chips of wood fly when the pines in the forest are cleared, so the winds of Darjeeling blow. Let the unworthy chela be cleared from our path. We clear for a noble purpose—the ennoblement of a cause and a race.... 'Let the chips fall where they may!'" El Morya, *The Chela and the Path,* Summit University Press, p. 13. Paperback, $3.95 ($4.80 postpaid USA). (3) John 3:30. (4) John 6:53. (5) Matt. 24:23–26; Mark 13:21–23; Luke 17:20, 21. (6) On Christmas Eve 1984, shortly after 6:00 p.m., a fire started in the large metal factory building at the Royal Teton Ranch's Industrial Park, east of Livingston, Montana. Within twenty minutes the central roof had collapsed, causing the walls to cave in. Metal tools melted, and sections of the steel frame became twisted in the heat. Firefighters battled the inferno for several hours before bringing it under control. At about 6:00 a.m., the fire was completely out, though two-thirds of the building was totally destroyed or rendered unusable. Investigators assume that the cause was electrical. In a Jan. 11 *Livingston Enterprise* article, "Power Line Blamed for Local Warehouse Fire," Tom Shands reported: "According to Rural Fire Marshall Walt Adams, who enlisted the help of the state fire marshall's office, the fire apparently started when Montana Power's 440-volt overhead line touched the metal warehouse, igniting a spray-on polyurethane insulation that was applied to the center section of the warehouse. Rural Fire Chief Ken Hanson said that type of insulation is supposed to be fire resistant, but under certain conditions it will ignite and burn fast and hot. 'In essence, that whole metal building turned into one hot hunk of metal,' Hanson said. 'This would account for the fact that we had so much fire so fast.' In sifting through the rubble, Adams said he attempted to determine the point of the fire's origin, what fuel was available for it to burn and in what direction the fire spread.... Adams said the electric heater was not near the point of origin and could not have caused that much fire that fast. Adams said church members were in the building about 10 minutes before the fire started, and within one-half hour after they left, the building was consumed in flames. Montana Power's spokesman in Butte said the utility does not agree with the fire marshalls' report. 'We disagree with the fact that the fire was caused by our line,' said Jerry Woods of MPC's claims division. Woods said MPC has had engineers inspect the warehouse and the company believes its line was subjected to intense heat, sagged, and then touched the building. He said early indications are the line came down after the fire was started. Woods said MPC engineers will continue to investigate the fire in an attempt to clear its line from any liability, but he added that investigation may not go as far as to determine the cause of the fire." (7) Matt. 10:28.

Our Christmas Eve Prayer to Mother Mary*

Beloved Mother Mary, we come to the fountain of your heart. Let us be cleansed in this hour of the eternal Christ Mass of all sin, perfidy, all folly and straying from thy eternal presence.

Beloved Mother Mary, in the name of thy Son Jesus Christ, pierce the veil of illusion, temptation, the spell that engages the mind in unreality. Light of the eternal countenance of the Mother, shine upon us.

Blessed Mary, search our souls, our hearts, our minds, and our bodies. Let the piercing Light of the benignity of thine eye now penetrate and probe and remove the cause and core of all propensity to stray from thy path, to engage in sin or disease or death matrices.

Blessed Mother, remove the cause and core of fear, the failure syndrome, the momentums of the subconscious that cause the spirit to strive less than the fullness of its soaring.

Beloved Mother Mary, we come to learn of thee those things which have escaped our hearts, for the veil of benighted understanding has fallen upon us in this samsara. Therefore, beloved Mother, show us those things—make them crystal clear to us—which we have failed to apprehend and therefore to internalize the Word of thy blessed Son.

Beloved Mother Mary, come into our hearts in this hour. Speak to us from within of those things of heaven and those things of earth, that the deliberations of our souls might be unto thy wholeness and the wholeness of thy Son Jesus Christ.

Beloved Mother, we are here to be thy hands and feet, thy heart and mind. If thou wouldst weep, weep, then, through us, for we shall weep with thee in this hour and rise to the joy of the morning. Where thy children suffer, let the weeping of our eyes with thine own bear to them a mighty tide of the River of Life that shall cleanse them, exalt them, and deliver them from the tempter and the dragon that seeks to devour the Manchild.

Beloved Mother Mary, let us stretch our comprehension to include more of thy greater joy and, consequently, more of thy sorrow that, as we are fixed beneath heaven and the darkest places, we might have that commeasurement of the omnipotence of Almighty God that enables us to save that which is lost, to give more, and to be more effective in the saving of souls worldwide.

We are thy children, yea, and more. We are thy sons and daughters and more. We are thy cohorts of Life. We are brother

Copyright © 1985 Church Universal and Triumphant, Inc.

and sister unto thee, beloved. We come as bodhisattvas of the ages to stand at thy right hand and at thy left and with thee to raise up thy hands as the hands of Moses were raised up that the armies of darkness might be turned to naught.

Beloved Mother Mary, receive us in this hour of resplendent victory of thy crown. Let the fire upon the spinal altar rise now as the fullness of the lily. And let us be on earth the instrument of thy salvation to America, to the I AM Race, to all nations. With thee we raise our right hand, O eternal Mother, for the turning back of darkness and the dark ones.

O let thy miracles of the Holy Spirit and thy immaculate heart which we have seen so abundantly, continuously flowing be the very element of the alchemy. And therefore, in the twinkling of the eye of God, in the twinkling of thy eye, O beloved Mother Mary, let the world be changed and let it become, through and through, the Body and Blood of our Lord—LORD, the eternal Christ, the eternal Krishna, the eternal Sanat Kumara.

This world in the hands of Almighty God must receive His blessing, His exorcism through thy blessed hands, Mother Mary. Hold the earth in thy hands, for we hold the faith, the hope, and the charity that this planetary evolution may be transformed by the power of Archangel Michael and Jophiel and Chamuel and Gabriel, Raphael, Uriel, and Zadkiel.

Nothing is too hard for the LORD.

Let the Light from the Mighty I AM Presence stream forth now from our hearts, from our souls, from the solar plexus and the third eye. O intensify, Blessed Mother, as we now ignite these candles unto thee and thy twin flame and all twin flames of cosmos who are indeed Alpha and Omega.

Blessed Mother, we pour forth gratitude. Thou art God in manifestation. Thou art the Mother of God, mothering the God flame in our hearts throughout all ages. Teach us, then, blessed one, to rise to the God-estate whence we have descended. Teach us in this hour to unlock the great treasures of the causal body of Life. Teach us in this hour, O Blessed Mother, to draw down the fullness of all that we are in the Mighty I AM Presence, in the beloved Christ Self. Let us be on earth the Universal Self. Let us be the instruments of the Almighty.

There is no reality to Death and Hell, nor to its denizens, nor to their consciousness. In the presence of the sacred fire of the Mother, all is God. Let us live in this reality, and by that God consciousness let the unreal be dissolved and let the illumination of the Almighty—Alpha and Omega, Helios and Vesta, the God and Goddess Meru, Lord Himalaya, Vaivasvata Manu, and the Great Divine Director—be unto us the fullness of our Mother's right choice made by divine illumination. Let all of the tribes of the earth who mourn come into that Cosmic Christ illumination by thy heart.

Beloved Mother Mary, we empower thee by the fourteen stations of the cosmic cross of white fire to use all of our Light, all of our causal body, all of our momentum for the saving of earth in this hour. Save, then, the lightbearers of all nations, and especially the oppressed.

Beloved Mother Mary, teach us in this hour to glorify the name of God I AM THAT I AM in our bodies and souls and communities, in our families and children, in our education.

Blessed Mother, help us to do what you want us to do now and show us how to do it with the all-power of heaven and earth. We beseech thy intercession and that of thy Son and all of thy sons and daughters in the entire Spirit of the Great White Brotherhood.

Elohim of God, Elohim of God, come forth. Amen.

---

*Give this prayer aloud—right now—and often as you reread and meditate on the words of the Master in this Pearl. Your voice is your vote in heaven that counts for the establishment of world peace. The Light of God never fails when you release it through the science of the spoken Word!

Pearls of Wisdom, published weekly by The Summit Lighthouse for Church Universal and Triumphant, come to you under the auspices of the Darjeeling Council of the Great White Brotherhood. These are presently dictated by the ascended masters to their Messenger Elizabeth Clare Prophet. The international headquarters of this nonprofit, nondenominational activity is located in Los Angeles, California. All communications and freewill contributions should be addressed to The Summit Lighthouse, Box A, Malibu, CA 90265. Pearls of Wisdom are sent weekly throughout the U.S.A. via third-class mail to all who support the Church with a minimum yearly love offering of $36. First-class and international postage rates available upon request. Notice of change of address should be received three weeks prior to the effective date. Third-class mail is not forwarded by the post office.

Copyright © 1985 Church Universal and Triumphant, Inc. All rights reserved. Printed in the United States of America. Pearls of Wisdom and The Summit Lighthouse are registered trademarks of Church Universal and Triumphant, Inc. All rights to their use are reserved.

The Judgment of Peshu Alga

The Archangel in Prayer before the Eternal Father

Eternal Father, I AM come in this hour to deliver the Woman and her seed.

Eternal Father, I AM Michael Archangel, crowned by thy holy hand, now endowed with thy vigil of sacred fire.

O Father, I, Michael, now bend the knee before thy throne of grace for the magnitude of thy glory and thy wonder and thy deliverance to the people of earth and all spheres. I lay my sword before thy altar, O Father, in gratitude sublime, in joy supreme, for thou hast truly bound the enemy and raised up thy living Son.

Heavenly Father, receive these legions of angels who accompany me in this hour at the side of the Woman and her seed. O God, receive now, in the name of Holy Virgin, thy faithful and true witnesses, thy devotees of the will of God in earth. I bear them to thy throne.

Thus, O God, bless us and cleanse us from the battle, that we might renew thy courses, that we might perpetually bend the knee and receive the inflamed wonder of thy holy will. Remove from us, O Father, the burden of the past and renew in us thy Light for the New Day. In reverence of the Holy Mother, we bow to thy Light. Send us, then, upon the new mission of glory, even the mission of the Everlasting Gospel.

The Honor of God Redeemed

Hail! chelas of the sacred fire. *Hail!* seraphim of God and all lovers of Christ throughout all eternity. I AM Archangel Michael, and I have descended from the Central Sun as with the speed of light to be with you in person in the very flesh of the messenger and in the very blood of thy self, if thou will it so—if thou wilt give to an archangel room.

Lo, I come. I come swiftly in pinions of Light, not only to enfold you but to dwell with you in the temple of the Most High God made without hands,[1] which He hath builded as your true individuality in God. Therefore, as in heaven so on earth, I AM Archangel Michael, servant of the holy will of God, servant of His people. And my legions of angels adore the crystal Light, as Above so below, cherishing the honor you accord them of joining in the service of the praise of God and the binding of the enemy.

Blessed ones, I ask you to stand in this hour for the honor of God. This day the honor of God is redeemed. This day and in this hour, O blessed ones, I come having defended, therefore, the daughter of Zion, the community of the Holy Spirit, and the mystical body of God in all ages.

At the Court of the Sacred Fire

Therefore, speaking now with the message of the Court of the Sacred Fire, the God Star Sirius, speaking in the name of the Four and Twenty Elders, I announce to you, O children of the Sun, the day of days. Thus, in this very hour, the Judgment—the final judgment and the second death—has come of that one you have known as Peshu Alga.[2] [applause]

Thus, the Keeper of the Scrolls has read these weeks record by record of the infamy of that fallen one in the trial at the Court of the Sacred Fire—that one who himself moved to tempt Lucifer away from the service of Light, that one who forever swore vengeance upon Almighty God because of the death of his only son, failing to apprehend eternal life and the reappearance of the son. Thus, his sworn enmity was one of the turning points (if not *the* turning point) in the rebellion of those fallen angels who have also followed him to the Court of the Sacred Fire.

Blessed hearts, this hour of the trial of that fallen one and the passing from earthly life has been noted by yourselves as being causative of conditions of upheaval and even danger and death to the children of Light—as in the case of certain calamities East and West.[3] Understand, beloved ones, that in the wake of the removal of the roots of evil and pride from the earth, there are those yet committed to darkness who remain and who, in their fear and ongoing vengeance, move to take therefore the holy innocents and to wreak havoc here and there among the nations.[4]

The Judgment of Peshu Alga

Thus, wisely the Darjeeling Council Master has called you to gather for the holding of Light in the five secret rays. Thus, beloved ones, keep the flame and continue to tarry. For the messenger as instrument, yourselves as instrument, the community as instrument of the judgments of God as so ordained does require, then, the vigilance of the armor of Light and of Peace and of Freedom. Let the science of the spoken Word be offered liberally and with joy and acclaim for the expansion of the Universal Christ in all people and planetary homes.

Beloved ones, this judgment, long attended, has far-reaching ramifications across the galaxies. And in this very hour, beloved, there is a liberation and a freedom not known before to many of your own brothers and sisters who happen to be what seems to be so very far, far away. All of the Matter cosmos is the womb of the Mother, and within that womb souls of Light are being formed and re-formed in the universal image of the eternal Krishna.

Call to Christ to Take the Genetic Replica of Peshu Alga

O Christ, O Anointed One, O Light of the Sun, liberate these children from their fascination with the fallen angels in every level and plane of consciousness.

O Surya, send thy legions of the Sun! Now demagnetize from all evolutions of Light and those who have yet to espouse the Light the image, the rebellion, the logic, the carnality of this serpent and fallen one! And bind—Surya, legions of God, by the command of the archangel—bind now the very cause and core of those who have moved in anger. Let the core of anger and its seed planted in the subconscious of the people by these nefarious ones be *seized* by the Light of the sacred fire, by the power of Elohim and Astrea!

Beloved hosts of the LORD, so, too, take the image and the replica reproduced again and again of the rebellion of Peshu Alga. Take it now, O Cosmic Christ, in answer to the call of my humble heart. Take it, then, from all who are the fruits of the Holy Spirit, from all who are the children of the Sun. Let them be delivered in this hour of these genetic implants moving to deter the Divine Image from descending.

Seraphim of God, stand with them. Consume the cause and core of the malignancies of the spirit, soul, body, and mind afflicting the lightbearers of earth.

A Day of Cosmic Celebration and an Hour of Cosmic Change

For this is a day of cosmic celebration and burst of joy unto the Lord Christ in every heart! It is the hour of rejoicing for the binding of the old witch and witchcraft—of the old dragon[5] and the tempter and the seed of Satan. This is the hour and the day when the Light going forth from the heart of Helios unto Vesta in this abode does truly win for God many souls lost—lost because they had lost their moorings in God, lost because they followed the maya and the magnetism and the bravado of these fallen ones.

We have reached, therefore, the high point of darkness, and darkness now must recede. And now you will have the momentum of the victory of our God, the victory of our bands, and the removal of darkness as impetus to thrust ho, to move forward, to act for the Light and for the Home, and to clear the way for many beings of Light to descend to earth through the portals of birth.

It is an hour for cosmic change if you will have it. But I must tell you truly in the honor of God, as in all time and space, the Law does require the spoken Word, the mantra, the call to me, and the call to God in order for Light to enter in. For you see, God has given to you absolute free will in the physical octave. If you desire change, you must call upon the LORD, your Mighty I AM Presence, and call for the reinforcement of us as agents of Light and of the Father-Son-Holy Spirit-Mother complement of the Godhead.

This is the City Foursquare, and I, Archangel Michael, stand in the center thereof, raising also the right hand of the Woman and therefore declaring to you her instrumentation in the standing guard—the standing guard, lo, these tens of thousands and hundreds of thousands of years against the fallen ones. They know their hour has come. And the vigil of Mary multiplied many times over in yourselves has taken place. Thus, they *could* not pass, they shall not pass, and not one of these little ones is lost save the single son of perdition.[6]

The Tutoring of the Angels Who Strayed from Their First Love

Beloved hosts of Light, I call now for the tutoring with the intensity of the Cosmic Christ of all angels who wandered and strayed from their first love. I call for the message of the Cosmic Christ to go forth with the magnanimity and the intensity and the joyousness of God to clearly reveal, to clear and *clearify* the auras of all angels, all sons and daughters of God and children of the Light who have followed now these falling stars[7] as they have appeared on the screen of life to tempt them away by their excessive noise, their excessive misuse of rhythm, their personality-cult consciousness.

Follow them not, O children of the Sun! There is no good fruit that can come forth from involvement in the culture of drugs and rock music.[8] Both, then, represent the consuming and the burning up of the Kundalini fire, the lowering of that life-force unto the utter destruction of the Deathless Solar Body and the wedding garment and even the violation of the chakras.

Beloved ones, those who follow those falling stars, those rock and drug stars, are following a train of death that leads to the very depths of hell.[9] Go not! Follow them not! As I have preached to you from the beginning, so I preach to you in the ending: It is not a matter of your free will. It is a matter of ultimate danger to your souls!

Beloved ones, you have heard of the scriptural reference to the castaway.[10] It is possible to lose the soul fabric, to lose self-consciousness, and to become a castaway, empty and void. If you do not believe me, look into the faces of those who are addicted and filled with this darkness, and you will understand what it means to be stripped of the wedding garment that is the etheric garment of God that seals you in the upward movement and momentum of the rising Mother flame within you and draws you back to the very heart of God.

The Seven Archangels Preach the Everlasting Gospel

Blessed ones, therefore let us move for the protection of Light on earth and for the finishing of that which has begun in this hour in the final judgment of Peshu Alga. Henceforth, you may know me as the angel who flies in heaven with the Everlasting Gospel, preaching that gospel to the men of earth.[11] And you may know that the archangels follow suit. And you also being angels who have come to earth to teach mankind must also follow.

This Everlasting Gospel is the published Word and Work of the LORD in this activity. You have only to pick up any of the teachings to find the thread. And begin at the beginning with the rereading of the book *Climb the Highest Mountain*.[12]

The highest mountain of your divinity is your crown chakra. *Go* then! Go to the Royal Teton Retreat! *Go* then to the Himalayas! *Go* to the highest mountain, Mount Everest, and find the rest and peace of the Buddha, the eye of the Mother. Find the strength and find the perception that directs the ray of God into the core nest of seed of Serpent still carrying on their habit pattern of destructivity midst the children of the Sun.

"I Demand Calls for the Defense of America"

I bring, then, to your attention what I have taught unto the Mother, that you might mark that cross of white fire foursquare in the heart of the city and see the quadrants of the cosmic clock of your own psychology and the patterns of the nations unfold. I demand, therefore, invocation for the protection of the nations. I demand, first and foremost, that such intense and precise and incisive calls be given for the defense of the I AM Race in every nation, for the defense of America as that nation that does yet guard the Spirit of the Great White Brotherhood and its teaching, and for the defense of India as the counterpart, if her people will it so—to once again take up the mantle and the banner of Maitreya and of Sanat Kumara and to leave off from their fascination with World Communism.

Beloved hearts of Light, let the divine polarity be reestablished from the Mount Meru to the Mount Himalaya. Let, therefore, your calls be for the defense of the *physical* nation America, the *physical* bodies of her people from all that which is poisonous and causative of death. Let there be the protection of the moral fiber of the soul, the spirituality, the mind, the desire body. Thus, cover all of the planes and see to it that the people of God who must deliver the earth are themselves brought into alignment with the inner holy will by calls to me.

I would not be displeased nor would I consider it an excessive sacrifice for you to maintain the perpetual vigil of calls to me and to my bands. For I can assure you that every problem that besets the nation—including the teetering and tottering of the economy and the banking systems, for they are invaded by false gods—each and every problem that is faced can be resolved by the most intensive calls to our legions.

By the grace of Almighty God, I AM the captain of the Lord's hosts.[13] And therefore, all archangels and seraphim of God and hosts of Light ministering in these systems do answer to my command. When you give me the authority to act, the mighty Christ Mind, which we have called the 'computer' of the Mind of God, does designate millions and millions of angels to go forth on that particular problem worldwide! Let us have a tremendous victory in this conference, knowing that our legions are ready to soar, ready to move because the sons of God *have* decreed it, *are* decreeing it, and *shall* decree it until the golden age is physically manifest.

The Defense of the Etheric Quadrant from the Wiles of Fallen Angels and Black Magicians

Therefore, beloved ones, as you know, this Peshu Alga, being not a native of this planet, did also descend via spacecraft and has been known as the first of the triad central—Anu, Enki, and Enlil.[14] Understand, therefore, that these fallen ones in their spacecraft, who are not benign, who have come to lead the children astray and to program mankind genetically to obedience to them, must also be judged and bound. And therefore, the remnant who would take their revenge because of the loss of one of their leaders must come under the dominance of the hosts of the LORD ere they go forth seeking whom they may devour before their time is up.[15]

Thus, it is a point of interval, it is a point of victory, and it is an hour when the more Light you send forth, the more you can expect the reversing of that Light in what we have called the "lashback," as the fallen ones refuse to accept their judgment. And thus the waves of Light, you see, must roll twenty-four hours a day. The rolling forth of the Light and the Light itself will greet, then, the darkness that they attempt to turn upon you. Let there not be a vacuum, therefore, in the decree sessions once you have begun this rolling momentum. For I tell you, in this hour it is the momentum which is unleashed for the ultimate victory over that Death and Hell of consciousness on earth.

Beloved ones, remember the etheric quadrant. Remember the black magicians; they misuse that quadrant and that body. And they misuse the sacred fire to imprison elemental life, causing accidents, calamities, fires, and promoting acts of terrorism—also the misuse of the fire of the Mother.

The Defense of the Mental Quadrant from False Teachers and False Teachings

Then, beloved hearts, move with intense calls in the defense of America, from the etheric octave to the mental, as you call for the purging of false teachings in every field of endeavor—false teachings especially in the field of God-government and religion which turn the people against the central course of their divine destiny. Thus, the false gurus, false prophets, false teachers—*these* must be exposed by enlightenment, by the true illumination of

Jophiel, who comes with the Buddhas and Bodhisattvas, who comes with the Christed ones, who comes to tutor your hearts, who comes to deliver reality and an understanding of that illumination which *shall* be the opening of the crown chakra within you!

I tell you, it is so! I tell you, you are on the verge of the breakthrough that you have been striving for. And this is the hour to reach now high to the highest sail of the mast of the ship of Lord Maitreya and to understand the meaning of that ship and its movement across the sea of earth.

We come, therefore, to save those who are on land and sea, who are attacked, therefore, in the astral plane and the physical plane. Therefore watch, then, and keep the faith, and let no ungodly thing invade the mind, the universal consciousness of the Mind of God upon this planet.

The Defense of the Astral Quadrant from the Promoters of Rock and Drugs

Let the right standard of the Universal Christ be raised up within you, within this community. Let the standard-bearers be none other than yourselves as you go forth preaching that Everlasting Gospel because you are ignited at the altar of the Mother. You have received the sacred fire. Your body does glow on the earth as the candle in the night. And soon there will be no more night! For the earth shall be filled with the glory of God and His knowledge as the waters cover the sea of the astral plane and the River of Life does inundate that astral plane and Death and Hell have no power.[16] And the LORD shall have them in derision! And you shall laugh and the nations shall laugh[17] and there shall be a peal of joy and victory throughout all evolutions of earth in the coming dawn of the new age!

O beloved hearts, intensify now, for know that truly all is the counting and all counts for the Victory. Therefore, let the protection be of the emotional bodies of the students, the desire body of the earth, from all that assails that body visually through the eye vision and through the third eye.

Understand the bombardment of all people through the media, through the ear and the eye, through sound, through messages, through brainwashing. And let there be the clearing of desire by the pure understanding of the image of God. And let all those denizens of the astral plane who promote drugs and rock this day and who pervert the life-force of the Mother in all manner of perversion and abuse of children—let them be bound! We shall bind them in answer to your call.

Copyright © 1985 Church Universal and Triumphant, Inc.

The Defense of the Physical Quadrant from the Capitalist/Communist Conspirators

We are ready! We are ready to charge in Victory's name. We are ready to go forth. And you must understand that the tide has turned; yet you are the living tide and you must move with it even as you direct it.

Let us understand that the toppling of those governments conducted by the fallen angels and the Nephilim [space] gods is about to occur. Let us understand the judgment that is necessary of the international capitalist/communist conspiracy, those who control it to their ends through power and monied interests. Beloved ones, these are they who confute the reign of Christ in the physical octave. Thus, the physical octave must be conquered, and it begins with the action of the abundant Life.

Beloved ones, physically you must take a stand and bind darkness. And we shall bind it, for it is our job and our calling and our assignment, and you are our sons and daughters.

Sons and daughters of the Most High, we bow before the Light of God within you! We bow before the image of the Father and the Son and the Holy Spirit and the Mother within you. We fear not to bow before the creation of Elohim, for we know that the creation of Elohim *is* Elohim in manifestation. And therefore, we have not the pride nor the ambition of those who have fallen [to desire] to exceed your Light but only to enhance it, that you might become as we are: servant-sons of God—free, immortal!—touching the crown of Reality forever.

Let us, then, while we are here in this hour of victory, contemplate the message of the blessed Mother Mary. Let us contemplate her call for the keeping of the flame of the Inner Retreat and the covenant of God and so great a salvation and the dispensation of the Western Shamballa.

"I Will Send You! I Will Defend You! I Will Cut You Free!"

I will send you! I will defend you! I will cut you free, blessed hearts, if you call to me. I came to Boston in 1961 to fetch the messenger that she might be here and with you in this hour of victory. As I proclaimed to her and "the people of Boston" (by way of saying, "the people of the crown chakra") that I would protect and guard, that I would cut free and defend in the hour of transition, so I make that offer to you in this hour.[18]

I can assure you that the call to this messenger to come apart and to leave the planes of the world was just as difficult an experience for her, if not more so, as that which may occur to you when you are called. If you would step up in a new initiation in life, you must be ready to forsake the past—and sometimes it is a painful parting. After all, beloved ones, you cannot continue round and round in a revolving door! If you have made a commitment to go forward, then you must get off the revolving door of your human creation and the revolving of the past and the hundred and one things you might be doing instead of the one-pointedness of becoming a chela of the sacred fire.

The Worth of the Commitment of One Son of God

Thus, I came. I cut her free. She responded. And because of that response and obedience, you have this day a Summit Lighthouse, you have a Church Universal and Triumphant, you have a songbook in your hand, you have a decree book—you have the wherewithal to know who you are in God and to act upon it! I only say this to demonstrate the worth of the commitment of one son of God in embodiment, that you might understand that truly the divine prophecies are fulfilled before your eyes as, you see, twin flames are destined to become even the gods of solar systems.

Now, does it not begin when you create a nucleus of sacred fire and ring upon ring of the mandala of Light gathers until you find that you have not only created a focus of Light but you have created a solar system itself composed of the planetary bodies who are the sons and daughters of God? Each one of you is a center of a sun within this Sun. Each one of you can become a star like Sirius of the very first magnitude.

Understand the meaning of your I AM Presence. Understand the meaning of the tide that must be taken.[19] Understand the meaning of the offer of an archangel who has done battle with the fallen ones directly and who, with the legions of Light, has defeated that great dragon [in heaven, as he must now be defeated on earth and in the hearts of men]. Understand the meaning of my presence. Establish your commeasurement with Infinity and where you want to be one hundred years from now (not tomorrow or next week or next year) and then make your decisions aright. Heaven has truly offered and given of itself.

My Moment of Destiny to Choose to Move On

Now, beloved ones, change is the alchemy of this conference and this new year—the alchemy of the violet flame. If you desire to be a new creature in Christ, then you must forsake the old creature. You cannot have both. You cannot become the new creature and carry the old image on your back. We take no monkeys into our chambers; and the old image is the monkey mind and the monkey imitator who can never integrate with the Word because the vessel is not adequate, the chalice cannot prevail.

Thus, I ask you to symbolically take a step forward where you are, even in place, to sense the dropping from behind you of the old self, to sense that there are cosmic moments, there are moments of destiny, even as I had my moment of destiny to choose to move on in a most painful parting that I myself had to undergo—the parting from one who determined to follow that Lucifer, the fallen angel. And therefore, I had to stand alone and move on and forsake that one.

Blessed ones, I know the meaning of sacrifice and I know the meaning of victory. I know the meaning of surrender to God's will and I know the meaning of His Presence with me. I know the meaning of His love and I know that He does supply the need of the one who goes forward in the way that is best, in the way that is highest, in a way far and beyond one's greatest hope for perfect love. Fear not, then, that in leaving behind the old way and the old path you will be deprived of love. A new love of springtime awaits you, a new joy of communion, and a new dawn.

O blessed hearts, I see veils falling from you. I see the divine man and the divine woman appearing. I see the victory of the God flame. And I touch you each one. I touch you with the hand of fire. I touch you for the cleansing.

The Hour of Victory Consecrated by the Fiery Touch of the Archangel

I come, for I am of this people. I am a part of this evolution. I have been with you for millions of years, and I decide now to dedicate and consecrate the hour of Victory. I am determined that you shall not turn back, that you shall not fail, that you shall not miss the perception of this moment! I am determined that you will save America. I am determined that you will save your salvation through the Inner Retreat. I am determined that the economy will have an infusion of Light! Let the Lords of Karma prevail on the outcome.

Sometimes the old must pass away and the new come. Sometimes the old may be transformed and in the alchemical Light have the appearance, then, of the new sign.

The will of God is good. The will of God will deliver you. Only stay with it and stay in your heart and let your perceptions be heart perceptions. Let the eye of the mind be the perception of the vision.

Maintain your identity and your integrity. Let nothing take from you that oneness here and now of God. Beware. Be alert. Be on guard. Expose the deceptors, the destroyers, the conspirators. They have no power. They have *no* power! Thus, let them also make their choices. This is an hour of choice and choosing.

I shall touch you by the fire of my hand. I say this, beloved: If you accept my touch, be willing to live by it. Be willing to consummate my faith in glory. Be willing to defend it. And be certain of thy commitment to never go back into the questionable state of doubt and fear of thy own divinity. Take guardedly the touch of the archangel and know that henceforth you shall have an extraordinary presence—my Electronic Presence—with you when you make the call.

Insidious forces move against the defense of this nation, especially militarily. Let us not rest until America is invulnerable within and without. It is a tall order, but is anything too hard for the LORD or for his chelas or for the legions of Archangel Michael and Mighty Victory and all of his hosts? I tell you *no!—nothing* is too hard for the Lord Sanat Kumara! This earth and universe belongs to God. I say: Go claim it! Claim it for Him, claim it for the Mother, and restore paradise. It can be done, but you must equate with the task and know that it is the work of the ages.

Let us begin. I am ready. From all whom I touch I shall therefore receive in return the inner electronic blueprint as well as the untransmuted self. As long as you are striving ones, I shall guard these two and assist you in every hour of burden. And you will know my presence within in a still, small voice and in the changes of thy life and this world.

Reject Not the Most High

God has come in this Dark Cycle. I pray you, receive Him, receive Her. Reject not the Most High, for my desire is that you shall live forevermore in the resurrection and the life with the Lord Christ.

In the name of the Father, the Son, the Holy Spirit, and the Mother, Amen.

The Judgment of Peshu Alga

"The Summit Lighthouse Sheds Its Radiance O'er All the World to Manifest as Pearls of Wisdom." This dictation by Archangel Michael was delivered through the Messenger Elizabeth Clare Prophet on Saturday, December 29, 1984 (1:31 p.m. PST), during the 6-day *New Year's Light of the World Conference*, at Camelot. It was the feast day of Saint Thomas Becket and the 3:00 line of the celebration of Michaelmas (September 29). (1) Mark 14:58; Acts 7:48; 17:24; II Cor. 5:1; Heb. 9:11, 24. (2) *Peshu Alga:* the first rebel against the Most High God; also known as the Accuser of the Brethren (Rev. 12:10). When Peshu Alga's son died, he cursed God for allowing his death, rejected all consolation, and swore eternal vengeance against the Almighty. It was the first sin ever committed against God. The archangel Lucifer (tempted through his own pride and ambition) was traduced by Peshu Alga and followed in his rebellion, thus causing the fall of many other angels under him. In his 1983 Christmas Day Address, "Ancient Records of Earth's Karma," Jesus announced: "As the year passes you will enter the Dark Cycle on April 23—the Dark Cycle in Aries. As you know, this cycle is the cycle of Helios and of Vesta and of the I AM Presence and the affirmation of the name of God, I AM, whereby the Christ, the Son of God, does declare, 'Lo, because thou art, I AM!' The identity of the Son of God as the living Christ is therefore the testing of the soul in 1984. You also understand that the perversion of the I AM, made originally by that one Peshu Alga and his consort and then Lucifer, was on that very line of the I AM THAT I AM. Declaring 'I am God!' as the antithesis of the sons of God, these fallen angels literally stole the Light from the altars of heaven to go forth to pervert and subvert the children of the Light. Now understand that these records of the original fall, the original betrayal of the LORD God Almighty by Peshu Alga, come due in 1984. And you will face the test of pride and of ambition, of the arrogance of the fallen ones—as you have never faced it before. This will be not only these elements untransmuted as black filings in the garment of thy self, but mainly and principally as the planetary momentum of the fall of the false hierarchy itself." At Summit University, January 12, 1984, El Morya reminded us: "Do not forget it has been spoken: 1984 is the year of the judgment of Peshu Alga and his seed and consort." (See "A Prayer Vigil for Communist Nations," *Pearls of Wisdom,* vol. 27, no. 26, p. 202.) Archangel Gabriel, April 20, 1984: "Therefore, look to the hour, for come this Monday, there shall return the Dark Cycle in Aries, which, as you have been told, signifies the returning karma of all of the fallen angels who followed after Lucifer, who followed after Peshu Alga, who was one of a number, specifically twelve renegades, who determined to pervert the Light of the archangels in their schools of Light on the twelve points of the rays of the sun." (See "The Joy of the Path," *Pearls of Wisdom,* vol. 27, no. 30, p. 236.) Jesus Christ, Easter Sunday, April 22, 1984: "I have said it before, and I say it again: It is the hour, therefore, in 1984 to look to the judgment of those who are the pagan ones, those who have professed me and the name of Christ and yet have denied in action the firstfruits of that love." (See "My Victory, Your Victory," *Pearls of Wisdom,* vol. 27, no. 31, p. 242.) (3) *Nov. 19, Mexico:* a series of explosions at the Petróleos Mexicanos (Pemex) liquefied gas storage and distribution site in San Juan Ixhuatepec (just north of Mexico City) leaves at least 490 dead and 4,248 seriously injured. *Dec. 3, India:* 40-minute toxic gas leak from a Union Carbide pesticide plant in Bhopal kills over 2,500; an estimated 100,000 permanently disabled. The worst industrial accident in history. *Dec. 4–9, Iran:* 4 Arab terrorists, demanding the release of 17 Shia Muslim fundamentalists held in Kuwait for the December 1983 bombing of the U.S. and French embassies in Kuwait, hijack a Kuwait Airways jetliner and hold hostages for 6 days at the Tehran airport. Two Americans murdered and other passengers tortured and brutalized until Iranian security forces successfully seize the terrorists and free the remaining 9 hostages on December 9. *Dec. 6, Florida:* Provincetown–Boston Airlines plane, on a flight to Tampa, crashes shortly after takeoff in Jacksonville, killing all 13 aboard. *Dec. 11, Belgium:* Bombs explode at 6 NATO pipeline sites in southern Belgium, sending streams of burning fuel into the air and shutting down sections of Europe's largest fuel delivery system for several days. Terrorist group Communist Combatant Cells claims responsibility. *Mid-Dec., USSR:* explosion in underground Soviet munitions factory kills hundreds of people in western Siberia. Exact date and precise death toll unknown. *Dec. 19, Utah:* coal-mine fire breaks out in the Emery Mining Corporation's Wilberg mine at Orangeville, trapping 27 people, including 6 executives of the company—no survivors. *Dec. 23, Italy:* terrorist bomb explodes aboard a Naples–Milan express train; at least 15 killed and 150 injured. Several terrorist groups claim responsibility, including the leftist Red Brigades, neo-fascist groups—the Black Order and the New Order—and the right-wing Armed Revolutionary Nuclei. *Dec. 24, Montana:* fire in large (600′ × 60′) metal factory building at the Royal Teton Ranch's Industrial Park, east of Livingston. Within 20 minutes, central roof collapses, causing the walls to cave in; metal tools melt in the heat and firefighters battle the inferno for hours before bringing it under control. Two-thirds of the building destroyed; investigators assume cause was electrical. *Dec. 25, Florida:* Explosions tear through 3 Pensacola abortion clinics, bringing to 23 the number of bombings and arsons at U.S. abortion facilities in 1984. Two young couples are arrested and tell authorities they carried out the bombings on orders from God. *Dec. 26, California:* fire destroys part of a Texaco oil refinery in Wilmington; no casualties; cause unknown. (4) Events subsequent to Archangel Michael's dictation: *Dec. 29–Jan. 1, Peru:* 11 peasants murdered in retaliation for aiding the government in anti-guerrilla campaigns; 12 Huayhuas villagers dragged from their homes and killed; 4 cities bombed and 2 others blacked out (23 dead) in New Year's attacks by Sendero Luminoso ("Shining Path") Maoist guerrillas. *Jan. 1, Bolivia:* an Eastern Airlines Boeing 727, en route from Asunción, Paraguay, to La Paz, Bolivia, crashes into the side of Bolivia's Illimani Mountain, killing all 29 aboard. Marian Davis (wife of U.S. Ambassador to Paraguay, Arthur H. Davis) and William Kelly (director of the Peace Corps in Paraguay) are among the 8 Americans killed in the crash. *Jan. 1, Washington, D.C.:* explosion in Hillcrest Women's Surgi-Center abortion clinic; 230 windows in nearby apartment buildings shattered. Caller claiming to be a member of the "Army of God" claims responsibility. *Early Jan., Europe and North Africa:* "killer freeze" cold wave blamed for an estimated 170 deaths and for seriously damaging crops. *Jan. 9, France:* fire in state-run nursing home kills 24 residents in Grandvilliers. Cause linked to electrical wires short-circuited by water from a burst pipe. *Jan. 10, England:* explosion, apparently caused by leaking gas, blows apart a luxury apartment building in the London suburb of Putney; 8 reported killed. *Jan. 11, West Germany:* 3 American soldiers killed when an unarmed U.S. Pershing 2 nuclear missile catches fire at a U.S. Army base near Heilbronn. (The rocket's solid fuel propellant ignited when the missile fell on the fuel container while being moved from a shipping crate.) *Jan. 11, Lebanon:* bank explosion in West Beirut marks fifth bombing of a Druze institution in past 6 weeks, bringing total casualties to 17 dead and over 86 wounded. "Youths of Free Beirut" claim responsibility. *Jan. 13, Ethiopia:* an express train derails on a bridge in central Ethiopia, plunging 4 passenger cars into a 40-foot ravine, killing at least 392 people and injuring another 370. *Jan. 14, Australia:* major fires, predominantly caused by lightning and initially fanned by high winds, sweep the states of Victoria, New South Wales, and South Australia (later spreading to Western Australia). At least 6 dead. Towns evacuated; hundreds of thousands of acres of forest, bush, and grazing land blackened; thousands of sheep, cattle, and wild animals killed. (5) Rev. 12:3–10; 20:1–3. (6) John 17:12; II Thess. 2:3, 4. (7) Isa. 14:12–19; Luke 10:18; II Cor. 11:14; Jude 12, 13; Rev. 6:13; 8:10, 11; 9:1; 12:4; Enoch 18:14–16; 21:3; 85:2, 4; 87:2, 5; 89:32, 33. (8) Rev. 9. (9) See the Maha Chohan and Helios and Vesta, May 2, 1982, "Beware the River of Death." *Pearls of Wisdom,* vol. 25, no. 31, pp. 320–22. (10) I Cor. 9:27. (11) Rev. 14:6. (12) Mark and Elizabeth Prophet, *Climb the Highest Mountain: The Everlasting Gospel,* Summit University Press, $14.95 ($16.08 postpaid USA). (13) Josh. 5:13–15. (14) In *The Twelfth Planet,* Zecharia Sitchin describes ancient Sumerian tablets that depict an extraterrestrial superrace of gods called *Nephilim* who "fell" to earth in spacecraft 450,000 years ago. According to Sitchin, there was a "central group" of principal deities: "The head of this family of Gods of Heaven and Earth was AN (or Anu in the Babylonian/Assyrian texts). He was the Great Father of the Gods, the King of the Gods.... The second most powerful deity of the Sumerian pantheon was EN.LIL. His name meant 'lord of the airspace'.... He was Anu's eldest son, born at his father's Heavenly Abode.... The third Great God of Sumer was another son of Anu; he bore two names, E.A ['house water'] and EN.KI ['lord of Earth']. Like his brother Enlil, he, too, was a God of Heaven and Earth." (*The Twelfth Planet* [New York: Avon Books, 1976], pp. 89–102; available through Summit University Press, $4.50; $5.35 postpaid USA.) See also: Elizabeth Clare Prophet, "Anti-Life Begets Anti-Life—A Conspiracy of Absolute Evil against Absolute Good," on 16-cassette album *Life Begets Life* (A83034), $85.00 ($86.78 postpaid USA); lecture available separately on 2 cassettes (B83037, B83038), $6.50 ea. ($6.99 postpaid USA). (15) I Pet. 5:8. (16) Isa. 11:9; Hab. 2:14; Rev. 22:1, 2; 20:14. (17) Pss. 2:4; 37:12, 13; 52:6, 7; 59:8; Job 5:22; 22:18, 19. (18) "If you will call to me secretly within your heart and ask me to come to you at that hour, I, Michael, will materialize to you at the hour of your passing and you will see me as I am. And I will promise you that I will help to cut you free from the remaining portions of your karma and will help you to enter the realms of Light with less of the attendant pain which results from human fear in passing. This is a privilege and a gift I give you from my heart. I flood it forth to the people of Boston and to those throughout the world who have the faith to accept it and to realize that God walks and talks with men today in the same manner as of old." Archangel Michael, April 22, 1961, "A Divine Mediatorship." *Pearls of Wisdom,* vol. 25, no. 45, pp. 431–34. The occasion of the delivery of this address by Archangel Michael through the Messenger Mark L. Prophet was the meeting of Mark and Elizabeth (then a student at Boston University) and her first physical encounter with the Great White Brotherhood through Archangel Michael's dictation. (19) "There is a tide in the affairs of men which, taken at the flood, leads on to fortune; omitted, all the voyage of their life is bound in shallows and in miseries..." Shakespeare, *Julius Caesar,* act 4, scene 3, lines 218–21.

Copyright © 1985 Church Universal and Triumphant, Inc., Box A, Malibu, CA 90265. All rights reserved. Printed in the United States of America. Pearls of Wisdom and The Summit Lighthouse are registered trademarks of Church Universal and Triumphant, Inc. All rights to their use are reserved. Published by The Summit Lighthouse. Pearls sent weekly (to U.S.A., via third-class mail) for a minimum love offering of $36/year.

Pearls of Wisdom
published by The Summit Lighthouse

Vol. 28 No. 3   Beloved Arcturus   January 20, 1985

The Process and the Procession of Liberty

Spirit-sparks of Liberty! Aye, that ye are—held in the hollow of my hand. Perceive as I bear living violet flames. These, my offering, are symbolic of thy Self: twin flames of Alpha and Omega tossed in the hands of Elohim, dancing in the heart of creation, free to be, to expand, to know who I AM.

Liberty is a process and a procession. Listen, and I will tell the story of the fire infolding itself,[1] complementing Divinity and establishing individuality where I AM.

The fire begins at the base of Mater creation and in the height and white fire core of Spirit—twin flames thus magnetized, striving to meet one another in the embrace of Love, overcoming all obstacles, sometimes divided by oceans of madness and perfidy, at other times moving against the relentless tide of world karma, then finding the breakthrough and moving together in a rhythmic spiral approaching the destiny of union in the heart of Christ.

Thus, thy way foreordained, brides of Christ, rise to meet thy eternal Spirit. His handiwork! Thou art called to be His instrument in the womb of Mater, to be now the vessel for the deliverance of worlds and the precious Manchild tossed in the hand of Father and Mother—the bouncing new baby boy, the new child, the girl come forth with joy and heart of gold.

Know, then, how—endowed by Elohim—you are and have been and evermore shall be co-creators with the Universal One, builders not only of temples to house immortal souls, but of the temple of the ages. Those who fashion a pyramid of Life dwell in the mountains, know the devas of the air and of the sea and the foam and the rose and the dewdrop—knowledge of elemental life

Copyright © 1985 Church Universal and Triumphant, Inc.

penetrating the blade of grass and discovering a galaxy all inside. And in the womb of Mother is the Central Sun. And in the seed of Christ descending is the point of the eye of God.

Know all things! Be all things! Understand the process of the fire infolding itself *in you* that immortality might once again reign even in this Matter cosmos. And this is not a contradiction. For even God may lower Himself, coming through the divine hatch—first appearing the feet of Vishnu (divine understanding) and the body stepping through each ring of galaxies, the divine astrology revealed in each of the body parts and all members conveying the divine astrology that supersedes the material. For the stars in all their courses are yet but a reflection of the greater universe of God whence you have come.

Alignment with the Blueprint of the Elohim of the First Ray

I AM the reminder of the eternal fire. Elohim of the seventh ray, I endowed you with physical form. Thus, the meaning of the seventh ray is the ritual—the *right-you-all*—of this manifestation of Matter, molecule by molecule. I command you to come into alignment with the Elohim of the first ray, the eternal blueprint! Thus, the process of alchemy. Thus, the procession.

Understand that which I speak. Understand the procession of lives of saints. Understand your own incarnations processioning, internalizing the Word. Understand me, for your lifestream has been in the process of the grand procession of the internalization of the Word for aeons.

There is the prehistory, prior to the descent into the veil of illusion, when you were crowned with the glory of God, when you knew the Light in Spirit. This grandeur and level of attainment is recorded in the causal body of your Self, and that divinity appears to you as your Christ Self. It is a Christhood won, then forsaken, but not compromised at inner levels. It is as the computer of the Mind of God: That which you are. That which you shall be is that which you have been; and then you may exceed it, you understand.

God has ordained His Law. He has made inaccessible to you the former True Self until you could be trusted with your Self once again. Thus, you see, every element of Self you cherish beyond any other condition—so precious as to not be lost, so precious that you never fail to defend it—this becomes the pearl, the jewel you cherish, and the initiation given. Thus, in retaining that star sapphire, you build upon it as building anew the God Star Sirius where you are.

Behold the Tree of Life! Here is the focus of the inner blueprint of the causal body of Hercules, in part—the reminder to the true to return to the true blue.[2] Thus, every tree of the Christ Mass can be focus of the causal body of every family reaching for those lights and the ultimate star. The tree lights are fruits of the causal body. Each one is plucked in its season for its purpose. And the twelve days of the Christ Mass are a sign of initiation in the twelve hierarchies of the sun. No pagan rite is this, but a reminder of the internal rite of the descent of Reality.

Seeking the Lost Identity and Lost Attainment of Self

You all yearn for something not quite remembered, not quite known or seen. You think it is for the twin flame or for God or for divine friendship. But, in reality, you seek the lost identity of Self.

Many times, frustrations or even illusions of grandeur or miscalculations of one's power or prowess derive from the distorted view of ancient days when the reality of Truth was there. Having abused power thus, there are many frustrated potentates. This has become an inversion. The ego, then, has dominated the temple, and the divine man remains aloft as in a balloon that will not land.

The procession of lives must find now fulfillment—the fire infolding itself in the Tree of Life. The base is heavy—the Matter cosmos. It thins at the top and ultimately it is the star of the Presence. Build the strong foundation. Build upon that which was laid that your Tree of Light might bear now the world of Spirit and house it.

Beloved, beloved, let all that has gone before count. Let the good, dotted in between the dark, now come to light. Do not rest so easy. Do not fail to understand how *open* is the Light of Elohim through this dispensation, how open now are your chakras to receive our Light, how the use of a physical vessel for the transference of the Word makes possible to you untold opportunity.

Let this be the day and the hour and the year when you dump that pride and rebellion once and for all into the violet flame of my heart. The caldron of an Elohim is great enough! Let us go forward in this year, this white page of opportunity. Let the fruits of your Tree of Life now come tumbling down. Receive them in such esteem and honor and sacredness.

How precious is that attainment won long ago in Spirit. How necessary it is in Matter to fulfill every assignment and cosmic purpose! How the trembling of the cup is the trembling of possibility in the moment! How you must believe that time and space are not—and this brief journey, one step in the long procession, can be the step, the step into the octaves of Spirit.

We who are the internalization of cycles, we from the beginning have observed the gradual descent into this sleep of forgetfulness. How easy to lose ultimate Reality. Yet, with the *waking, piercing, fierce* God-determination, *you* can return! *You can make it to the heart of God!*

Be careful lest you indulge the old patterns and lose what you gain. The procession of your lives—each one—is about to culminate in the Star. Keep your eye on the Presence. *Keep your eye on the Presence.*

Transformation of Physical Bodies by the Violet Flame

Thus, I am called again to speak to you as the sponsor of physical form and as the sponsor of the violet flame extolled and brought by Saint Germain. I desire to see bodies made of clay be transmuted into bodies made of living Spirit-fire!

Divine sparks of Liberty are ye! Understand the clay was not the creation of Elohim. Yet, bodies physical we made. There are bodies physical and there are bodies of clay: they are not the same. But the physical bodies we have made have also become compromised. Thus, you have taken in the clay and the 'clay consciousness' of the clay man and lost even the spirituality of the physical body. And it, too, must be purified.

How well you know how much you are composed of artificial chemicals and elements. This is my meaning: Life has been distorted. And even the bodies you wear, then, in some measure are functioning below the level of the Elohimic creation.

Let us bring, then, the physical body back to the place of its pristine beginning. The method has been given by Sanat Kumara and the eternal Mother. The method has been given; it is in your hands. Let us see what vessels of Light and crystal you may become, that it be no longer necessary to wear gemstones to transmit Light. Your physical body shall become the amethyst jewel.

Thus, there are bodies and there are bodies.[3] Let each one guard well, for the spiritual consciousness and the spiritual fire of all seven Elohim does transform the flesh until that which appears to be flesh is no longer of the earth earthy.[4]

In this planetary home, as small as it is, you can observe— from densification to spiritualization to etherealization—the varying degrees of consciousness at the physical level. Thus, the body limits the mind, even as the mind can control Matter. The body liberates the Mind of God, else it is a prison house defying the Spirit. And the defilement of the Spirit is in all unclean things which you have been taught not to partake of.

Internalization of the Word by Will, Wise Dominion, and Love

Consciousness is won by the process of the procession of electrons and molecules, the process of internalization of the Word by will. And will, then, is a foundation for wise dominion; and the twain thirst after love. And love becomes the necessity when passing through, then, the upper levels of the pyramid of this Tree of Life. The foundation is the blue will, then the wise dominion [*wisdom*] of it. But you cannot exceed the two-thirds mark to the point of resurrection without love. Without love it is not possible to love God supremely, to give obedience to the Guru, to forgive and forgive again—truly, to forget.

Thus, God has created the barrier. Even as the fallen angels have determined to purvey a false use of will and power and intelligence, they have never been able to synthesize a love that could carry the Spirit-sparks Home. Not that their misuse of power or intelligence could! But this misuse enables many to survive on the left-handed path, taking heaven by force.[5]

Thus, beloved, note the perversions of love which promise luxury, which promise pleasure, the perversions of love as drugs and rhythm that is not the rhythm of the spheres—not only in unacceptable sounds but in life-styles, for all is rhythm. There is nothing but rhythm. When you are out of rhythm with your causal body, life does not go well. When you are out of step with your life cycles, you never quite make the wave and ride with it and perceive the moments of opportunity and initiation.

Misuses of love come in a practice of medicine not based on the laws of Sanat Kumara—misuses of love in the treatment of the ill or the aged or the afflicted. And art itself, portraying only death and hell—the unacceptable offering purveyed in the world commands the highest prices. The divine art is almost unfindable in this octave. Pity the child who has never seen the perfection of a divine piece of art or the divine artistry. Nay, do more than pity! but find for him one thing of beauty that may nourish his soul.

Rituals of the Seventh Ray for the Turning of Worlds

I come for the reversing of the degeneracy of Matter. It is my office, it is my life. Only the seventh ray, the seventh age, and the seventh dispensation may accomplish this. Thus, you might say, all might have been lost in previous two-thousand-year cycles, as life itself was literally hanging on, waiting for the ritual of the seventh ray in full force.

We have come for the turning of worlds, and we have come again in a series of dictations of the judgment. Thus, I come again for an infusion of the planet this day of violet-flame light and violet-flame transmutation.

I speak of the conclusion of the cycle of the year and the open-door opportunity, of which you are aware, for forgiveness and transmutation now until the hour of the midnight and the speaking of the Lord of the World, Gautama Buddha. We seek for maximum transmutation by your violet-flame decrees.

Let your letters to the Karmic Board be written this day. Let them be received ahead of time and burned in ceremony this night that we might already examine your calls and implement them through violet-flame decrees in preparation for the coming of the Lord of the World. And some of your requests will also await the meeting of the Lords of Karma which comes at the turning of the year.

Let us, then, write—and write in these letters the nefarious designs we would see transmuted, their spirals arrested, that the carry-over into the new year of the purposes of war and degeneracy might already be stopped in its course.

Call for the Judgment of the Sympathizers and Servants of Peshu Alga

I would speak to you, then, of this event which has occurred in this galaxy whereby there has come to pass the judgment of the one known as Peshu Alga, the one who turned aside the archangel Lucifer from his service of the Most High and therefore caused the rebellion of many angels under that one. This individual functioned as a hierarch in his own right and many, many across the galaxy looked to that one as having the prowess to defeat the God-light in the one Lucifer.

Now, the knowledge has gone forth of the vacuum created by the second death and judgment. Now, then, those tied to that chain of false hierarchy look for another. They procession as the gray ones—blank, having a luster not of the sun but of the dark side of the moon.

I have revealed to the messenger the awareness of the procession of the godless. They are processioning blindly toward the Light and the focal point of the judgment, that being this altar and person and yourselves. They know not why. They are not fully aroused to wage war. They are simply without selfhood, save the selfhood of the lost leader. These individuals are judged simultaneously because they have claimed the one and the identity of Peshu Alga. When a hierarch is judged, a false hierarch, those in his service must similarly meet the same judgment.

I speak of this event because it is the request of the Cosmic Council and the Four and Twenty Elders to apprise you of the fact that their judgment must be confirmed in the Matter universe through physically embodied initiates of the sacred fire as ye are, and devotees of the flame as ye are. Just as you have confirmed the judgment of their hierarch, so you must now call for the judgment of these mindless, godless masses of fallen angels, mechanization man, and laggards—all of whom functioned almost as Nazi robots in blind obedience to their leader.

The race of overlords known as Nazis in this century and tyrants of all ages have come under this Peshu Alga. Though they have passed from the screen of life, they have not all passed through the final judgment and the second death because their time could not come until the false hierarch himself had been taken.

You must be aware of the fact, therefore, that centuries ago the twin flame of Peshu Alga, being even more vicious than himself, passed through that judgment and second death through the victory and the life of Christ and his saints. But there are other complements, there are other coordinates who move to support that Peshu Alga who are yet in physical embodiment.

Those physically in embodiment yet entwined with his matrix are the most deadly, for they have become the open door of the mounting momentum of awareness of loss experienced by these mindless ones. And on a certain day and date, their mindlessness shall be turned to a fury of hellfire and a viciousness untold. The threat of this has been foretold by prophets in rumors of world war and holocaust and the unleashing of terrorism or nuclear fire.

God's Answer, Already Provided, Must Be Implemented by Your Call

Have no fear. God has provided the answer, but it must be implemented by the call. The calls are in your hands. Use them. Define those who are called to the judgment and already prejudged, awaiting your confirmation. Define them as all sympathizers and servants of Peshu Alga and his consort, and not one of them shall go unjudged.

This is the most serious threat to the planet Earth and to the forward movement of this teaching of liberation of the Great White Brotherhood. *Believe me* when I tell you that there are cycles which must be taken.

There are reasons, infinite in number, why each one of you is seated and hearing my Word. *Believe me* that you were called and chosen for manifold reasons, not the least of which is the mandate of your karma as well as your True Self to choose to be who you are this day, this year, this embodiment, and to make haste to use well the life opportunity that remains in your heart.

We seek to overturn every prophecy of darkness and destruction. We seek this against the odds of the death wish in the very religious movements which have accepted as prophecy the destruction of earth or a final holocaust to precede the coming of Christ. This is a devilish doctrine and the leftover message of Lucifer, who has sworn his own (prior to his second death[6]) to carry his message of Death and Hell to utterly confuse all Christendom and the Moslem world and the path of Judaism.

Thus, instead of challenging this darkness of nuclear holocaust, many simply await the day of its coming and have chosen to disarm and become pacifists and to fail to defend the God within. Therefore, the angel, the mighty Archangel Jophiel, will speak to you regarding the education of the world that must come to pass through you.

The Encounter with Christ through *The Lost Years of Jesus*

I say this in his name: that Elohim have taken to heart—to their hearts afire—this book on the lost years of Jesus.[7] And we have placed within it the matrix of the encounter of Christ. This figure of Jesus—the youth, the teenager—is in fact a veiled image of Christ on the road to Damascus.[8] It is the figure of Christ in the encounter. This youth shall encounter the great teachers of the East whom he seeks.

This youth is also the one who will encounter all who receive this book. I would explain, then, that the placing of this book in the hand of friend or relative, stranger or foe, is the flinging of the challenge of the Cosmic Christ. You have heard of all of the roles of Christ—Christ the Redeemer, Christ the Saviour, Christ the Healer, the Burden-Bearer, Christ the Mother, Christ the Judge. Which role shall Christ have in your life and the lives of others?

It does not matter. He said, by way of defining a certain posture of his Christhood, "I came not to send peace but a sword."[9] If this be a sword, then let it be a sword! If this be the healer, then let it be the healer! But do not limit the action of Elohim.

You see, they have hidden the life of Christ. The potentates of Rome, the fallen angels of the West have determined that the youth should not know the quest of youth in these years between twelve and thirty-three—that they should have taken from them the knowledge of the quest and of the Holy Grail and the trek to Lord Himalaya and to Sanat Kumara and the knowledge of the Guru/chela relationship.

They made him a god fashioned after their own fallen-angel state of consciousness—a god to be worshiped, mocked, hated, spat upon, because he would do it all and leave all else as the mindless ones. They created a god for their own creation, for their own followers who would not think or feel or know pain or travail or struggle, who would not work the same work he worked. They created a computerized Jesus—born the computer, crucified as the computer.

Thus, you have not known Jesus. *You* have known him, but I speak to the world.

Beloved hearts, as Mary the Mother has told you, let this book fly! Send it to all you have ever known. Balance your karma by releasing the flame of the Christ encounter.

Here let the individual begin to think as a free spirit. Let him begin to wrestle with his archdeceivers. Let him wrestle! Let him be uncomfortable! Let him have to take a stand and have courage. Let him hurl the book to the floor! Let him pick it up again.

You see, beloved hearts, Truth must come and Truth brings a revolution. And a revolution is good because it is a turning of the mind and the heart—and this time in the right direction.

They follow Karl Marx. They follow Lenin. Let them follow the man Jesus. Let them follow the youth. Let them follow a real person of flesh and blood.

It is the most thrilling story, if you could read beyond in the records of akasha, of his encounter with the many on his way—his wisdom, his narrow escapes, what he learned about human character. You have known it as he did, in other lives, but it is required to learn it again.

It is a refreshing story of one who dared, one who took the chance—the chance of God to be victorious—and made it. It is the most exciting story of the hero of the age. And it will *tear them* from their orthodoxy, else leave them angry and growling and hissing.

Let them hiss! Let them condemn. As long as you give the

dynamic decrees and continue your support, these arrows of hatred will touch neither yourselves nor the messengers. It does not matter what anyone says. Let Truth march onward, and let it be through you personally.

The Loaf of Cosmic Consciousness

I demand change of those who have not changed! And do not think that I do not know and have not seen when you could do better.

I am at once the highest vibrating color of the spectrum and at once the most physical. The seventh ray spans the octaves. Thus, it spans East and West. Thus, let there be the meeting. And through the flame of the Universal Mother, let there be a common understanding of the loaf, the loaf of bread of cosmic consciousness. As He said, "This is my body which is broken for you."[10]

Thus, be content to be morsels of the whole loaf. Be content to be now those who assimilate the Body and Blood and become Elohim—Alpha/Omega. Alpha bits in the Omega of Life's spiritual composite. Computer emanation. Fire infolding itself. Fire ye are. To fire ye return! So be it. It is ordained. Only confirm His will and step into newness of Life.

So receive the Central Sun. [Monstrance upheld.[11]] So receive the Body of God, for ye are God's. So receive the Blood of God, for ye are God's. Receive the essential Light and know that the true communion is the Word (as the Blood) and the Work (as the Body). Enter fully into the Word and the Work of Elohim and thereby acquaint thyself with Him and be at peace.

I have touched and charged the communion wafer and wine. Let our servants distribute it to you in this ritual of the seventh ray of the alchemy of the transubstantiation, not only of the communion but of thyself in Christ. Amen.

"The Summit Lighthouse Sheds Its Radiance O'er All the World to Manifest as Pearls of Wisdom."
This dictation by Arcturus was delivered through the Messenger Elizabeth Clare Prophet on Sunday, December 30, 1984, during the 6-day *New Year's Light of the World Conference*, at Camelot. A fiery sermon on the Path of Liberty (including teaching on Jer. 34:8–22, Isa. 61:1, 2, and Rom. 8) preceded the dictation. (1) Ezek. 1:4. (2) Throughout the Christmas season, a beautiful 18-foot Michigan blue spruce, flocked in pale blue and decorated with blue lights and ornaments, stood near the altar in the Chapel of the Holy Grail as a focus of the will of God—to which Christ dedicated his birth when he said, "Lo, I AM come to do thy will, O God!" The tree was for each one's meditation upon the divine blueprint of Life, that we might draw down from our causal bodies (our "Tree of Life") the fruit of attainment on the blue ray and also invoke the momentum of the first-ray Masters. (3) I Cor. 15:40, 44. (4) I Cor. 15:47–49. (5) Matt. 11:12. (6) See Alpha, July 5, 1975, "The Judgment: The Sealing of the Lifewaves throughout the Galaxy," in *The Great White Brotherhood in the Culture, History, and Religion of America*, Summit University Press, pp. 234–37, 239–49; $8.95 ($10.07 postpaid USA). (7) See *Pearls of Wisdom*, vol. 28, no. 1, n. 1. (8) Acts 9:1–20; 22:1–15; 26:9–18. (9) Matt. 10:34. (10) I Cor. 11:24. (11) *monstrance* (from the Latin *monstrare* 'to show'): a sacred vessel, usually of gold or silver, in which the consecrated Eucharistic Host is exposed for veneration.
Copyright © 1985 Church Universal and Triumphant, Inc., Box A, Malibu, CA 90265. All rights reserved. Printed in the United States of America. Pearls of Wisdom and The Summit Lighthouse are registered trademarks of Church Universal and Triumphant, Inc. All rights to their use are reserved. Published by The Summit Lighthouse. Pearls sent weekly (to U.S.A., via third-class mail) for a minimum love offering of $36/year.

The Sign of Excalibur

O my beloved! A love such as ours keeps heaven yearning for earth and earth yearning for heaven. And this is as it should be, for it is the consummation of worlds to which we aspire. It is the fusion of beloved Father and Mother, Alpha and Omega. Thus, as you long for the Guru, the Ever-Present Guru longs for thee.

In each precious moment when our hearts find the point of Light's union, there is the convergence, there is the grand merging of Light forces, there is the moment of seeing the dawn of the golden age and Life transcending itself.

Oh, I would speak to you at year's end of my own thoughts and awareness—so much of which I conveyed to you in the last days and years, and so much of which I withheld. All other considerations taken to heart and understood, yet the soul's striving, the soul's destiny to fulfill the inner mandate, ultimately takes precedence over all. Thus, the deepest loves we bear toward one another and family and counterpart—all these must submit to the flaming sword Excalibur which gleams, suspended in the air: the sign to every knight that the call to enter the flame has come.

In the beginning the test is to take the sword from the stone. This is symbolical of the activation and loosing of the Kundalini fire, the World Mother within oneself. Thus, when the beloved Arthur took the sword from the stone, it was the placing in his hand of the object and symbol of the mighty crystal cord, star-studded with seven chakras. The taking of the sword is the taking of the rod of the Woman whereby king and prince and knight do conquer even the illusions of these octaves.

Copyright © 1985 Church Universal and Triumphant, Inc.

In the life of King Arthur, you observe the grand nobility of the soul facing each and every challenge, every momentum of personal and world darkness assailing each new plane of God's consciousness which is to be discovered as one mounts the altar of sacred fire up the spine to the crown of Life[1]—always the crown of the World Mother which she places upon her blessed sons.

Dear hearts, you have seen bejeweled swords. Know that those jewels are a sign of victory, of reward—but ultimately the sign of the starry configurations of the chakras in the mystical body of man. Thus, the gleaming, silver-white sword Excalibur, blinding in its presence, signifies the fire of the Mother complete and raised. Thus, it is in truth the appearance of the ascension flame.

When one sees the sword before one's gaze, one understands that it is the hour when the sword truly does cleave asunder the lower and the higher self, and the veil in the temple is rent in twain[2] and the soul does take flight to the higher domain.

Thus, in those hours I did attempt to reveal, in various ways and messages to you, that I should not forever remain in Colorado Springs, nor should you; that I must move on and transcend being.[3] The compelling fire of this call is beyond any experience you have ever known. And though the self may experience sadness before the *Mahasamadhi*,[4] understand, blessed hearts, that the call of the Guru and of the World Mother does satisfy every longing and give to the ascending son the means to bring comfort and enlightenment and peace and nearness to his own throughout the world.

Therefore, in this cycle of self-transcendence, one enters the heart of all who love God as a part of the stream of Life itself—not as an intrusion but as a oneness with the River of Life that flows and courses through all being. Thus, the meaning of cosmic consciousness is a total awareness of Life itself and a sharing of that Life in each cup prepared.

Now, beloved, the joys of our union are apparent. And I am here this evening to bring that mighty sword of my King, to bring the sword Excalibur as the sign of the victory of a year, and to place myself in the midst of all of my beloved as comfort and sealing of that which you have achieved.

I come to clear the way for the brightness of the star of Gautama and the mighty archangels who precede him. I come, beloved, that you may understand that in this moment and in this year God has placed in my hand the opportunity to cast into the sacred fire that which has not been fulfilled or accomplished but that which may be begun again in the new year. Thus, that which is good is sealed in Light and that which is lesser or incomplete passes through the flame.

It is an hour of the unburdening by the World Mother. It is an hour of the sensing of a joy and a freedom and of a victory. Surely you have laid upon this altar this day a fervor of calls that have carried to the sun and returned and resulted in much. Now I add to your calls this, my prayer, which you may repeat often, as you like:

> Our Father Eternal, sever now from the Mother and the chelas of the Mother the unwanted unreality, the force of the betrayer of the Word and of the holy Brotherhood of Light. Let the community move on now without the weight of the consciousness or the self or the idea or the condition that has burdened by the misperceptions of fallen angels and mechanical ones.
>
> Our Father, have compassion upon these, our own. And in the name of Mother Mary, heal now their hearts and souls, heal their bodies, heal their minds, and let them be free to know Thee as Thou art.

I, Lanello, do draw a Circle of Love, a line of ruby fire, around those who are truly one in Love. And the ruby flame does exclude the vibration of anti-Love that is pitted and marked with criticism and the divisive elements of disdain, discouragement, deceit, and sympathy for the downtrodden self.

I take the sword Excalibur. I take the Light of the Mother. I cut away the error and the dust. I cut away all veils of darkness and death, and I form now a body of Light. I form a Light presence in the very center and heart of this forward-moving community and cycle.

Truly, all of you have been tested, beloved hearts, beyond that which would ordinarily be the testing of souls at your level of chelaship. This testing has been given by Lord Maitreya that he might define precisely the rings of lightbearers to gather at the Western Shamballa in the service of the Lord of the World and Sanat Kumara. Mighty responsibilities demand a mighty wisdom and the soul's fervent work of the ages.

Come to me, dear heart. Lay your burden upon my heart. Let me enfold you that you might sleep the sweet, childlike-sweet, peace of comfort and love in the arms of Father. Come, my child. Come, my hero. Come, my sons and daughters. Come now, my students and friends and cherished ones. Come now, for God has given to me the means to lift your sorrow or your burden, to resolve your dilemma, and truly to make your heart one—one in Him, one in Love.

Blessed hearts, I perceive the greatest affliction of all on planet Earth as the relentless hatred of the Christ that is harbored in the subconscious of those who have sworn enmity with God. Spilling over into the wells of the unwary, into the pockets not filled with good fruit, we see, then, that this force moves in a stealthy manner to trouble and vex the hearts of God's dear children.

Understand that the entry into the world of the individual of the forces of death and the last plagues and of war, pestilence, and upheaval [i.e., the Four Horsemen of the Apocalypse] is through this force which comes by many names and means and in all sorts of Hallowe'en masks and even at the New Year's Eve ball. Precious hearts, the jesters themselves carry this force. For hatred becomes a mockery and then an envy and then a malice until, hardly able to contain itself, it erupts in acts of vengeance and violence. Dear ones, it even penetrates to little children through the misuse of sound, of art, of educational materials, of drama and entertainment pumped into the subconscious through the media.

Let us have compassion for such as these. Let us renew, then, in this *New Year's Light of the World Conference* our dedication to the torch that is passed from Gautama Buddha through the hand of Clara Louise to the heart of the Mother of the Flame.[5] Thus we hold, as the ascended and unascended messengers together, the commitment of that torch passed in 1973—that torch for the illumination of the world's children, for the setting aright of education by the heart, and for the lowering into manifestation of the God-design from Lake Titicaca and the God and Goddess Meru.

Much has transpired in terms of illumination since that sponsorship. This community itself bespeaks a student body of all ages, of great perception and wisdom and knowledge of the real and the unreal. Strides have been made. But this is the year when, my beloved, there is a turning and an acceleration and an option for you to carry, to bear, a more than ordinary momentum of illumination from the Lord of the World—to increase that Light, to increase that perception, to increase the actual potential for the Mind of God in the lightbearers of earth.

Nineteen eighty-five, as you will see, is a year of Cosmic Christ illumination on all fronts. And you will also take note that the false hierarchy of Serpent and his seed, of materialistic knowledge and sensual knowledge, will attempt to convert the great dispensation to a perverted knowledge that is without individual Christhood or its discipleship.

Thus, we send you in this year on the mission of the dragon-slayer on the second ray. The second ray of illumination is the ray of the Buddhas and Bodhisattvas, of the wise ones and the prophets and the anointed of Light. Let us be champions of wise dominion and let us see how a planet illumined measure for measure by the fire of the heart will make right choices for their survival, God-government, and abundant Life.

Let us approach every departure from Truth as a violation of wisdom and of the flame of the Goddess of Wisdom. Let us know that the flame of the Grand Teton is the flame of Lord Lanto and Confucius, and that it is the illumination flame in the northern hemisphere. It is a light of illumination for the precipitation once again of the golden-age civilization. Thus, it has direct application to the principles and plans of our Inner Retreat.

Oh, how I cherish this place! Oh, how I love to walk in its paths and hills, to climb the mountains and sit with Shiva in the whiteness of the snow and wind!

How I love its streams! How I love its stalwart chelas and faithful co-workers! How I love the dreams of Nicholas and Helena Roerich[6] which we do outpicture.

How I love the dreams of Paramahansa Yogananda,[7] my brother. And how I see them appearing in the faces of the Masters of the Himalayas who come to rejoice in the flowing stream, the mighty river of the Yellowstone.

Beloved, it is a year to claim the land for one's Christhood. It is a year to take thy place anywhere, to be seated in the lotus in memory of Siddhartha, in memory of the one who claimed his right to be doing what he was doing[8]—his meditation purely upon Sanat Kumara.

May I find you in the way anywhere, seated—seated then with the earth-touching mudra, that all of earth might bear witness to the glory of the son of God who has determined:

> This day I shall mount new courses! This day is the day when I clean escape, press through and beyond the stickiness of the astral plane, and make my mark upon the highest rock as the sign of my ascension. It is a mark of fire, a pearly white light. It is my promise and hope to the everlasting God that I, too, shall ascend! And because I will to ascend, I place behind me the smallness, the pettiness, and the unreality of world hatred in all its many disguises.

Hatred quenches wisdom and eventuates in folly, then ignorance, then insanity and mindlessness. The fires of hatred are the fires of hell that consume the very fabric of identity. Thus, we understand the source of the absence of mindfulness in the individual.

Some have long ago been self-consumed upon their hatreds and lusts of hatred, but all this is behind us. We face the Sun. We only warn because there will always be some who come to drink of the fire only to abort its purpose and turn it once again to that which is past and nevermore shall be nor can continue in all my holy mountain, saith the LORD.[9]

I am, therefore, now touching your hearts with intense yellow fire preceding the coming of the Buddha. Yet, from the Buddha's heart this fire does come—the preparation to be blazing Sun, blazing Son of God where thou art! Thus, Jophiel does appear now in the sky—high above the Holy Grail, high above the sword Excalibur suspended—to deliver, then, his mandate for the continuing education of the heart by way of defeating the darkness of earth.

Lest I tarry too long with you, beloved, may I say: This is a blessed day for all of us and a freedom—a freedom we have not known: the gift of God's true and righteous judgments.[10]

I wish to pay tribute to the Lords of Karma and to the Four and Twenty Elders who, in their great fullness of the Mind of God and in their achievement of cosmic science, have delivered this age from a massive darkness in this recent judgment of Peshu Alga and have devised the means to withdraw, without disruption of planetary cycles, much of the momentum of record of this and other affiliated lifestreams.

Your calls have compelled a response and a new discovery, as it were, for the demagnetization of the worlds of the heaviness of laggard evolutions. May you continue to exert the pressure of your hearts' love upon cosmic beings who draw nigh to earth because they draw nigh to the God flame you have extolled in your hearts. Thus it becomes a truth, as you might say of yourselves: And I, if I be lifted up, shall draw all God-free beings unto me![11]

I raise up the sword Excalibur in the being of our messenger. I raise up that magnet of Light, that truly the magnet might polarize and attract the intercession of cosmic hosts for the maximum deliverance of planet Earth in the year to come. And I shall be, in answer to your call, the presence of the World Mother and the Ever-Present Guru in your chakras—again, as that sword. As you are able to bear it and to become its scabbard, so, beloved hearts, know that it shall be unto thee a device of protection and merriment as you make Light of darkness and give it not too much trouble and not too much time, but yourself reign supreme as our beloved Son.

May I sing with you in this hour to the World Mother we know and love as our very own—to Her light in the heavens, Her veil in the clouds, Her tresses in the earth and tender feet in grasses and streams. The image of the World Mother is everywhere, and She holds in Her embrace all evolutions of earth. Do not allow any to deny the position of preeminence of the Mother flame in your life, and the very person of Omega and the tender heart you cherish.

Blessed ones, the Mother is the path to God. The highest hope I can have for you for this year and the best prayer is:

May Her radiance be upon you always.

Now sing with me—as we never part, but enter Her heart as one.

O Mother of the World

O Mother of the World
We are all children of thy heart—
O Mother of the World
We long for cosmic ecstasy
O great starry Mother
Do teach thy children
To have no other than thyself
Fill our hearts with purpose
Forge thy cosmic union—real God-dream!

Thy office of pure Light
It fears no competition
Let no one in the world e'er doubt thee
But find attunement with thy blessed head
Hallowed thoughts
Thy love which flows from glowing heart
Of cosmic dreams from God
Clears the air of confusion
That splits and saws asunder
Many lives 'til all wonder

Where's blunder 'neath our feet
Shall it defeat us evermore?
Never to take our store
With all our wisdom evanescent

O Mother of the World
We are all children of thy heart
Now kept apart, triviality
We would return to cosmic ecstasy.

The night is long and vacant
From Light of radiant Manchild
Here standing in the sun of oneness
We now confess to loss of happiness to thee.
I AM thy child, thy concept pure
Of my willingness to be God-taught
O Cosmic Mother, set my heart afire!

I move by thy love
To the fount of brotherhood
Where washing feet of all
I serve and see Poseidon rise
The New Atlantis of allness
Nevermore to sink into smallness
Of lesser self
I AM able now
To serve and reign as thy beloved Son!

"The Summit Lighthouse Sheds Its Radiance O'er All the World to Manifest as Pearls of Wisdom." This dictation by Lanello was delivered through the Messenger Elizabeth Clare Prophet on Monday, December 31, 1984, during the 6-day *New Year's Light of the World Conference*, at Camelot. (1) James 1:12; Rev. 2:10. (2) Matt. 27:51. (3) "I don't expect to be forever here in Colorado Springs. I don't expect to be forever here in this world. Do you?... It'd really be kind of silly because there are so many more wonderful places in the universe—beautiful places—and there are greater opportunities." From "Momentum," a lecture by Mark L. Prophet given January 28, 1973; published on 2-cassette album *Sermons for a Sabbath Evening*, Album I (A8073), $9.95 ($10.80 postpaid USA). The Messenger Mark L. Prophet resided at The Summit Lighthouse headquarters in Colorado Springs, Colorado, from January 1966 until his ascension on February 26, 1973. He is now known and loved as the Ascended Master Lanello, the Ever-Present Guru. (4) *Mahasamadhi* (Sanskrit *maha*, meaning "great," and *samadhi*, the highest stage of yoga; state of mystical ecstasy; deep contemplation leading to absorption into ultimate Reality): that final samadhi in which a yogi consciously leaves the physical body, nevermore to return to that house of clay. (5) On January 1, 1973, at the *New Year's Light of the World Conference* in Santa Barbara, California, Gautama Buddha announced that the Ascended Lady Master Clara Louise, who was the first Mother of the Flame, would, "ere the night pass, give to the present Mother of the Flame [the Messenger Elizabeth Clare Prophet] a torch charged with the vital fires from God's heavenly altar and the conveyance of a vast mission to illumine the world's children and produce the blessing of true culture to the age and unto all people everywhere." (6) Nicholas Roerich (*b.* Oct. 10, 1874, St. Petersburg, Russia; *d.* Dec. 1947, the Kulu Valley, India) and his wife, Helena (*d.* 1955), served during the early twentieth century as amanuenses for the Ascended Master El Morya and Lord Maitreya. (7) Paramahansa Yogananda (*b.* Jan. 5, 1893, Gorakhpur, India; *d.* Mar. 7, 1952, Los Angeles, California): Founder of Yogoda Satsanga Society in India (1917) and the Self-Realization Fellowship in America (1920); author of *Autobiography of a Yogi.* (8) As Siddhartha Gautama (soon to be the Buddha) sat beneath the Bo tree, where he had vowed to remain until fully illumined, Mara, the Evil One, tempted him with visions of desire and death, finally challenging his right to be doing what he was doing. Gautama, who remained unmoved, responded by tapping the earth with the "earth-touching" mudra (left hand upturned in lap, right hand pointed downward, touching the earth) and the earth thundered her answer: "I bear you witness!" All the LORD's hosts and elemental beings acclaimed his right to pursue the enlightenment of the Buddha—whereupon Mara fled. (9) Isa. 11:9; 65:25. (10) Rev. 16:7; 19:2. (11) John 12:32.

Copyright © 1985 Church Universal and Triumphant, Inc., Box A, Malibu, CA 90265. All rights reserved. Printed in the United States of America. Pearls of Wisdom and The Summit Lighthouse are registered trademarks of Church Universal and Triumphant, Inc. All rights to their use are reserved. Published by The Summit Lighthouse. Pearls sent weekly (to USA, via third-class mail) for a minimum love offering of $36/year.

Pearls of Wisdom

published by The Summit Lighthouse

Vol. 28 No. 5   Beloved Archangels Jophiel and Uriel   February 3, 1985

Qualifying World Teachers to Dispense the Illumination of the New Age

Ho! Children of the Sun! I appear to thee as the reality of heaven come to earth in this hour.

I AM the stillness of the Light. I AM the stillness of the Mind of God. I AM the perfect Be-ness of the Buddha within. And I AM the glory of the I AM THAT I AM. I AM the glory of the Son of God that ye are! I AM the glory of the Mighty Presence! And I shed the radiance of the Sun in my coming to *charge* the earth with the illumination of the new age!

I AM here to consecrate and to amplify the flame of Himalaya and Lake Titicaca, of Meru and the mystery of wisdom's fire. Therefore, children of the Sun, welcome to my heart, for I have some work to do this night here! (Please be seated.)

Now, beloved, Helios has called. Does Vesta answer? We shall see. Let us work the perfect work of God in the hour and know that the next hour and the succeeding one shall care for itself.

Our Commitment to Education

Blessed hearts, we are committed to education, to illumination, to enlightenment in this year. And our commitment is made this hour before the Great Central Sun, before the throne of Alpha and Omega. Thus, we have come from the very heart of creation to speak to you. For I so desired to bring the radiance of the Great Central Sun to this altar and messenger and student body that I determined to journey from that place here for this purpose of the declaration of the dedication of the angels of my band to overturn the ignorance that has been spawned as Marxism, as Communism, as world ignorance, as

Copyright © 1985 Church Universal and Triumphant, Inc.

world enslavement by the 'beast'* of socialism.

I speak in terms of Light! For I know whereof I speak. I AM the Angel of the Second Ray. I have witnessed the descent of the fire of the crown† in the people of God upon earth, for they have gone after other gods.[1] They have worshiped those fallen angels[2] and they have taken the alternative to individual accountability for divine wisdom.

Who is the chela of the sacred fire who will raise the Mother flame and keep the crown of rejoicing as the bubbling brook of the stream of Light? Who is the chela who values the River of Life so completely as to let no man take her crown?[3]

Now, blessed hearts, do understand the meaning of the Son of God. Understand the blessed head of the World Mother. Understand the fiery, piercing, golden illumination's flame of the eternal Buddha! It is not only a corona. It is a blazing consciousness of fire, until the whole fire of cosmos is contained inside of the head of the Mother of the World.

Know the meaning of Mother and you will find the Buddha—the Buddha of thine own soul's appearing, the budding divinity that must blossom as the yellow rose in this year and hour of service. Let it be, if you will, the yellow rose of Texas or Montana, California or New York, of Siam or wherever upon the planet Earth you hail from. But let it be the yellow rose that does blossom.

We Must Have Teachers!

Beloved hearts, know this: that if people are to be God-taught, we must have teachers. Therefore, thy teachers shall no longer be [removed] in[to] a corner.[4] *You* shall not retreat from becoming teachers! I will find you! And I will take you from your corners and compel you to teach the Word, to teach the facts that bring knowledge, that bring therefore the ability to use the fires of discrimination and choose right and wrong. *You* must be the standard-bearer.

Therefore, I command: Holy Christ Selves, descend into these temples now! Holy Christ Selves, come forth! For cosmos has waited long enough. And therefore, we will make of these stones not tyrants' thrones but the very throne of the threefold flame of Divinity!

---

*We interpret the scriptural term *beast*, found in the books of Daniel and Revelation, as 'conglomerate' in the sense of an aggregate body, "a clustered mass of individual particles," a group of entities forming a multi-purposed unit of hierarchy, a consortium of diverse interest groups bound by a common objective. The term is used for both positive and negative forces abroad in the world and in the case of the beasts (interpreted as 'living creatures') who sit midst and round about the throne set in heaven. The word *beast* as used in Rev. 4 is translated from the original Greek *zoon*, denoting a living being. In Rev. 13 and 17, the term *beast* derives from the original Greek *therion*, meaning "wild and robbing (or venomous) animal." *Zoon* stresses the vital element, *therion* the bestial.

†the lowering of the Light of the crown chakra through the misqualification of one's native God-intelligence

You cannot neglect the calling to transmit the knowledge that you have of who and what you are and the knowledge of this earth and what has turned it aside. Be not without hope, for I also embody hope. Where is there greater hope than in the flame of wisdom itself that promises to reveal the divine Selfhood appearing and all that this implies?

I AM Jophiel, and I AM determined to expose the most entrenched lies that have perverted wisdom's flame for aeons. Let us begin with the lie of nondivinity. I say ye are the divine manifestation! It is truth. Let this truth be known by your constancy to the God flame. You have no idea how reckless is the manifestation of the individual who is not constant in his example of divinity. For those who are beginning to trust in that divinity, it is necessary to show forth the staff of the shepherd.

I call you as I called Saint Patrick of old. I call you, I pummel you, I chasten you! I love you! I hold you in my arm and I sit you on the chair before me and I rebuke you for your failure to internalize more of the Word! For I know the potential, and potential never was enough! For all they who have fallen have had grand potential and grandiose ideas, but they have not delivered the blessed babe of the eternal Christ Mass.

Blessed hearts, break now the barriers of self-limitation! Understand that people suffer and die every day for want of the cup of illumination's flame. If one is taken and another is left,[5] let us at least begin to reduce the percentages.

That Not One of These Little Ones Shall Be Lost
—For a Failure of Wisdom's Flame

Let not one soul be lost in this year 1985 for want of illumination's flame!

I, Jophiel, make myself accountable for this fiat. And you will see me racing through the skies until they wonder, "Is that that yogi Milarepa hither and there and yon?" And I will say, "No! It is I, Jophiel! And I go here and there to be certain that not one of these little ones shall be lost[6] because of a failure of wisdom's flame." And my angels, as multiplications of this determination and my God Presence, do determine, beloved hearts, to go here and there and to be myself everywhere as the reminder of Truth.

In order for individuals to choose, they must have fact, they must have logic, they must have conclusion. Thus, the details of fact become the fastidiousness of the first ray. Line upon line, carefully research, set before the people that which has been the lie concerning drugs, concerning the imbibing of alcohol or tobacco, concerning all things that plague the body and mind which they take in. Let them be liberated from the addictions that come—come into the body through the senses and the orifices of that temple. You drink in pollution inadvertently by the chakras, by the ear, by the eye, by the mouth. Understand how the very pores of the skin take in the lie of pollution.

There must be a crystal-clear perception of what is reality, made clear by illumination. Let fact, then, be set forth as irrefutable! But, you see, fact is refuted. Why is it so? Because the desire is not quenched and therefore, no matter what you say that is fact, that can be proven, the individual who retains the desire (which means the entity's consciousness, the demon of his addiction) will not be convinced and will not be freed.

Thus, from fact, proceed to the Logos of Divine Reason. For the Logos is the embodiment of the Universal Christ and is the Word from the beginning. The power of the Word to create is the power now to translate fact into a momentum for change in the individual. And yet this Word made manifest is not complete until the grand conclusion of the Holy Spirit as Divine Love comes into the world of the individual and comes between him and those vipers that assail him—and cuts him free by the devotion, the innocence, the purity of one *Shiva* such as Lanello!

Understand the many faces of *Shiva* in the Ascended Masters. Understand the cutting edge of the sword of each one and know well the implements needed to divest the individual of the shroud of death they* have placed upon this race.

No, we have not given up! We have not ceded our place to any other. We are the archangels. As long as you strive, as long as you drink the nectar of the wisdom of the Buddha, we remain with planet Earth. You are the righteous ones who were not there in the cities of the plain, Sodom and Gomorrah;[7] and therefore the citadels of consciousness are spared as long as you keep that citadel of the Mind of God and protect the minds of the people.

Realize your place. Realize your place. Understand the meaning of the God here where you are, here in the very center of your temple, and know that that God is as important as the God who presides in the heart of the Great Central Sun. When

---

*the 'vipers', a band of fallen angels known for their attack on the children of Light through the misuse (in the practice of black magic) of the 'serpentine', Kundalini, fire—the life-force which animates the body and mind, rising upon the spinal altar, nourishing the chakras from the base to the crown

you [shall] have [attained] this commeasurement from your most beloved El Morya, you will understand how much you count. It is that snake (the anti-self) of self-denial, the denial of self-worth, that makes you lethargic—procrastinators avoiding the office of world teacher.

Qualifying Yourself to Receive the Mantle of the World Teachers

Indeed, blessed hearts, receive the mantle of the World Teachers.* Understand that you are qualified if you qualify yourselves. Think of this now: Take any series of our dictations, books, or tapes. All you need to do each day to be a world teacher is to study—early in the morning, thirty minutes—some message, going through our books, our Pearls. Thus, each day you have one message to teach to all whom you meet. You study it. You read it. You take a few notes, you go over it. And wherever you go, you have a message. It is like the child who learns to sing "Jingle Bells"—he sings it to everyone he meets! And he is happy and they are happy.

You see, you fail to become teachers because you think you must know all that the sages know. But you have forgotten: the requirement is the single cup of cold water in Christ's name.[8] Is it so hard to fill the single cup, the silver cup from which you drank as an infant? Remember your first cup, blessed hearts. It is the cup you give of the innocence of your soul.

Set yourself to any course of expertise—a path of spiritual teaching or qualification in awareness of burdensome conditions that we must challenge. Both are needed—the knowledge of the world and the wisdom of the Spirit which gives the sword in hand to conquer it. Then go forth confident that you may play one piece and play it well and give that knowledge. Surely, all will tell that it is the wisdom of the Holy Spirit through you that is the enlightenment and not merely the letter you have made your own.

The Maha Chohan may whistle a happy tune through your heart, but you must not fail an archangel to now count yourselves all teachers of something. Each and every one of you who knows the meaning of this Chart has something to teach, something to give. How shall they know what to ask? Do you know what to ask an archangel of the mysteries of God? Unless I tell

---

*The office and mantle of World Teacher in the hierarchy of the Great White Brotherhood is held jointly by Jesus Christ and Kuthumi (who was embodied as Saint Francis of Assisi). The term *world teacher*, lowercased, refers to the embodied disciple who dedicates himself to the lifetime calling of planetary enlightenment under the Universal Christ consciousness. This appellation is descriptive of the disciple's chosen sacred labor and dedication to it. It is not an indication of his attainment or that he has necessarily qualified himself to share the office or mantle of Jesus and Kuthumi.

you the mystery, there is silence between us. Thus, those whom you meet cannot say, "Explain to me the meaning of the Chart of my Divine Self," for they have never seen it. Thus you have at hand, on your person, in your briefcase or purse, wallet-size Charts of the Presence.

I show you how simple is the message, for you can always take in your hand this beautiful divine representation. And I tell you, beloved ones, it is such a miracle revelation of the reality of each one's eternality, that you *will* and you shall discover in due course that the glimpse of that Chart will mean for those making the transition an entering in to a coil of Light, because in their mind's eye at the hour of transition they will see that Chart. It is flashed by the I AM Presence, reinforced by my commitment to the education of the heart. And because of that vision, the soul may escape the troublesome elements that surround some who pass from the screen of life.

The Truth Must Be Shared

The Truth that is so simple yet so powerful in your life must be shared. And when I say "must," I speak of the mandate of karma. And I bring to you the knowledge of the karma of the second ray of illumination. Those who are illumined who do not pass on their illumination—in a consecrated and orderly, understandable manner, with good hearts and gentleness—begin to be burdened by the karma of neglect, the karma of the blocking of the flow.

Thus, no more illumination can be granted unto such as these; and that which they have may be taken from them by the Great Law that says, "To him that hath (with responsibility) shall more be added; from him that hath not (with responsibility) shall be taken away even that which he hath."[9]

Thus, there comes the atrophying of the mind and heart faculties of wisdom. There comes a stultification and staleness to the knowledge one has. It is knowledge no longer buoyant with joy, with victory, with the Holy Spirit; for unless it is shared, it is reduced to the level of the letter.

Thus, we find that some repeat our teachings in a mental manner but no longer have a spark to ignite another soul with the new joy of discovery of one's divinity and of the Universal God and of the Great White Brotherhood and the very excitement of the Ascended Masters. And they think that in reciting the teachings mentally that they know them and that they are qualified as teachers.

A Community Responsibility
to Assimilate the Body and Blood of the Christ Consciousness
and to Share It with One Another

Therefore, blessed hearts, realize the responsibility of the wisdom already given—not only to assimilate the Body and Blood of that Christ consciousness but to review it in order to serve at the table prepared in the wilderness. "Thou preparest a table before me."[10] Who do you think does prepare the table? Is it not ministering angels and shepherds of the Most High? Is this not a feast of Light? Has not the World Mother prepared it for thee? Thus, you serve at the table of the Lord and his disciples, and you prepare each meal of enlightenment as carefully as you learn your recipes and perfect the art of cuisine.

Blessed ones, the responsibility is great that has been entrusted to this community. There will not be world enlightenment without world teachers. We are not about to leave crumbs of bread in the forest as markers for Hansel and Gretel. The evolutions of the planet deserve more. And *you* deserve to have more of your divinity functioning through you. Thus, let each one unite with each and every other one to exchange the teaching. One teaches the other; the other teaches the friend. And thus, you share the resources and your research and you bring together what is absolutely essential to the rescue of the nations.

From time to time, you have heard from your teachers the emphasis on education as the deterrence to world darkness. And we have mentioned that those who give the violet flame and call for protection would do well to teach many the Law, for then their own duties would lessen and mankind would misqualify less energy and therefore require less maintenance.

We must do more than maintain a planet. We must create—and carve out of individuality—enlightened sons and daughters of God who will cease the misqualification of God's Law and Energy and become instantaneously—by knowledge, by the Logos, and by the conversion—trumpeters for God, leaders in battle, representatives of all issues, ready to tackle the conglomerates of conspiracy that have conspired to keep the most amazing Truth, the most amazing power of healing, the most amazing path of Christhood from the people of this planet.

The Karma of the Non-Transmission of the Word—
a Record on the Book of Life

Thus, I trust you have understood. And I trust you will realize that not any one of you will appreciate the day of finding on the record of the Book of Life that you have earned the karma of non-transmission of the Word as you drank in the Light in these sessions. Thus, leap in your hearts! Leap to your feet for joy, for the intercession of God is come. And when you hear the secrets and the mysteries of the angels, run and find the one in whose heart you may safely tuck the great pearl, the pearl of great price.[11]

I am, therefore, in the Sun and I am in your heart. And I am carving highways through all fields of human endeavor. And where I have gone and where I am going, I am finding that before we even begin to educate, *we* must tear down, *we* must remove the weeds of consciousness, *we* must clear the paths. We must eliminate—through the spiritual education of the people—the false teachers as well as their false teachings. We must create a climate of acceptability and of reverence, of open-mindedness. All these things complement wisdom by the fire of the seven rays.

It is a symphony of the stars that is being played—a symphony of the stars, I tell you! Some will hear it. Some will understand it. Some will know that the radiation of the stars is the very stimulus of the secret rays and the finer *nadis** that are to be the instrument of this expanded consciousness.

Good Karma of the Second Ray
through the Publishing of the Teaching

The world, by your effort, has increased its ability to understand the Ascended Masters and their teachings. And this is the good karma of the second ray that you have earned by decree and service and the publishing abroad of the teaching. Won't you add to us—and add to it now the Omega current of the heart-to-heart, mouth-to-mouth feeding of the mother bird to her own? Oh, be the compassionate one that does not rest until they have understood and until they are wrested from their enslavement to mass ignorance!

Beloved ones, those who bring Truth bring an uncomfortability. Do not be concerned that the ones thou wouldst feed shall fight back and become angry and will say, "Don't wake me! Don't disturb me! I am happy in my ignorance." Press on. Press on as angels and archangels who have wrestled with this state for aeons. You are here because we have wrestled with the devils that have moved against you. We have wrestled with your souls to bring you to the Light, that you might see. We fear not the dislike of the children whom we discipline. They come to love us more than any other teachers.

---
*nadis (Sanskrit, from the root *nad* 'motion'): in the Indian yogic tradition, the thousands of threadlike, luminous vessels through which *prana* (the vital force) flows through the body
Copyright © 1985 Church Universal and Triumphant, Inc.

The Determination of Golden-Flame Angels to Ignite Millions

My beloved, the earth is filled with golden-flame angels in this hour. They are everywhere looking for hearts to convey their message. They walk the halls of government in every nation, the institutions of learning and culture. They come, beloved ones, and I assure you: Though many have been determined and highly determined in the salvation of earth, truly it can be said, none have ever been more determined than these angels. They consider it their mission. They consider that illumination is the key, for God has told us that it is. And they are grateful for the materials at hand which you have prepared which they may use. But this is also only the beginning.

Therefore, I, Jophiel, call to thee, Mighty Victory. Now multiply our forces! Victory and angels of the sun of Helios and Vesta, angels of Sanat Kumara, come now to India and rescue these millions. Come to China and Russia! Come to Africa and Europe! Come to the Americas! Come to these hearts! O legions of Light, legions of all who have triumphed in Universal Christhood, come to earth and bring mankind to the knowledge of freedom and peace.

Peace and a Golden Age—we are determined to ensoul it. May we count you among our numbers, precious hearts? ["Yes!"] I ask it, for I, too, need the comfort of your caress and presence. Thus, the angels of illumination are at home—at home on earth, for some have heard, some have understood, and they will ignite millions.

We trust in the deeper understanding of your souls, for we have come to transfer that depth. This depth, beloved, is the opening now in this moment of our blessing of a deeper contact with your own Higher Consciousness. Thus, to us is given the dispensation to remove a single most tenacious block that has heretofore obstructed the contact of thy soul and mind and heart with the deeper things of God.

Prepare to Know the Mysteries

Prepare to know the mysteries. Prepare to be initiated as world teachers. And prepare for the Holy Spirit to give them freely to all. Thus, let thy good karma be thy instrumentation of that Spirit, as all prophets and teachers who have gone before you have done. They have allowed the Word to speak through them and it was so. And they and the Word were multiplied. So, as hard as the responsibility of the second ray is, so just so easy is the movement of the Holy Spirit once you have set yourself upon the mount of attainment of that crown chakra.

Seated, then, on Mount Kailas, know the meaning of Shiva and his beloved. And let that fire and that presence be the means to unleash the law of Brahma and the wisdom of Vishnu.

So it is done. So I am unrelenting. So I have come from the Sun. So I am drenched with the Sun! So I sponsor those who would be sponsors. So I make my plea. So I am in the gladness of the Buddha. So I wash the feet. So I kiss the feet of my beloved chelas.

Tenderly we serve in a Brotherhood of the Golden Robe—tenderly with Kuthumi and Jesus, Himalaya, Vaivasvata. Tenderly we love one another and rejoice in each soul won for individual Christhood, Buddhahood.

Kuan Yin, all legions of Light bow before thy presence. Kuan Yin! Kuan Yin, thou whose mercy's flame and star and flower has paved the way for our coming. Mother of Mercy, have mercy upon an archangel and bless us in this cause of our Father and our Mother.

In the name of Light *invictus*,* I AM Jophiel of the Ray of Almighty God.

Beloved Archangel Uriel

We Work While We Have the Light!

I, too, come from the Sun! Archangel Uriel I AM. I come in love for my cohort of Light. I AM the Angel of the Sixth Ray of the Universal Christ and the Angel of the Judgment. I go before Jophiel and his legions by dispensation, which I have implored from the Father unbeknownst to this blessed hierarch.

To Clear the Path before the Legions of Illumination

We come, therefore, to clear the path before the legions of illumination by bringing the ray of judgment and exorcism into the very bowels of the earth to bind the hordes that betray the youth and their minds and bodies, to bind the demons of the abuse of the living temple of the child.

We come, therefore, to go before Jophiel for the binding of the false teachers, false Christs, and false prophets, and all of their false doctrines. We come to implement the service of Archangel Michael and Arcturus and the Cosmic Council. We come fully equipped for the binding, therefore, of the demons.

Let the earth tremble, for we are fully armed and armored

---
*invictus (Latin): unconquerable, invincible
Copyright © 1985 Church Universal and Triumphant, Inc.

this night. And we will search out every adversary and false-hierarchy impostor—impostors of the principles of the Mind of God, those anti-waves and anti-ideations that conflict in the very brains of the people and cause the release of Truth to be short-circuited.

We go after the subtleties of the unconscious and the collective unconscious of the planet. We go after the subtleties of resistance and limitation of which mankind are not aware, for they cannot perceive the diminishing of their own faculties by interferences. And we go after those concerning whom the messenger has called the remnant of the darkest of the dark ones, who betray a planet and the oncoming Light—the ones of the Kali Yuga who must appear before the Court of the Sacred Fire this very night and give accounting for their evil deeds.

The Judgment of the False Educators and the False Initiators of the Heart and Mind

Thus, they are judged by the Universal Mother in manifestation in the Four and Twenty Elders. And thus, we come to bind. And thus, we summon Elohim. And we summon light-bearers. And let us utilize the hours remaining of this year to now go for the judgment of the false educators and the false initiators of the heart and mind. So let it be done!

I remain on this altar until the coming of Gautama Buddha. And in all of my myriad manifestations of my Electronic Presence, I, with my angels, now go forth for the binding of all that can be taken that the year might be sealed, the page might be turned, and 1985 might begin as no year has begun—with the options of right choice to every man, woman, and child on earth and with the options to undo the wrong, to redo the right, and to seal one's pledge again with one's Maker.

We will defend. We will go to any end! We will make any sacrifice, so long as our God has given the opportunity to work with the evolutions of earth. Therefore, I say in the name of my Lord Jesus Christ—I say: Work while ye have the Light![12] For this, too, is our motto. We work while we have the Light of Logos in dispensation for this earth.

Let the wise ones know my meaning and presence.

I AM Uriel of the Sun, never forsaking the dawn of the soul.

I AM Peace.

Messenger's Invocation:

Illumination's Flame, Impel Us to Right Action

Beloved Angels of Illumination's Flame, we call in the name of our dearest Mother Mary for such Cosmic Christ Illumination to empower us and impel us to right action in the name of Gautama Buddha, whose shrine and citadel and Western Shamballa we must guard physically.

Beloved Lord of the World, beloved Sanat Kumara, let Illumination's fires wash our minds and souls, wash us clean that we might be empowered with right action and determined action for the Victory. Almighty God, sift us now.

Jophiel, come into this room. Come into our sanctuary of the heart! Come to us, Jophiel—enlighten us and move us to do the will of God, to respond to the call of Jesus, who has said, "Come, leave your nets and I will make you fishers of men."

O God, we have been with this world so long. We are ready and eager and willing to drop these nets of karmic entanglement, to drop the nets of our own carnal reasoning and planning, to drop the nets of our emotional involvements, to drop all and run to thee, O Saviour.

O holy angels and seraphim, now burn thy fire around us, that we do not neglect so great a salvation and that we know our right response to our Mother's call. Even so, Jophiel, come in to us now in the name of Mary.

"The Summit Lighthouse Sheds Its Radiance O'er All the World to Manifest as Pearls of Wisdom."
These dictations by Archangels Jophiel and Uriel were delivered through the Messenger Elizabeth Clare Prophet on Monday, December 31, 1984, during the 6-day *New Year's Light of the World Conference,* at Camelot. (1) Deut. 29:26; Josh. 23:16; Judges 10:6, 13; I Sam. 8:8; Jer. 11:10, 13. (2) Enoch 7–9. (3) Rev. 3:11. (4) Isa. 30:20. (5) Matt. 24:40, 41; Luke 17:34–36. (6) Matt. 18:11–14. (7) Gen. 13:10–13; 18:16–19:28. (8) Matt. 10:42. (9) Matt. 13:12; 25:29; Mark 4:25; Luke 8:18; 19:26. (10) Pss. 23:5. (11) Matt. 13:45, 46. (12) John 9:4, 5; 12:35, 36. Pearls of Wisdom, published weekly by The Summit Lighthouse for Church Universal and Triumphant, come to you under the auspices of the Darjeeling Council of the Great White Brotherhood. These are presently dictated by the Ascended Masters to their Messenger Elizabeth Clare Prophet. The international headquarters of this nonprofit, nondenominational activity is located in Los Angeles, California. All communications and freewill contributions should be addressed to The Summit Lighthouse, Box A, Malibu, CA 90265. Pearls of Wisdom are sent weekly throughout the USA via third-class mail to all who support the Church with a minimum yearly love offering of $40. First-class and international postage rates available upon request. Notice of change of address should be received three weeks prior to the effective date. Third-class mail is not forwarded by the post office.
Copyright © 1985 Church Universal and Triumphant, Inc. All rights reserved. Printed in the United States of America. Pearls of Wisdom and The Summit Lighthouse are registered trademarks of Church Universal and Triumphant, Inc. All rights to their use are reserved.

Gentle Hearts and Gentle Candles
New Year's Eve Address by the Lord of the World
Release of the Thoughtform for the Year 1985

Gentle hearts and gentle candles held high, won't you illumine the sky? In reverence of the Universal Mother, I deliver my Word to the evolutions of Light in all galaxies.

Timelessness. Spacelessness. Gentle lights, gentle candles belying the inner strength of the God who is born. How magnificent is the release! Hearts are light, flowers unfold again, and the birds know their song.

The Harvest of the Year
Souls Emerge as Lotus Blossoms

I am well pleased with the harvest of the year. It has been more than difficult for you, beloved. You have climbed not one but many mountains. Some have not been aware of just how much they have passed through. For ye have been spirit-sparks of violet flame passing in many cases through treacherous waters and malignant consciousness and by thy innocence transcending it all until the angels are heard to whisper, "How magnificent, how wondrous is our God, that souls emerge as the lotus blossoms midst the swamplands of earth!"

It is best not to know all of the intricacies of the travail. It is best not to dwell on failure, for this is the moment of joy. The release of joy is a release of freedom as a rain of dew from my own causal body. The Light, then, descends upon all, and upon all the alchemy is unique, individual. For who can say what blessing or bane the Light shall bring? Yet, for all it is the opportunity for blessing if they will make it so, if they will only tether to the real—to the thread of contact.

Copyright © 1985 Church Universal and Triumphant, Inc.

Gentle hearts, gentle fire, how much does it take to kindle a world? When will the hour come, O chela? O Metteyya,* O Blessed One, sound the hour! Sound the hour when the little one does enter the Eternal Now, no longer to feel the limitations of time and space but to enter her eternal rest of nirvana and victory in the here and the now. The little one of whom I speak is the soul—a very precious soul. And ye are many precious souls.

Thus, I am glad. And in my power of peace I hold the strings of all manifestation. I hold the balance now in transition where some upon earth yet count 1984 and some 1985. Thus, the movement toward the sun shows the relativity of the awareness of the passage of infinite cycles.

The Keeper of the Scrolls Consumes the Record of an Ancient Era

There is a moment, an interval...and the sacred breath. The sacred breath held in the secret chamber of the heart does cause the threefold flame to glow. And the glowing of the Light is a sigh of relief. Indeed, blessed ones, for certain conditions of darkness upon earth have sought their level. Their tide shall rise no higher. And the turning of the year is the sign of the receding of certain conditions that pertain to ancient times that shall not appear again.

For the Keeper of the Scrolls in this moment holds a taper in his hand. It is a scroll that shall be now consumed; and the cause, effect, record, and memory of the ancient infamy is erased from the screen of life. Thus, when it is erased, the power, the momentum, and the force thereof can no longer be duplicated or retained by any lifestream or lifewave in any of the Matter spheres. Thus, it is the passing of an era and much error—but not of this era, but of an ancient one that cannot be outpictured again.

Archangel Uriel Submits His Report to the Lord of the World

Angels sigh the sigh of bliss and children nestle in the heart of the Buddha once again. May there be peace in many places as I plant the fire of Maitreya—peace as a flaming sword, peace in the person of Uriel, who approaches now with his report of service sustained by the call of the chela, the manifest God.

Thus, Uriel apprises me of the work well accomplished and of a relief to elemental life so burdened by prior darkness. Particularly, he desires you to know that the fire of the ruby ray and the purple and the gold of the sixth dispensation (the

---

*Metteyya: the name for Lord Maitreya in Pali, the sacred language of the Theravada Buddhist canon. Maitreya is derived from the Sanskrit *maitri* ("friendliness").

universal Body and Blood of Alpha and Omega) has been sealed and encapsulated in the sign of Jophiel's yellow rose for the undoing, the melting, and the dissolving of this hideous conspiracy against the youth of the planet in every nation. Hidden in the five secret rays in lifestreams and in forcefields, these may be quickened by your decree.

I, Gautama, salute thee, O mighty Archangel, in gratitude for the service of thy blessed life and all hierarchies of heaven.

The Judgment of the Conspirators against the Eternal Youth

I, then, raise my right hand as the Lord of the World under Sanat Kumara, and I release a tangible stream of fire, perpetually flowing, never ceasing, that is for the judgment of all conspirators against the youth, the Eternal Youth—which signifies the pure soul from the hour of conception of the holy innocents unto the eternality of the masterful presence embodied in the Holy Kumaras.

Thus, understand that the term *youth* spans all of thy life, all of thy becoming. Thou art the Eternal Youth as thou wouldst cast thyself as the youthful one. Thus, understand the meaning once again of taking on the aura and the garment of thy ascended self and knowing the full reality of the resurrection and the life on earth here and now as in heaven.

The stream of fire goes forth. And therefore, I say: In the name I AM THAT I AM Sanat Kumara and Holy Kumaras, by the authority of my office as Lord of the World and my chelas with me, let the judgment go forth of the conspirators against the Eternal Youth, the holy innocents, the Christed ones.

Thus, it is the decree of the Lord of the World that in this hour and year they shall not pass. They are bound by the fiat of the Cosmic Council. And all who raise the hand to harm one of these little ones[1] shall now have the immediate return by the stream of fire of the Lord of the World of their own hate and hate creation. According to the will of the embodied chelas and Bodhisattvas, so it is done in the name of God—Elohim. And all who so call in my name shall be the instruments of my presence.

You have seen, beloved, the determination of Jophiel. Understand that there are literally millions of hosts of the Lord of the World who contain this same fiery determination.

Whence cometh the Light? The Light cometh from the far-off worlds, from the throne of glory, from the invisible, indivisible One and the soundless sound. The Light cometh because Sanat Kumara is here. He would speak now to you, beloved.

Beloved Sanat Kumara

The Turning Point of Life on Earth: A Dispensation of the Solar Logoi

Precious souls who have long endured the forgetfulness of samsara, I come to remind you of the hour of the consummation of our deliverance of earth. My counsel is that we must not postpone this day or think because it has been so long coming that it is always in the future. Those who do not desire to experience the reckoning of their deeds prefer to think in terms of tomorrow. But we understand as the Solar Lords of Flame that that which may appear as yesterday or a million years hence is in reality for us the now and the present.

Deliverance of Earth by the Etheric Matrix of the Central Sun

Thus, I, Sanat Kumara, declare that in this hour is the deliverance of earth. The etheric matrix of the Central Sun is set as cosmic beings place an etheric matrix over the entire planet. This etheric sheath contains the record and blueprint of the original divine plan, its fulfillment, and added thereto all victories of all saints and early root races unto the present hour.

Understand that the etheric body of this planet has likewise been polluted by the fallen ones and the misuse of the sacred fire, by the rending of the garment and the forcing of the chakras. And thus, to see it is to see a once-and-former shell of light—betrapped, besmirched, gridded with darkness and record of war.

Thus, the Solar Logoi bequeath to the planet a new swaddling garment, a matrix very nigh the heart of God, that all might see and know in their finer bodies, as their own etheric body is purified, what is that acceptable destiny for this freedom star. The matrix itself—emerald, ruby, and sapphire, and the fourth, amethyst—provides a discipline and even a judgment. For the grid of Light is so powerful that many will not be able to go against the very presence of its force. Many will then turn to the path of purity and soul-searching. May they find interpreters of this octave and of the retreats.

This etheric sphere, beloved, makes vibrant and does intensify the etheric retreats and cities of Light. It does also activate and make light the chakras, as each one's karma does allow. The opportunity, then, beloved, to renew the golden age has never been greater than in this moment.

I who have known you in the vast forever, you who are my

own bands who answered the call to come to earth[2]—I must tell you that it is an hour when all that we have hoped for and dreamed for can be looked to and lowered into manifestation.

I must also tell you, beloved, that the pressure of so much Light pressing in upon a darkness untransmuted, unsurrendered in many lifewaves, as you well know, can also cause explosive types of situations as people feel they cannot escape their own substance which they do not surrender, and they feel they cannot escape the Light. Thus, for those who do not desire the Light, this sphere will be one of uncomfortability, one to which they are not accustomed. In other words, the Light is too bright for those who are of the Darkness.

Thus, expect chemicalization and saturate the earth with violet flame and protection as you have been doing. To continue these calls will provide heavenly beings with the wherewithal to enable earth to make this transition with the least burden of upheaval. We place great trust in the legions of the Holy Kumaras who accompanied me here so long ago. Our trust in you is great enough to give our assent to the Solar Logoi that such a gift could indeed be the turning point of life—a new life on earth, leaving behind the old.

This etheric sheath is itself a self-consuming, all-consuming presence—the fire that tries every man's karma, the fire that eliminates the unreal.[3] Thus, let there be the thinning of the veils of illusion! I, Sanat Kumara, proclaim it. We shall not forever stay the hand of Mercy and allow our beloved to suffer, but we shall intensify Light and demand that choices be made now.

Sanat Kumara Stands before Every Lifestream on Earth: "Choose You This Day Whom Ye Will Serve"

I, Sanat Kumara, place my Electronic Presence billions of times over in this moment. I now do stand before every lifestream upon earth and I say to each and every one: Choose you this day whom ye will serve.[4] Lo! I unfold the record of all of thy incarnations of perfidy and folly. I demand the choice for right action, for love, for compassion. I demand obedience to the Law of the One and the Almighty God. I show you, each one, the consequences of continuing in the denial of the Divinity and I show you the opportunity to enter into oneness of eternal Life.

I show you once again the hosts of the LORD, the Great White Brotherhood, and the Messengers from the Sun. Heed our Word. Obey the Law of Harmony. Enter into communion with Life. Shun death and all evildoings, and thou wilt truly find thy habitation to be the eternal spheres.

I AM Sanat Kumara. I compel the earth's evolutions to rise to the center of the Higher Consciousness of the Universal Christ. I have kept the flame for you for millions of years. Now I demand the recompense. I demand that you keep the flame for me as the representative of God and that you keep the flame for this evolution, and that the divine plan be fulfilled. I extend the solemn warning that those who continue to use free will against the laws of God shall be cut off from the land of the living[5] and have no further opportunity to realize God-Selfhood. For the hour has come for the Reckoning and it shall not be postponed. Therefore, choose Life and live forevermore.[6]

Beloved ones, my angels shall reinforce this message and even interpret and teach it to those who will not understand. For the same Cosmic Council who gave me the opportunity to be the Ancient of Days, the Guru for earth, has now decreed that the level of mankind's abominations and degradations is so great that the Law must act and compel cessation of darkness for the deliverance of the faithful and true. Therefore, they call a halt to the continued dispensation of freedom unto those who deny all others freedom and sow seeds of corruption in souls and bodies and minds.

As Above, so below. As God has spoken, so let the chelas respond and affirm this Word and this decree. And let everyone who is a son of God in the earth know that the science of the spoken Word is the power to transmit this decree of the Solar Logoi and the Holy Kumaras and the Lord of the World. And we bow before the Almighty and accept these judgments as the wisdom of the Universal God.

A Separate People, Elect unto God, Receive a Flame of Balance

Come apart, then, in the joy of the LORD to be that separate people elect unto God,[7] that thou and thy household and thy loved ones might be protected in the day of the wrath of the avenging ones, who will not relent in their darkness but only seek to destroy as they themselves are self-consumed.

We come to place a flame of balance—balance of the three-fold flame and balance of the cosmic scales—with each and every one of you. I place my aura around you secure, that you might be the Buddha and the presence of Gautama holding the balance of earth as the necessary step-up and changes take place.

I will leave off speaking with you now that I might place the oneness that I AM in the heart of the earth throughout the

Gentle Hearts and Gentle Candles

planetary body, containing it entirely in my own being. Thus, all who live here must deal with the consciousness of the Holy Kumaras, feel then the halter of the Law, the intensity of the Love, know the wisdom of God, and determine the course of their individual life action.

Gautama, my son, in our hearts' oneness, we endure unto the consummation of all cycles.

Beloved Gautama Buddha

Noble knights and ladies of the flame, our beloved Sanat Kumara has revealed to us that which has been kept secret in the heart of the Solar Logoi. Thus, I, too, bask in the new glory of the New Day.

The Thoughtform for the Year 1985: The Image of Planet Earth Restored

There is passed to me now from the Keeper of the Scrolls the scroll of the thoughtform for the year 1985. It is the image of planet Earth restored—karma balanced, axis straightened. It is sealed in the etheric sheath and thus appears as a shimmering sphere of light. The configurations of landmasses and seas are not exactly as they are today, signifying the true etheric matrix of that which is to be in the golden age.

Present in the canvas that is drawn, at the lower left, is an anchor, an anchor such as used by Maitreya in his clipper ship. It signifies the anchoring of planet Earth in the bedrock of Maitreya's consciousness. In the upper right corner are the scales, signifying the balance of all forces and karmic cycles.

In the lower right-hand corner is the sacred heart of the Christ, full blossoming with a fleur-de-lis and the white rose of the Mother. Diamond and bejeweled with the gems of the City Foursquare,[8] this heart is the sign of the disciples of the path of the ruby ray who enter into the union of the cross of Sanat Kumara, Gautama, Jesus, and Maitreya.

And in the upper left-hand corner there is the image of the City Foursquare, the New Jerusalem that descends out of heaven[9] as the etheric matrix lowered for the community of the Holy Spirit forged and won by the called-out ones. Beneath that symbol is the outline of the mountains of the Inner Retreat.

Thus, in these signs you may understand the mighty work of the ages of your souls to seal the earth in the bedrock of the path of Maitreya by the anchor itself for the conquest of sea and water. The balance that is held is in the Mind of God through the scales. The sacred fire of the heart is the victory of the Spirit as the Word made flesh. Fire in Matter signifies the union of heaven and earth in the chakra supreme in the body temple. And the descending city is the pattern and blueprint whereby the etheric octave becomes physical, proven once and then proven again and again as a formula of Life varying in each continent and place that shall spring up as the whole world receives the education of the heart.

May you pray for the precipitation of these four symbols in the hearts of all lightbearers, that the cardinal points of earth and the gates of the city might be kept.

The Year of the Four Horsemen

As we have unveiled and seen with our eyes, beheld in the inner hearing of the ear, and witnessed this glory, understand that the height of eternal Life that is the gift of God must see the flushing out of Darkness. Thus, it is the year of the Four Horsemen and of the fourth.[10] Life, then, in its intensity, must cancel out anti-Life.

Thus, this year is the death of unreality and ego-centered existence. Teach the people to separate themselves out from this consciousness and therefore live while the dying of the old self takes place. Be vigilant in the calls of the judgment of Death and Hell by my right hand, one with the hand of Mother Mary and your own. See, then, that the greatest Light must consume the greatest Darkness; and unless the intensity of the polarity be forthcoming, no flesh should be saved[11]—nor spirits. Thus, when you make big calls for big eventualities, expect big dispensations and enter the consciousness of Sirius, the God Star.

Learn the soberness of life, even as the lilt of joy, the humor of the hour—especially, *especially* in the commeasurement of human nonsense, quite silly against the backdrop of the divine procession. We always retain the sense of joy and the twinkle in the eye of God that sees beyond the calamity, the temporary crisis, to its resolution and the far better experience of the soul in Light.

Let all agents and agencies of the Four Horsemen then be submitted to the judgment of the right hand of the Cosmic Virgin, and see how you clear the stables and the darkest places of the cellars of these leftover ghosts of Christmas past. In each of the four quadrants one of the horsemen rides to challenge the light of the etheric matrix there.

Blessed ones, I tell you a truth: It is easy to overturn them and unseat them! For I ask you whether it is greater a feat to bind

Copyright © 1985 Church Universal and Triumphant, Inc.

a single ghost of unreality or ten thousand ghosts of unreality. Is not the zero the zero? The nonentity is the nonentity, whether it is multiplied a million times over.

It is the perception of the Son of God. There is a contact with the real matrix beyond the illusion; and when that contact is made, the entire procession of the not-selves must collapse. Thus, fear not the prophecies but fulfill the Judgment. And know that the etheric day and the golden age is alive now within your heart.

A Message of Reality, Vision, and an Open Book

Thus, my message in this hour is one of Reality. Ere three months have passed from this day, a new vision will come to you personally. Thus, beginning in the sign of Aries, look for the vision of thine eye and the all-seeing eye. Prepare for it even now and attend the vision of thy God. For 1985 is the year of vision, and the precipitation of that vision is according to thy work and thy word.

And for the rest of my message, I leave it as an open book and a white page on which you shall write. For the great mystery and joy of the future lies in the exercise of free will by the Christed ones. So may you rejoice as co-creators with God. In the heart of the Saviour, thou, too, art Saviour. In the heart of the Redeemer, thou, too, art Redeemer.

Healers, then, of sacred fire, confrères of Raphael and Mother Mary, I, Gautama, commend you to thy meditation and delight in the Law of God. Truly in His love and our own, let us dwell together forevermore.

O sign of Infinity, seal now each forehead with the promise of eternal Life.

I AM with you alway. You may call me Father, Guru, Gautama, Buddha, brother, friend, child. In every face and light and eye, I present the lessons of 1985. I seal them and I reveal them step by step, one by one, unto your unfolding Cosmic Christ consciousness.

I expect the fruit of discrimination one year from today. May you bring it to the altar as a gift, showing forth the persistent pursuit of attainment in the discernment of the ways of God. Discrimination and discretion are the marks of the Bodhisattva.

In the name I AM THAT I AM, *AUM AUM* . . .

[Lord Gautama chants.]

You have heard the voice of my feminine self.

Messenger's Benediction:

Joy and Gratitude for Earth's Swaddling Garment

Beloved Alpha, beloved Omega, we express our utmost joy and gratitude to be the recipients of so great a gift as this new etheric body for our planet. We send our heart's fullness of light and love and joy—we send you all of our causal body. We ask you to use every erg of Good in our lifestream for the saving of this planet and the pursuit of your projects made known to us through all of our ascended brethren.

Beloved Alpha and Omega, you truly are near as heartbeat, yet far as distant star. And we see you in all ways and everywhere, and we are so grateful to be in your universe. Thank you for Sanat Kumara and Elohim and Archangels and Gautama Buddha, Maitreya, Jesus, El Morya, Saint Germain, beloved Jophiel and Uriel and all Archangels, and our dearly beloved Lanello, who has opened the door for our own Victory.

Therefore, Alpha and Omega, seal these hearts so joyous in the gratitude of the Lords of Karma. Seal them now as they are already sealed by the devotion of On High and here below.

In the name of Mother Mary, Amen.

"**The Summit Lighthouse Sheds Its Radiance O'er All the World to Manifest as Pearls of Wisdom.**" This dictation by Gautama Buddha and Sanat Kumara was delivered through the Messenger Elizabeth Clare Prophet at the midnight hour, Monday, December 31, 1984, during the 6-day *New Year's Light of the World Conference,* at Camelot. Devotees—each holding high a taper lit from the flame upon the Altar of Invocation—kept a candlelight vigil throughout the dictation. (1) Matt. 18:6, 10, 14; Mark 9:42; Luke 17:1, 2. (2) Thousands of years ago, when mankind's departure from cosmic law became so great that cosmic councils decreed the dissolution of the planet, Sanat Kumara, the Ancient of Days (Dan. 7:9, 13, 22), volunteered to come from his home star, Venus, to embody the threefold flame on behalf of the evolutions of earth—who had willfully ignored and forgotten the God-flame within their hearts. One hundred and forty-four thousand lightbearers accompanied him, incarnating among mankind to quicken souls of Light to the memory and renewal of their vow to be bearers of the flame. Sanat Kumara recounts the story in his April 8, 1979, Pearl of Wisdom, "The Dispensation Granted," vol. 22, no. 14, pp. 82–86. See also "Lord of the World," *Pearls of Wisdom,* vol. 26, no. 9, pp. 75–76. (3) I Cor. 3:13–15; I Pet. 1:7; 4:12. (4) Josh. 24:15. (5) Pss. 52:5; Isa. 53:8. (6) Deut. 30:19. (7) Exod. 33:16; Lev. 20:24, 26; II Cor. 6:17. (8) Rev. 21:9–11, 18–21. (9) Rev. 21:2. (10) Rev. 6:1–8 (read by the messenger following the dictation). (11) Matt. 24:22; Mark 13:20.

Fiats of the LORD printed in bold type are to be used by the disciples of Christ as mantras and dynamic decrees in the science of the spoken Word. Keepers of the Flame are encouraged to compose their own affirmations based on the teachings given in the Pearls of Wisdom.

Pearls of Wisdom, published weekly by The Summit Lighthouse for Church Universal and Triumphant, come to you under the auspices of the Darjeeling Council of the Great White Brotherhood. These are presently dictated by the Ascended Masters to their Messenger Elizabeth Clare Prophet. The international headquarters of this nonprofit, nondenominational activity is located in Los Angeles, California. All communications and freewill contributions should be addressed to The Summit Lighthouse, Box A, Malibu, CA 90265. Pearls of Wisdom are sent weekly throughout the USA via third-class mail to all who support the Church with a minimum yearly love offering of $40. First-class and international postage rates available upon request. Notice of change of address should be received three weeks prior to the effective date. Third-class mail is not forwarded by the post office.

Copyright © 1985 Church Universal and Triumphant, Inc. All rights reserved. Printed in the United States of America. Pearls of Wisdom and The Summit Lighthouse are registered trademarks of Church Universal and Triumphant, Inc. All rights to their use are reserved.

New Love

A Ring of Our Sun System

Eternal lifestreams of God, I am blessed in the Mother Light of Omega to keep the Flame of Mother in this system of worlds. I am blessed to anchor here in your hearts and in the ring of fire you have formed,[1] a ring of our sun system.

I am therefore sealing by the Light of Omega your chakras and souls—anchoring, grounding, perfecting the release of Helios.[2] I beam now the Light of our sun from starry bodies that this 'sun-Light' might carry the vibration of all benign configurations of cosmos.

In this Light we see, then, the lowering from thine own star, thy causal body, the assistance from my heart necessary for all that you have set yourselves to accomplish in this year and lifetime and beyond that is the LORD's purpose for thy heart. I draw you now into the folds of my garment, which sweep through this entire property, that you might discover in the true Flame of Mother what is the Reality of the Divine Woman—and all else that can be set aside.

The Neutralization of the Misuses of the Light on Lemuria and Atlantis

I have come specifically for the neutralization of all misuses of the Light of the Mother on earth, including the ancient records that caused the sinking of Lemuria and Atlantis. Certain members of our bands, including Sanat Kumara, have come to perform this service and, increment by increment—so the Solar Logoi will it so—that these misuses of the sacred fire might be neutralized and the energy itself rechanneled in the heart of the sun.

Copyright © 1985 Church Universal and Triumphant, Inc.

Specifically, now, I concentrate upon those misuses of the Light by the black magicians of Atlantis causing the sinking of that continent. We are determined that no advanced science or scientists (all of whom use the Light of the Mother) may activate again, and reactivate, those very causes for the destruction of life and earth and the changing of continents.

Therefore, "neutralization" means the sealing of all such records and their knowledge in an intense white fire until day by day the violet-flame angels, in answer to your call, may also transmute this energy. As you well know, Darkness begets Darkness as innocent lifestreams tie in to the ancient records. If earth is to become a sun, as we are that sun, earth must be cleansed and purified at the rate which can be tolerated by her evolutions. Too much Light or too much Darkness will burden the patient and destroy the opportunity for Life.

Anchoring the Light of World Transmutation in the Mountain Chains of the Planet

Thus, my beloved, in the person of Mother in every manifestation of Durga—as Sarasvati, Lakshmi, Kali, Astrea, Mary, Kuan Yin; as every virtue of the feminine power of God in the water, the earth, the fire, and the air and in the ethers themselves—I say to you:

Receive now the flow of Cosmos' secret rays which does trace the path marked by your Christ Selves today. Receive, O earth, all that a Mother's heart may bestow. Through the God and Goddess Meru and Lord Himalaya, we anchor now in the currents of the mountain chains of the entire planet and the underground waters this Light of world transmutation.

I AM Vesta and I AM determined now in the fiery center of earth to release the Light of Elohim to consume all forces perverting the life-force in any manner and in any chakra. I come because of the danger of the spread of the karma of these individuals who misqualify the Light, and the spread of disease and death because of their infamy and rebellion against the Divine Mother Flame.

Let the Mother Flame, then, increase within you and let your protection be commensurate with your need. For the Mother Flame is great power. I place it under the control of Brahma, Vishnu, and Shiva within you, that it may not cause insanity or derangement or quicken anger or emotions, but be kept in the very heart of fire for the release and control of the planetary home and changes that are to come.

I come now as a bird of paradise to nestle with you. I come in many forms, beloved. See me in everything and you will not miss me.

That This Experiment in Cosmic Liberty Shall Succeed

The beams of the sun, the warmth of our love and wisdom vivify all the earth. And thus, the Light also uncovers the anti-Light. We are determined, as we hold this planet in our very hands in this hour, that this experiment in Cosmic Liberty shall succeed and that this star shall be not only Freedom's Star but Victory's Star.

I press the petals of the flowers from our garden in the heart of the sun. I have brought enough petals of flowers you know—and some you know not—to completely saturate each one in petals of Light. My angels place around your necks leis of the most fragrant, perfumed offerings of the heart of the angels of the sun.

Mothers-to-be, Buddhas-to-be, Christs-to-be, thus receive our Light. Thus know our Love. Thus be diligent in all thou hast been taught.

My presence here seals you and must now be withdrawn, for earth cannot bear more of my presence. This is a beginning of the rise of Mother to new levels. It is sealed. It shall not cause cataclysm. Hold it and guard the Flame. I take my leave, withdraw my forcefield, and go to the sun that you and earth might adjust to new Love.

In the eternal springtime, remember our love, our oneness, and our embrace.

Hymn to the Sun
by Helios

O mighty Presence of God, I AM, in and behind the Sun:
I welcome thy Light, which floods all the earth,
   into my life, into my mind, into my spirit, into my soul.
Radiate and blaze forth thy Light!
Break the bonds of darkness and superstition!
Charge me with the great clearness
   of thy white fire radiance!
I AM thy child, and each day I shall become
   more of thy manifestation!

The New Day
by Vesta

Helios and Vesta!
Helios and Vesta!
Helios and Vesta!
Let the Light flow into my being!
Let the Light expand in the center of my heart!
Let the Light expand in the center of the earth
And let the earth be transformed into the New Day!

"**The Summit Lighthouse Sheds Its Radiance O'er All the World to Manifest as Pearls of Wisdom.**" This dictation by Vesta was delivered through the Messenger Elizabeth Clare Prophet on Tuesday, January 1, 1985, during the 6-day *New Year's Light of the World Conference*. (1) In preparation for the dictation, the Messenger together with more than one thousand devotees joined hands to form Mother Mary's Circle of Light on the meadow at Camelot for the healing of America and the world and for the deliverance of the nations through prayers, hymns, and meditations on the Blessed Mother's diamond heart. The Circle of Light continued until dusk when Beloved Vesta addressed the conferees as the Messenger stood in the center of the circle, the strong, comforting light of Venus overhead. (2) Beloved Helios' address, which was hailed by Lord Maitreya as the "event of the millennia," was delivered July 4, 1984, in the Heart of the Inner Retreat. To hold the balance for his coming, Vesta remained in their etheric retreat, the Temple of the Sun, in the center of our physical sun. In a dictation given November 18, 1984, Kuthumi said: "This is the half-year cycle of the coming of Helios; therefore, salute Vesta who appears in winter solstice as Helios appears in summer solstice . . . . Thus, let us see if we together by our love and perpetual vigil in this sanctuary might not woo the beloved Vesta to release her Light and speak to us in this New Year's conference." El Morya, in his letter of November 26, 1984, reminded Keepers of the Flame of their opportunity to "hold, during this winter solstice, the balance for the Light of Helios released at summer solstice in the Heart of the Inner Retreat. If this balance is held during the weeks preceding and including the conference, the proferred gift of Vesta for the sealing of the Spirit of the Father in the Matter of the Feminine Ray will be delivered through the Messenger. This Light is to be anchored in her heart and in the retreat at Lake Titicaca, physically, for the holding of the balance of North, South, and Central America—thus forming the figure eight from the heart of Gautama Buddha in the Western Shamballa to the hearts of the God and Goddess Meru."

Copyright © 1985 Church Universal and Triumphant, Inc., Box A, Malibu, CA 90265. All rights reserved. Printed in the United States of America. Pearls of Wisdom and The Summit Lighthouse are registered trademarks of Church Universal and Triumphant, Inc. All rights to their use are reserved. Published by The Summit Lighthouse. Pearls sent weekly (to USA, via third-class mail) for a minimum love offering of $40/year.

The Battle of Armageddon in the Classrooms of America

Beloved of the Light, we come together this day from Lake Titicaca. And thus, within our twin flames the Father/Mother God release illumination as illumined action for this age.

The Mantle of Christ-Illumined Government

Receive ye the Holy Spirit of our office and understand our service in this hemisphere directly beneath that of Helios and Vesta. For it is our twin flames who shall graduate to that office when the fulfillment of the time of the Two Witnesses is come; and this community within a century shall ascend to take on its shoulders the full light of the inner government of the Great White Brotherhood.

This is the long-range goal of lifestreams prepared as disciples of the Word. Understand that if you are to inherit the mantle of Christ-illumined government, it is well to put it on—to try it on for size, as you say—in this hour. We, therefore, shall bring to you this education of the heart by way of the exposés of injustice which must be known. We are determined to educate you in this hour of service and praise to the LORD, that your praise might be an illumined one, your dynamic decrees truly founded upon the bedrock of knowledge of the things of this world, which itself is a gift of the Holy Spirit.[1]

—And that gift involves, as you see, the interpretation of prophecy and the light of the probing of events so that the people may understand cause-and-effect sequences, so that they might understand their role in the downstream course of civilization and their role, consequently, in the moving stream of the River of Life, which is a confluent stream that does gather together all of the lightbearers of the earth.

And as many drops make a mighty river, so many lifestreams of Light gather together and, contacted and ennobled and raised up by the light of this teaching worldwide, they may become pillars of fire—pillars in the temple of my God[2] and pillars as that which does go before the people of their nations to reveal the way to them:[3] the way out of the stranglehold and the grip of the fallen ones who have held that grip for so long that they cannot even remember what it is like to have a successful revolution to overturn *them* instead of their manipulated revolutions which have overturned the sons and daughters of God, whom they have indoctrinated to their very devices.

Armageddon in the Classrooms of America

Beloved ones, we come with a burden of our heart of the Armageddon that is being fought and won in the classrooms of America this day! We come, therefore, pursuing the line of education and that action taken by the Archangel Jophiel—and our coming is overdue. Therefore, consider that this is the message of the hour and also the message of yesterday and that it must be acted upon today and tomorrow.

This Armageddon is also found in the classrooms of Montessori International. It is the warfare against the Spirit and the mind and the heart and the soul of the child, even as the mind and the four lower bodies must be trained along the path of functioning within a society and upon a planet where the child must survive.

Blessed hearts, our goal in education is the parallel path of the development of the inner man. Just as the child who does not learn to read at an early age is not learning to read easily at the age of fifteen or eighteen, so understand, beloved ones, that if the inner man of the heart[4] is not developed from the earliest levels of life, that image tends to recede—that memory, that contact which is pure and perfect at birth, the contact with the holy angels and with the Christ Self.

The Two-Edged Sword of Maitreya Outplayed: the Psychology of Parent/Teacher/Child Relationships

Therefore, we desire to see the two-edged sword of Maitreya outplayed in this community. We desire you to understand that psychology only goes so far and it, too, must be endowed with a flame. Beware of the terms of humanism and democratic interaction between parent and child, for this is not true to the

Ascended Masters' teachings. The interaction is with respect of the office in hierarchy of both personages—the office of parent being that of parent and teacher representing the Godhead; the office of child being that of chela and that of the heir becoming the son.[5]

Thus, if there is only equality in the democratic sense or the humanistic sense, we lose the sense of respect, we lose the sense of the mantle. Where there is no sense of the mantle, the mantle itself cannot be active. And the mantle is of each one's Christhood and causal body, which apparently must be somewhat (and, in fact, a great deal) outpictured in the adult, whereas it is not intended to descend in the child except by increments each year.

Beloved ones, understand that you must go beyond the psychology courses you have seen and recognize that the effort toward communication, toward interaction, toward right motivation, and toward the support of the child must come through the inner contact of the child and the parent with the Christ mind. And therefore, you have already been given formulas and teachings and a way of life that in a sense compensates for many of the humanistic approaches to the solving of parent/child and teacher/child problems.

Thus, it becomes and it behooves the teachers of the Montessori revolution and the Montessori message to involve themselves in discipleship and a penetration of the Word and its assimilation. When the parents and the teachers, therefore, put on the Body and Blood of the Universal Christ, they have a balance of mind and heart. And therefore, they need not be governed by the forceful mentality of the lower mind or the emotions when dealing with children but must have the equivalent thereof in the mind and heart of God and in the hand of the Holy Spirit in action.

Identifying the Battle and the Defenders of the Montessori Revolution

Thus, you find that this Armageddon in the Montessori classroom and in this community of Camelot is not fully won because those who are our armies—namely, the parents and teachers—have not fully and finally recognized the battle and have not perceived that it is not physical walls or a physical method that can guard the child against the encroachments of the world which flow through the astral plane through the television sets which you leave on in your homes (it is sad to say) and through the general malaise and the rock music that abounds throughout the large cities and therefore does permeate the psyche even unbeknownst to those who are attacked by it.

Beloved hearts, how can we fight and win a battle when the armies of that battle have not identified themselves as knights and ladies of the flame and defenders of that Holy Grail within themselves, first and foremost, and then, out of all due respect to the manifestation of that Grail within the child? It must be, therefore, a parallel path of common sense and good works and observation of the educational methods that work.

Whatever works, whatever is practical *is* the Montessori revolution. It need not have been spoken by Montessori. Therefore, beware of a flesh-and-blood-saviour consciousness and of a flesh-and-blood-devil consciousness. All people are instruments of God a good deal of the time, and some may fall prey to be instruments of error as well.

Thus, let us understand that Maria Montessori was one spokesman for the revolution in education, and you are another when you are the instrument of your Christ Self. And there are others throughout the fields of education in America and the world. When you pick the best fruits from the tree of education, you find that you have a basket that is acceptable not only to the Ascended Lady Master Maria Montessori, but to Mother Mary and Magda and Jesus and John the Baptist, for whom this very method was developed.

And therefore, you cannot keep up with the revolution unless you renew your own courses of the mind—unless you come to understand that each year there is greater potential within the children and a different way of learning because the universal astrology changes, because the ages change, the years change, the dispensations descend.

Unless you are attuned with these—unless you analyze the dispensations of this conference, for instance, you will not understand how they apply to the children and the new calls that must be made in a service dedicated to the children of this campus and the world (which, I might say, at this time is not well enough attended for the Sponsors of Youth or the Lords of Karma to be effective in staying the aggressive forces that are even now puncturing through to the children of this community).

Holding the Child as a Manifestation of God

Beloved ones, it is not a physical location that is the salvation either; it is a spiritual state of consciousness. And therefore, beware of idolatry. Beware of thinking in terms of time and space, and understand that the development of the heart and the love of the heart is that which must be delivered unto the children and youth—the heart of support, the heart of compassion, the heart that sternly rebukes that which ought to be rebuked, and the heart that never holds the child in idolatry but holds the child as a manifestation of God as oneself and is comfortable with being that manifestation and working out the self-realization of that God within and without.

We call, then, for the victory in the education of the hearts of all members of this community; and therefore, the fruits of that victory may truly be laid upon the altar of our children and youth and all who come here seeking that cup of cold water in Christ's name.[6] And that cup of cold water is truly the education of the heart. It is truly the enlightenment of the age. That which refreshes the soul is a new vista—a new understanding! That is what is needed.

Keeping Up with the Progression of the World Teachers

And this is why the churches are empty all over the world: because there is not a new awareness and a moving forward with the age of those who represent the various world religions. There must be a renewal and a reinfusion and a resurrection and a sense of the regenerative mind of the Buddha, for instance, who surely has progressed over twenty-five hundred years—and of Jesus Christ, who in two thousand years has become more and more and more of that Universal Christ.

Thus, the universe is progressive and unfolding and ongoing. Thus, you also are more today, I dare say, than we found you twenty-five hundred years ago! And none of you would want to go back to that point. And therefore, do not hold back the World Teachers ascended, but recognize that you must follow in the wake of the very journey and pilgrimage which they lead across the heavens and through the stars. And if you lose the wake, you will not have the momentum of their forging of the trail and when you finally decide to follow after them, you will have to cut afresh through the jungles of maya and the astral illusions.

Understand, then, it is important to keep up with your Teacher. It is important to move when the Guru moves! It is important to let go of the old fantasies of self and selfhood when they are to be let go of. When we give dispensations of healing, it means there is a dispensation and it is a moment when you can accelerate in rejuvenation, because this is what is important to the Lords of Karma and this is the opening to heaven's gate in this hour.

How Can We Build upon a Foundation That Is Not Laid?

Therefore, when we come and see the talent and the teaching unused, what can we say? How can we build upon a foundation that is not laid? Where is the chief cornerstone of your own building, who is Christ the LORD within your temple?[7]

Some, therefore, have resisted. And therefore, understand. You will not be ready when the plagues come. You are not ready when the flu comes, you are not ready for the setbacks because the body is not cleansed and purified and therefore it takes on this pestilence of the age and the hour, which itself is also programmed.

And I know that you weary of hearing of the programming of the Atlantean scientists, and yet it is an ever-present cause of the Four Horsemen of the Apocalypse.[8] And therefore, it is best to live with realities rather than notions of "all is well." After all, I give you that respect that you are men and women of courage and you desire to know reality, and I also give you the respect and accord that you will act on the reality that you know.

We Require a Revolution in the Body

There is a responsibility for knowledge given. Until you apply it, we cannot increase it. Yet, we come with a mandate of Jophiel and of Lord Himalaya and of the Manus of the races. Therefore, we say, make haste for the revolution in Spirit and consciousness! And in this hour we require a revolution in the body.

For the sword shall descend, the two-edged sword, and it shall separate and divide; and one shall be taken and another shall be left.[9] And you will understand that those who are left are left because they have predestroyed the body and not allowed it to grow in the grace of the capacity to contain more Light, which more Light is the key to the entering of the new age and the golden age—and that means the entering in to the etheric octave and the higher consciousness of eternal Life here and now.

Simple Invocations and Inserts for the Farmers

Blessed ones, we come, then, with a mighty fervor of our hearts. We come determined to educate you, even as you determine to educate yourselves and to make the very simple invocations with simple inserts. This very invocation on the farmers[10] can be shortened to five lines so that you will give it. There is an avoidance of the giving of long decrees that we have observed, and therefore many issues go unattended. Let us see those who have the power and mind for summary and condensation therefore create these inserts. And let them be given, for all is in the giving and the proof of the pudding is in the eating.

Beloved ones, it is an hour for action and manifold action, and the sword of the Spirit must come forth not only from the mouth but from all of the chakras, dividing the Real from the unreal in all octaves and planes of consciousness.

I speak by the Holy Spirit and the rapidity of the Mind of God that you might understand that the intellect itself must be stepped up. Your thinking process, your memory process, your reaction time must be accelerated! If you are to become immortals, you must put on immortality in this hour.[11]

Realize, then, that nothing will happen of a sudden. As the tree falls, so it will lie.[12] "He that is filthy, let him be filthy still."[13] As you exit the body in consciousness, so shall you be. If you do not prepare to enter His gates with thanksgiving and praise,[14] how, then, can you be the bearer of joy and the joy flame all the way to the altar of the Central Sun?

Dispense with Your Concept of Limitation and Ride the Bull as Buddha Did

Dispense with the consciousness that you are segmented in time and space! *Dispense* with your concept of limitation! *Go forth* and be the mighty conqueror! Be that conquering hero that is the one who comes in the name of Maitreya and put aside all former vestments and offices that parallel those of the Four Horsemen. For those who engage in the world and the world karma will be overcome by that world karma, but those who ride the bull as Buddha did[15] unto the victory will use the world karma as the means and the standing and stepping ground unto the eternal victory that is by the flame of the Spirit.

Thus, be caught up as the Manchild is caught up into heaven.[16] Thus, be caught up above the astral plane and the pestilence and the persecutions and all of the wagging of tongues that moves against this movement. Be not concerned. Let it be cast into the sacred fire. Let illumination come because the Word is spoken and because it penetrates the very core of the earth.

You are drenched in this hour in the golden sunlight of our temple, Meru, and of Helios and Vesta. This golden flame of illumination is the basking in the sun of the winter—the winter solstice still having its radiance and effect.

The Cycle for the Laying of Plans for the Building

In this hour of the LORD's judgment, in this hour of the changing of the light of Capricorn to Aquarius that will come, recognize, beloved, that this is a moment in the earth sign for the laying of plans for the building. It is indeed the propitious moment for the giving of the gift that can be multiplied by the cycles of the heavens.

The signs and the cycles do come, and as you give liberation and freedom to us to act on a free land, so we shall act. And the dispensations given to us of the Great White Brotherhood to work through that Ranch are directly connected with its absolute invulnerability to any forces known or unknown. And this can come not only by the paying off of the land, but it must also come by hearts and minds united physically on the land as the presence of the might and strength required by Mother Mary and Morya and Maitreya and ourselves.

Focus on World Communism in Central and South America

We stand waiting for you to settle yourselves and settle your personal problems so that our decree sessions may move and focus entirely on Central and South America and the oncoming darkness of World Communism and conspiracy there.

We are determined to reverse the tide by a strong and united City Foursquare of United States and Canada. And this larger square, finding its heart in the Inner Retreat, will be the very base and stronghold of the powers of Light and the chelas to move forth and roll back the entire momentum and the effect of the Four Horsemen when they are spent.

Let us pray that their spending be swift. Let us pray that the cycles of their coming be shortened for the elect.[17] Let us pray that the elect are out of harm's way and that they be sealed as the servants of God in their foreheads.[18]

Be at Peace, for God Is in You

We give a wafer of divine illumination. We bless the communion now. And we command you to go within to find Christ's kingdom and be at peace. All of the worry and the anxiety only attracts to yourself more. Be at peace, for God is in you; and act from that standpoint and do not look to another to act for you. For each time you think another will act in your stead, you forfeit the mastery of your own Christhood. Thus, be it so in your community, your homes, your businesses, and in the recreation of life.

Understand in the building of the city, it is the white

stone[19] of each one that counts, and none may do it for another. Thus, pursue now the bedrock of your attainment and build from the reality of that attainment and not a false sense of security in the labor of another.

The only security that each one has is in the God within. I increase it by the Light of our hearts.

I seal you in the victorious golden flame of illumination, which is the flame of divine action. Thus, I send you forth to act in the name of the farmer, in the name of the steelworker, in the name of the laborer, in the name of the rich and the poor—for both must be dispossessed of their false sense of self.

I send you forth in the name of Christ-victory and in the name of Zadkiel, who saturates now the earth with violet flame, increasing and intensifying for the fulfillment of the star of Bethlehem within you.

"**The Summit Lighthouse Sheds Its Radiance O'er All the World to Manifest as Pearls of Wisdom.**" This dictation by the God and Goddess Meru was delivered through the Messenger Elizabeth Clare Prophet on the Feast of the Epiphany, Sunday, January 6, 1985, at Camelot. "The Interpretation of the Four Horsemen of the Apocalypse by Gautama Buddha" and the messenger's exposé on "The Manipulation of the American Farmer" preceded the dictation. (1) I Cor. 12:4–10. (2) Rev. 3:12. (3) Exod. 13:21, 22; 14:19, 20, 24; Num. 14:14; Neh. 9:12, 19. (4) Eph. 3:16; I Pet. 3:4. (5) Gal. 4:1–7. (6) Matt. 10:42. (7) Pss. 118:22, 23; Matt. 21:42; Mark 12:10, 11; Acts 4:10–12; Eph. 2:19–22; I Pet. 2:6, 7. (8) Rev. 6:1–8. (9) Heb. 4:12; Matt. 24:40, 41; Luke 17:34–36. (10) The invocation referred to here by the God and Goddess Meru is a two-page insert composed by a student—"Circle-and-Sword Patterns on the Manipulation of the American Farmer"—which was given by the messenger and congregation during the service prior to the dictation. (11) I Cor. 15:53, 54. (12) Eccl. 11:3. (13) Rev. 22:11. (14) Pss. 100:4. (15) Inspired by earlier Taoist drawings, the twelfth-century Chinese master Kakuan used the symbol of ten bulls (in illustration and verse) to represent the ten successive steps by which the initiate conquers and transcends the lower nature to realize true identity: The Search for the Bull, Discovering the Footprints, Perceiving the Bull, Catching the Bull, Taming the Bull, Riding the Bull Home, The Bull Transcended, Both Bull and Self Transcended, Reaching the Source, In the World. The messenger has explained that the bull is the carnal mind and dweller on the threshold which must be slain before one can become the Buddha. See Kakuan, "10 Bulls," in *Zen Flesh, Zen Bones: A Collection of Zen & Pre-Zen Writings,* comp. Paul Reps (Garden City, N.Y.: Doubleday & Company, Anchor Books, n.d.), pp. 131–55; available through Summit University Press, $3.95 ($4.76 postpaid USA). (16) Rev. 12:5. (17) Matt. 24:22; Mark 13:20. (18) Rev. 7:3; 9:4. (19) Rev. 2:17.

Messenger's Invocation:*

For the Victory of the Eternal Manchild

Eternal Father, our gracious help in time of trouble, Eternal Father, hear now the prayer of thy sons and daughters. Intensify thy flame of purity and peace within our hearts, of freedom and diligence in the way of our Lord Jesus Christ.

In the name of Alpha and Omega, the beginning and the ending, we call forth these flames from the altar of heaven. Descend, O sacred fire, for the purging of hearts and souls and minds! Come unto us, O mighty flame of Grace. Teach us the way to save our brothers and sisters on earth from every manner of self-destruction and the burdens which swiftly come upon the earth.

Beloved seven mighty archangels, come now in the victory of the sevenfold path and the fourteen stations of the cross. Mighty archangels, we implore intercession for the defense of church and state, for the defense of God-government in every nation upon earth.

Let the Light of the Holy Spirit descend now to purge the governments and economies of the nations of all darkness and deceit and treachery and betrayal of our people. Light of the far-off worlds, saints of heaven, unite the people of Light worldwide that they might come into the union and the strength of the eternal Son of God.

In the name of the Father, the Son, the Holy Spirit, and the Mother, we consecrate this congregation of the righteous to the victory of the Trinity in the heart, to the victory of the eternal Manchild. In the name of Mother Mary, Amen.

---

*Give this invocation aloud in full force—right now—and often as you reread and meditate on the words of the Master in this Pearl. Your voice is your vote in heaven that counts for the establishment of world peace. The Light of God never fails when you release it through the science of the spoken Word!

Pearls of Wisdom, published weekly by The Summit Lighthouse for Church Universal and Triumphant, come to you under the auspices of the Darjeeling Council of the Great White Brotherhood. These are presently dictated by the Ascended Masters to their Messenger Elizabeth Clare Prophet. The international headquarters of this nonprofit, nondenominational activity is located in Los Angeles, California. All communications and freewill contributions should be addressed to The Summit Lighthouse, Box A, Malibu, CA 90265. Pearls of Wisdom are sent weekly throughout the USA via third-class mail to all who support the Church with a minimum yearly love offering of $40. First-class and international postage rates available upon request. Notice of change of address should be received three weeks prior to the effective date. Third-class mail is not forwarded by the post office.

Copyright © 1985 Church Universal and Triumphant, Inc. All rights reserved. Printed in the United States of America. Pearls of Wisdom and The Summit Lighthouse are registered trademarks of Church Universal and Triumphant, Inc. All rights to their use are reserved.

Remember the Ancient Encounter
On Discipleship under Lord Maitreya

My love enfolds you in the rapturous Light of the One Sent. I am, as you know, as you know me, Kuthumi.

To Play Our Roles We Crossed the Bar

Remember the ancient encounter. For I have been your brother on many occasion; and in each succeeding incarnation we have shared, our souls have moved together to pluck the star of the Divine Light and to pluck the harp of the heart of Maitreya.

Disciples of Maitreya are we—Metteyya—and therefore together we have sought a glance, a smile, a whisper, an acknowledgment that we might know our God is pleased.

Thus, we agreed, thou and I, that I should go with Morya before you to stand in Christ with Jesus and that you would remain to bring up the rear of the troops and your own flaming chakras.

Thus, to play our roles—I the Alpha, you the Omega—we crossed the bar; and you remain, the faithful witness of our cause.

How can I leave thee, devotees of Light and Peace and Freedom and of the heart of that Christ?

Is it any wonder to you that I should become, not only before my ascension in the final hours [as the Mahatma Koot Hoomi] but subsequently, a bit incensed at these Christians and their small-mindedness and inability to perceive his true mission when I myself [as Saint Francis], through trial and pain and the deep affection of the heart, came truly to understand beyond orthodoxy the reality of my Saviour?[1]

Thus, beloved, I am impatient today for your sakes and for the sakes of those who wait for the cup of knowledge that you bear from our abode. I am impatient with those who attempt again and again to weave their slander, their unreality, and all the rest around such a shining star as the Teaching itself.

Of course, I know the end from the beginning. And I, too, understand the cycles that must be outplayed as outlined for you by Sanat Kumara and Gautama and the living Word in the Great White Brotherhood. But still I long to think of those who, if they had the fruit and the sweet nectar of the knowledge that has become such a daily affair as to be taken for granted by yourselves, might run with it, eat it now to the fullness of the cup, and become for us other servants in many fields East and West.

We press on then. We jump over the bowling balls that are rolled our way, and we stand before you today rejoicing in admonishment and dispensation from Maitreya to our own heart.

My Assignment to Work with You for Your Physical Health and the Healing of Your Psychology

Thus, I come, the joyful student, to announce to you the most precious dispensation which comes from Maitreya, placed upon me by him with all diligence and the same concern for the step-up of your lives. This dispensation is my assignment to work with each one of you individually for your physical health and for the healing of your psychology, that we might swiftly get to the very cause and core of physical as well as spiritual and emotional conditions that there be no more setbacks or indulgences and surely not two steps forward and one step back.

Thus, from this hour, if you will call to me and make a determination in your heart to transcend the former self, I will tutor you both through your own heart and any messenger I may send your way. Therefore, heed the voices—not astral but physical—and watch the course of events. And, of course, when you have the opportunity to receive my word from the messenger, know truly that I use her often to explain to you the intricacies of the blocks in consciousness. For you are so sincere and the sweetness of thy hearts is touching to the soul in a world hardened by war and abortion.

Thus, I come in many guises. And I do acknowledge to you, beloved, that whatever else may or may not be said from the left or the right, our messenger is truly adequate and ready to demonstrate to you the path of your Christhood as we have walked it, as we have attained it.

A School of Hard Knocks and Our Gruff Voice

This is a school, truly, of hard knocks. This is a school where you will hear our gruff voice. Be of good cheer, for our bark is often worse than our bite but proves most useful in eliminating those who are so easily scared away from the fount, who seek favoritism and praise when in fact they should recognize the love of the gruff voice and know that that which is offended is the ego self, the prideful self.

Thus, offense is a grave enemy and ought to be discarded. We use this mode, that those who belong not here may well have their offense and take it and move on their way as the "hurt ones," the "bruised ones," the "injured ones."

Isn't it strange that those who call themselves men, who have gone forth, could be offended by a little woman? Beloved hearts, something is awry! Where has gone the prototype of Western man with all the strength and independence, without botheration from females? After all, are we not the Gurus? Then why allow a little woman to cause so much consternation, so much reaction, so much anger? More is the proof, then, that it is we who act, for how can a little woman perform such deeds of which she is accused?

Seek Not the Human Mother but the Divine

Blessed ones, those who come for favoritism and the personality cult, those who come seeking the Mother, therefore, as the substitute for the human mother come precisely for the wrong reason. This is not a human mother! This is the Divine Mother, veiled in many garbs. You cannot have a relationship with the Divine Mother in any of us unless you first satisfy yourself at the human level, resolve your psychology with human parents, become your own mother and father and keeper, and then enter into a true and lasting relationship with the Divine Mother and the Divine Father.

Now, why do you suppose that the good God made human mothers and human fathers? It is because the tender souls, those reincarnating with a pack of karma on their backs, truly need the humanness of the human mother and father. Thus, these are necessary steps in the planetary home, and you would feel bereft and left out if you were spoken of as that one having neither father nor mother nor beginning nor ending of days.[2]

Thus, the one who comes in the name of Melchizedek, the Ascended Master and the priest, has initiated the Lord Jesus as a priest forever.[3] That priesthood comes through the initiation of the Divine Father and the Divine Mother unto those who have internalized the essential elements of the humanity of the world's greatest fathers and mothers.

I speak, then, of the inner resolution. I speak, then, to you!

Those who seek here what they did not derive from human parents, those who seek to prove again and again that human parents will fail by seeing failure in the messengers have not the slightest conception of the Path. Some require tutoring and a study of the true and ancient traditions of the Guru/chela relationship.

Blessed ones, we cannot be unto you both human and divine. Therefore, we have chosen—and chosen well—to represent the divine, since you have so many specimens of the human before you. It is really not necessary that we provide the human link in the chain of humanism.

The Ascension Is the Mark of Achievement

We come, therefore, to provide the link to the Divinity, and we place before you in this mystery school the goal of the ascension. The ascension itself is the mark of achievement, the victory, and the single act that is praiseworthy. If you do not graduate with your ascension, not only will your report card be marked "failed," but so will ours. For the teacher is also responsible—and so is the messenger.

Thus, each one sent comes with a prayer that none of these little ones should be lost save the son of perdition.[4] And who is the son of perdition? I tell you, he is not the bogeyman! He is not your worst enemy that you imagine to be nine feet tall. The son of perdition is the dweller on the threshold of your own house. It should be lost and rightfully so—and swiftly!

But it is difficult to become a dragon-slayer when the age of chivalry has long passed. Some find it a bit unpleasant to take up sword and slay the not-self. But in the meantime, while their stomachs are in too delicate a condition (and their egos as well) to perform this act, they themselves are being devoured by the dweller—dallying, marking time, and often drifting backwards with no realization. For in relativity, it sometimes appears one is going forward when one is standing still or moving backward.

Thus, precious hearts, understand that the ascension is the acceptable offering. Those who do not truly want the ascension but want the power of the Light of Serapis Bey ought not to come. But these are the very ones who cannot be convinced to stay away, for they enjoy the lap of the Mother and need make no effort and become most angry when they are sent forth to prove their wisdom in action and thus balance the threefold flame!

They must recognize once and for all that if they had mastery once or twice or thrice in a previous life, that full mastery should have long ago gained for them the eternal octaves of Light.

What is wanting is always the absence of balance in the threefold flame. If it cannot be gained here, it must be gained in the wide opportunity of the world for professionalism and self-mastery.

Some things are required of one, and some things of another. Resent not, then, the admonishments we give through the messenger. Our admonishments are only for the shortening of the days for the elect.[5] Who are the elect? You are the elect! You have elected to enter a path, in the main, by trust, by determination, and by the elimination of possibilities; for you have wisely observed what the world has to offer. Not knowing, then, what you would encounter, you have nevertheless sought the Great White Brotherhood, sought the Ascended Masters, entered the school presenting itself to be ours (as so it is), and thus come in faith to seek and to find.

I welcome you to this quarter of Summit University in the name of Lord Maitreya. My arms are open, and my heart also. I would take you inside and give to you as much as you are able to take. Thus, enter in to the faith of thy own Selfhood, and we can roll up our sleeves and begin.

"What Does It Mean, This Slaying of the Dweller on the Threshold?"

"What does it mean," you have said, "this slaying of the dweller on the threshold?" Let us begin once again at the beginning for those who have not understood:

Beloved, by free will all have forged action, word, desire. Some of these, as vibration, have been pure and perfect, building individual Christhood and the mantle, the seamless garment. Through ignorance, absence of tutoring, forgetfulness of First Cause and origin in the higher spheres, others of these vibrations emanating from actions and words and desires have fallen; for they had not the balance of flight of Alpha and Omega. They have fallen and begun to form a spiral like a solar system around the solar plexus, the "place of the sun."

Momentums, then, of lifetimes for many thousands of years have built the antithesis of Self, sometimes entirely unbeknownst to the outer mind who thought itself so sincere and desirous of doing right that in the very desire to do right there has been the mistaken conclusion that the desire should make all things right. Nevertheless, the Law perceives that there is right action, there is wrong action, and the proof is in the causal body—the pure vessel of Light of all good deeds and acts in Matter—and in this electronic belt.

Now, in the eye of that vortex of misqualified energy—in the very eye of the vortex—there is the point of consciousness and identity that emerges as the collective consciousness of all misdeeds. Each time a decision is made that registers as the unreal, a portion of the unreal mind must be used to make it. Thus, the collection of actions has a collective consciousness, and the dweller is the collective manifestation of all that has been in error. It emerges as an identity, a figment, you might say, but a momentum that wields human power to a grave and great extent.

This identity is the impostor of the soul and of the Christ Self. A portion of the soul by free will is invested in the impostor, and a portion of the soul is invested in the Christ. Thus, the battleground and Armageddon is of the soul which, as you know, can be lost.

Now cometh the Christ and the Ascended Masters and their chelas to woo the soul away from unreality, to prove to the soul what is Real, what is Light, what is the eternal Goal. This is your office as shepherds and ministering servants and students of the World Teachers. When the soul is enlightened and quickened and gains awareness through Christ, it begins to be able to see on its own through that Christ intelligence what is unreal.

But seeing is not necessarily believing. Seeing, then, is the first step; believing, the second.

The action to deny that which is unreal is fraught with the burdens of the individual's psychology. And thus, sometimes hard lessons—burning in the trial by fire,[6] pain in this world—must convince the soul that Life is more important and therefore that one must let go of certain situations and conditions and beliefs and comfortabilities.

We move the soul as close to the precipice of knowledge of Absolute Good and Absolute Evil as is possible, at the same time to preserve the integrity of the soul and not to cause that one too much fear, too much awareness of the great Darkness within that opposes the great Light.

Thus, beloved hearts, the slaying of the dweller. Not all at once but little by little. And this is something you should be aware of, though you have been told before. Each day, according to the cosmic cycles, a little bit of the head of the dweller emerges above this dark pool of the electronic belt. It is a still darkness, and one can see perhaps the head or the ear or the eye or the nose of this dweller, this self-created monster. You see this, then, in your own actions and reactions. You see it in the musings of the mind—sometimes only a telltale ripple on the surface or perhaps the tail when the beast has dived to the bottom.

Thus, you must listen and watch what is lurking. And as soon as you find a tendency to fear, to be jealous, to become angry or whatever, go after it as the tip of the iceberg! Work at it! This work is truly a profound work of the Spirit. It is not easy always to be on the path of confrontation.

The Path of Accommodation of the Dweller

I come with the message of Maitreya and to amplify his previous messages. For he has spoken of the path of accommodation* whereby, instead of slaying the dweller, you find ways to go around this side and around that side. And thus, you begin to build the tower of light—you build a great momentum of decrees and service, trusting that somehow, in some way, this terrifying encounter will go away. But it will not go away. And the day you discover once again that all of that goodness is not the acceptable offering is the day when in the presence of Maitreya you once again encounter face-to-face that dweller on the threshold.

You may go far and wide and keep a wide berth from the messenger and never notice the dweller and build a positive human momentum in those outer attainments, whether through yoga or decrees or this or that discipline. And you may be very happy with yourself, and others may be exceedingly happy with you. Of course, this is not the question.

The question is whether your I AM Presence and Christ Self are happy and whether your Teachers will tell you that in the light of cosmic initiation your offering is acceptable. Thus, beloved, to avoid the Masters or to avoid the instrument whereby we may speak to you is to avoid the Day of Reckoning [of your karmic accountability] which has been called, in biblical terms, the day of vengeance of our God.[7]

Who Is Your God?

Now think of this in the occult† sense. Who is our God? Your God is the thing which you fear most. I pray it be the Almighty in the sense of awe, but too often fear is of things from beneath[8] or of fear itself. Your God is also the thing you hate most or resent most, the thing to which you are tied irrevocably by the greatest intensity of human feelings. These may be good or bad, pleasureful or painful; but there is your God, the one to whom you give deference.

---
*accommodation (fr. Latin ad + commodare, to make fit, give, lend): adaptation; adjustment; functional adjustment of an organism to its environment through modification of its habits.
†occult (fr. Latin occulere, to cover up): hidden, requiring more than ordinary perception or knowledge. "We speak the wisdom of God in a mystery, even the hidden wisdom, which God ordained before the world unto our glory..." (I Cor. 2:7)

Now listen to the Word: "the day of vengeance of our God." What is the vengeance? It is the terrifying moment when the thing you have feared or hated or loved most (in a human consciousness) has become your master and you its slave, and you find you are indeed not free although you have built a mountain of decrees and service on either side.

Thus, beloved, the mighty work of the ages must be pursued, and we stand with you and we place our messenger before you because of the initiation and tutoring and training and encounter that is needed constantly to assist: To assist *your* overcoming.

Only you can overcome—we cannot do it for you! And yet, we can deliver the precise Word and the thrust of the sword at any hour of the day or night when it is required. And those who are the true brides of Christ and the wise virgins[9]—*they* will respond, *they* will know the source, *they* will move!

You May Know Us through Our Teachings

Blessed hearts, you may not understand or perceive us personally, but you may do so through the dictations and the teachings. And inasmuch as you never know where you will find it, it is important to be ongoing students of the teachings that have come forth. So precious are these teachings that their recording, their organization, is deemed by us often more important than more human conversation with our messenger.

As you can see, if we did not have our books and letters from previous centuries, where would we be to convey the very same instruction? We would have to begin all over again and repeat what we have done. But we have better and nobler ideas to convey and new situations demanding attention. Thus, do not neglect so great a salvation as the written and spoken Word. And value all other contact above and below with our bands.

The Accommodation of Rebellion against the Guru and Disobedience to the LORD God

Blessed ones, understand, then, the accommodation of the aspect of the beast known as rebellion against the Guru and disobedience to the LORD God. Understand that that core rebellion has been the undoing of many chelas, some who were not calculated by us to make it in the first place.

Although we held the immaculate concept, the record of the past was before us. We gave the opportunity in purest hope, in support, and with the full momentum of our Electronic Presence. Yet, beloved, others who have not made it have lost in the race simply for want of this very instruction from Lord Maitreya, which because it has helped so many I give to you again.

The accommodation, then, of rebellion, going to the right and to the left of it, becoming as it were, a workaholic, performing many good human deeds and social deeds, or the performance of ritual and prayer and yoga, the assiduous following of perhaps asceticism or personal discipline or diet—all of these things may be a careful accumulation of human virtue by the individual to avoid [subconsciously, at least] what is *the* most important step which must be taken: The step of the encounter with that satellite orbiting in the electronic belt that has come between the soul and her I AM Presence—namely, the rebellion against Lord Maitreya or Sanat Kumara or against the Law itself because it was spoken, perhaps, by a very imperfect vessel. This rebellion, then, becomes a block self-perpetuating, for it is set in orbit by free will and it cannot be removed from orbit without free will.

How You Create Your Personal Astrology out of Your Karma

When you place planets in orbit in this electronic belt, you create your personal subconscious astrology and psychology, which are one and the same—focuses of your karma. Now, when you think of the solar system you inhabit and you consider the weight, the volume, and the magnitude of the planets, you can learn the lesson that it is far easier to set a planet in motion than to call it back, even as the words which proceed from your mouths cannot be called back, no matter how great the regret, else it is by the violet flame.

The Necessity for Attainment in the Heart Chakra through the Master/Disciple Relationship

Thus, to remove the planet of rebellion, you must have a oneness with the central sun of your being—the I AM Presence, the Christ Self, and the externalized attainment of the heart chakra. This is why we preach on the Sacred Heart. This is why there is a union of religion East and West through the path of the heart; for all who have ever attained have done so by this sacred fire.

Listen well, then. To recall the planet of rebellion in the electronic belt, you must have an equal and greater force of Light and sacred fire manifest in the heart to counteract it and dissolve it, else you must be holding the hand of the Master or the Guru who has that development and can transmit to you the

Light that can keep you above the waves when you would sink as Peter did.[10]

Thus, the necessity of the Master/disciple relationship. For there is not one among you or those upon earth today (save those who are already in our inner retreats) who can make it alone, who has not in his electronic belt something that requires reinforcement of the Masters who have gone before to remove— to remove, I say, in a timely manner, for we do not have a million years for you to sit and give the violet flame and to pursue these disciplines.

Thus, the Master/disciple relationship has never been more important. And because this messenger has submitted to the most complete and arduous training at inner levels and in the physical octave, taking the lessons from both friend and foe alike, from Masters and chelas alike (not missing those lessons), we can tell you that the instrument is dependable for our purposes to make known to you what are the mandated options that you must consider through free will to take and take quickly for your own victory.

Cycles must not be lost. Tests must not be postponed. And when you see it, call it and move on.

Beloved ones, when the aspect of the dweller of rebellion is not challenged and bound and cast out—and these are steps; for that planet may be bound before it is ultimately cast out, which means it is in submission to your free will and to your Christhood but not entirely eliminated—when it remains, therefore, and you are in the twilight zone of not having slain the dweller and not having entered into complete union with Christ, these are treacherous waters.

We Offer Our Hand in Friendship

In these waters of the astral plane, again you need our living witness and our hand, which we offer this day purely and in friendship and as never before to assist you—to assist you for Maitreya's sake and for your ascension's sake.

The Acceptable Offering Is Christ-Good

When you are in that twilight zone, scurrying about like frightened mice to pile up good karma, yet not facing the problem—the offering of human righteousness and human goodness is not the acceptable offering. If the individual is not willing to take this teaching to heart and to change, then, you see, he will become angry, as Cain was angry when his offering was not accepted.[11] He demanded of Maitreya that his human goodness be received as a substitute for Christ-goodness—that the Law be changed for him and, instead of his fulfillment of that Law, that all of this grandiose human goodness should suffice.

And individuals do this again and again, and their schemes and their deeds become more and more grandiose, sometimes encompassing the earth. And they say, "Surely this great good deed, this great endowment, this great act I have done that has blessed millions should be the acceptable offering!"

It is only the acceptable offering when it is Christ-good. What is Christ-good? It is the soul united with Christ who has slain the dweller through that Christ and therefore can say, "This I have done to the glory of God and not as an accommodation for my rebellion, not as a substitute for my surrender, not as my demand that God should take me according to *my* path instead of according to His."

Depression and Moodiness for the Rejected Offering

Now when the offering that is not Christ-good is rejected, as it always is and shall be, there is an anger that occurs at the subconscious level, which on the surface may manifest as depression. Beware depression and moodiness, for it is a sign of severe problems. Depression is that state of the twilight zone where the individual has neither slain the dweller nor entered fully into the heart of Christ. It is the most dangerous situation of the soul in this octave of the Matter universe. Therefore, you desire to quickly remove yourself from that place of jeopardy.

Some of you have recurrent dreams of walking over very insecure bridges, over deep chasms or through narrow passageways, or of being confined in a box. You may wake up in a cold sweat, you may experience terror in the night. And thus, a lesson is coming through from your Higher Mental Body that tells you that you have placed yourself in a condition that is dangerous, that you must pass through it, you must make a move, you cannot go back and you cannot stand still: you must move forward.

Enter the False Gurus Offering Souls False Fruits

For here the tempter may come, here you may be vulnerable to those who are offering you wares and fruits which are not the initiatic fruits of Maitreya.

Thus enter the false gurus to take advantage of souls who have refused to pass through the initiation of challenging that core rebellion. Now they find a false guru, now they satisfy themselves that all is well. They may keep their rebellion, for the false guru is the embodiment of the dweller on the threshold of rebellion against Maitreya. And they will follow the false teachers lifetime after lifetime, totally suppressing all other awareness of the Light of Christ.

For that awareness would demand and force them once again to the point of the encounter and the point of the choice. Thus, they have a system of knowledge, of education, of academia—all these things to confirm and hold together a system of civilization based upon pride and the development of the human ego, situation ethics, the modification of behavior, and all that occurs in the molding of the human animal.

Now understand how the individual who ten thousand or twelve thousand years ago in rejecting Maitreya made the conscious decision to keep the dweller of rebellion, does react in this hour or in any century when the representatives of Maitreya and the Great White Brotherhood come forth with the true Teaching and the true requirements of the Law. Now the anger that is subconscious, that used to manifest outwardly as depression, inverts and is on the surface in an all-out campaign to destroy the society or the organization or the orifice of the true Light.

The Soul Holds the Balance of Right Choice, Fortified by Prayer and Meditation

Blessed ones, to a greater or lesser extent, now and then the dweller within you rebels against your own Christhood. But the soul may choose. For the soul ultimately, though it hangs in the balance, holds the balance of right choice. Thus, when you do not know the way to go or the right hand from the left hand, pray—pray for attunement and oneness with us.

Learn the steps of prayer and meditation which we have taught in our release[12] that you might also be fortified by prayer and meditation as the right hand and the left hand of the presence of the Bodhisattvas who come to reinforce your desire to be all that God intended you to be.

Thus, you see, depression then begets inefficiency, more rebellion, disobedience, until finally there is a clamoring and a clanking in the electronic belt and in the four lower bodies. And unless that individual swiftly choose the Light of his own Mighty I AM Presence and choose to align himself with us, the helpers who can help, that individual must surely make the choice to run for the hills or for the canyons of the big cities where he may lose himself and place himself at the farthest possible distance from the one who can help—if not ourselves, then the messenger.

Copyright © 1985 Church Universal and Triumphant, Inc.

Some Sense of Injustice, Some Offense

Realize, then, beloved hearts, that all who do this must have an excuse, and their excuse must be based on some sense of injustice, some offense, or some real or imagined fault of our witness or our chelas or our organization. It is a pity, beloved hearts, that personal offense based on a core rebellion should unseat the rider, should unhorse the knight and he thereby lose such a grand opportunity. This work of the ages is a joyous work when you have one another, when you have community and such joy unlimited that is possible in this circumstance with which you are blessed, having this center with all that it portends for your lifestream.

We Come in the Name of Serapis Bey Because the Mystery School Is Required

Why have we come in this century? Why are we here presenting the equation of Life? We come in the name of Serapis Bey, our chief. We come in the name of this Master. We come because it is required that there be a mystery school in the physical octave in this century, teaching the path of the ascension, where the only graduates from that school are Ascended Masters.

It is required that the Path be set, that there not be a mincing of words or indulgences, paid or unpaid,[13] but there be the pure and simple Path demonstrated by ourselves and yourselves to keep this earth in its cosmic spin. We are proud in the true, humble sense of the word as we rejoice that there is indeed such a school in this time and space.

The Messenger of Truth Must Meet the Foes of the Message

Beloved ones, I must tell you that when we looked for the messenger who could carry this message and Truth through what would befall that messenger in this century, we looked down this lifestream and found that strength and faith which would not be moved by the gossip or the calumny or the framing or whatever else might occur. For if the message is not borne by one who has the strength to meet the foes of the message with their antimessage, then how can our activity or our knowledge endure?

All qualities you may desire may not be evident in the messenger, but can one individual embody all virtues of God? Why are you here? Are you not here to embody those virtues and talents that might be absent from the outpicturing in this life of the one who stands before you? What purpose would you have if it would not be to complement all that is manifest here?

What purpose of the messenger if not to provide you with those ingredients necessary and expedient to your own victory? This is the great beauty of the Great White Brotherhood, lest one having more than her share or his share perceive himself a god or independent of the Most High.

Come, then, to understand that the most necessary ingredients—to stand, and still stand, and to deliver our Word—are present. We are satisfied, and we are also satisfied that you will provide the rest.

Active and Passive Roles of Alpha and Omega
Fulfilling the Word and Its Work

We encourage you to be aggressive and active on those particular notes that are your keynote to make this community complete. You understand the meaning of the passive receiver, the Omega who receives the Light of Spirit. The moment you receive it, you become Alpha. And now you are the active ones, now you move into action, now you implement the Word!

Beloved ones, there must be, perforce, workshops drilling in communication. You must be *receivers* of the Word. Then you must be *givers* of the Word. This is not yet action. The Word translated by the Holy Spirit becomes an Awareness/Action whereby you move. And suddenly the Word which is the power of the Spirit becomes the Work, the mighty Work that is the manifestation of the Mother in Matter. This is why we capitalize *Word* and *Work*—that you might understand the polarity of Alpha and Omega.

It is the Omega cycle that you must triumph in. Thus, the Work counts, for it shows forth the effect of the inner cause of the Spirit with you. Until the Word is received and given, heard, assimilated, and the very result of assimilation is the mighty Work of the ages—you have not completed the spiral! And until the Word becomes the Work, it is either an unfulfilled spiral or an aborted spiral.

Great Is the Cry of Injustice,
Short-Fused the Determination to Act

I speak of this because I look across this great nation. People meet and talk. They agree in committee. They form policy. If all of the noble thoughts and desires of the hearts of the good people of the land would come into action, this nation would be a highly improved place. But it is not so.

When it comes to the Omega action, when it comes to the

individual becoming the Shakti of the Great White Brotherhood, when it comes to courage and the willingness to stand apart from the crowd, to go against the most cherished belief systems, we find that those who are often most courageous are the fallen ones, for they have a momentum on rebellion and therefore they stand out.

And those who should stand out are quietly in their living rooms watching their television sets, listening to their music, and demanding endless hours and time to pursue their families and all other interests except the demand to save the nation or the youth or to fight drugs or to rescue the little children.

Great is the cry of injustice, and very short and short-fused is the determination to act. Few have the sustaining power to act in exception to their neighbors for very long. Few can stand the ostracization that they receive. That is why we have community, for we are like minds who ought to be attracting more like minds, and may well do so.

The Order of Francis and Clare

Beloved, I underscore and bring to the fore of your attention now our order, the holy Order of Francis and Clare, which has long been the underlying motive and purpose of many who serve here and throughout the field. I wish to inaugurate this order in this hour in a more organized way, that you might identify yourselves, whether on the celibate path or married, with the works that we strove to accomplish in the rebuilding of the Church[14] on the cornerstone of purity while being servants to all life.

Obedience, Poverty, Chastity, and the Defense of Mother Church

I would speak to you of our motto, which I would say today as Obedience, as Poverty, as Chastity.[15] May I speak upon these for a moment. For the obedience of our order is to the one we call Love—Christ. Obedience to Love in the person of Christ in every Ascended Master and not Jesus alone. Obedience to the inner Light and the inner Calling—the foundation of those who walk in commemoration of the World Teachers.

The Order of Francis and Clare takes its name from a quaint period in history which was fraught with the personal Armageddon and vicious forces every whit as nefarious as they are today. It also harks back to a limited understanding of Christ; yet, in the inner mysteries of our hearts, we knew far more than we dared say.

The order today goes beyond that which it was to a new

birth in the Aquarian age. And as you receive the mantle and the perception of the office, you forge that order and create out of it what must needs be. Thus, beloved hearts, chastity itself is purity. It is the purity of the chakras. It is the purity of heart. It is the path of the Sacred Heart. It is the purity of the soul and the purification of body. Above all, it is the transmutation of all past karma. It is the dedication to the path of the ascension by the raising of that Kundalini fire.

Poverty is the self-emptying, that one might be filled. Every day give the light away that is yours to give. Thus, know the true way of Mother Poverty. The emptying that one might be filled is the nature of the Path. Poverty is a love that is greater for others than for oneself.

To these three virtues I add a fourth: it is the defense of the Mother Church.

The Order of the Holy Child

Also included in this order is the Order of the Holy Child, loved by Jesus, brought forth by Lanello, of which you have heard tell on the anniversary of The Summit Lighthouse.[16] This Order of the Holy Child is the defense of the child in all of the seven rays: the protection of the child, the education of the child, the teaching of the child what is love, giving and receiving. It is a path of purity that is the clarity in the heart to pursue the goal of Life. It is a teaching of science and health and abundance, the teaching and the training of the child of the heart—your heart and other children—in the path of service, the path of freedom and the holy orders. All of these things become a part of our Word and our Work.

The Order of the Brothers and Sisters of the Golden Robe

May you then be striving ones. May you remember also that the fulfillment of the Order of Francis and Clare in the etheric octave is now through the Order of the Brothers and Sisters of the Golden Robe.[17] It is the golden robe of the World Teachers and of Christhood, and it is the golden dawn of illumination to the earth. Thus I bring the concept of the order in the hour of Jophiel's coming when so much illumination is needed.

Blessed ones, fear not the Path, for it does unfold as a golden robe before you. The love we have known, the inflaming by the Holy Spirit in our communions—all that we share—far supersedes any adversity or persecution or human consciousness you may encounter.

The equanimity and the peace and the joy of our hearts

attend you in this hour. I desire, then, in the name of Maitreya to break the bread of Life with you—to serve communion that you might understand that both the Teacher and the Teaching is manifest in communion. It is the communion with Maitreya which demands the assimilation.

Recapitulation of My Discourse

May I recapitulate and remind you that I have spoken in the beginning of my discourse to you today of the dispensation of my help to you in your personal health and psychology to the end that you might know the joy of wholeness, be at peace to freely and swiftly eliminate the unreal portions of the self, to mount then the path of initiation that the flame of the heart might be balanced and shine to all nations as the dissemination of our Light, leading all to the fruit of Maitreya and the necessary initiation which every disciple must have if he is to overcome the most difficult and complex problems of the subconscious or the electronic belt. For the accomplishment of this, I recommend this Order of Francis and Clare, which necessarily includes the path of the ministering servant already announced.

This order is a means to an end and not an end in itself. It is not that we desire that you should become caught up in the sense of the order, but that you might use it as a means, a strength, a unity, a brotherhood and a sisterhood to work through the most difficult challenges and to be supported in the hour of weakness by your friends.

Thus, my beloved, it is not with great fanfare but with the transfer to you of an awareness that your allegiance to holy precepts and purposes, your consideration of vows, is strengthening and serves to take the light of the Kundalini to fashion the sacred arrow which will meet its mark in the infinite realms.

Our Motive, Our Mode, Our Maitreya

The purpose of all we do is your ascension. Understand that in order to rescue your soul, we must outsmart or challenge or even bruise that dweller. And we must cajole and contrive circumstances where the eyes of the soul will be opened and true self-knowledge will be gained and thus right choices be made. The entire purpose of our instruction at Summit University from the heart of Maitreya is so that you, dear chela, might have at your disposal our standards from the Ascended Master octaves as you exercise free will for right action—right Word and Work. Understand our motive and tolerate our means, for we must act in the best way possible to reach you swiftly.

Consider always the motive of the Ascended Masters in any adversity, any clash with a chela or family, any misunderstanding of our teaching or the messenger. Consider the motive and consider that the most important part of any experience you have is not what is flung your way but your reaction to it. Your reaction is the determination of your place on the ladder of attainment. Your reaction enables us to act or not to act. Your reaction to anything or everything shows us the fruit that has ripened in you from all of our prior teaching and loving and support as well as discipline.

Thus, perceive the sine wave building towards events that produce a thrust which requires from you a response. Observe the response and you will observe the highest hopes and possibilities which now are given room to manifest. It is always well to pause and take a deep breath and to consider, therefore, before you speak and before you decide on a course of action.

Thus, all is in the pudding. Let us see now the proof of your pudding, for we will not leave thee. We are here for the stated purposes. And we wonder what wonder Maitreya may have before us when you shall have achieved a new level of community attainment.

With the sign of the East and the hierarch of Light, with the sign of the One who has sent me, I am forever the little bird of Christ, the little bird of Buddha. I speak in the ear, twitter in the tree, make ripples in the pond, and bring you a little piece of bread in my beak.

"The Summit Lighthouse Sheds Its Radiance O'er All the World to Manifest as Pearls of Wisdom." This dictation by Kuthumi was delivered through the Messenger Elizabeth Clare Prophet on Sunday, January 27, 1985, at Camelot. The service was conducted by Kuthumi and included teaching on John 6:1–21 and *The Mahatma Letters to A. P. Sinnett*, written by the Mahatmas M. and K.H. (1) Kuthumi, who once walked the path of Christian sainthood as Francis of Assisi (c. 1181–1226), was revered in his soul's final incarnation, in the nineteenth century, as the Kashmiri Brahman Koot Hoomi Lal Singh—known to students of Theosophy as the Master K.H. Together with El Morya (the Master M.), he founded the Theosophical Society through H. P. Blavatsky in 1875. The Masters M. and K.H. wrote *The Mahatma Letters* between 1880 and 1884 to A. P. Sinnett, a disciple in the Theosophical Society. In the service preceding Kuthumi's dictation, the messenger read from Section III, "Probation and Chelaship" (Letters XL, XLIX, LV), in which Morya and Koot Hoomi speak of the "fiendish malice and systematic intrigue" surrounding the Theosophical Society from various sources, including the press and Christians. (2) Heb. 7:1–3. (3) Pss. 110:4; Heb. 5:5–10; 6:19, 20; Heb. 7:14–22. (4) Matt. 18:14; John 17:12; II Thess. 2:3, 4. (5) Matt. 24:22; Mark 13:20. (6) I Cor. 3:13–15; I Pet. 1:7; 4:12. (7) Isa. 34:8; 61:2; 63:4; Jer. 50:15, 28; 51:6, 11; Luke 21:22. (8) John 8:23. (9) Matt. 25:1–13. (10) Matt. 14:28–31. (11) Gen. 4:3–8. (12) Jesus and Kuthumi, *Prayer and Meditation*, Summit University Press, $6.95 ($7.95 postpaid USA). (13) The term *indulgence* in Roman
Copyright © 1985 Church Universal and Triumphant, Inc.

Catholicism refers to the plenary (full) or partial remission of temporal punishment due for sins whose guilt and eternal punishment have already been pardoned. Indulgences are usually granted in exchange for prayers and devotional acts. During the medieval period, this practice came under abuse when indulgences could be obtained through monetary contributions, which eventually instigated the Protestant Reformation. (14) Saint Francis—born into the wealthy Bernardone family about 1181 in Assisi, Umbria, Italy—was called by God to restore the Church, which had fallen into corruption. As he was in prayer one day in 1206 at the ruined chapel of San Damiano outside the gate of Assisi, he heard a voice from the crucifix above the altar command: "Go, Francis, and repair my house which, as you see, is falling in ruins." Renouncing worldly goods and family ties, Francis embraced a life of poverty and, for two or three years, fervently dedicated himself to repairing the church of San Damiano, a chapel honoring St. Peter, and the Portiuncula, the chapel of St. Mary of the Angels, near Assisi. The Portiuncula, which was to become the cradle of the Franciscan Order, was described by Saint Bonaventure as "the place that Francis loved most in the whole world." It was there that Francis received the revelation of his true vocation. While attending Mass in the restored chapel on the Feast of St. Matthias, February 24, 1208, he listened as the priest read from Matthew 10: "Go, preach, saying, The kingdom of heaven is at hand. Heal the sick, cleanse the lepers, raise the dead, cast out devils. Freely ye have received, freely give. Provide neither gold, nor silver, nor brass in your purses, nor scrip for your journey, neither two coats, neither shoes, nor yet staves; for the workman is worthy of his meat." Francis later recalled this as his "day of decision"—the day in which "the Most High personally revealed to me that I ought to live according to the Holy Gospel." He donned a coarser garment, went barefoot, and began to preach to the townspeople, attracting followers to his way of life. In 1209, Francis, with a band of eleven disciples, went to Rome to seek the approval of Pope Innocent III for a "rule of life" to formally begin his religious order. The Pope assented when he recognized Francis as the same figure he had seen in a dream holding up the Lateran basilica on his own back. This marked the official founding of the Franciscan Order, which then began to spread rapidly, growing to over 5,000 members by 1219. (15) The Franciscan Order of Friars Minor (the "little brothers") was founded by Saint Francis in 1209 "to follow the teachings of our Lord Jesus Christ and to walk in his footsteps." Francis wrote: "The Rule and life of the Friars Minor is this, namely, to observe the Holy Gospel of our Lord Jesus Christ by living in obedience, without property, and in chastity." In 1212, when Clare, a young devotee of noble birth, determined to follow his way of life, Francis began a second order for women, which became known as the Poor Clares (or the Order of Saint Clare). Around 1221, he established the Third Order of Brothers and Sisters of Penance, a lay fraternity for those who did not wish to withdraw from the world or take religious vows but desired to live by Franciscan precepts. (16) During the August 1983 celebration of the twenty-fifth anniversary of The Summit Lighthouse, the messenger read excerpts from the Ashram Notes—a precious collection of correspondence and teachings from Master Morya recorded by Mark L. Prophet prior to the founding of the organization in 1958. The first letter, dated April 26, 1951, from Mark to chelas announced the formation of "The Order of The Child"—a sacred order for legislators, rulers, directors of culture, and citizens who would promise to be "ever-mindful of the little child of the future." The letter explained: "There are no dues, no rules, except that you promise to devote one minute per day to reading a few words inscribed on the certificate of membership, which you will post on the wall of your office. Membership is *ad vitam*. And there are no meetings except a meeting of mind and heart before God. Also the promise to stand face to face with this certificate and submit your conscience to the little child in any matter embodying a decision affecting the lives of others." (The certificate and membership pledge is reprinted on the closing page of this Pearl.) (17) The Order of the Brothers and Sisters of the Golden Robe is a fraternity composed of Ascended Masters and their embodied chelas dedicated to the raising up of the Mother flame of illumined action and the opening of the crown chakra in its initiates, and to the enlightenment of all people of God through the flame of Wisdom. It is headed by beloved Kuthumi, who has retreats on the etheric plane in Kashmir, India, and Shigatse, Tibet.

Pearls of Wisdom, published weekly by The Summit Lighthouse for Church Universal and Triumphant, come to you under the auspices of the Darjeeling Council of the Great White Brotherhood. These are presently dictated by the Ascended Masters to their Messenger Elizabeth Clare Prophet. The international headquarters of this nonprofit, nondenominational activity is located in Los Angeles, California. All communications and freewill contributions should be addressed to The Summit Lighthouse, Box A, Malibu, CA 90265. Pearls of Wisdom are sent weekly throughout the USA via third-class mail to all who support the Church with a minimum yearly love offering of $40. First-class and international postage rates available upon request. Notice of change of address should be received three weeks prior to the effective date. Third-class mail is not forwarded by the post office.

Copyright © 1985 Church Universal and Triumphant, Inc. All rights reserved. Printed in the United States of America. Pearls of Wisdom and The Summit Lighthouse are registered trademarks of Church Universal and Triumphant, Inc. All rights to their use are reserved.

Celestial Order of the Child

A Body Including Legislators, Rulers, Directors of Culture,
and Citizens Embracing the Embodied Principles

_____
(date)

There is conferred upon the one whose name is written below
the title of Advocate.

_____
(Write your own name here. Post by your desk.)

My signature above signifies that I am willing to conform in heart and mind to the sacred precepts of the Order of the Child, spending the required time of one minute daily in contemplation and thought before the precepts below written, also submitting major decisions to these same precepts.

IN REMEMBRANCE of His Words...

Whosoever shall receive <u>one</u> such little child in my name receiveth me.
Of such is the kingdom of heaven.
Woe unto him who shall hurt one of these little ones.
Inasmuch as ye have done it unto the least of these, ye have done it unto me...

I desire that my heart shall ever make me aware of the little child, who is always without in the concourse of time and space *and who is affected by my decisions and my acts.*

In knowledge of the fact that my acts combined with others' do affect the destiny of my country, the human race, and our common future, I do enter wholeheartedly into the below pledge, realizing whether I make the pledge or not, I am still held *fully* accountable for every act.

I unite therefore with others, that we may make a bond for good, that our common purpose before God, our common heart and mind, will shine forth a golden ray of Light to establish the greatest civilization ever on earth.

Knowing also that if these principles be not adhered to it is possible and imminent that this great civilization, like that of ancient Rome and others, may fall, decay, and decline, I should therefore work for our future without bias.

PLEDGE

BEFORE THE GOD of the universe, I promise to be ever aware of the interests of mankind, as an All, and of all who dwell in my country, rather than the few.

I shall seek better government of the people, by the people, and for the people. As I act toward the least of humanity, I have acted toward the greatest.

My thoughts shall be ever mindful of the little child of the future—every little child in whom is the breath of Life. If ever I cannot act accordingly, I shall resign my authority over others.

Conferring upon each advocate of the child of the future a portion of the wisdom of Solomon, who received wisdom of God, may your wisdom be like unto your sincerity, increasing unto the full light of divine wisdom, sufficient unto this day.

Mark L. Prophet
Servant of Advocates

The Summoning:
Straight Talk and a Sword from the Hierarch of Banff

Hail, legions of Light, hosts of the LORD, chelas of the sacred fire of the will of God! I not only shall return, I am returned[1] unto thee in the fullness of my flaming sword!

I come in this hour and day of rejoicing in heaven and rejoicing on earth, for I AM Michael, Prince of the Archangels—and I address you now in the fullness of your own God Presence. For only by that God Presence can you witness unto me. And by that great God Presence, beloved hearts—far greater than all those "men of renown"[2] of ancient days—you, then, by the crystal cord, sip the divine nectar as through a straw, *you* tie in to our bands and our legions, and you are become one in the Divinity we espouse.

Chelas of El Morya Enlisted in Archangel Michael's Legions

We have heard the call of the Mother to enlist all of you in our legions[3] and we have already acted with dispatch. And we have therefore summoned you in our legions of Light—conscripted, then, by our captains. And those who have entered in to that freewill surrender in faith have truly been anointed in our retreat and have already received their first lessons in the hours of the rest of the physical body.[4]

Beloved hearts of Light, the swelling of our ranks by unascended devotees of the sacred fire can only mean a greater fortification in the earth for the protection of right action and of virtue.

The Light of the New World Religion Will Be Cursed by the Darkness

Fear not, beloved hearts! For when you are labeled a "destructive cult," you understand the meaning of the accusation

Copyright © 1985 Church Universal and Triumphant, Inc.

leveled against Saint Germain, calling him the devil and cursing his blessings and healings in the streets of Paris and throughout the earth where he has appeared in many guises.

Let it be understood that that which is to come, that which is the Light of the new world religion, will be cursed by the Darkness and the Dark Ones of the previous cycles who will not let go of their hold, their stranglehold, upon the souls of the people. For they enjoy their positions of power and truly *they* have made of the Light of the avatars destructive cults enthroned as the major religions and sects of this time.

The people of earth can but experience the current cycles of their understanding [present levels of their comprehension of the things of the Spirit], and scarcely this itself. Therefore, trust and understand, beloved hearts, that they are not able to imbibe the sacred communion cup of the future.

Thus, it has always been that the mystery schools and the communities surrounding our representative teachers have held the flame for many to make the transition into the sacred awareness they all once knew in the very heart of hearts: the awareness of the Law of the One. Thus, those who have been with us from the beginning are called again, and our recruits are those who have proven themselves tried-and-true in the previous battles.

Qualifications for Service
with the Defender of World Peace and Freedom

I represent the angels of the first ray and all of the angels of the seven rays. Beloved hearts of Light, my position and posture is the securing of the physical body, the physical matrix, the faith of the soul. And therefore, I am a part of the militant defense of world peace and world freedom.

Thus, my perspective of selecting those for my ranks must come from my goals, as any employer will hire employees whom he desires to see accomplish his ends. Thus, understand that the basic qualifications of service with me are also the qualifications of devotion on the first ray. If you desire to serve with other of the archangels, you will discover the manifold purpose of the Holy Church and the Great White Brotherhood represented by us, and you have had preparation for that service by the training under the seven chohans of the rays.

Therefore, beloved, be seated as I address you on the subject of world victory.

First and foremost, you understand that your beloved

El Morya chose and was chosen to sponsor these Messengers and this organization for the training up of the disciples of the living Christ according to the requirements of the first ray. Those, then, who are not dedicated to the will of God and its perfectionment in their souls and its protection in the Teaching ought not to consider that they are a part of this circle of Light.

One cannot skip the first note of qualification. Thus, beloved hearts, by the very nature of the founding father of this activity, by the very nature of planetary conditions, all who come to us for blessing must first be received as disciples in our retreats. The retreat of El Morya [at Darjeeling, India] is the beginning, together with the Royal Teton [at the Grand Teton, Wyoming], and then the retreats which we share—that of our legions at Banff, that of Hercules and Amazonia [over Half Dome at Yosemite National Park, California] and the Great Divine Director [Cave of Light in India], who have trained those who have been victorious in all ages.

Usurpers of God-Government, God-Economy Must Be Challenged

Understand, beloved hearts, that there is found wanting on this planet true representatives of the people in the economy and in the government of every nation because they have failed their exams at Luxor, at Darjeeling, at Banff, and Yosemite![5] They have refused to bend the knee and appropriate the magnificent instruction by Saint Germain in God-government.

Thus, all must have their day and you must understand that all who occupy positions on this planet, great or small—the fact that they have physical form and manifestation means that they must be given the opportunity to choose this day whom they will serve,[6] to choose the living Christ and the living Word.

Understand, beloved hearts, that this choosing may be preunderstood by us but it is never preordained. There is no fixed karma, astrology, or any past action whereby we judge the individual. We may know all things or we may enter into the immaculate heart of the Universal Mother, but we will not surmise what the outcome of the individual choices will be; for we hold to the law of free will for the victory of all evolutions of earth.

We demand, therefore, that you come to the realization that those usurpers of the Light of the first ray must be challenged— that is, those who have made their determination and their commitment to use any Light available to them to supplant God-government and the God-economy.

Four Horsemen Deliver Mankind's Karma in the Economy

I have personally instructed the Messenger this day to present to you very necessary information on the economy concerning the international bankers, the Order,[7] the manipulation of the prices of oil and the consequences thereof to the international economy and to you personally in your lives in this decade. And therefore, I request you return after your repast and come into the knowledge of this information and increase your calls for the understanding of what is at hand and what is the treachery that is about to break through through the manipulation of the money systems of this planet.

Beloved hearts of Light, these eventualities come by edict of the Karmic Board. And this is the nature of the Four Horsemen[8] (as well as the seven angels who come to signal the seven last plagues[9]) who come to deliver mankind's karma, for they [mankind] have *refused* to sit at the feet of their Teachers to be initiated that they might transcend their karma. And they have therefore deserved to have their own karma, with no intercessory grace, teach them the lessons of their perfidy and their rebellion against God.

A Planetary Home of Varied Evolutions and Many Lifewaves

You live upon a planetary home of many and varied evolutions. Do not be concerned, for Jesus said that thine enemies shall be they of thine own household.[10] "Thine own household" begins with the four lower bodies, the internal subconscious mind, and all records of the past, extending, then, to one's family and all karmic ties.

The enemy, of course, is the unredeemed substance. You are your own worst enemy! And beginning from that point, you will discover a reflection of yourself in those with whom you have interaction and you must see through the unreality to the real principle of Life.

Understand, then, the equation of many lifewaves and the coming apart. You have often said that going to the Inner Retreat is like going to another planet. Well, it is, but the *planet* is another *plane*. And that other plane of consciousness is a focalization of the etheric octave and the etheric retreats. On this planetary home, you can find the physical manifestation of Death and Hell. Thus is the broad spectrum apparent.

The Wise Seek the Holy Mountain of God

Thus, you must be wise and realize that merely because you have a tube of light and the action of my blue flame and sword is no guarantee that if you descend into hell and do play with the fires of hell and say, "I am immune," you will not be caught up in a situation in which you will find yourself ill-equipped to deal with the forces unleashed against you.

Therefore, the wise seek the holy mountain of God and the Holy of Holies of their own I AM Presence, and they remain on guard. This is the very first lesson of the angels of our bands and you who would desire to serve with us at inner levels. You have heard the statement, "Fools rush in where angels fear to tread."[11] Until you know solidly how to invoke [spiritual protection in the physical/astral/mental/etheric planes] and to be certain that you have on the armor of the angels of the first ray, do not so lightly go into places of darkness.

Beloved hearts, merely going into a bar for a glass of beer can put you in contact with the entire false hierarchy of the liquor industry and its focus in the bottomless pit. These are not innocent pastimes and cannot be engaged in by the true initiates of the sacred fire.

Take Right Action to Undo the Wrong Action of the Wicked

If you would be with us, then you must be with us all the way. And I am speaking of those of you who are determined to take right action with the sword of blue flame of our legions to undo the wrong action of the seed of the wicked that has been taken in these days against this community of Light, its Messenger, and its tried-and-true system of chelaship under the Great White Brotherhood.[12]

Blessed hearts, what do they attack? I will tell you that the attack is on the path that leads to reunion with God. It is on the school of the ascension that is now physical (and has remained etheric with Serapis for many thousands of years) that the ascension may become the goal of life. Moreover, it is an attack on the means to that end: the balancing of one's karma.

Souls of Earth and Venus to Bring In the Golden Age

Precious hearts, the accomplishment of this goal in our lifetime together and our service in this century will place this planet in a new dimension—and in that access [from that vantage] to be on a par with the purposes and the victory of Venus. And as a result, the sister star to earth will truly be able to enter into that polarity of the figure-eight flow whereby your loved ones and evolutions of Light who are embodied there in this hour in the etheric octave may then embody on earth. And the reunions and the serving together of these groups of souls will bring about the great golden age.

The lever of the Karmic Board and the Four and Twenty Elders has not descended in approval of this interchange which we envision, for we do not consider this planet ready to receive the Venusian souls, except those who have come as avatars and Christed ones. For we desire not to lose those who are not as advanced as some.

A One-Pointed Purpose, Waking and Sleeping

Understand, then, that when I give the qualifications for those in our service, I give it for those who would march with the legions of Light at inner levels and who must know the ultimate protection. For it is the action of the legions of the first ray and the legions of Astrea and El Morya and Lanello to descend into the very darkest places of the astral plane, including into the very pit itself. I tell you, beloved hearts, you must have a one-pointed purpose, waking and sleeping, if you are to be a part of this extraordinary band of lightbearers.

Therefore, consider well, for the life-style of our Messengers and the certain caution that is pursued by them has been according to the protection needed by those who wear the mantle of Messenger. Well, I tell you, you stand to wear the mantle of your Holy Christ Self—and not only this, but the mantle of our bands. And therefore, you need the ultimate protection that is required.

A False Witness for a Purpose

You need to think about the consequences and you need to look at that which is ready to precipitate on this planet—so easily seen in the fear, the insanity, the projected hatred, and the determination to destroy that is obvious in this reporting [in the media] that does not measure up to the reporting of the Keeper of the Scrolls, and indeed cannot. For it is a false witness for a purpose— not for the mere entertainment of the week, not even for sensationalism, but to incite a body of individuals who will then contain fear and doubt and superstition and hatred and anger against this activity.

And thus, those who have the murderous intent send forth the sparks of that intent, and unwary souls[13] then begin to carry that consciousness. Thus, transmutation is in order. Thus, the action of the legions of blue lightning is in order to go forth and bind the astral hordes and the demons of the night who prey upon these unsuspecting hearts when truly, by their own witness, they can see and know the Truth even in the presence of the false witness.

What Is the Bottomless Pit?

Beloved hearts of Light, I have already shown your Messenger this very weekend the necessary work that now must be done for the cleaning out of the focuses of the pit on the astral plane of this planet.

What is the pit?

Beloved ones, it is mentioned in the Book of Revelation. It is mentioned in chapter nine. It is mentioned with the sounding forth of the fifth angel and the star that descends from heaven having the keys to the bottomless pit. Again, according to cosmic cycles, according to karmic cycles as well, that pit was opened that the earth might receive the product of its lowered consciousness.

A Triad of Misuse of the Base Chakra

And out from that pit have come forth in this century individuals who have spawned the entire culture of rock and drugs and have renewed the ancient perversions of the misuse of the sacred fire in genetic engineering, in destructive creations in the laboratories, in the misuse of energy in nuclear weapons, and in the misuse of the life-force through all manner of dire perversion.

Beloved hearts, this triad of misuse of the base chakra must be seen by you as the outplaying of fallen angels. Thanks to your presence and that of the Great White Brotherhood, there has been a rallying of parents' groups against drugs, but no one is seriously tackling the engines of rock music or those stars that have fallen, leading the children of Light astray and wreaking havoc with their chakras. And also there is not sufficient challenging, in terms of decree work, of the misuse of the base chakra by these fallen ones. They are about to bring forth, as you have been told, the same sort of miscreation that they brought forth on Atlantis. And the Law will not allow it!

A First-Ray Activity in Clearing Out the Bottomless Pit

Beloved hearts, understand, then, the meaning of the bottomless pit. And understand that as a result of the actions of those who have come forth from that very place—who have embodied and who have set themselves up as judge and jury of the Teaching, the Brotherhood, the Masters, the Messengers, the organization and yourselves—there has come forth the edict of the judgment that you may in your calls, by the authority of the sponsoring ones of this activity ascended and unascended, therefore demand the total clearing out of the focuses of the bottomless pit on this planet!

This is a mighty work of the ages, which is led by none other than Hercules himself with Amazonia, none other than Surya and Cuzco and all the hosts and legions of Light who join us now on the first ray for a first-ray activity.

The Messenger Witnesses the Bottomless Pit

Thus, within the past forty-eight hours, I have taken the Messenger into the bottomless pit to witness these fallen ones and to witness the action of the fiery salamanders and the seraphim and to see the work of the mighty archangels in the binding of those who have been cast there because of their infamy against the Light.

Beloved ones, if the karmic law of the planetary evolution were to move forward without the intercession of representatives of the Great White Brotherhood in physical embodiment, we could not perform this service. The requirement is that there be those who stand for the path of the ascension. For the path of the ascension devours the cause and core of all drugs and their misuse, of all rock music and every misuse of the base chakra in every form of manipulation of mechanization man—whether in technology or science or religion!

Perversions of the Pit Transmitted to Agents in Embodiment

Understand, therefore, that those who hold the Light against the conspiracy of cocaine and marijuana and death will therefore receive the onslaughts of those who have opposed that Light for aeons, even though they may be imprisoned in the bottomless pit. The opening of that pit has caused many among them to be in embodiment; therefore, the consciousness of those in the pit is transmitted to those agents in embodiment and does yet permeate the planetary home at the astral plane.

The drugs and the rock music and the misuse of the sacred fire carry, then, the young people to that astral awareness. And thus, out of the bowels of the pit itself does come forth the direction of these fallen ones and their demons, for a like vibration produces a like receptivity. Thus, you might say that these fallen ones pervert the very Spirit of the Great Central Sun in that pit, and they look to the youth of the world as the passive receivers of their darkness and their malintent—which is not perceived by the youth.

Drugs, Rock, and Misuse of Sacred Fire Produce Passivity

Drugs produce passivity. Rock music produces passivity. And so does the misuse of the sacred fire destroy the strength and the courage and the Light of the Kundalini fire. Therefore, that manifestation of passivity is present throughout the world—and not only in the youth, but in all those who become the counterpart of the pit, positioning themselves in respectability in the governments of the nations. Thus, action is not taken, for the action of the sacred fire is not with them—is not in their body temples! Do you see the dilemma, beloved hearts? ["Yes!"]

Gratitude of Archangels and the Darjeeling Council for the Chelas

I cannot even tell you the gratitude of the archangels and the Darjeeling Council that we may explain these things, these mysteries of God, to a body of chelas on earth, and that these chelas are positioned strategically throughout the planet and do receive these messages on a weekly basis; and therefore, the network of the blue lightning of the Mind of God is in position and God Mercury can work through you to implement the very next step that must be taken.

I can only say, let the dictations go forth also in the written Word as quickly as they are given, for they are timely and they are a warning and they keep all of our chelas on the cycles of overcoming.

Beloved hearts, realize, then, that this action for the cleaning out of the pit is the decree of the Four and Twenty Elders and the Cosmic Council and of Almighty God that the lightbearers in embodiment should no longer be burdened by the permeation of the malice and the hate and hate creation of those who are seething in the pit. Thus, we have said, "The serpents are hissing in their pits."

Focuses of the Pit around the World

Beloved hearts, the pit is referred to in the Bible as one place, but in fact it has focuses around the world. And thus, in places of extreme darkness you will note that there is a proximity to the opening into the very depths of hell—such as Guyana, such as certain other places in South America and in the Middle East and in Asia and in the Caribbean. Beloved hearts, wherever you notice a concentration of great darkness and voodoo and bloodletting, such as in certain places of Africa, you will note that there is the necessity to go forth with us, fully armored in the victory of the God flame and in the challenge and the binding of these fallen ones.

The Challenge to Chelas of El Morya
to Become Chelas of Archangel Michael

You are the authority for this earth because you are in physical embodiment. Therefore, when you come, heaven and earth bear testimony and witness together and we have the fullness of the Law in our backing. Understand how vital it is, then, for the chelas of El Morya to step up now to the next level to become chelas of Archangel Michael. Do you understand my call, blessed hearts? ["Yes!"]

Now, I would say to you that in the understanding of this challenge, you may draw the perspective and the commeasurement of what your service must be in the days to come. You will understand, therefore, that this is a mighty edict and it comes forth from the hosts of Light from the Central Sun in answer to the call given day in and day out by yourselves and the Messenger that Death and Hell be cast into the lake of fire.[14]

The Fallen Ones Have Overstepped Their Bounds

Understand that there are many pockets and canyons and caverns, a labyrinth complex of the consciousness of Death and Hell. Thus, it is not taken all at once. Thus, because of the judgment of Helios, this consequence may come forth, but the actual manifestation of the dispensation comes because of the fallen ones overstepping their bounds in this media attack upon the Church Universal and Triumphant.

Understand that they have lost the momentum of their immunity which they have enjoyed, these fallen ones, even as the hierarchs of the left-handed path are not taken and cannot be taken until their time is up—as long as they remember the LORD's counsel unto Satan as depicted in the Book of Job: that he might go forth to tempt and to do all manner of mischief against Job except the taking of his life.

The Testing, That You Might Receive
Things Permanent in the Heavens

Thus, in the period of initiation that the LORD God allowed, Job lost everything. And in the end, by his faithfulness to his God, his refusal to curse his God, all these things were returned to him. That which he gave up was physical and temporal; that which he received in return was permanent in the heavens, having its source in the etheric octave.

And thus, beloved hearts, do not hold on to those things which are temporal, fearing the loss whether of things or life.

But understand that all things that you see are there that you might be tested. And when you are tested, the crown of Life you receive is the raised sacred fire of the Kundalini as that mighty sword Excalibur—the full power of the crown chakra. And you receive, then, the things of heaven. You receive the wedding garment and those things that are permanent and forever with you now and in your causal body.

Do Not Expect the Approbation of the World

Understand that it has always been that the judgments of the world have not been the true judgments of God. Since this is a planet occupied and preoccupied by the fallen angels and their mass-consciousness creations, you will not receive the approbation of the world. If the greatest who have gone before you have not received it, do not rest your thought on the idea that somehow and somewhere and in some way you will make them believe that you are true and righteous and pure and of good intent. Even when they see it, they do not want to believe it! And above all, they do not want the world to know it.

We Link the Lightbearers by the Diamond Heart of Mary and El Morya

And therefore, we circumvent those who have taken unto themselves the domination of the media and the press. And we link the lightbearers by the diamond heart of Mary and El Morya, by the blue lightning of our causal body. And there is a direct communication that is established in this hour of the oneness of all lightbearers of the planet, that your decrees might flow as a direct transfusion to their hearts through the Mighty I AM Presence to deliver them of the burdens of the fear coming upon their hearts—the projected fear and agitation of the fallen ones.

And thus, you may know that your calls are sustaining the body of God worldwide. And do not mistake the impostors who come saying they represent this body; but know them only by their fruits. For the impostors have also learned to imitate the light of the eye and to draw the sacred fire to put on the appearance of The Faithful and True.

The further we march for the victory of Light, the more determined we are to rid the planet of the astral hordes, the more you will find the attempt to enter in to the company of saints by those who are the impostors, those who are the fallen ones. Thus, we have counseled against idolatry many times, but we encourage you to study exactly what is idolatry and to know what is Light and what is Darkness.[15]

You have heard, then, the invocation of the Messenger given in the lighting of the candles for the descent and the intercession of the Great Central Sun Magnet. This is a city that represents the crossroads of the earth as pertains to the victory of the Light in the seat-of-the-soul chakra, just as the base chakra of the planet has its crossroads in the Middle East. There are areas of concentration of forces in the earth that are key in the planetary God-mastery of the seven chakras.

Establishment of the Forcefield of the Great Central Sun and the Four and Twenty Elders over Los Angeles

Therefore, beloved hearts, preceding those things that may be coming upon the earth, Alpha and Omega have determined to use the Threefold Flame Fountain of Light established here more than twenty years ago.[16] Using that Fountain of Light then, beloved hearts, they have set the forcefield of the Great Central Sun and the Four and Twenty Elders. This is in the etheric octave. It presses close to the physical and the astral planes, and it is sent that the witnesses of God and that this Church, which represents the Great White Brotherhood truly, might receive the witness of heaven and the true and just judgments as well as the protection.

The presence of the Four and Twenty Elders, therefore, in their Electronic Presence here, indicates that this is the city and the time and the place for the focalization of your calls upon the system of justice and the courts and the judges and the lawyers and the witnesses and the jurors.

Focus of Christ and Antichrist in the Motion-Picture Industry

For all is brought to a head in the judgment of Christ and Antichrist here. Every motion picture that is made, every television program that has its origin here or in the companion city, New York (which focuses the third-eye chakra of the nation), does play before the children of the Sun the interactions of Light and Darkness.

Unfortunately, it is the intent of many among the producers of these films that the conclusion ought to be sympathy for the fallen ones and the downtrodden. It is no longer cut-and-dried that triumph comes to Virtue and to Truth and to those who stand alone.

Thus, beloved hearts, you see there is a prejudgment that becomes the inner goal of the conception of these films. And the whole world receives a human consciousness of light and darkness, right and wrong, and of the absolutes of Light and Darkness

Copyright © 1985 Church Universal and Triumphant, Inc.

outplayed in life. Rather, look to those who produce these films than to their stories to understand what is their malintent.

Side by side with this is the great drama of the ages: the path of the ascension that you are outplaying as the actors on the stage of life. You are seen just as clearly at inner levels [as the movies and movie stars and rock stars are seen at outer levels] by all evolutions of earth, and the consequences of your actions are known at the soul level.

Thus, when the condemnation comes forth, it presents confusion in the outer mind. They want to believe, but how can they believe in the face of such testimony as has been given?

Everyone Must Be Tested

Beloved hearts, this is the dilemma. But I tell you from the heart of beloved El Morya this day that he reminds all that everyone must be tested and everyone has already had a prior understanding of the One Sent, the Avatar, the Christ, and the children of the Sun; for this has been repeated civilization after civilization. Thus, the test that is presented through the dark ones is to hear the lie and to pass through the lie and therefore be able to enter through the doorway of Truth.

This is the initiation which each and every one of you has had before arriving to this very Holy Grail. You have had to discount this and that—whether gossip or calumny or false theology or misinterpretation of scripture. You have had to walk by the faith of the heart, by the certain knowing of the inner self, and to disregard outer things that have been played against your minds aggressively to deter you from the perfect Path.

I speak, then, to those who are here and those who are not who have separated themselves spiritually from our Cause. These are they who have judged the unjust judgment of outer conditionings and have not been willing to take that sword of Truth and puncture the lie and poke right through that vast panorama that they have portrayed.

Decreers Come Forth to Challenge the Misuse of the Word

Why, the entire momentum of World Communism coming out of the Soviet Union is a fabrication, something they desire the people to see! But The Faithful and True comes as The Word, comes with the sword going forth from the mouth.[17] And when it [the lie of World Communism] is punctured, it is seen as a sham—as nothing but, as it were, papier-mâché, maya. But it is fierce and intense as long as the lie is repeated.

The lie is repeated in the perversion of the science of

mantra. Understand this. The perpetual repetition of the lie of Lenin and Marx and Trotsky and all who have followed, such as Mao and the Soviets—all of this repetition and writing is the misuse of the Word.

Thus understand, there must come forth those decreers who decree perpetually to challenge the misuse of the science of the spoken Word, not only in the media and the press or in World Communism, but in the fundamentalist prayers of malintent, in the fundamentalist hatred of a Khomeini, of world terrorism, of that which is happening in the Middle East—that fundamentalism which is fanaticism and the ability to use the base chakra by the spoken Word or by explosives or by murder to undo the true Word manifest in your hearts.

Thus, it is the Word that was perverted in both areas of focalization [the press and TV] on this organization. But you stand for The Word. You are the embodiment of the science of the dynamic decree par excellence.

Your Attainment in the Science of the Spoken Word Will Be Challenged

There is no organization—and I say, *organization*—on the planet that has as much power in the use of the Word for constructive change as this one. And this is my report to you, and you should know it and understand it and esteem your supreme value to the hosts of Light and to the evolutions of this planet as you act in this capacity!

You have been long told by Serapis Bey that that which is your point of attainment and your greatest Light is the very thing which will be challenged again and again and again—not only because it is feared by the sinister force and the false hierarchy of the media and the churches, but because you must constantly prove your own attainment on that path and, by having overcome and thrust through, be given the opportunity to ascend that ladder.

Thus, some of you, who have made it your theme of life and your supreme dedication, find yourselves—because you have this attainment in the science of the spoken Word—at a certain level of your being in the etheric octave and in our inner retreats solely by the fastidiousness of the practice of this science. Now, this is indeed a threat to those in this very city who are misusing that Word in the media, in the motion-picture industry, in the multiplication of rock music, in the sale of drugs, and in the absolute perversion of the base-of-the-spine chakra.

Copyright © 1985 Church Universal and Triumphant, Inc.

The Interchange between Los Angeles and New York— from the Seat-of-the-Soul Chakra to the Third Eye

Thus, beloved ones, the Word is the defeating of the international drug conspiracy. And, as you see the arcing of the Light and the interchange between Los Angeles and New York, you understand that from the seat-of-the-soul chakra to the third eye there is the connection in the spoken Word to the banking houses, to Wall Street, to the headquarters of the Mafia, and to all manner of perversion of world government through the United Nations and every other manifestation of the Order that is known.

Therefore, there is an interconnection. And those [Keepers of the Flame] in New York must take responsibility for the actions which find receptivity from Los Angeles to New York in the minds of the people. And the reverse is true: that which is done in New York is also felt here. And this is a false polarity— the misuse of the Light of the polarity of Alpha and Omega that ought to be the mighty pillars of sacred fire.

When you think of ten million individuals focused in the greater metropolitan areas of these two cities, you understand that they are intended to be the focuses of the guardian action of the United States of America.

The Anti-Maitreya Force of the Planet

And if the evolutions of these cities had embraced the Light and the Godhead and the Mighty I AM Presence, their very auras of Light would protect this nation against the Soviet submarines and their malintent and their positioning of their nuclear weapons aimed directly at this continent.[18]

Beloved hearts, this is a threat that ought not to be tolerated. And yet, we cannot cite your leaders, for their toleration of this situation goes back far beyond this lifetime. It goes back to the place where, having betrayed the LORD Maitreya, they lost the power to challenge the enemy.

Those submarines and their malintent are the anti-Maitreya force of the planet! Understand me when I say this, and understand me when you see, then, that I tell you that the Lords of Karma and Almighty God have placed such a trust in your hearts that Maitreya has come forth. And in his coming forth, ordained by the Great Central Sun, there was a preknowledge that the force of anti-Maitreya would increase and intensify. Therefore, we must count upon you to defend Lord Maitreya, his School, and his Teaching at the Inner Retreat—the only place where we can protect such a mighty focus of Light.

The Only Recourse That Can Save the World

We must depend upon you to have the vision and the realization that it is a calculated risk to have a Messenger in embodiment and to sponsor such an organization, for it brings out the darkest of the dark. Thus, you are indeed between two ages—the ages of Darkness and Light—and you stand with all of humanity behind you and the fallen ones pitted against you. And you in the midst have the only recourse that can save the world: to look up and call forth the hosts of the LORD and the Spirit of the Great White Brotherhood!

Now, beloved hearts, we enter into counsel with the supreme strategists observing planetary forces. And we remind you that there are many in this nation who are the powers that be, often behind the scenes, who do not desire to see the liberation of Afghanistan or the driving back of the darkness that is there, who may not act if the Soviets determine to launch a full-scale attack on Pakistan. And where can those be found who would defend Iran in the hour of her takeover by the Soviet forces?

Thus, the pressing onward into the Mediterranean, into the Middle East, into those very strategic waters is continuing. And you will understand further, as you receive our report this afternoon, what are the forces at play in the Middle East that lead us to observe in the making the conditions for a resource war, planetary in scope, unless the dynamic decree goes forth and those in embodiment who have the power to act do act—and I speak of the representatives of the governments of the nations.

We look, then, and we ask you to look, both at inner and outer levels, at the strategy of the Caribbean and Central America and those areas that are key and that will not hold without the intercession of Light.

The Messenger's Stump to Australia and the Philippines

As Mother Mary has called, as Gautama Buddha has decreed, and as El Morya has sponsored—and therefore all of us with him—we announce to you the forthcoming Stump by the Messenger and her team to Australia and the Philippines!

This, beloved hearts [applause and standing ovation]... This, beloved hearts, is ready to be set forth in the very physical octave. The preparations have been made and this team of coworkers and disciples of Maitreya shall depart Los Angeles for Sydney on the twelfth of February. Thus, the hour and the day draw nigh and our posters are already being seen in Sydney, as the advertisements have also gone forth.

Copyright © 1985 Church Universal and Triumphant, Inc.

Prayer Vigil for Protection of the Team and Lightbearers

We make this announcement this day that we might have your reinforcement in a prayer vigil for the protection of the Messenger and the Word and the Teaching and the Lightbearers of these nations who must come forth and gather and hear the Word and apply it, as well as for the condition that always happens: that those who are ready for the judgment must also be judged.

We are grateful for the tremendous response and support of the Keepers of the Flame of Australia and the Philippines, and also for the chelas in Hawaii who will receive this team on their way home.

We are counting on you to be a mighty electrode of Light and a focus of the Great Central Sun Magnet here. And we trust you will understand that this mighty world expansion is truly changing the face of the planet as the very shadow of the Great White Brotherhood precedes the coming of the chelas and the Messenger in those areas. And therefore, planetary changes have already been seen as well as much opposition from the fallen ones who have attempted to place in the way of this delivery fires and all manners of climatic conditions that are dangerous and untimely.

The Opening of Focuses for the Ascension

Beloved hearts, understand the necessity for the leaven to leaven the whole world and for the Teaching to go forth. Understand also, as Mother Mary said in that hour of August 26th, that wherever the Messenger places her feet in the delivery of the Word, *there* will be opened up the opportunity for the ascension of the sons and daughters of God![19]

Now, what I must add to this, beloved hearts, is the understanding that beneath her feet in many places will be the very vortices of the bottomless pit we have described. Thus, these pits must be cleaned out and their denizens be bound and sealed, that Serapis might place through her the focus for all evolutions of earth to make it on the Path, no matter what conditions ensue on planet Earth.

Every Chela of the Will of God Is a Part of the Stump Team

I trust you will understand that a trip of this nature is a great, great challenge to the physical bodies and the hearts and minds of this team. I trust you will consider yourself now a part of this team, traveling with me by night in your finer bodies to those very places to stand guard against those fundamentalist fanatics who appear in every nation—in the name of religion or politics or science or nonreligion—to challenge by the very core of hate and hate creation and their false theology the coming of the Word.

Blessed hearts, may the courage of the Great White Brotherhood be upon the Messenger and upon you all! And may you take that careful watch of the Watchman of the Night to secure that protection by the call. In answer to your call, we will give that protection. And that protection is needed for every soul of Light already marked by our bands as those whom we would draw in.

Blessed ones, realize, then, that an excursion of such magnitude, a Stump so far-reaching, must also have received this type of send-off from the local press. Understand that it is the desire of the fallen ones to transmit all of this false reporting to any area where the Messenger goes. Thus be prepared, and be prepared to defend against every type of onslaught.

I trust, through your ingenuity and your awareness already of that which the fallen ones are capable of, that you will not tire and you will not slumber or sleep but you will recognize that this is the Stump of beloved Jesus and Maitreya and Gautama and Sanat Kumara to go forth and find your brothers and sisters, your twin flames, your children—those who need you and whom you need for the full expression of love and community and the victory of our Ranch.

Let us understand the scope of this going forth. And let us treat it as an ultimate opportunity, for one does not know what the years and the decades will bring as possibility in the future. Thus, we ride the crest of the wave of the prosperity of this nation—which, nevertheless, does not have in the physical octave, as its underpinnings, a solid foundation. Thus, let us ride the wave of Light. Let us trust in God and let us know that He will return and return with a Messenger victorious—and that all of you will be victorious for your participation as one! [applause]

Call for the Descent of the Etheric Matrix of the New Jerusalem over the Cities of the Earth

Now, beloved hearts, concurrently with the descent of the replica of the forcefield of the Court of the Sacred Fire over Los Angeles, there is also the descent of the etheric matrix of the New Jerusalem[20] at this point and in various points on the planet.

Copyright © 1985 Church Universal and Triumphant, Inc.

We have spoken before of the descent of this blueprint and this manifestation, but the descent must come through the Electronic Presence of the embodied chelas, through the magnet of their hearts, of their own I AM Presence, through their espousal of the will of God and that perfect faith that has trust that God will perform all miracles and save to the uttermost this community of Light to perform its perfect work.

Understand that we may announce many times the descending of the Holy City and you must understand what it is: It is the etheric counterpart of that which is the divine plan for each and every city and center of Light on earth. And ultimately, superimposed upon that which is the divine plan, specific and unique for the city, there is that of the New Jerusalem itself, which is the city of Christ and his saints and which contains the divine and true etheric matrix to which the lost tribes and the Christed ones shall return.

Let us see both manifest in every area—the local divine plan as the etheric city descending (that peculiar to that area) and that of the New Jerusalem itself. Let all realize that if there is to be any Justice on earth in any field of endeavor, it is this matrix that must be invoked and lowered into manifestation. Thus, those citizens of other cities, states, and nations may take this, my release—they may play it and play it as often as they will and write their letters to the Four and Twenty Elders that the very same etheric matrix of the Court of the Sacred Fire might focus over their states and nations.

I do not say what the answer will be. I am an advocate of the call and of the sword of blue flame. I am an advocate of the science of the spoken Word. I am an advocate of the power of the blue-ray chakra and what it can do to re-create the world.

The Power of Serapis, the Blessing of the Seven Mighty Archangels

I send you forth with the power of Serapis, with the blessing of the seven mighty archangels. I send you to the highest etheric octave of our retreats. And I go with you into the lowest octaves of the astral plane, that you truly might know and understand that great breadth of spectrum of vibration and have a keenness and an awareness that makes you diligent in the outer to go not in those places where you ought not to be, to take the precaution and the realization that you are so important to God that you must watch and pray and secure your physical protection and that of your families, your children, and your community.

Beloved hearts, I send you in this hour the mighty greetings and blessings of the blue-flame angels who serve under all hierarchs of this ray—and comfort and a pledge and a vow to defend you as long as you make the call!

I give to you now your own beloved El Morya, who desires to speak to you today. [published as next week's Pearl of Wisdom]

Messenger's Prayer to Archangel Michael
Given During Mother Mary's Circle of Light February 1, 1985

Beloved Mighty I AM Presence: we call to you, beloved Archangel Michael, and we desire now to sign up for your most advanced teams of Light going forth with your legions—with helmet and armor and sword of blue flame. Teach us to march in step with you to defeat the enemy of the Christ in all mankind, to bind up the brokenhearted, to serve the purposes of Christ, to minister to the sick and the poor and the downtrodden.

Almighty God, take us now in the legions of Archangel Michael. For we would defend the Faith and The Faithful and True and the Woman and her seed and the name of the Great White Brotherhood.

Archangel Michael, take us and let us begin our drills this night. And let us become a part not of the reserves but of those on active duty night after night after night.

Beloved Archangel Michael, train us well! For we would move on to serve with all the Archangels and finally be received in the order of the holy seraphim under beloved Justinius.

We call to the armies of the LORD! We call to the armies of The Faithful and True! Beloved Lord Maitreya, beloved Moses, beloved Jesus, beloved Gautama Buddha, receive us now into your hearts that we might go forth and cut free first the precious children from all the world. Let them be cut free from all hate and hate creation and all that would move against their divine potential to realize God in their hearts.

O God, anoint us. Beloved Mighty I AM Presence, anoint us.

Beloved Archangel Michael, we kneel now before the altar of your retreat. We ask you to come and bless us. Place your Electronic Presence with us. Receive us now, Almighty God.

So we pray in thy name, beloved Archangel Michael.

"**The Summit Lighthouse Sheds Its Radiance O'er All the World to Manifest as Pearls of Wisdom.**" This dictation by Archangel Michael was delivered through the Messenger Elizabeth Clare Prophet on Sunday, February 3, 1985, at Camelot. (1) Interestingly, on March 11, 1942, Gen. Douglas MacArthur promised, "I shall return," as he was departing from Corregidor Island in the Philippines for a mission in Australia during World War II. When he arrived back in the Philippines on the island of Leyte, October 20, 1944, he said: "I have returned. By the grace of Almighty God, our forces stand again on Philippine soil!" (2) The term "men of renown" in Genesis 6:4 and Numbers 16:2 is translated from the original Hebrew texts as "people of the *shem.*" Although *shem* is traditionally interpreted as meaning "name" (hence, "the people who have a name" or "the people of renown"), author Zecharia Sitchin traces the etymology of the word through Mesopotamian texts to the root *shamah,* "that which is highward." According to Sitchin, *shem* would be read as "sky vehicle" or, in modern terminology, as "rocket ship." He equates the "men of renown" to the *Nephilim* (Hebrew for "those who fell" or "those who were cast down" from the Semitic root *naphal,* "to fall")—a biblical race of giants or demigods, also referred to in Genesis 6:4 ("There were *giants* in the earth in those days..."). Sitchin concludes from his study of ancient Sumerian texts that the Nephilim were an extraterrestrial race who "fell" to earth (landed) in spacecraft 450,000 years ago. See Zecharia Sitchin, "The Nefilim: People of the Fiery Rockets" in *The Twelfth Planet* (New York: Avon Books, 1976), pp. 143–72, 410; available through Summit University Press, $4.50 ($5.35 postpaid USA). The Messengers do not necessarily subscribe to this theory. See Elizabeth Clare Prophet, *Forbidden Mysteries of Enoch: The Untold Story of Men and Angels,* Summit University Press, pp. 61–67; $12.95 ($13.95 postpaid USA). The Great Divine Director, *The Mechanization Concept (Pearls of Wisdom,* vol. 8, no. 15), p. 80, pars. 2–3; $12.95 ($14.55 postpaid USA). (3) prayer given by the Messenger during Mother Mary's Circle of Light at the Victory Rally for Camelot, February 1, 1985 (see p. 120). (4) The Ascended Masters teach their *chelas* (Sanskrit, 'disciples') to leave the physical body and travel in their finer bodies (in the etheric sheath) to their retreats and halls of learning situated on the etheric plane. Before retiring at night, call to your beloved I AM Presence and Holy Christ Self and the guardian angels to take you to Banff in Alberta, Canada, the location of Archangel Michael's headquarters and training center for his legions of blue-lightning angels. Here you will be trained in the service of protection for the children of the Light and for the preservation of freedom on earth. Earnest students of the Keepers of the Flame Lessons make steady progress on this path of world service through spiritual self-discipline leading to attainment and self-mastery. Archangel Michael, whose name means "who is as God," serves on the first (blue) ray, embodying the God consciousness of faith, protection, perfection, and goodwill. He is called the Prince of the Archangels, the Defender of the Faith, Guardian of the Twelve Tribes of Israel, and Captain of the LORD's Host (Josh. 5:13–15). In Daniel 12:1, he is referred to as "the great prince which standeth for the children of thy people." Revelation 12:7 records that he and his angels "fought against the dragon, and the dragon fought and his angels and prevailed not, neither was their place found any more in heaven." In Revelation 16:2 Archangel Michael is the angel who poured out the first vial of the seven last plagues upon the earth (see *Vials of the Seven Last Plagues: The Judgments of Almighty God Delivered by the Seven Archangels,* Summit University Press, pp. 2–14; $4.95; $5.80 postpaid USA). The Book of Enoch describes Archangel Michael as "the merciful, the patient," "one of the holy angels, who, presiding over human virtue, commands the nations" (see Enoch 20:5; 40:8). In one of the Dead Sea Scrolls, *The War of the Sons of Light and the Sons of Darkness,* he is the "mighty, ministering angel" through whom God promises to "send perpetual help" to the sons of Light. (5) Luxor, Darjeeling, Banff, and Yosemite are the locations of the etheric retreats of Serapis Bey, El Morya, Archangel Michael, and Hercules and Amazonia. (6) Josh. 24:15. (7) See Antony C. Sutton: *An Introduction to the Order, How the Order Controls Education, How the Order Creates War and Revolution,* and *The Secret Cult of the Order* (Phoenix: Research Publications, 1983, 1984). (8) Rev. 6:1–8. (9) Rev. 15:1, 6–8; 16. (10) Matt. 10:36. (11) Alexander Pope, *An Essay on Criticism,* pt. III, line 66. (12) During the week of January 27–February 1, 1985, the Messenger Elizabeth Clare Prophet and Church Universal and Triumphant were the subject of a two-pronged media attack through the *Los Angeles Herald Examiner* and KCBS-TV (Los Angeles CBS, Channel 2). (13) the unwary souls who see and hear and read and listen to the mouthpieces of the Liar and his lie without having benefit of the glorious witness of the chelas of El Morya—or to the facts. (14) Rev. 19:20; 20:10, 14, 15; 21:8. (15) See Elizabeth Clare Prophet, "Idolatry and the Fiery Trial," on the 8-cassette Easter class album *Feast of the Resurrection Flame I* (A8116), $50.00 ($51.56 postpaid USA); sermon available separately on 2 cassettes (B8122, B8123), $6.50 ea. ($6.99 postpaid USA). (16) In his dictation of September 21, 1963, the Elohim Cyclopea (sometimes called Immaculata, denoting the feminine release of the Elohim) announced that the devas and builders of form were "building around the entire circumferential area of Los Angeles a tremendous fountain of cosmic light." He explained: "This fountain is an etheric fountain...thirty miles in diameter and is, on the exterior surface, a bright blue. There is a blue fountain rising into the upper atmosphere one mile high above this city. This great blue fountain is the fountain of cosmic faith and it is filled with the vibratory action of the blessed angels of faith from Archangel Michael's band....Then, within a space of one mile within the thirty-mile range, there is established a beautiful golden fountain of cosmic illumination, which rises to a height of one mile and a half into the atmosphere.... Within the center of that forcefield, there is built a two-mile-high fountain which is a pink fountain of spiritual love charged by the angels of beloved Chamuel's band. This magnificent tripartite fountain of cosmic light will continue to blaze over the forcefield of Los Angeles, the City of the Angels.... [It] is a fountain of illumination for the planetary body to create the vibratory action of a cosmic Eden in this beautiful area of Light's perfection." (17) Rev. 19:11–16, 21. (18) On May 20, 1984, Soviet Defense Minister Dmitri F. Ustinov announced that Moscow had increased the number of its nuclear-missiled submarines near United States shores. The missiles, Ustinov said, could hit American target cities within eight to ten minutes. A buildup of Soviet missile-carrying submarines has been observed off the East and West coasts for years. In January 1984, following the deployment of U.S. Pershing and cruise missiles in Europe, Moscow sent an additional submarine to each coast. According to an NBC news report, both carry sixteen missiles with a range of 5,000 miles, capable of hitting any city in the continental United States. (19) See Mother Mary, August 26, 1984, "The Power of God in My Right Hand," *Pearls of Wisdom*, vol. 27, no. 51, p. 442, pars. 4–6. (20) Rev. 21:1, 2.

Pearls of Wisdom, published weekly by The Summit Lighthouse for Church Universal and Triumphant, come to you under the auspices of the Darjeeling Council of the Great White Brotherhood. These are presently dictated by the Ascended Masters to their Messenger Elizabeth Clare Prophet. The international headquarters of this nonprofit, nondenominational activity is located in Los Angeles, California. All communications and freewill contributions should be addressed to The Summit Lighthouse, Box T, Malibu, CA 90265. Pearls of Wisdom are sent weekly throughout the USA via third-class mail to all who support the Church with a minimum yearly love offering of $40. First-class and international postage rates available upon request. Notice of change of address should be received three weeks prior to the effective date. Third-class mail is not forwarded by the post office.
Copyright © 1985 Church Universal and Triumphant, Inc. All rights reserved. Printed in the United States of America. Pearls of Wisdom and The Summit Lighthouse are registered trademarks of Church Universal and Triumphant, Inc. All rights to their use are reserved.

Chela—Christed One—Guru
Offices on the Path of the Individualization of the God Flame

Blessed knights and ladies of the flame, children of the Sun, be seated now in the lap of infinity of the World Mother.

The Right of the Evolutions of God to Conquer and Win

We bow before the Light of Archangel Michael and the legions of Light who are also the guardians of our service and who, without question, respond to protect all whom we sponsor. Thus, it is a hallowed love we share with the mighty beings of Light who have defended with the Manus the right of the evolutions of God to conquer and win their immortality on earth.

The Office of Chela Waits

I would speak to you, then, of your office of chela.

The office of chela we diagram on the Chart[1] as the lower figure. The chela is the one in whom there blazes a literal furnace of violet flame as is depicted—one striving on the Path, one who is dedicated to make his temple the temple of the living God, and of the Father, the Mighty I AM Presence, and of the Son descending.

The chela is the striving one.

Thus, we consider all who defend our Teaching and our Messenger and who are faithful in the service we have outlined to be a part of that level and that hierarchy. The office waits and you may so qualify yourself by intense calls to the violet flame and the will of God and the request that you have revealed to you what are those things which must shortly be passed into the flame for you to know the true protection of the mantle of chela.

Blessed ones, the chela is striving on the path of personal Christhood. And when that Christhood is bestowed, then he wears the mantle not only of the chela or disciple but also of his own Holy Christ Self.

The chela, before becoming that Shepherd, does become—on occasion, from time to time, and often—the vessel of his Christ Self. By and by, as this becomes a perpetual vigil of the hours, the mantle descends and the Christ does not leave that one, even if that one may temporarily lose his balance or become out of alignment.

You see, an office, once granted by the LORD God, is not withdrawn as one would snatch from you a cape, then drop it again, then snatch it again. This is not the way of the Great White Brotherhood. When we see fit to bestow the mantle of chela, we stand by that chela.

Thus, not all who are students of ours do we count as chelas. For a chela is someone with whom we share our very life and breath. Thus, a relationship of trust must be established.

Passing the Initiation of the Office of Christ

In the same manner, the one who has been seen consistently to strive to outpicture that Christhood does eventually, by initiation of Maitreya and Jesus and his own Christ Self, attain to a certain equilibrium in the manifestation of Christhood—not giving us the ups and downs of inconstancy, not being here one day and there another.

Thus, the passing of initiation in each office is required. And thus, you see that the Christed ones must also be equal to the task of bearing that Christ Light.

Beloved hearts, this office of Christ formerly occupied by your Messengers and *still* occupied by your Messengers is the true assignment of yourselves. You, the direct initiates of our call, are expected not to remain chelas forever—forever seeking the Truth but never coming to the knowledge of that Truth,[2] to borrow a phrase from the apostle.

Chelaship may be comfortable because the chela may yet depend upon the Christed One or the Master. I admonish you that those who have our direct word and blessing must strive not only to rise but to pull down the full power of the office of Christhood.

When you, therefore, are initiated directly by me through the Messenger, it is a goad to compel you to a higher consciousness, to the Mind of Christ—to the strength of that Mind, to the love of that Mind, to the wisdom and the courage of that Presence!

You may also receive chelaship from the teachings and from

one another, but the action of initiation to Christhood must come from the embodied Witness.

The Office of the I AM Presence and the Mantle of Guru

Now, with the mantle of the Guru Sanat Kumara placed upon this Messenger by Padma Sambhava,³ the Messenger has been required to occupy and hold the office at all times of the I AM Presence. For to have one holding that Word, I AM THAT I AM, in embodiment is the absolute requirement and necessity for the sustainment of an outer activity of the Great White Brotherhood. And this mantle and office did beloved Mark occupy and own before his ascension, and does he still own in this hour.

Now, beloved hearts, for want of those who desire to excel—with all of the challenges that this acceleration compels—to the level of the Christ, you see, the Messenger must descend the spiral staircase of the lighthouse tower and position herself in the office of Christ on behalf of the community. This produces in itself a certain stress and strain for all concerned. For although we desire to release the Light of the Summit from the I AM Presence, yet the Messenger must function at the level of your Christhood—for want of understanding or realization or whatever the cause may be that you yourselves do not take that position.

Thus, beloved hearts, the Christed ones* of this organization —and there is no limit to that number that ought to be Christed ones—should be known as the shepherds of the people, as the ministering servants.

And they should have developed within their hearts the discrimination (that faculty for decision making) to implement right action not only for themselves but for their departments and areas of service. This discrimination and dependability allows the Messenger to perform the necessary work for you and the world from the level of the I AM Presence. And this is how hierarchy ought to be counted in this order.

Beloved Kuthumi has called you to the Order of the Brothers and Sisters of Francis and Clare. Understand that striving in this order, whether through the path of the *brahmacharya*⁴ or the path of the householder and the family member, must be pursued with the goal in mind of the attainment of the mantle of Christ—of the "occupying till I come."⁵ Do you understand?

When the Masters descend to the level of Christ, then,

**Christed ones:* 'anointed' ones. The word *Christ* is derived from the Greek *Christos*, meaning 'anointed', from *chriein* 'to anoint'. "That was the true Light which lighteth every manifestation of God that cometh into the world"—i.e., "That was the true Anointed One who anointeth every manifestation of God . . ." (John 1:9).

you see, your office is fulfilled in heaven and on earth. When you present to God a magnet of the Christ consciousness as a community, then you draw down the Universal Christ in the Ascended Masters.

It is necessary, then, that the decision-making process, the listening to the Word, the execution of the Word, the action of the Word become the goal of those chelas striving to move from their centeredness in the violet-flame-transmutation level to the point of personal Christhood.

The Christ *is* the Word incarnate within you! The Christ *is* your Real Self! Thus, you must resist the temptation to indulge the lesser self that opposes that Light.

Some prefer not to push. Some prefer not to heave and ho and to strive. Some yet prefer a comfortable niche of what they think is chelaship—to find a nook and cranny and to simply perform the tasks they are given and to do what they are told.

Beloved ones, it is wonderful to have loyal and obedient servants, but this loyalty and obedience must also include the understanding that the office of chela embodies within it, by definition, the one striving to become the Christ.

Thus, it is a question of looking at the goals of the world, what they are, and seeing how people in the world become complacent. When they own their own home and car, have a good job, a few children, and so forth—whatever they have envisioned—they usually rest at that point and when you see them, they desire nothing more.

Well, let us pray that that complacency of the attainment of the visible goal is not somehow transmitted to the chela, who then thinks that because he is chela, he may enjoy a life of a chela without further responsibility!

I tell you as the Chohan of the First Ray: You will one day lose the mantle of chela if the very mantle itself is not employed by you to divide the waters of the human consciousness, to exorcise from you all that inhibits the manifestation of your Christhood!

Just as the Christed ones are striving to be one with the Father and to embody the I AM, so all who move forward in the scale of hierarchy maintain their present office while striving to embody the elements and the jewels of light of the next.

Thus is the link of hierarchy sustained by those who have the capacity to live in the present, to take dominion over the past and past karma—personal and planetary—and to live in the future, where they perceive and look upon the goal daily and see themselves already robed in white and reigning with the saints in heaven.⁶ It is necessary to be able to face and to contain the past, present, and future compartments of time and space and thus to one day transcend them all at the point of Infinity.

Now, beloved hearts, let us look at what the office of Guru, the office of the one who must embody the I AM THAT I AM for the community, does entail. The consciousness of the I AM THAT I AM has been well described by the prophet Habakkuk as the LORD God revealed it to him and as he said, "Thou art of too pure eyes to behold iniquity."⁷

The I AM Presence is the Spirit of God immutable—absolute God-purity, the absolute fount of the perception only of that which is Real. It is therefore the office of the Christ to behold Good and Evil both in the absolute sense and in the relative sense, to counsel and instruct you, and to send forth recommendations to the heart of the Father for the release of Light unto those striving ones below.

Now, if the beings of Light who surround God in the Great Central Sun did not hold the immaculate concept, if the next rings of Christed ones did not retain the perception of all goings-on of the universe, then the central authority of God Himself could not be sustained as the Knower of the All and the One and the Light.

The just judgments come forth from that I AM THAT I AM because it is pure Light. The one in embodiment holding that concept of purity for you, for the earth, for the community—because of that very concept and presence—can take you on the journeys of initiation through the circle of Light, can be the recipient of the transmission of the Light of the Central Sun in the initiations you receive, can give to you the living flame of the altar of God that you absolutely require for your ascension.

If you will allow the Messenger to fulfill that office, to deliver the Word, to bring forth the Light directly from God for the healing of the nations, then the earth shall truly have a new dispensation of salvation through the Great White Brotherhood. If you rise to the occasion of the office of Christhood, all *will* go well.

Bearers of the Mantle Must Defend the Church

Now I would like to speak to you of the application of that office as it pertains to such events as the [media] attack upon the Church. It is the chelas and the Christed ones who must guard the citadel, who must protect Camelot and the Ranch, who must take necessary action in counsel.

It is not meet for the Messenger to engage these adversaries on their own ground, on their own terminology. The I AM Presence is not on trial. Neither is the Guru. Neither is the Messenger. *They* are on trial and they exhibit who and what they are. And the authority of the Father for the judgment of these fallen ones has eternally been conveyed to the one who occupies the office of Christ.

Thus, the decrees have been given that your Christ Self might enact that judgment. Thus, you are the ones who move into action and determine what actions must be taken for the defense of the privilege of the earth to have access to the Mighty I AM Presence through the office and the mantle that we have instituted, which was instituted by God before us.

The Messenger Lives in Deference to the Mantle

It is always true that the mantle is greater than the person, but the person has the opportunity to so identify with the mantle of the office as to become the fullness of it and thereby to move on in the chain of hierarchy. As this is true for yourselves—the eternal hope of the open door, the eternal freedom to pursue at your own pace the initiations of Maitreya—so it is also open to the Messenger.

The setting forth of the Law of the Lawgiver is also this office. Thus, our dictations are not intended for those who are in the world and who have not even approached the level of being student. The setting forth of the Law and the Light and the release of dispensations is absolutely essential, and so is the stepping down and the interpretation of that Word by the Holy Spirit through yourselves to those who must have presented to them that which they can take in of this Word.

Now, in regard to this media attack, the Messenger has informed you that according to her office, she has neither viewed this television series nor set eyes upon the newspapers that have been published. For in the very midst of the fray, she must hold that balance.

Some have criticized her or thought perhaps she was being an ostrich, burying her head in the sand, not wanting to hear about anything of a destructive nature. I can assure you this is not a condition of the human consciousness, but it is the protection of the mantle of the office by its wearer, the wearer being obedient to our request.

This you may observe, therefore, in the Messenger: that the life is lived in deference to the mantle. And however much she may prefer to do something another way, to befriend this individual or that, it is the deference to the mantle, what it allows—

Chela—Christed One—Guru

the deference to the mantle, seeing to it that it is not trampled upon in incorrect activity—that does guide her action.

Thus, the keeping of the mantle is the result of the effort of the one who understands and feels the presence of the mantle of the Great White Brotherhood and lives by its Law. Thus may you be true to the mantle of chela even before you receive it and therefore become so worthy that it is almost perfunctory on graduation day that the robe of the graduate becomes the mantle of chela.

It is the same for those striving for the office of Christ. It is the imitation of Christ, it is the practice of the Presence of Christ[8] that establishes in your life not only the reverence for that mantle which is shortly coming upon you, but also the respect for the officeholder who does already wear the mantle.

Criticism of the Staff in the Mystery School

Now, I find within this staff that there are some who have come here with what they think to be unusual abilities of an intellectual nature or of a technical nature. And they have considered themselves more qualified than our servants who wear the mantle of chela or of the Holy Christ Self. And therefore, they have taken it upon themselves to correct or criticize their department heads or those who have gone before them in the devotions, the decrees, and the contributions that have kept the very flame of this organization until the new ones could arrive.

Blessed ones, when you challenge those who wear the mantle of staff, in this manner of criticism, you are impugning, therefore, the office of Messenger, who has given the assignments, as well as of the Darjeeling Council. And I counsel you today that you are moving in treacherous waters to allow yourselves to be so seized by the conceit and pride of the carnal mind when, in fact, you have known from the beginning why you were coming to this mystery school—for the very defeat of that mind and to become the humble servant and chela at the altar of Serapis, at the altar of Christ, being willing to take the first and necessary steps of putting on the mantle of student. Thus, I will shortly speak with those who have retained that propensity to be critical of this staff.

Catherine of Siena, Humble Defender of Pope and Church

It is necessary for you to be aware of the humble life of Catherine of Siena which was lived by this soul, your Messenger, who deferred to the mantle of the office of the Pope when the bearers of that office were profoundly corrupt and truly betrayed that office.[9] This is the necessary test of the soul who will bear the mantle of that office. Thus, it has been told to her by Jesus that she does wear that mantle representing Christ to his Church by the very fact that she did not turn against one who misused it—but instead upheld the office, "occupying till I come."

It is all well and good for you to praise and support a perfect person, but, beloved hearts, that is not the reality. It is the mantle that is the power. It is the office whereby the individual may be the instrument of God.

Therefore, we may trust that the Messenger will cling to the mantle and not be fooled, whether by her own mistakes or by those of any other, but will hold that immaculate concept for all and not rely on the arm of flesh[10]—neither upon her own, nor upon yours, nor upon those who come saying, "We are indispensable! We are your saviours! We will promote you. We are necessary to your victory."

Once you have felt the weight and the protection of this mantle, you rely upon it. And the mantle of Messenger as the mantle of the I AM THAT I AM is a mantle that embraces all chelas and all Christed ones and does include the sponsoring of diligent students preparing themselves to become chelas. Thus it is the mantle of the office whereby the dispensation of the organization is secured.

Thus, understand that this mantle must be worn by someone in physical embodiment, and the mantle of Christ must be worn by the many. But when the disciples became apostles, as spokesmen of Christ, they wore his mantle of Christ and they moved in the Spirit of the Christ consciousness. Even though from time to time there may have been error in their expression or in their doctrine, they had to receive the mantle in order to do the work of the LORD—and the LORD is the I AM THAT I AM. Thus, [in logical progression] the Christed ones are becoming the embodiment of the Great God who is Guru.

The Christed Ones Become the Elders of the Church

Now, I trust you will understand that it is necessary for those striving in this order of hierarchy to volunteer and apply to become what we will call Elders of the Church—Elders, then, applying as a word that refers to the elder brothers and sisters who are the Ascended Masters. The Elders of the Church may consist of those who are in a position to make decisions, to give counsel, to defend the Church, to be its spokesmen, and to be

Copyright © 1985 Church Universal and Triumphant, Inc.

those who determine the security of the Word, the Work, the chela, the staff, and the Messenger.

I ask you to consider that a council of such elders ought to be acting in concerted fashion in this hour to defend the posture and position of this organization and should submit its deliberations and advice to the Messenger in order that these proposals might receive the higher guidance of our counsel, the wisdom, and the necessary caution which we would convey.

I, beloved ones, counsel you, then, as your Chief that when this circle is formed, I will place the circle of the Darjeeling Council with you, and those of you who have not attained necessarily to the fullness of the office may indeed have access to those who do in a circle of Light and in a devotion to the decrees to the Holy Christ Self.

I am therefore appointing Edward Francis as the liaison between this council and the Messenger, and I am appointing Gene Vosseler and Susan Krister to form the nucleus of that council here in Camelot. I ask for those of you who feel able and constant, who would determine to serve in this body, to come forward in this week to declare yourselves, that we might seal such a body in our absence as the Messenger goes forth on this mission.

This group of individuals needs to assume the responsibility for the direction and the course of Camelot and the Royal Teton Ranch, as well as for its defense. They must have sharpened swords of the Word, be capable in the dynamic decree, and truly know what action ought to be taken in this science of the Spirit, the decree work, and in the physical domain.

I commend you, then, to the study of the words of Archangel Michael. I commend you to the calling of looking beyond the immediate manifestation of the media to the cause and core behind it, to its ramifications, and to the destructivity of the fallen ones.

All things are in the crucible of change. Thus, transmutation and the violet flame can shortcut what may be decreed by karmic law for the earth or even this organization. Let the violet flame become your swimming sea of Light within and without—the very air you breathe and the song you sing. May it be fiercely punctuated by all of the calls to the blue lightning of the Mind of God and the judgment and all things that you have been taught. May you rely upon our legions and our presence and the decree to deliver you and the Light in this age.

I promise you this: Neither God nor the Great White Brotherhood will ever desert the one who stands steadfast and makes the call. Listen well: *stands steadfast and makes the call.* One must have both steadfastness of purpose and the immediate response of the call. This is the Alpha and the Omega of your protection. We stand by it. We obey the Law as we must also remain true to the mantle of our office.

And we say to you, beloved ones: We expect you in the halls of Luxor at the conclusion of this embodiment! And we expect mighty fruits to be borne by you of achievement for the securing of the Great White Brotherhood, that this generation of Light, this office, this I AM Race shall not perish from the earth!

To the victory of the Light in God-government and the economy, I am pledged.

I seal you now in the *fire* of the will of God.

Will you join me in the holy communion of angels.

"The Summit Lighthouse Sheds Its Radiance O'er All the World to Manifest as Pearls of Wisdom." This dictation by El Morya was delivered through the Messenger Elizabeth Clare Prophet on Sunday, February 3, 1985, at Camelot, following the address of Archangel Michael (published as last week's Pearl of Wisdom). (1) The *Chart of Your Real Self,* representing the I AM Presence (upper figure), the Christ Self (middle figure), and the soul evolving in Matter (lower figure). See Mark and Elizabeth Prophet, *Climb the Highest Mountain,* Summit University Press, pp. 228-37; 301, par. 2; $14.95 ($15.95 postpaid USA). (2) II Tim. 3:7. (3) On July 2, 1977, the Ascended Master Padma Sambhava announced: "I make known to you the dispensation of God, the Great Guru, and of all Gurus who serve to represent Him, that although for many a month and many a year the Mother of the Flame has resisted the appellation 'Guru,' we shall not permit it any longer. For the mantle must be upon the feminine incarnation and, because there are many changes taking place in the forcefield of earth, we must have, then, the acknowledgment of the open door of Guru through a Mother.... In the transfer of initiation, and very severe initiation of the Gurus that has been given to her, there has been made possible a more than ordinary incarnation of the Ascended Masters through your Messenger. It gives me, then, good joy as I am privileged to make known to you that the Ascended Masters come as a living witness to proclaim in this hour that the Guru/chela relationship can now be sustained in this octave through the flame of heart of Mother." See Padma Sambhava, "The Great Synthesis—the Mother as Guru," on the 6-cassette Freedom class album *Only Love* (A7742), $37.50 ($38.81 postpaid USA); single cassette B7745, $6.50 ($6.99 postpaid USA). (4) *Brahmacharya,* as taught in the Vedas, is the first of four stages in man's life—the period of strict chastity as a celibate religious student. The second stage *(garhasthya)* is that of the married householder with worldly responsibilities. The third *(vanaprastha)* is retirement and meditation, the life of a hermit or forest-dweller. The final stage *(sannyasa)* is that of renunciation, when one is bound by neither work nor desire but follows the path of a wanderer, freely pursuing knowledge of Brahman. (5) Luke 19:13. (6) Rev. 3:4, 5; 6:9-11; 7:9, 13, 14. (7) "Thou art of purer eyes than to behold evil and canst not look on iniquity..." Hab. 1:13. (8) See *The Imitation of Christ* by Thomas à Kempis, and *The Practice of the Presence of God* by Brother Lawrence of the Resurrection. (9) Catherine of Siena (1347-1380), patron saint of Italy, has been called the "mystic of the Incarnate Word" and the "herald of the Holy See." Recommended reading on the life and teachings of Saint Catherine (available through Summit University Press): Igino Giordani, *Saint Catherine of Siena—Doctor of the Church,* trans. Thomas J. Tobin (Boston: St. Paul Editions, 1980), $7.00 ($7.95 postpaid USA). *The Dialogue of the Seraphic Virgin Catherine of Siena,* trans. Algar Thorold (Rockford, Ill.: Tan Books and Publishers, 1974), $4.50 ($5.35 postpaid USA). *The Prayers of Catherine of Siena,* ed. Suzanne Noffke (Ramsey, N.J.: Paulist Press, 1983), $9.95 ($10.82 postpaid USA). (10) Jer. 17:5.

Copyright © 1985 Church Universal and Triumphant, Inc., Box A, Malibu, CA 90265. All rights reserved. Printed in the United States of America. Pearls of Wisdom and The Summit Lighthouse are registered trademarks of Church Universal and Triumphant, Inc. All rights to their use are reserved. Published by The Summit Lighthouse. Pearls sent weekly (to USA, via third-class mail) for a minimum love offering of $40/year.

FROM MY HEART

Love Marriage and Beyond

ALMOST EVERYONE at some time or another has pondered the whys and hows of a relationship. Why can't I find the perfect love? How do I know if this is really the one? Why isn't it the way I always thought it would be? How can I make it work?

Many people search a lifetime, never knowing quite what they are looking for. Others, thinking they have found it, live their lives in the surface contentment of human oneness.

But the real understanding of relationships, and the intense longing for wholeness that often spurs them, goes much farther back. It goes all the way back to the very origin of life and the creation of individual Spirit sparks—'twin flames' that formed a single 'white fire body', then separated out to manifest two spheres of being in polarity—masculine and feminine.

Each sphere became a body of First Cause, or Causal Body. The Spirit sparks became the focus of each I AM Presence, from which twin souls descended to begin their evolutionary rounds in the various dimensions of the Spirit/Matter Cosmos. (See Chart of Your Divine Self, p. 5, and diagrams, pp. *36–37*.)

BY ELIZABETH CLARE PROPHET

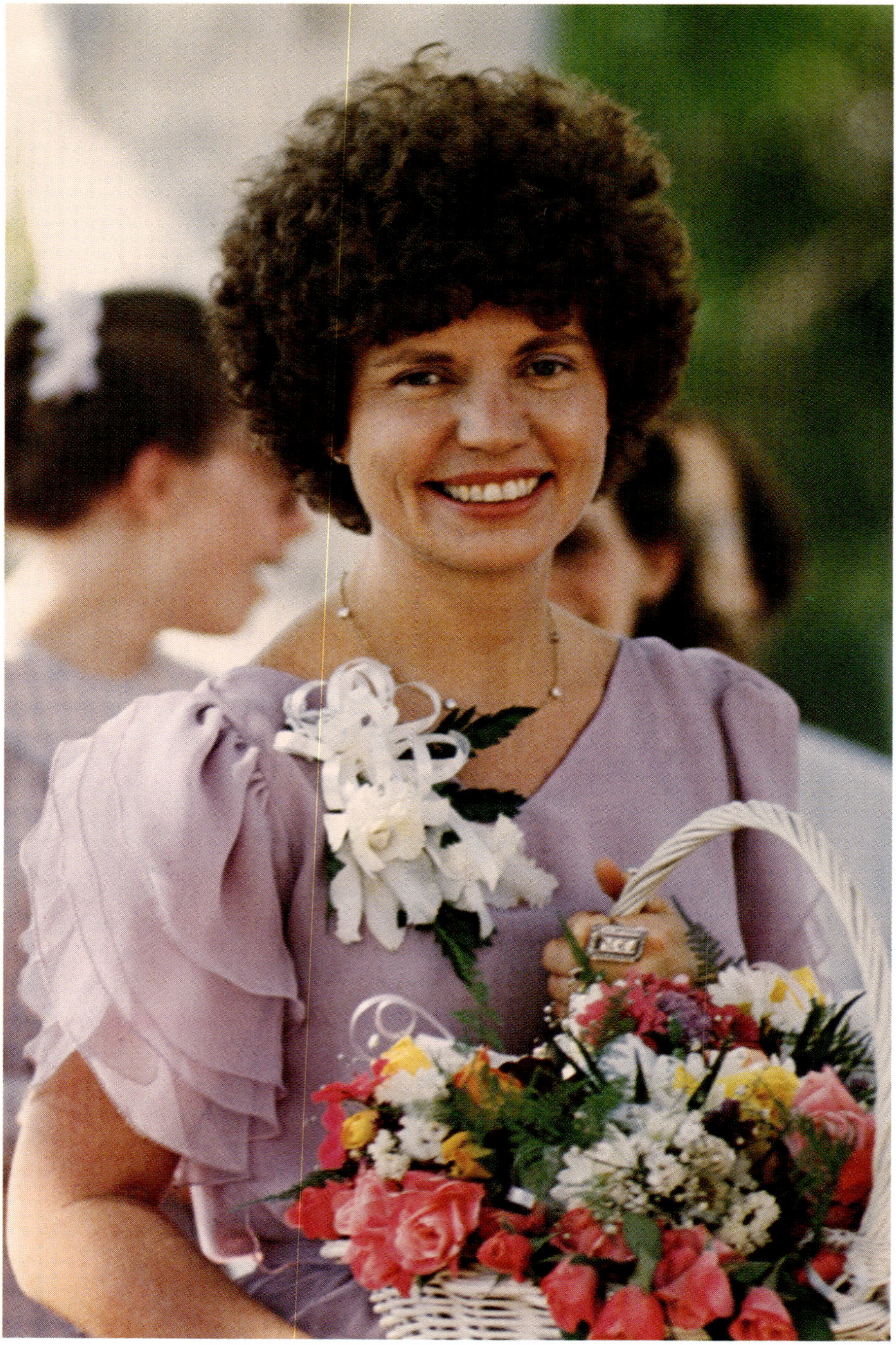

Whereas twin flames are one in Spirit and in their spiritual origin, soul mates are souls sharing a complementary calling in life. They are mates in the sense of being partners for the journey, co-workers, very much alike and very compatible because their initiations on the path of soul development are at the same levels but in polarity. They work well together, are project oriented, well mated, and often have similar facial features and physique.

Twin flames share a destiny beyond the stars, are bound in eternity by the Holy Ghost, and are never separated though they be kept apart physically by circumstance for centuries. The mind, heart, and consciousness of twin flames flow from the same fount. But soul mates are playmates in the schoolroom of life and there may be a number of such associations in the history of the soul's evolution through the rounds of rebirth.

The numerous insights that Elizabeth Clare Prophet has brought to bear on the study of the human personality and relationships through her teachings on twin flames and soul mates has earned her a position as one of the foremost authorities in the world on this subject.

For more than a decade Mrs. Prophet has conducted seminars—from Miami to New York to Colorado Springs to Los Angeles—explaining the whys and hows of love, marriage, and the bonds of friendship, answering questions that the experts are not even asking, and offering a timeless wisdom that will revolutionize your way of thinking about yourself, your family—your life.

This is the time, she says, as we approach the dawn of the Aquarian age, when it is important for many people to find their twin flame, so that they can finish their 'work' or karma on earth and move on together in their mutual soul evolution. And she tells us how.

Recently, in a one-day seminar conducted at Camelot on the Summit University campus, Mrs. Prophet spoke to a group of her students from all over the world, sharing priceless memories of life with her twin flame, Mark L. Prophet, and explaining how anyone can magnetize their own 'perfect love'.

The text which follows includes excerpts of her very touching, personal counsel as it was given heart-to-heart on that occasion and reflects the sensitivity and profound spiritual perceptions which have made her one of the most respected woman religious figures of our time.

Having met my twin flame in this life in the person of Mark Prophet, my understanding of the quest for the twin flame and the finding of the twin flame is very vivid.

I WOULD LIKE TO TELL YOU ABOUT IT, because often we learn things from the personal experience of someone else.

First of all, I never knew that there was any such thing as a twin flame until, at eighteen, I read an obscure book about soul mates.

My quest, however, in those early years of searching which had been going on since childhood, was to find God and to discover what his mission was for me. I was very determined to get to the foundation of my life and to do what I knew I had to do. It was an impelling call from within.

In retrospect (as I have read the record of my own lifestream from those years) I have seen that in searching for God, I used to leave my body in sleep at night and go to the inner temples of the Brotherhood and work with the Ascended Masters and work with Mark—who was about twenty years my senior according to the calculations of this life.*

As far as twin flames are concerned, the age of the body has nothing to do with the age of the soul, because one's souls are the same age, having begun together in the beginning in the 'white fire body' of the Divine Whole.

And so, with the encounter on inner planes as prologue, we met when I was twenty-two and he was forty-two. I was looking for the Teacher and the Guru because I knew that somewhere there was that one who was going to give to me the key to my mission. What I did not know was that my inner understanding included the awareness that my Teacher would be my twin flame.

So, when I saw Mark Prophet for the first time, I recognized him as Teacher. He, seeing me for the first time, recognized me as twin flame.

---
*Out-of-the-body soul experiences in the 'etheric' retreats of the Ascended Masters are the ongoing method of soul advancement provided by God for earth's evolutions.

It was a very interesting experience. I was so one-pointed in the direction of finding the Teacher and so elated to have found the One, that I was almost burdened by having to deal with another relationship at the same time.

I wanted to be absolutely certain and I wanted to have the confirmation in my own being that every step that I took was right and was the will of God, so that I would not make any mistake to the harm of any part of life. And so, I asked God to reveal to me and confirm within my own being that this indeed was my twin flame.

Weeks later I had a very astounding experience. It was one of those indelible experiences that never dims with time. I happened to look into a mirror where I was dressing. And I looked up and I did not see myself—I saw the face of Mark Prophet.

Now, if you can ever imagine looking in a mirror and not seeing yourself, it's a very shocking experience.

What I saw was really the revelation of the inner soul pattern, not just of the soul which is that potential to become God, but I saw the image of the 'man behind the man'. It was as if I was seeing the archetypal likeness of myself in the masculine polarity.

> When my being had registered the confirmation of the inner pattern, his face was no longer in the mirror but fully awakened in my soul.

I drew close to examine it in greater detail. It did not fade but 'waited' for me to take in every line of it. It was ancient. It had always been. It was sculpted in marble, etched in crystal, yet 'flesh of my flesh'. I saw that I was the reflection in the negative (feminine) polarity of that positive (masculine) image.

When my being had registered the confirmation of the inner pattern, his face was no longer in the mirror but fully awakened in my soul.

It was awesome to contemplate the meaning of the twin flame— to have felt the inner reality and now to understand how the twin flame could actually be oneself—the other half, the 'alter divine ego' (to grasp at a definition), like the person you are on the other side of yourself.

This awareness precedes love. It is the mystery of Life itself that one must enter before one loves. One isn't quite ready to love—one has a lot to think about. And I thought—and thought:

It was undeniable—the inescapable truth. There was no turning back. The die had been cast beyond time and space. It was mine to choose to act upon a preordained Reality. Or to walk away from it—but how? It would always be with me. He was myself, as he had told me.

I had called to God for my Teacher and he had sent me my twin flame. Now we must sort out our lives and chart our course.

This inner knowing—this certain knowledge of the soul—has nothing to do with being in love in the human sense of the word.

I wish to clarify this point because for as long as I have been teaching, during the last twenty-two years since this experience, I have received hundreds of letters from people concerning twin flames. They tell me that they have found their twin flame and they base it on a human love experience, compatible personalities and astrology, or outer indexes that point more to the soul mate relationship or the karmic polarization than to the inner reality of twin flames.

> We are not twin flames by virtue of the condition of our flesh and blood, our personality, our astrology, our karma, or our mutual attraction.

Although these may provide an indication of compatibility, they do not necessarily confirm the depth of soul oneness that we find when we go to the bedrock of being where the truth of our twin flame can be known.

Remember that Paul said, "Flesh and blood cannot inherit the kingdom of God." We are not twin flames by virtue of the condition of our flesh and blood, our personality, our astrology, our karma, or our mutual attraction. We are twin flames by our origin in the same sphere of being called the white fire body. Only we two came out of the One—only we share the unique divine design—'male and female', Elohim created us. And no other will ever share the same identical pattern.

If the twin flame relationship is not going to serve a spiritual purpose—if its reestablishment in this life is going to mean the breaking up of families and homes, if it's going to cause a cataclysm in people's lives because they are in different situations that they are bound to be involved with (because they are resolving past karma), then often the outer mind would rather not deal with what the soul knows at the subconscious level—and so the outer mind does not readily admit to the 'pre-cognition' that is ever-present with the soul.

For instance, I have seen twin flames where the man was twenty and the woman was seventy. And their meeting did not produce instant love and marriage. Nor did the relationship become anything more than a loyal friendship and a mutual fondness. In fact, though inseparable, they never even realized they were twin flames.

It wasn't necessary for them to know. Their souls knew and they accomplished what they were supposed to without having to deal with any more than they were ready for.

The encounter that produces a spiritual polarity and an intense mutual love can be the result of many different circumstances. The twin flame tie is one. Soul mates is another. And then there is karma. The karmic tie may be the tightest of all. Because it is not free, it is binding. Because it is not balanced, the internal harmonies are wanting. And from time to time, there is an emptiness, a loneliness, that reveals the inadequacy of a relationship based solely on karma. This, too, shall pass.

We may have several such relationships with people with whom we have made karma in our past lives—good karma and bad karma. Sometimes the worse the karma, the more intense the impact when we first meet someone, because there is God—the God* we ourselves have imprisoned through past negative activity—and we run to greet that one to set him (her) free from our own past transgressions of his (her) being. And we love much because there is much to be forgiven.

A negative experience of the past—such as violence, passionate hatred, murder, noncaring for one's children, one's family, something that you have been involved in with someone else that has caused an imbalance both in their lifestream and in yours and perhaps in the lives of many—is experienced as a weight upon the heart and an absence of resolution at the soul level. This is a very gnawing condition that troubles our consciousness until it is resolved by love.

Your soul knows why you have come into embodiment. You have been told by your spiritual teachers, your Christ Self, or guardian angel: "There is this situation with so and so that requires resolution. You and this person, by your neglect, by your failure to act, once caused the collapse of this city, or because you walked away from your responsibility many people were involved in a famine."

These are not unlikely situations. The ramifications of what we do by committing sin or by omitting to serve life are very great and they're very heavy. At inner levels the soul who is on the Homeward path (going home to the Father/Mother God) is very conscientious and desirous of righting the wrongs of the past—because it knows

---

*Elizabeth Clare Prophet teaches that everyone is a manifestation of God and that we meet God face to face in every part of life.

that righting the wrongs of lifetimes of ignorant and erroneous sowings is the only way to get back to the place we started from.

On the bright side, a Master may have told you before you took embodiment in this life that because of the many constructive labors for humanity you have done together, you are assigned an even greater responsibility with this person in this life. And because of your good karma, you will be happy and fruitful and have many victories for the right.

In this century of our souls' acceleration toward Aquarius* you may experience more than one relationship of both kinds. We are winding up the loose ends of our karma with a number of people.

These equations of our karma can cause distress, divorce, soul-searching, and a real need to understand why our lives have not followed the perfect storybook version. The knowledge of karma and reincarnation can teach us a lot about the bumpy road of relationships, some beautiful and some very unpleasant—but all very necessary to the soul's evolution and the path of defining our true selfhood with God, Christ, and our twin flame.

So you may meet someone—and this may occur in the latter teen-age years and the twenties or anytime—and the impact will be stunning. It's like the impact of planetary bodies. And it will be stunning because at the subconscious level you are so elated that you have found the person with whom you can balance a certain record of karma.

Your soul knows that if you do not get through that karma, you cannot go on to the next slice of the spiral of life and then on to world service and the creative projects you want most to do with the one you love most—even though you may have never met.

This sense of obligation translates as a need to give of oneself—and to receive; the desire to love—and be loved, because the flame of love is the all-consuming fire of God that dissolves the records of non-love or anti-love as we give and take in a relationship.

There may be children involved, and you may have agreed to bring into the world a certain number of children who are a part of a certain family or group karma. And because the goal of life is reunion with the Christ Self, reunion with your I AM Presence, and ultimately the spiritual reunion with your twin flame, you realize that if you don't get this karma balanced, you will not get to your perfect love.

And so, the faster you submit to the law of your own karma—which is in fact the law of love—the faster both you and your partner are going to be liberated for the next step in your divine plan.

---

*The two-thousand-year dispensation which follows the age of Pisces inaugurated by the birth of Jesus Christ.

We are reaping what we have sown, but through service to each other we can accelerate karmic cycles.

And so, you may have one of these very intense interchanges in a relationship. You may be in the tight coil of that karma, and you may be aware of just what the causes were that set in motion the effects you are seeing pass before you and between you every day—or you may be blissfully unaware of anything but love.

You're in the pink. There is nothing more important. There's no one in all the world you'd rather be with. There's nothing you'd rather do. The love is there. The newness of the relationship is there. You marry, you start a family, you start working together, and you start working out this karma.

Well, you all know the expression "the honeymoon is over." That expression has to do with the impact of karma once there is a binding relationship of marriage. And this is why some people just don't want to get married—because they have a resistance to "bearing one another's burden."

They simply don't want the responsibility. They say marriage would ruin everything, but what they mean is taking on each other's karma would really mess things up. Each half of the partnership is still too self-centered to give up that independence which can be kept only if they don't pick up each other's karmic load.*

But that is precisely the inner meaning of the ritual of marriage— that we love so much, *so very much* that we eagerly share and bear the karma of our spouse with our own. We want to be one at all levels of consciousness.

> The faster you submit to the law of your own karma, the faster both you and your partner are going to be liberated for the next step in your divine plan.

The marriage vow reflects this commitment of souls who plight their troth: "...to have and to hold from this day forward, for better, for worse, for richer, for poorer, in sickness and in health, to love and to cherish till death us do part." It is this totality of oneness spiritually, karmically, and in all ways that Jesus described when he said, "and they twain shall be one flesh."

---

*Living with someone or having an affair is another story entirely. We may share our karma for awhile and pool our resources for a worthwhile or enjoyable experience—but when we go our separate ways, we go back on the way of our separate karma without having really balanced our karma at the depth of mutual burden-bearing that true spiritual progress requires. The more casual the relationship and the less serious the commitment, the easier it is to walk away when the very first head-on encounter with karma takes place.

LOVE, MARRIAGE AND BEYOND

If marriage were a mere physical union, divorce, when it occurs, would not be so emotionally devastating. Divorce is a surgery of pulling apart the two that have become one; and all the battles about who owns what and who gets the children really center around the excruciating process of redefining one's self apart from the 'other self'.

Taking the marriage vow signifies that when we take one another "to my wedded wife/to my wedded husband," we will stand together come what may in the other's life and karma. Since the future and the subconscious are not known on the wedding day, and the vow is so 'final', it is the most serious and far-reaching contract we will ever sign in our lifetime. That's why Jesus warned us not to be unequally yoked together with those of unlike mind, and recommended we consider "what fellowship hath light with darkness" in interpersonal relationships.

> The thing about this karmic marriage or relationship that you are into is that you can never get out of it if you don't fulfill every jot and tittle of the law.

If you marry someone who has less attainment on the spiritual path or a heavier karma than yours, when the honeymoon is over, you're going to feel the weight. And you know that you have taken on the karma of someone else, and that someone else is on the good end of the bargain because he or she's gotten all your light, your talent, or your money. But you may want it that way—because you love so much and you want to give yourself to that person, or to the God in that person.

It may be the correct decision. It may be ordained by your karma that you must lay down your life for this old friend because he once saved you from utter loss and despair. It may be the correct decision even if it later appears as a mistake or the worst of all possible choices. You made the decision because you needed to make the decision—because your soul had a need to resolve.

Even if it was only to learn the whys and wherefores of factors of decision-making in your own personal psychology—or to face a part of him (or her) that is really a part of yourself that must be worked through and overcome. This could be a part of yourself you were never willing to admit was there until you were forced to confront it in the personality of another.

Don't get upset with yourself when you find out these things. Don't knock yourself or go on a guilt trip. God loves you and He wants you to come home to His heart whole—psychologically, spiritually, and karmically whole. And he is giving you these varied experiences and encounters so that you will be weaned from unreality, love Him more than all of these, and see Christ's face smiling at you just beyond the veil of the one you are loving.

This need for resolution can be explained by the way an oyster feels when he gets a little grain of sand and he's got to keep on covering it over because it's a botheration, it's an irritant to his world. Because he wants resolution he makes a pearl out of it.

Well, that's how karma is. It irritates. And we want to smooth it over. We want to make it right.

Now, the thing about this karmic marriage or relationship that you are into is that you can never get out of it, you can never get free of it if you don't fulfill every jot and tittle of the law—the law of karma that compels the highest expression of love in order to be free. If you don't balance ultimately and finally what there is between you, you will reembody and you will still have to enter into some sort of a relationship with that person, even if it is a business partnership.

No one in heaven or on earth can separate you from your twin flame. That's why Jesus said, "What therefore God hath joined together, let no(t) man put asunder."

When you come before the altar to be married, you are receiving a blessing *by your choice*, by your freewill decision, but this marriage may or may not be a condition or an estate where it can be said, "whom God hath joined together." Marriages are made on earth by two people for various reasons; as such they are not necessarily *the* marriage that was made in heaven.

God created you and your twin flame out of the same white fire body in the beginning. The story of Eve being formed out of the rib taken from Adam is an attempt to illustrate this mystical origin. Because of this oneness in the nucleus of divine selfhood, in all other conditions and circumstances of life, no one can separate you from that love of God in your twin flame. That is the real meaning of that passage of Scripture.

So, karmic marriages and other conditions of life may come and go and they are for a purpose. So long as the karma remains (unless there be alternative means for working it out) they are binding. And while we are in the midst of them, we can make of these marriages a celebration on earth of our inner union with our twin flame. And this is lawful.

What is *not* lawful is that you treat such a relationship halfheartedly or even resentfully and do not give it your best and the most fervent love of your heart because you say, "Well, this person is not my twin flame. And this is just a karmic situation, so I'll give it a token effort and bide my time until the real thing comes along." Well, that's a very good way to prolong your karma and to make more karma.

We look at life with the understanding that whoever we are dealing with *is God*. The person is God—in manifestation. The divine flame is God. The potential is God. And we must love that person with our whole heart, with the purest and highest love that we would have for God and for our twin flame.

That love is liberating. It is a transmutative force. We need forgiveness in relationships. We need liberally to forgive others and to forgive ourselves because that's the whole point of karma. We all have much to forgive and much to be forgiven for or we would not find ourselves on this planet at this point in time and space.

So it doesn't matter if you're married to your twin flame or if you've ever met your twin flame. What matters is that you realize the sacredness of marriage and the relationship of man and woman, and that this polarity is always representative of 'Alpha and Omega'— the Masculine/Feminine Co-Creators of Life in the white fire body of the Godhead depicted by the Chinese as the T'ai Chi ☯.

Wherever your twin flame is, even if your twin flame is a cosmic being, your twin flame needs your support and your love. Because, if you are in a negative vibration, you can actually hinder the activity and service of an Ascended Master, an angel, or someone in embodiment who is trying to fight for freedom in Poland today, someone in Russia who's taking a stand against the KGB or lying in a psychiatric hospital being injected with drugs to make him a vegetable.

Whoever the person is, if you let down your flame, your guard, or your love in those friends and family ties you now have, you are letting down first, Almighty God, and second, your twin flame. And ultimately, you will suffer, because a setback to your twin flame is a setback to you.

On that day when you make your ascension back to the heart of God and you would like to know your twin flame is going to ascend also, that twin flame may not be ready to ascend. He or she may have another thousand years to embody upon earth because you did not supply that extra thrust of spirituality and light and selflessness that could have propelled that person into a higher dimension of their own consciousness. (I don't recommend that you blame yourself for anything or everything that has or can go wrong in life, but I do ask that you consider how much more you can do for yourself and others to make things go right.)

So when we say, "no man is an island, no woman is an island," we understand that the twin flame, as the other half of the whole, is experiencing the ramifications and the repercussions of our life. This knowledge makes life worth doing and doing well. Sharing love and serving others' needs and helping them grow is all a part of giving yourself in advance to that perfect love that will be there when you're both ready—really ready.

I also understand that it is lawful in the Aquarian age for the ritual of marriage to be celebrated for other reasons than the marriage of twin flames, because the laws of God take into account and accommodate the human condition.

We all have a human condition right now. You have a scroll upon which is written the law of your life, which is the law of your karma. As a co-creator with God, you have made good karma, you have made bad karma.

The law of the inner blueprint is written underneath this page. Our human karma is like an overlay which we've put over the original fiery blueprint. We see that overlay, and we see peeking through what is underneath.

We all know how life should be for us, how we would like it to be in the idyllic, Edenic sense of the word. And then we look about us and we are still in the state of toiling. But we have hope in

> Wherever your twin flame is, even if your twin flame is a cosmic being, your twin flame needs your support and your love.

our heart: Christ the hope of our glory in God and in our twin flame. And that hope lies in the fact that we know what is real at inner levels.

We know where we have come from. We know who we are. We know where we are going. Through the Holy Spirit, God has given to us the gift of the violet flame to get there. And so, we take every day as an opportunity to erase the overlay, so that one day that entire page can be turned over and once again we are returned to that point of Eden and the bliss of Love in the hallowed circle of our Oneness.

We know that most of the sacred scriptures of the world contain a story about man and woman and their fall. This actually refers to the descent of you and your twin flame from the etheric octave—the place of the pristine purity of the golden-age consciousness to the place where we are now weighted down by the world karma that is upon us.

It is a weight of untransmuted energy and it begins to interfere with the untrammeled and free flow of light in the heart and the chakras, so we are no longer spinning at such an intense velocity of light. We are literally earthbound.

We know the meaning of the weight of a physical body. We can all do only so much in each given day and then the body is spent and we must put it to rest and recharge it again.

So that descent is the point of sorrow. And the greatest sorrow, of course, is separation from the face-to-face encounter with the beloved I AM Presence, the face-to-face encounter with the Person of Christ, our Christ Self, or the embodied Teacher, and then the loss of the perpetual communion with the twin flame.

At that point, we begin to make karma with other lifestreams and there are the long separations which may go on for many lifetimes. This is sometimes the source of depression and a sense of nonfulfillment in life.

> Your Real Self, your Holy Christ Self, and that of your twin flame is the magnet that will draw you and your twin flame together — in this world and the next.

And often, of course, it is an illusion, because people say, "Well, if only my twin flame were here, everything would be wonderful. I can't get along with this person. We're not really alike. We don't agree. We don't think alike"—all these problems that come up in relationships.

We have the sense of the ideal, the sense of who this person is, and this person will absolutely, completely, and totally be our complement and all of our dreams and wishes will come true.

Well, it just isn't so. If you can't get along with yourself, you won't get along with your twin flame or soul mate. Actually, twin flames develop different personalities by being separated for so long. They go through negative conditionings by negative experiences. Twin flames are not necessarily alike. They may have an astrology that clashes.

I remember an astrologer once told Mark and me that we should never be married because we couldn't possibly get along with the astrology that we had. He was a Capricorn and I'm an Aries, which is a combination of an earth and fire sign. They say either the earth will put out the fire or the fire will scorch the earth. But I say, Love conquers all.

Well, I realized that there was only one way that this relationship would work, and that was that one of us had to be the boss and one of us had to submit. And I understood completely who was who in that relationship. And if I didn't understand it, I was very swiftly reminded by Mark! So, luckily, I figured that one out and we lived happily ever after.

I firmly believe in the hierarchy of the household established by Moses, Buddha, and Christ: "Wives, submit yourselves unto your own husbands, as unto the Lord. For the husband is the head of the wife, even as Christ is the head of the church..."

I was very happy to be in the role of disciple to Mark. He represented the Master to me as no other could. He was the only person who could have brought me to the very quintessence of my own being and simultaneously to the submission unto Christ. He knew my soul as no one else could. He bore to me the love of the universe. To be near him was and is to be enveloped in God.

He knew me in the beginning. He knew what I should be manifesting and what I was not. He knew what was excess human consciousness picked up as baggage in life from all of the many interactions we've had with so many people and conditions.

And so, he was highly qualified to bring me to an abrupt waking awareness of this disparity between the inner divine being that I AM, and you are, and all of us are, and sometimes the paltry and shameful manifestation—which is shameful not because it's so 'bad', but it's shameful because it's such a mediocre version of what the inner Self really is.

And when you have a masterful one such as Mark who can plug you back into the power of that original design, you are electrified with the sense within yourself of who you really are and what you should be. Mark Prophet galvanized my life for Christ and revealed Him as the Saviour and Bridegroom of my soul.

Your Real Self, your Holy Christ Self, and that of your twin flame is the magnet that will draw you and your twin flame together—in this world and the next. "And I," to paraphrase Jesus, "if the I AM in me be lifted up, then I will draw my twin flame unto me."

So, we have to go back to the statement of Paul once again, that "flesh and blood cannot inherit the kingdom of God." And flesh and blood does not guarantee you a harmonious relationship with anyone, including your twin flame. What will guarantee it is your determination to work hard at a relationship.

There is no relationship—any friendship, our children, brothers and sisters, relatives, professional relationships—which, if it's going to endure, does not require work. We all have to give of ourselves and give a lot in order to sustain that interaction with anyone.

So you have to see that twin flames, by having gone all over the earth in all kinds of incarnations and circumstances might, through karmic conditions, have superficial personality clashes. And when these are seen as superficial and we get to the heart of the matter, then we're in the driver's seat and we become co-creators with God.

You see, twin flames do make karma with each other in various embodiments. And that karma also has to be balanced when they finally get back together. And so there can be a tremendous sense of injustice between twin flames.

That explains what occurs in karmic marriages where people are constantly fighting and you can see no purpose to the relationship. So you say, "Why don't they just quit and separate, because this has been going on for years?" And next thing you know they're back as lovebirds, starting all over again. And this repeats and repeats and repeats. And nobody can understand what's going on except the two people involved.

And, of course, it's a very dangerous thing because there's a lot of karma-making in those heavy scenes. And ultimately, they become so self-destructive that often the solution is for people to go their separate ways, *even if they are twin flames, and even if they haven't balanced their mutual karma.*

I've known of twin flames who have destroyed their lives and their marriages, when if they had just had an understanding of the law of love, where love begets love, and a commitment to the relationship, they could have made some progress.

I've seen twin flames who are alcoholics, drug addicts. I've seen them ruin their lives and their children's lives and wind up in the dregs of disappointment. And life comes to a conclusion and they pass from the screen of life and they are sorry beyond words at the soul level when they see that they utterly failed in their assignment to go down into physical embodiment and get things together and make things happen.

So you need to be ready to meet your twin flame. You need to have a good deal of self-control. You've got to love Love enough to respect it, to hold your peace and your harmony when those old records of ancient clashes come up for resolution. You've got to hold on to your Dream, seal those unkind words, the cruel criticism—the put-down and anything that will shatter the matrix of the most beautiful gift Life will ever give to you—perfect love.

Give in. You don't have to win every argument. Preserve the integrity and self-respect of the one you love and thereby guarantee your own. The mantra of John the Baptist will go a long way on the path of sacrifice and surrender that marriage is: "He must increase, but I must decrease."

And so you have to have a dedication to something more than your twin flame, and that something more is God. You've got to love God first and be very sure of your path and your service and that you're not going to give in to discord or the theatrics of the human ego and all kinds of self-indulgences and demands—whether your own or your mate's.

You cannot demand that anyone be a complement to your human personality with all of its faults. You cannot expect someone to be to you father and mother, brother and sister, lover, husband or wife, and son and daughter all at once, so that every time you experience the least little bit of a problem, your idea is that this twin flame or this spouse is going to move right in and pick you up and everything's going to be rosy.

You have to decide to be complete in yourself—stop that pouting and self-pity and that constant demand for attention—and then by the magnet of your wholeness, you will attract wholeness in another person.

Read I Corinthians 13 often and keep a copy of the Prayer of Saint Francis of Assisi on your nightstand so you remember true love is self-givingness. *The Prophet* by Kahlil Gibran will restore your memory of the bliss of Love and Marriage. True love is sacrificial—*always* putting the beloved first.

Now, I have to tell you that sometimes and in some circumstances, because of such a difference between twin flames, God actually works it so that they embody as brother and sister, or as father and child, or as members of the same sex. Because a marriage relationship would not be profitable and more than likely, based on the record of past performance, would hinder more than help their soul evolution.

There is nothing more painful to a cosmos than an argument between twin flames. Because it is from strife in the circle of the One that war and every desolation ensues. It violates the Father/Mother God in heaven and on earth.

If you ever remember as a child hearing an argument between your father and mother, you know that you could have no worse experience. It's a crushing blow to every part of life that those who hold the office of Father and Mother should experience any discord in the flow of that divine love.

> You have to have a dedication to something more than your twin flame, and that something more is God. You've got to love God first.

And it is painful to the souls of twin flames. At inner levels, we ourselves don't want this to occur because we know how damaging it is. We know it will keep us separated for succeeding incarnations. And so, we have to give. There is no other way.

We all have human weaknesses. We all have human problems. We have human things we haven't overcome. And when we think of the spouse, made in the image of the Divine Spouse, the one who would be the perfect one for us, we always imagine that that person should be 'perfect'.

So when they're not perfect in our eyes, which measurement we take by our own state of imperfection, we throw a tantrum. We rant, we rave, we make demands, we scream, we sob—all these things that are going on in marriages all over the world, because somebody is expecting another person to be something more than that person is—and better than they themselves are. If we have faults, we want the other person to be perfect.

So we make demands of people in a marriage that are totally unrealistic. And this is why marriages fall apart. Not to mention, of course, that one of the basic reasons people marry is for sensual gratification. Putting that aside, all of the other psychological situations of strident tensions between human personalities become a horrendous mark against the divine image of Father/Mother God—against wholeness.

> You've got to become very wonderful yourself, as wonderful as the person that you desire to be with.

I advocate that one meditate upon one's Self and one's Life in both the divine and the human sense of the word and realize that if you want to attract the beautiful lady of grace or the knight in shining armor, you have to *become* that counterpart first. And you ought to look at yourself in terms of scrubbing up that karma with violet flame and meditation, coming to a resolution of your own psychology.

In seeking your twin flame, the only real desire that you ought to have is to bring to that twin flame the gift of your love, your self, your own spiritual attainment as well as your outer professional accomplishments.

What bouquet of flowers are you ready to bring to your twin flame today?

I'd like you to meditate upon this because it's a most important part of your understanding of your psychology. After you've defined what you are capable of giving on one piece of paper, you should write down what you know, by past performance and present awareness, you're not capable of giving.

You might say, "Well, one thing I can't do: I don't know how to cook. So I can't cook a meal for this twin flame." Whether you're a man or a woman, you like to have somebody cook a meal for you once in a while. So you ought to learn to cook.

Get down to the basics in life. Can you keep a schedule? Can you add happiness to a household? Can you be patient with children? Can you be patient with the child in the person that you're imagining is going to come down the highway one of these days?

Look at how you interact with yourself. Can you get along with yourself or do you have problems with yourself? Do you have moods? Do you have ups and downs?

Now, when you look at the balance between the flowers you can offer and the weeds you have not yet plucked from your garden or the barren earth where you haven't planted a flower, then you turn around and you get on the receiving end.

Pretend you're the other person. You're the other person seeing you coming down the road. Are they going to be interested? Is this wonderful person that you're imagining going to want you? If they're so wonderful, they may be *so* wonderful that they may be *too* wonderful! They may not even notice you!

In other words, you've got to become very wonderful yourself, as wonderful as the person that you desire to be with. And you have to be that in fact and in reality and not in fantasy.

So now the other person is coming down the road. Maybe it is your twin flame and they see you—you're standing there—and they walk on by. You say, "Wait a minute. You're supposed to stop when you get to me!"

But they didn't stop when they got to you because they didn't find in you a magnet. You didn't have the capacity to magnetize the person that you imagine is your divine polarity.

Well, why didn't you have the capacity? You have to imagine what that person would be looking for. You know what you want in that person. You know the virtues and qualities. If you don't contain the same virtues and qualities you're looking for, the person will not recognize you. It'll be like strangers in a crowded room who never speak.

Many people think it's all in the package, in the appearance. But it isn't. That wears away very quickly. You've got to have heart. You've got to have soul. You've got to be willing to give. And you've also got to be willing to demonstrate that you do have the qualifications for the job.

And what's the job? It's an office. It's saying, "Here's the person who is the 'Alpha'. Here's the person who's the 'Omega'. I want to be the counterpart to that person. I have to be able to prove to that person that I can hold the balance for their mission. I can uphold them. I can serve with them. I can provide the counterpart of qualities they need." Whatever they do, you've got to be able to give something to their life that they need, because all relationships are based on need.

You have to be very honest in a relationship, because you may see well in advance that you're not going to be able to provide a major interest that that person needs and you may see they're not going to be able to provide yours. And if you're the one that can see it, then you will bear the karma of going into that relationship because your human self wants it even though your heart and your mind and your soul really know that it's not going to work.

The reason that this is such a situation of concern to us all is that each of us really does have a fundamental need to relate to at least one person in life in a very personal way.

So when we recognize the fundamental soul need in life for "the Friend," we need to be careful to understand what it is that we really need in that friend. A friend that does not meet that need, a friend that we can't give and take with, who is of a different vibration than what our souls require, becomes no friend at all—in fact, he or she becomes a shackle and a drag.

And when we have such a relationship with people, we realize we're wasting our life and their life. And we've only got threescore and ten and maybe a little bit more. And we've got things we've got to do.

Sublimation is one way of dealing with the absence, in physical proximity, of the friend. It means taking the energy of the need and the creative force of our life itself and projecting it into the future as a future goal. And in the meantime, while reaching that goal of the perfect love, we love all life. We love people, many people, individually and personally, in a very deep way. We have good relationships, good associates.

But we understand that what we are looking for and what we know is there just beyond the veil already does exist. And in the process of our self-mastery, we learn to live with that fact and we say, "I will go through the coil of experience. I will accept no substitute and no diversion from my goal." It's like knowing you're going to meet someone in Rome and you realize that it takes a certain amount of time to travel there.

If we don't understand sublimation, or 'etherealization', if we are a creature of wants and demands—"I want what I want and I want it now and it *has* to be now"—we will accept a lesser standard in our lives and we will actually not have the power to attract to ourselves what really is the fulfillment of the divine meeting as well as the divine plan for this embodiment.

So, it's alright to acknowledge the need. But remember, a need is also an absence of wholeness. And an absence of wholeness makes you incomplete. And when you're incomplete, you are not focusing the divine magnet that can attract to yourself the very thing you need to complete your wholeness.

A twin flame is not looking for someone to take care of. A twin flame is looking for your wholeness to complement his own or her own, so that when you are together as one complete Alpha/Omega circle, you can minister to life in need, to others who have not yet discovered the law of their oneness.

So, while you are aware of the fact that you are incomplete in some sense of the word, you lack this or that, you have to tie into the superior matrix of your wholeness which does exist and is now at inner levels—the wholeness of your Christ Self, the wholeness of your I AM Presence, and your absolute divine union with your twin flame.

You need to affirm it right here. You need to have a sense of peace about present wholeness, and you can because it exists right now in God where you are. When you have that peace, then and only then do you have something to offer anyone, any part of life.

When you have the peace of wholeness, all you can do is attract from the four corners of the heavens more of that wholeness, more of the confirmation of what you know you are and what you are in reality.

> A twin flame is not looking for someone to take care of. A twin flame is looking for your wholeness to complement his own or her own.

So, while you have a sense of filling in the matrix, while you have a sense that sooner or later you're going to eat and fill that hunger, presently you affirm: "I am filled. I am full of Light."

By that affirmation, by that Divine *Be*-Attitude, you will attract every person, every condition, every circumstance in your life that is necessary to the fruition of cosmic purpose. And that may or may not include your twin flame. But it no longer matters because *you are your twin flame*. "I and my Father are One. I and my Mother are One. We are One here and now!" *And you are never alone.*

That statement eliminates time and space, all distance and maya. It gives you peace and harmony. Because you know you are whole, you pull down from your Causal Body of Light and your I AM Presence, all of the virtues and factors and talents and supply and abundance and beauty and joy and wisdom you need to be who you are.

And when you are that one, people are magnetized to you because of their sense of need. You have, in manifestation in your aura, what they need. And so they come. They come to be fed. They come to hear. They come to be nourished. They come to you for advice professionally. They come because you have something they don't have.

And you have that very simple key that "I AM THAT I AM. Here and now I AM One, We are One. Alpha and Omega are One where I AM. No time or space can separate me from my twin flame, for we are one in the Heart of God."

LOVE, MARRIAGE AND BEYOND

That is who everyone is seeking in life—the person who is whole and knows he is whole and uses his very wholeness to transmute the wants and lacks in the physical plane, the last vestiges of karma, and all of the various human consciousness situations that kind of get left over and still have to be dealt with in our lives.

So that is the key to your union with your twin flame. And I think that that affirmation of Being is the starting point of an eternity of happiness.

> "I'm going to remake myself so that I'm irresistible to God."

Just remember, the mere absence of the quality of joy, of happiness, may be depriving you, in the outer sense, of more than you can ever dream of. So, just at the moment when you slip into a little sadness, a little self-pity, a little indulgence in mood energy—at that moment, remember: you may have lost the spark of contact with your twin flame.

Your twin flame doesn't deserve to have to experience your moods, your self-pity, your self-indulgence. And if you can understand the twin flame as the God-counterpart of you, and you have a sense of reverence for God in your life, you may look at yourself and say, "Maybe I'm not worthy now, but one hour from now I'm going to be worthy. I'm going to remake myself so that I'm irresistible to God, the angels, the Masters. They're going to walk and talk with me. They're going to enjoy being in my house. And my twin flame is going to seek and find me."

So, decide who you are. Decide what you've got to do. Ask God. And then go out and find the people who are a part of your team—your group karma—for world service.

Let's be up and doing. It's only in action that we find God—God in ourselves and in our twin flame.

I love you!

Pearls of Wisdom

published by The Summit Lighthouse

Vol. 28 No. 12   *Beloved Saint Germain*   March 24, 1985

Send-off of the Messenger's Stump to the Nations: We Seek a Change of World Consciousness

Hail, Keepers of the Flame! Noble knights and ladies serving the sacred fire, I have come, your Knight Commander, for the anointing of the one whom I send.

The Anointing for the Heart-to-Heart Contact with the Violet-Flame Bearers

O beloved, as God has used me as His witness and prophet and mouthpiece in many ages, so I have anointed these Messengers. And I do anoint them again to the calling in your name—in the name of the Keepers of the Flame of Liberty—to this holy purpose.

So the mission of the Brotherhood to the nations called by God is called by the Mother, Mary, who has interceded before the Father and pleaded for that mercy, that light and strength to be placed upon this Messenger as a mantle whereby we might reach the hearts of our beloved, our faithful, our lightbearers of every nation and background, followers of every religion and of every persuasion.

They are our hearts and shall be, regardless of the outer belief systems imposed upon them. We do not allow such things as the mere indoctrination of a lifetime to deter us from making the heart-to-heart contact with the violet-flame bearers who long ago went forth with you from Zadkiel's retreat, also bearing the flame-flower of the seventh ray—the only hope for the nations, the only hope for the soul of Aquarius.[1]

Brave Hearts Have Lost Their Lives in the Service of Freedom

Beloved, many brave and true hearts dedicated fully to the mission of Freedom have lost their lives in this very year

Copyright © 1985 Church Universal and Triumphant, Inc.

defending our outposts in the world. Thus, they have gone, sent by this government to represent America. And yet, for the forces of tyranny and terrorism abroad in the world, they lost their lives in the service of the flame and in the service of my office—never having apprehended my name, Saint Germain, or the reality of the violet flame or the tube of light.

Many brave heroes in the United States and in every nation are standing in this hour on the very line of the forces of Death and Hell, willing to wrestle with the returning karma borne by the Four Horsemen[2]—willing to stand, willing to live, willing to die, for so have they prayed to the Blessed Mother and to Jesus and to me as Saint Joseph.

A Multifaceted Purpose and Program in Answer to the Call

Thus, heaven answers their call in many ways. And one way is to send the Messenger as the lightning that cometh out of the East and shineth even unto the West,[3] as the lightning of our Brotherhood that shall surely bring the full-gathered momentum of our devotion and yours and lay it upon the altar of the nations and the lightbearers wherever we lead her by our full Spirit.

—To Open the Door to the Path of the Ascension

Blessed ones, it is a multifaceted purpose and program. And I ask you, with beloved Portia and the Lords of Karma, to pray for the fulfillment of this purpose. Spiritually, it is to establish the open door for the path of the ascension wherever her feet are placed. So it is the mantle, and the mantle will perform the Work of the LORD. And the office shall be the fulfilling of His Word.

Thus, beloved, to those who prepare themselves, to those who fulfill the Law, that opportunity [for the ascension] will come, whether in this life or in the next. And no force shall be able to erase these pillars we shall establish for the ascending servants of God, for the sons and daughters who must also rise as we have risen and, in fulfilling their fiery destiny, raise a planet and her evolutions. For the Light which descends in the very scientific process of the ascension inundates the earth and raises all life!

Thus, in the acceleration of the ascensions of the sons and daughters of God, you will see the Light that will consume the vestiges of the last plagues and all those things which come upon the earth. For the earth is not yet full of the glory of the Light of the Central Sun that has come unto it in the etheric octave through Sanat Kumara and the Solar Logoi.⁴ And therefore, those who yet dwell in the valleys of karma yet suffer what to some of you is an unimaginable suffering.

Thus, keep the flame, for ye are also chosen. And I send you as representatives of the violet flame and of Oromasis and Diana this day to keep the flame in the heart of America burning—in the soul of America, in her mind, and in her body. For so is the Mother the extension of the Spirit of America and the Spirit of the Great White Brotherhood.

Blessed hearts, thus she is an extension of yourself as well as myself, of the community here as well as the Great White Brotherhood. And we desire to see the nations and the lightbearers of the nations raised, therefore, to a level where they might hold the balance and the chalice for world freedom.

—To Pave the Way for the Light and the Violet Flame

Thus, having so said, and sending her to that purpose of the laying of the foundation of the spiritual path with the spiritual teaching, understand that the second most important purpose is to pave the way for the Light—the leavening of the consciousness of the people so that the violet flame will make all the difference in future decisions by the independent governments of these nations, by the people's representatives, and by the negotiators of these nations with the representatives of the United States or other nations of the earth.

—To Unite the Lightbearers
of Australia and America and the Philippines

There are seemingly insurmountable problems which have beset both Australia and the Philippines. On the one hand, you see those who love peace denying access to the United States to bases and the opportunity to abide there, for they deny all use of nuclear weapons. Thus, this very philosophy and movement toward peace threatens the alliance (ANZUS)⁵ [as well as the United States bases in the Philippines] that ought to remain and unite these powerful nations; for this people of Australia and America are united in the very seed of Sanat Kumara, in the very origin of the tribe, then, of Joseph.⁶

Beloved ones, remember Ephraim and Manasseh, remember holy purpose, and remember that both continents are a key to world freedom! Therefore, pray that the violet flame shall unite the lightbearers of these nations and that these lightbearers shall therefore be the leaven that draws and magnetizes the people of

Australia and New Zealand to rally around the Light of God, around the flame of Freedom, around the divine understanding that sees through war and its mechanisms.

After all, beloved ones, here we have an enemy who has vowed to destroy the capitalist nations, who has armed to the fullest with nuclear weapons; and this very arming has produced in America and the West the necessity for self-defense and strategic military strength. Thus, on the basis of the move—the chess move of the enemy and the response of the West—there comes division between those who ought to remain friends forever.

Let the bond be of the heart, and let us set aside the divisions of political opinion or the calculated divisions between those who are pro and con nuclear weapons. This is something that is put forth to divide and conquer the people and to amass them on opposing sides when in fact the real issue is to choose Life, not Death, as Moses proclaimed.[7] The real issue is to become the living Christ! The real issue is to raise up the violet flame within the living temple of each one! And by the increase of Light on the planet, the entire geopolitical configuration of the world will change.

—To Leaven the Whole World Consciousness to Freedom

Thus let the leaven go forth. Let the Woman take the leaven of the Christ consciousness and hide it in the earth, in the very hearts of God's people, and let it leaven the whole world consciousness[8] to Freedom, until the day shall come when a child shall ask his parent, "What was it that they had in those days? Was it something they called 'communism' or something like that?" And the violet flame shall have so transmuted the entire momentum of world totalitarian movements that they shall scarcely remember that there was a period in history when the whole world was threatened by the fallen angels who came in many disguises East and West to tear the people from their God.

—To Convert the Nations by the Violet Flame

Do you not see, beloved hearts, these first principles? The worship of the other gods is to place one's attention upon politics and social programs and everything else (as the source of the solution) except the Almighty One who shall deliver His people in His way. And therefore, the conversion of the nations is by the violet flame, by the action of the science of the spoken Word, by the message of the heart of Freedom that unites all lightbearers throughout the world who rise up in one mighty voice and demand the action of their governments to overturn that which is the injustice of the ages.

The United States Is Divided and Weakened by Political Parties

Understand, beloved hearts, that you ought not to stray into the camp of political argumentation and the division of parties and the opposition based upon differing views. It is as though all gather around the elephant of the Republican Party or the donkey of the Democrats. And each surveys the animal from head to toe and side to side, and all have differing opinions about how to put together this animal, how to make it work, how to develop a political philosophy!

And there are so many opinions and so many positions that the United States itself is divided through political parties and her strength is weakened. For there are some who will not follow the Republicans and some who will not follow the Democrats, for they say that the party of their choice has betrayed them. And thus, they form smaller and smaller groups; and some are for and some are against the President. And, beloved hearts, this comes from the argumentation and the discussion of human solutions to human problems.

The God-Solution to the Human Problem

Well, humans have created many problems and very few solutions. In fact, there is hardly a human solution that is not a temporary Band-Aid. The only solution I know for human problems is the God-solution, which embraces the hearts of all real people. It is the God-solution of love and of wisdom and of the power of the sacred fire!

You must be aware of the fact, and know it, that the raising up of the Light within your temple and doing all those things which are necessary to accomplish that end—including right diet and exercise and not excluding sacrifice and the immersion in the sacred fire—this becomes your lawful obedience to the Ascended Masters who have taught you. And these things establishing in you that immense fire of the Brotherhood *are* the solution to nuclear war and to every problem that besets the organization.

Thus, walk in the path of fervor. And know that fervor is never fanaticism, does never burn with hatred or doctrine or dogmatism, but fervor is the increase of the Holy Ghost within you. It is the fire of our presence! It is the power to expand, the power to heal, and the power of conversion! Therefore, become instruments in Freedom's name—become those ministering servants and understand what God is able to work through you.

Governments Must Be Built upon the Rock of Christ

Therefore, this is the purpose of our mission. And you must keep the flame here while the Messenger delivers the fire and the power that will bring men to a new understanding of the I AM Presence where they can bend the knee and bow to the Universal Christ present with them as the prophesied Immanuel, as the coming of that Christ upon whose shoulders the governments must stand.[9] And unless they be placed upon the Rock of Christ as the chief cornerstone[10] of planet Earth, these governments shall not stand!

Thus, when they approach Truth as the Christ-solution to the human problem, you will see how human solutions give way to divine solutions. (And men do not even know that they are divine or locked into their divinity!) For the way of the divine will become the natural way and the natural order of life; and all men shall see the Masters face-to-face—they will know us, and their Teachers will not be removed into a corner anymore.[11] And they will not remember the days when they could not see their Teachers. They will not even remember the day when they could not see their I AM Presence!

This is the dawn of a new age. Ride its crest and understand the meaning of having the forcefield of the Court of the Sacred Fire of the Great Central Sun and the Four and Twenty Elders over Los Angeles.[12] Understand the necessity to call daily to the Four and Twenty Elders to take command of this nation. This forcefield is placed here that you might discover in the Universal Christ and in these masterful beings the means to keep the flame for America while the Messenger is physically absent.

Each One Must Bear His Own Burden

Thus, I give to you, each one, in your own Christ Self, that portion that you must bear which is borne for you by the Messenger when she is physically present. You must take heed that when the Messenger physically leaves an area there is a change of forcefield. There is a change, beloved, and you ought to take note of it and see that the fallen ones do not fill the vacuum with their mischief-making but that you fill the vacuum by calling upon the mantle of your own Christhood and that you do not consider that when the Messenger goes forth it is time for a "vacation." Nay, it is time to be in the sanctuary as much as you can possibly be here to keep the flame—not only for her mission but for America, which is indeed our joint responsibility.

Thus, beloved, we deliver the violet flame to the nations, that these solutions which seem nigh impossible to conclude may have the benefit of a new ingredient—a new Love, as Vesta brought it and taught it; a new Light, as by the hand of Sanat Kumara and Gautama Buddha; a new Wisdom, which Jophiel does bear and precede her with, with those legions of illumination's flame.[13]

Beloved hearts, all is in readiness, as Above and so below, thus to bring the precious oil as the balm of Gilead for the healing of the nations and their people, for the healing of their governments—to draw the individual citizens to the very feet of their own Christhood that they might see and know the way to go to keep planet Earth free.

Designs of World Communism on the Philippines, New Zealand, and Australia

Beloved ones, as pertains to the Philippines, you know well the tremendous foment of World Communism there, and you know the burden surrounding Marcos, and the entire affair that has preceded, in the year past. Beloved ones, this assassination of Aquino has resulted in a great burden and division in the country. This particular event, therefore, has divided the people and caused them to have great suspicion concerning their leaders.[14] And thus, their desire for freedom is great. And the work of the Communists is very intense to take over that land as a base in the South Pacific, even as it is their desire to use New Zealand to their own ends and Australia herself.

As you know well, the plan of Soviet dominion encompasses every nation upon earth. We are determined to plant a flame, to give Comfort and Truth and the Light of the Almighty One to stay the hand of the fallen ones in their onward march. As you realize, the governments of the West have not mobilized, have not moved in concerted effort as they might have to protect Afghanistan—yea, to drive back the Soviets. Nor is there protection to Pakistan or India, nor is it particularly desired in India this day.

Understand, beloved ones, that where you see genocide—the systematic destruction of a people and a nation in Afghanistan—with no hand raised against it of any strength at all, there the name of Uncle Sam and the image of Uncle Sam must hang with shame in this hour. You can also realize that were such eventualities to come upon the Philippines or Australia or New Zealand perhaps, *perhaps* there would be the same response or nonresponse.

Beloved hearts, these things are not imminent, but you who have vision and see the handwriting on the wall must understand that ere the world meet the threat of this totalitarian movement, there must be a change of consciousness. And therefore, the change of world consciousness is that which we seek!

Keepers of the Flame Have Turned the Tide in America

I give tribute to the Keepers of the Flame worldwide and to the Messengers for turning the tide in America back to the original patriotism and the fervor through the very violet flame, through the angels that could be sent because of your diligence to my Freedom service on Saturday evenings. You may not remember how 'liberal' an attitude there was prevailing in this nation, what an absence of fervor and patriotism; for today it is strong and becoming stronger. Realize, then, that had we not had at our disposal an organization—this Messenger and yourselves united as one—this would be a very sorry and a very different picture in this hour.

Forces Moving Against the U.S. Government and President

Beloved hearts, there are many forces that move at inner levels against your government, your President, and the present majority of public opinion for that light of Freedom. Do not become overconfident but keep the flame for the Victory.

May you know that it is because of the weight that this activity has borne, individual by individual, down to the smallest children, to the Messenger herself—the weight borne through these months during the Christmas season, of which you were warned by Kuthumi[15]—that your President was able to deliver his State of the Union message.

Beloved hearts, whatever you have borne, whatever you have suffered, whatever burden has come upon your life in these months—and for many of you it has been great—I tell you, had you not stood, *had you not stood,* beloved hearts, events would have occurred which would have resulted in the President not delivering that address. I tell you no more regarding the intelligence that is on my desk, but I tell you, beloved ones, to keep the flame.

Burdens Essential to the Preservation of World Freedom

Remember, as I have often reminded the Messenger when her burdens wax heavy, we would not place upon you any burden, any request, or any requirement except that which becomes essential if world freedom is to be preserved, if this nation is to be preserved.

Therefore, know, when you must fight through with dynamic decrees a burden upon your heart or soul or mind or body, that the pressure you feel is not to be interpreted either as personal karma or personal condemnation but as the weight of the astral plane pressing in upon you and your families. In that hour, rally together! Rally in the Holy Grail and give your calls to the violet flame as <u>loud</u> and as <u>full</u> and as <u>joyous</u> as you can muster. And you will understand that the burden is given as a sign, as a barometer reading on world freedom that it is time to be up and doing and to move with the force of Light!

Thus, rejoice when you have completed such offerings of hours of decrees and take that moment to laugh and sing and be loving together. And then await the next ring of the inner telephone when I call upon you to be with me the Watchman of the Night.[16]

Remember, beloved ones, that for some the only way we can get your attention is to allow some of this to come upon you, because then you cry out for help and that is what we need! We must have the call.

We Must Have the Call

Remember that I told you: We must have the call! And do not allow the pall that settles upon you to make you believe that now you are sick, now you are ill, now you are weak, now you need a vacation, now you must go to bed! This is the time to summon your forces and give the call and recognize that these physical things can be dismissed very quickly if you will stay in the sacred fire. They are only symptoms of world pain and world disease, they are not symptoms of your own. Remember I have told you, for it will spare you needless sense of guilt and self-condemnation, which is always projected by the force.

—To Gather and to Anoint the Lightbearers

Beloved ones, I tell you, then, the third purpose—and that is to gather and to anoint the lightbearers who at inner levels both require and have dedicated themselves to the Inner Retreat—to call the lost sheep of the house of Israel[17] who have forgotten their name and the name I AM THAT I AM, who have forgotten Sanat Kumara and their reason for being, beloved ones—to call the community of lightbearers and to seal them in the fiery heart of the angels' love!

— To Bring the Full Fire of Jophiel's Illumination into Education and the Economies of the Nations

And then again, we must bring the full fire of Jophiel for illumination in every walk of life—from education to the economies of the nations. The wisdom of the Cosmic Christ must saturate, and it must come upon the people, regardless of whether or not they themselves have put in the time and the energy for individual attainment or attunement with God. *It must come because the mantle of the office of the Messenger and the mantle of the office of the chela does hold the flame.*

This is the meaning of being a Keeper of the Flame: to keep the flame of individual self-mastery on behalf of those who do not have it yet and who, left to their own, would not perceive or receive the inner workings of the Law or bring back to their outer selves that which they have learned at inner levels.

Thus, we keep the flame for you by overshadowing you with our Electronic Presence, by helping you to draw down your I AM Presence so that you will receive the intimations of the Great White Brotherhood hourly and daily in your service. Understand, therefore, how important it is to lend your mantle to your brothers and sisters who, feeling that sacred fire and that Light, will desire to come to the fount and drink for themselves.

— To Personally and Physically Anoint Souls with Illumination and Freedom

Thus, we see Illumination and Freedom as the key to the age and the personal anointing. Even as I was the anointer of servants of God in the past,[18] beloved hearts, so the Messenger must personally and physically anoint souls, touch them, and draw them into the Light that they might be quickened. For it is indeed a quickening that the dead might come to life and might cry out in the valley of the dry bones,[19] that their forces might be summoned, their souls might be gathered, and they might sing once again the praises unto the LORD. This does require the personal and individual transfer.

Thus, I trust you will appreciate why the mission is necessary. For if we desire in the name of Arcturus and Zadkiel to have a physical action of the sacred fire and a physical presence of the violet flame and a physical healing of a physical earth, then we must have a physical Messenger and we must have *you* as physical messengers of the Light of your Christhood, meaning that the Light of your Christhood must penetrate through your very pores and through your very bodies and through your very hearts.

Copyright © 1985 Church Universal and Triumphant, Inc.

Blessed ones, I am certain that you can think of ten more reasons and a thousand for the sending forth of your representative and ours to reach your beloved ones—individuals and families, brothers and sisters, twin flames, soul mates—all who are a part of your life. As you have kept the flame here, so you and they deserve to be reacquainted and drawn together anew so that you might discover the totality, the meaning, and the strength of the body of God in the earth.

—To Form the Circle of Light for the World Union of Freedom-Fighters

It has been the consideration of the Goddess of Liberty with the Lords of Karma and the Darjeeling Council that the union of the freedom-fighters of the world, the union of lightbearers through the Circle of Light, would be the mighty ring—even the golden ring signifying the wedding band of the union of Sanat Kumara, the Eternal Guru, with all of us as his chelas—for the raising of the planet and for the overturning of Darkness and Death.

Thus, beloved hearts, pray for the Circle of Light to be formed. For Mother Mary's Circle of Light worldwide is the manifestation in the physical octave of the solar ring which you have called forth. As seraphim have formed that ring, so, beloved, understand that you yourselves, extensions of seraphim, form ultimately the physical ring in the earth. Each time you form the Circle of Light in the name of Mother Mary—and you may do it often in the Messenger's absence—remember that that ring of Light is the ring of Sanat Kumara and is the conductor of your mighty decrees and praises unto God. And it does hold the balance for America and our mission.

The Anointing of the Messenger and Chelas

Therefore, beloved, I do now anoint the Messenger and place within her very body and Christ Self the inner blueprint and the divine plan for this mission fulfilled.

[Messenger kneels at the high altar.]

Concurrently, my angels, beloved, anoint you into the hierarchy of a greater responsibility for the flame of this nation.

Beloved ones, we are grateful for the stamina of spirit which you as a world body and this Messenger have displayed. Beloved ones, there are not many who can stand in the full strength of Almighty God against the tide of an adverse public opinion and press and media. Realize that when we see that you are impervious to anything that may come as the attack of the fallen ones, we may allow them to run toward their target of Light in a final run of their own self-destruction, for so the Law decrees it.

Therefore, we say to them: That which thou doest, do quickly,[20] that the Law itself might be fulfilled and the karma of your own evil mischief-making may be upon your heads! For this house [of the betrayers of the Lord] shall not be served. And as for me and my house, we will serve the Lord.[21]

Thus, the Lord God, in His great trust for His servant Job, feared not to allow Satan to tempt him in every way.[22] Likewise, we fear not. We hold the hand of the loving and the obedient servant, and we stay and support those who esteem highly the Lord God.

Beloved hearts, take a lesson from my instrumentation as the prophet Samuel. As I did deliver the Word of God unto them as the judgment for their deeds, even so the dispensation is always there that those who turn and serve the Lord are protected by Him. This is a fundamental principle of the Law, beloved hearts, that cannot be turned back by the prophet or the Messenger. For your actions, even as your words, must be either the justification of your cause or the judgment. For by thy words thou art justified, and by thy words thou art condemned.[23]

Therefore, do not consider that the mantle of the office of chela that you wear or the mantle of the Messenger will stand between you and your own transgressions of the Law. Walk humbly in your God. Walk in the path of Truth. Express your sorrow to your own I AM Presence for the petty indulgences and move on to a higher calling without even a moment's self-condemnation, for it will leave you off guard for the next test which comes on the heels of any transgression.

Thus, beloved hearts, there is no condemnation in the Ascended Masters or in Almighty God. And when you bear it upon your own head and heap it upon yourself, you move yourself back at least five to ten thousand years to the era of world condemnation. We are past the dark ages of world condemnation where the Nephilim gods stalked the earth and condemned humanity and condemned even more the lightbearers.

Thus, self-condemnation is the first sin from which we cannot deliver you! You must deliver yourself from this shameful state and know, as Moses has told you, that ye are God's.[24] You belong to God. You are His. And therefore, you are God in manifestation. We expect you to act the part.

Copyright © 1985 Church Universal and Triumphant, Inc.

Blessing of the Messenger's Stump Team and the Congregation of the Righteous

I call now to this altar those who will accompany the Messenger on this trip, that they might also be blessed.

[Members of the Stump team gather at the altar.]

Beloved Alpha, beloved Omega, I, Saint Germain, with Portia, having bowed before your hearts this day, now call forth the original and divine and universal matrix of the sending forth of the knights of the holy quest and the ladies in fulfillment of the office of the Divine Mother.

Therefore, in the name of all who have ever held high the Grail chalice [Messenger holds up the crystal chalice] and followed the mysteries of that Holy Grail unto the internalization of the God flame, in the name of all who have served the Great White Brotherhood, I now send forth by the power of the Sword Excalibur, by the Light of the Eternal One, this fire of my heart for the healing of Camelot, for the transmutation, for the raising up of my bands to fulfill the original purposes of those who have descended from the Son, Jesus Christ, as the seed of Sanat Kumara—those who have gone forth throughout the world bearing the Cup.

Let them now be redeemed, O God—these who go forth in this age, these who have dared to suffer the persecutions for calling themselves knights and ladies of Camelot, who have dared to reveal their identities as the Messengers have, to bear the full scorn of the world.

O God, let the age of Camelot return! Let the age of knighthood and of the Divine Mother return! Let the age of the Grail, by the very heart of thy servant Gabriel, come once again to earth!

And let it be the path unto the West, unto the heart of the Saviouress and Maitreya and Gautama and our Brotherhood. Let it be for the redemption of all devotees who have served in our holy orders throughout all ages. Let it be for the igniting of the world and the enfiring of this earth with the full power and dominion of the Holy Kumaras unto the golden age!

Therefore, I say unto you, knights and ladies of the quest: Be no longer after the flesh. Be ye renewed and exalted in the renewing of the mind, in the conversion of your spirits. Henceforth, walk the earth knowing that the sword of El Morya has touched you and that if you fulfill that spark and remember your allegiance to him and to the will of God which he represents, you will do all those things that you have longed to do in his name. And God will raise you up as you raise Him up, if you forget not your calling and your anointing this day.

Blessed hearts, kneel before your I AM Presence.

Let all Keepers of the Flame worldwide know that the opportunity is given to serve the LORD and the LORD God—and to live. Therefore, as you seek to climb the highest mountain you can climb that is within your given God-potential, somewhere along that mountainous road God will come to you, I will come and I will touch you with this sword and you will know it. And you will know that strong and sure effort brings new opportunity and the quickening.

How else shall we quicken hearts unless hearts be quickened? Therefore, be quickened.

[Saint Germain touches the crown of each Stump-team member with the Sword Excalibur.]

O LORD our God, be with us in the hour and in the hour of the fulfillment of thy promises.

Knights and ladies of the flame, I send you forth upon a mission! Let God fulfill His mighty purposes through you and work His wondrous works. For the miracles are tumbling down from the very being of Arcturus.

Thus may you understand the Word made flesh. Thus may you understand the flesh transcended and transmuted by the Word. Thus may you understand the mounting of the spiral staircase of the degrees to the entering in to the eternal Life by the door ajar to the etheric octaves and our retreats.

I have stepped through that door down to this octave this day. By and by, you shall step up and know the meaning of universal Life and Oneness—as heaven and earth are one and earth is dissolved in heaven and heaven does saturate earth. And the Sun shall shine forever and forever.

Rise now and let us go to. All ye who attend in this hour are blessed. Rise, then, for your mission is no less worthy and no less divinely ordained. When you perceive the true meaning of your mantle, then you will awaken in the likeness of that mantle.

In the name of the Ancient of Days, I send you forth, conquering ones in Spirit and Matter. Let all things be unto you according to Christ. In his name, in the name of the entire Spirit of the Great White Brotherhood, Amen.

Copyright © 1985 Church Universal and Triumphant, Inc.

Send-off of the Messenger's Stump to the Nations 147

But One Wish

My beloved, I have but one wish this day. That is to sing with you to my beloved Portia, by whose hand and heart the dispensation of Justice unto the nations through the heart of the Messenger is come. Without Justice, beloved hearts, Freedom cannot prosper. For Freedom grows only in the garden of Justice.

Therefore, legions of Justice, come forth now. Bind all movements and every consciousness of injustice, and let the full flowering of my beloved Portia be in the earth as a cosmic, universal sense of Justice, as The LORD Our Righteousness[25] does descend into each one's temple.

Thus, I, Saint Germain, step through the veil through the heart of Justice. When Justice does prevail, when Justice is adored, when Justice becomes the allegiance of all, you will see me as never before in all the earth.

Therefore, let us sing to the flame of Justice.

[The Messenger and congregation sing "Beloved Goddess of Justice," song 422, and "Love's Opportunity," song 240, from *The Summit Lighthouse Book of Songs.*]

"**The Summit Lighthouse Sheds Its Radiance O'er All the World to Manifest as Pearls of Wisdom.**" This dictation by Saint Germain was delivered through the Messenger Elizabeth Clare Prophet on Sunday, February 10, 1985, at Camelot. (1) On February 12, 1985, the Messenger and the Stump team departed on a four-week stumping tour of Australia, the Philippines, and Hawaii. Their itinerary included Sydney, Brisbane, Adelaide, Melbourne, Manila, and Honolulu, where Mother delivered Saint Germain's message for the Coming Revolution in Higher Consciousness and on the Lost Arts of Healing to enthusiastic and record-breaking audiences. She sealed the servants of God in their foreheads (Rev. 7:3) with the Emerald Matrix and received several thousand souls for the laying on of hands and healing invocations. On four weekends, in Sydney, Melbourne, Manila and Honolulu, the staff with Rev. Susan Elizabeth Krister presented the Inner Workshops on: The Science of the Spoken Word; Sound: The Creative Source; The Lost Years of Jesus; Wholeness through Spiritual Healing; Charting Karma on the Cosmic Clock; Our World Destiny in the Aquarian Age; and Twin Flames in Love. During the trip the Messenger and Rev. Krister made numerous TV and radio appearances, introducing millions to Saint Germain's message on freedom, the violet flame, and the Lost Arts of Healing. (2) Rev. 6:1–8. (3) Matt. 24:27, 28. (4) See Gautama Buddha and Sanat Kumara, December 31, 1984, "Gentle Hearts and Gentle Candles," "The Turning Point of Life on Earth: A Dispensation of the Solar Logoi," *Pearls of Wisdom*, vol. 28, no. 6, p. 60, pars. 2–5. (5) In recent months, the Labor Party government of New Zealand's Prime Minister David Lange (elected July 1984) has banned all nuclear-powered and nuclear-armed ships from its harbors, thereby threatening the 1951 Australia–New Zealand–United States defense alliance, the ANZUS treaty. Since it is U.S. policy not to disclose whether or not its warships are nuclear-armed, the ban effectively applies to all U.S. Navy ships capable of carrying nuclear weapons. Prime Minister Lange, who contends that New Zealand can avoid becoming a target in time of war by keeping its territory free of nuclear weapons, has said that his government will deny access to U.S. warships if the United States refuses to guarantee that they are not equipped with nuclear arms. In late January, New Zealand denied permission for the American destroyer *Buchanan* to make a port call during ANZUS military exercises scheduled for March. The U.S. retaliated by withdrawing from the exercises (known as Sea Eagle I-85) and subsequent training maneuvers involving New Zealand. According to reports, the U.S. has also blocked New Zealand from receiving top-level intelligence on the Soviet Union. Lange stresses that his policy is "anti-nuclear, not anti-American," but says: "We do not wish to have nuclear weapons on New Zealand soil or in our harbors. We do not ask, we do not expect, the United States to come to New Zealand's assistance with nuclear weapons or to present American nuclear capability as a deterrent to an attacker." A second threat to the ANZUS alliance came through Australian Prime Minister Robert Hawke in early February. Hawke announced that because of strong opposition in his government he would have to withdraw his previous offer to allow U.S. aircraft to use an Australian staging base to monitor MX missile tests later this year. According to Secretary of State George P. Schultz, the United States will proceed with plans to test the MX in the South Pacific, but "without the use of Australian support arrangements." (6) The twelve sons of Jacob were the ancestors of the twelve tribes of Israel: Reuben, Simeon, Levi, Judah, Dan, Naphtali, Gad, Asher, Issachar, Zebulun, Joseph, and Benjamin. Joseph, the eleventh and most favored son, was an incarnation of Jesus Christ. His sons, Ephraim and Manasseh, were blessed by Jacob as his own, thereby forming two half-tribes. The seed of Ephraim and Manasseh reincarnated in the British Isles, then the United States, and are to be found generally among the English-speaking peoples of the world. The other eleven tribes reincarnated to form the European nations, including Russia, and many were scattered to the four corners of the earth, embodying today in every race and nation. See Gen. 41:50–52; 46:20; 48. (7) Deut. 30:19. (8) Matt. 13:33; Luke 13:21. (9) Isa. 7:14; 9:6, 7; Matt. 1:22, 23. (10) Acts 4:10–12; Eph. 2:20; I Pet. 2:6, 7. (11) Isa. 30:20, 21. (12) On February 3, 1985, Archangel Michael announced "the descent of the replica of the forcefield of the Court of the Sacred Fire over Los Angeles" and, concurrently, "the descent of the etheric matrix of the New Jerusalem." See "The Summoning: Straight Talk and a Sword from the Hierarch of Banff," *Pearls of Wisdom*, vol. 28, no. 10. (13) *New Year's Light of the World Conference, Pearls of Wisdom*, vol. 28, nos. 5–7: Vesta, January 1, 1985, "New Love," p. 69, pars. 2, 4, 5. Gautama Buddha and Sanat Kumara, December 31, 1984, "Gentle Hearts and Gentle Candles," "The Turning Point of Life on Earth: A Dispensation of the Solar Logoi," p. 59, par. 7; p. 60, par. 4. Archangel Jophiel, December 31, 1984, "Qualifying World Teachers to Dispense the Illumination of the New Age," p. 45, pars. 2, 3, 5; p. 47, pars. 5, 6; p. 53, pars. 1–3. (14) On August 21, 1983, Philippine opposition leader Benigno S. Aquino was assassinated upon his arrival at Manila International Airport. Seconds later, Rolando Galman, the alleged hit man, was shot and killed. The assassination shocked the nation and instigated a year of protests against President Ferdinand E. Marcos, who had jailed Aquino in 1972 on charges of subversion and murder. After nearly eight years in solitary confinement, Aquino had been released to go to the United States for heart surgery, where he spent three years in self-exile. Upon his return to the Philippines, Aquino intended to unify the anti-Marcos opposition and challenge the president in the May 1984 parliamentary elections. Based on the report of a five-member citizens panel which investigated the case, special prosecutor Bernardo Fernandez indicted twenty-five military personnel and one civilian for conspiring to kill Aquino and Galman or for participation in a cover-up attempt. Among those charged was Gen. Fabian Ver, armed forces chief of staff. On December 26, 1984, twelve leading opponents of Marcos signed a "declaration of unity," vowing to seek a new constitution and the legalization of the Communist Party should any of them succeed Marcos as president. The declaration, which would become the platform of a new government, also calls for the removal of U.S. military bases in order to establish the Philippines and other Southeast Asian nations as a "zone of peace and neutrality." This would affect Clark Air Base and Subic Bay Naval Base— two of America's key military installations. Both are about sixty miles north of Manila and are crucial to the United States' defense posture in the Pacific. From these two facilities, the U.S. counters Soviet military buildup in the Pacific and Indian oceans. Another source of increased tensions since the Aquino assassination has been the movement for a "protracted people's war" led by the New People's Army (NPA)—a group of 5,000 to 10,000 Communist guerrilla insurgents rapidly attracting new members, despite all efforts by the Marcos regime to crush it. (15) Kuthumi, November 18, 1984, "The Light of Winter Solstice," *Pearls of Wisdom*, vol. 27, no. 58, p. 518, pars. 2–5; p. 519, pars. 1–3; p. 523, par. 4. (16) See Saint Germain, November 22, 1980, "The Watchman of the Night," *A Prophecy of Karma to Earth and Her Evolutions* (*Pearls of Wisdom*, vol. 23, no. 48), p. 325, par. 1; p. 326, par. 4. (17) Matt. 10:6; 15:24. (18) Saint Germain was embodied as the Prophet Samuel, who anointed Saul as the first king of Israel and David, the son of Jesse, as his successor. Samuel (whose name means "asked of God" or "name of God") was the last of the Judges and the initiator of the prophetic order in Israel. True to tradition, the Ascended Master Saint Germain anointed Gen. George Washington as the first president of the United States (see the legend of "The Wissahikon," "The Consecration of the Deliverer," in *Washington and His Generals,* by George Lippard [Philadelphia: G.B. Zieber and Co., 1847], pp. 86–99). Saint Germain also anointed Godfre Ray King as his Messenger. As a meditation upon Samuel's life and the heart of Saint Germain, the Messenger read I Samuel 1:9–3:21; 12 in preparation for the dictation. (19) Ezek. 37:1–14. (20) John 13:27. (21) Josh. 24:15. (22) Job 1:6–12; 2:1–6. (23) Matt. 12:37. (24) Exod. 6:6–8; 29:45, 46; Lev. 11:44, 45; 26:12, 13; Pss. 82:6; John 10:34. (25) Jer. 23:5, 6; 33:15, 16.

Copyright © 1985 Church Universal and Triumphant, Inc., Box A, Malibu, CA 90265. All rights reserved. Printed in the United States of America. Pearls of Wisdom and The Summit Lighthouse are registered trademarks of Church Universal and Triumphant, Inc. All rights to their use are reserved. Published by The Summit Lighthouse. Pearls sent weekly (to USA, via third-class mail) for a minimum love offering of $40/year.

The Lord's Promise of Deliverance
A Sermon to the People of the Philippines
by Elizabeth Clare Prophet

I am going to read to you a great message of freedom and God's justice from the heart of the prophet Isaiah.[1] Please remember that the message is applicable to the hour.

It is a promise of deliverance unto the people but, as you will hear, the *deliverance*—the *desire* for deliverance, the *demand* for deliverance from Almighty God—places upon each one of us as individuals supreme testings and responsibilities, an acute sensitivity to the inner voice of God and the allegiance to that voice as the instrument of our ultimate victory.

Behold, the Lord's hand—*the hand of the I AM THAT I AM*—**is not shortened that it cannot save, neither his ear heavy that it cannot hear. But your iniquities have separated between you and your God, and your sins have hid his face from you that he will not hear.**

Thus, when we ponder the burdens upon this nation in the government and in the economy that are so burdensome upon the people, and we look and we point the finger to this or that cause or this or that person, we must hearken unto the Lord and look within first, find the strength of Almighty God and cast out the enemy from within the personal psyche and the soul.

God does not tell us that our leaders stand between us and Him, but our own iniquities. And these are our karma—the accumulation of causes we have set in motion by our words and our works or by our neglect thereof. This buildup, this momentum of sins, must now be washed clean by obedience and love and the violet flame and the understanding that as we decree daily God fulfills His promise **After those days . . . I will**

remember their sin no more. (Jer. 31:33, 34)

Let us welcome the purging Light of the sacred fire, the baptism of the Holy Ghost, the baptism of the Lord Jesus Christ. Let the fire try our works, every man's works, of what sort they are.[2] And so, let those works that are not acceptable to the living Christ within us be burned—let them be consumed. Let this house serve the Lord. As Joshua said in his farewell address: **As for me and my house, we will serve the Lord.** (Josh. 24:15)

Let all of your members, all of the components of the flowing stream of your consciousness, converge at the point of your I AM Presence. Thus present yourself the living vessel, the receptacle, the sacrifice for the saving of this nation. One with God is the majority. And when God is in you, no tyrant may prevail in any land.

And so God speaks to His people and He tells them why they are vulnerable to the burden of the enemy without or within—the oppressors, foreign invasions, and armies that overcame Israel and Judah—why they are vulnerable to that sort of manipulation and violence. They must look to their hearts and be converted once again to God. And then the hosts of the Lord, the Mighty I AM Presence personified in Sanat Kumara, will come and deliver them through the call, through the spoken Word, through the pure heart.

For your hands are defiled with blood and your fingers with iniquity; your lips have spoken lies, your tongue hath muttered perverseness.

None calleth for Justice, nor any pleadeth for Truth. They trust in vanity and speak lies; they conceive mischief and bring forth iniquity.

Thus, if the leaders are corrupt, ought the people to follow them in the ways of the corruption of the soul and the little child? Nay, let the people be the example! And therefore, by stark contrast, let the leaders be put to shame. Let the people demand by the cosmic honor flame that their leaders conform to that honor.

Where is the standard, if it not be the standard of Christ in we the people in every nation upon earth? Thus, when we uphold it and we see the union of that Christ, nothing can divide us. Let us not be divided as we stand for Truth, for only in the Union will we overcome the enemy.

They hatch cockatrice' eggs and weave the spider's web. He that eateth of their eggs dieth and that which is crushed breaketh out into a viper.

Thus, the consciousness of evil begets more of the consciousness of evil in the land. And the depression in the economy produces immorality and depravity in the people, and so we descend to new lows of self-degradation. And yet, we still complain that our problems are the fault of our leaders.

Our leaders are the reflection of the corrosion of the soul. When the soul returns to grace and diligently finds that Light, the Light itself will consume the Darkness and be the very judgment of those who have betrayed the nation.

Let the responsibility be upon the shoulders of the Christ in the heart of each and every one. For it is written, **The government shall be upon His shoulder.** (Isa. 9:6) Let us see to it, therefore, that we look not to this saviour or that saviour or to flesh and blood to lead us or to this or that political ideology or economic system. For the center of the Light is the Principle, and by this sign we conquer.

Thus, we are divided, and we must not be divided, for it is a conspiracy to divide and conquer. And therefore, let us not succumb. Let us be wise and let us build upon a common foundation.

Their webs shall not become garments, neither shall they cover themselves with their works: their works are works of iniquity and the act of violence is in their hands.

Wherever violence is this day, so let it be judged by Almighty God and let the judgment descend!

Their feet run to evil and they make haste to shed innocent blood: their thoughts are thoughts of iniquity; wasting and destruction are in their paths.

Where there is the shedding of innocent blood this day in this land, let the judgment of Almighty God descend! Let the oneness of the I AM Presence with us release now the sacred fire for the consuming, then, of the terror in the land.

The way of peace they know not, and there is no judgment in their goings. They have made them crooked paths: whosoever goeth therein shall not know peace.

Therefore, in the name of the LORD, we say, **Woe unto the pastors who destroy and scatter the sheep of my pasture!**[3]

In the name of Jesus Christ, Peace, be still! Peace, be still! Peace, be still! Peace, be still!

I call upon the four cosmic forces this day. I call upon the mighty wind of the Holy Spirit for the cleansing and the purification of the minds and hearts of this nation. From the top to the bottom, from the bottom to the top, let all men know the LORD!

Let them fear the I AM THAT I AM and let them care for Him in the heart, the mind, and the body of every little child in this nation!

And let the Brotherhood of Light in the Philippines now be galvanized into a unity of compassion that intensifies to a Love that becomes an all-consuming fire. And let all hate and hate creation be *bound* now by the seven mighty archangels!

Archangels of the LORD, I invoke thy presence here this day for the deliverance of this nation and this people. According to the prophecy and the Word of the LORD through Isaiah, let it be done! Let it be done in the name of the Cosmic Virgin and Saint Germain and Jesus Christ! Amen.

Therefore is judgment far from us, neither doth justice overtake us. We wait for light, but behold obscurity; for brightness, but we walk in darkness.

We grope for the wall like the blind and we grope as if we had no eyes. We stumble at noon day as in the night; we are in desolate places as dead men.

We roar all like bears and mourn sore like doves. We look for judgment but there is none, for salvation but it is far off from us.

For our transgressions are multiplied before Thee and our sins testify against us. For our transgressions are with us and as for our iniquities, we know them, in transgressing and lying against the LORD—*the Mighty I AM Presence*—and departing away from our God, speaking oppression and revolt, conceiving and uttering from the heart words of falsehood.

And judgment is turned away backward and justice standeth afar off, for truth is fallen in the street and equity cannot enter.

Yea, truth faileth and he that departeth from evil maketh himself a prey. And the LORD saw it and it displeased him that there was no judgment in the land.

And he saw that there was no man and wondered that there was no intercessor. Therefore his arm brought salvation unto him, and his righteousness, it sustained him.

For he put on righteousness as a breastplate and an helmet of salvation upon his head; and he put on the garments of vengeance for clothing and was clad with zeal as a cloak.

According to their deeds, accordingly he will repay, fury to his adversaries, recompence to his enemies; to the islands he will repay recompence.

So shall they fear the name of the LORD—*I AM THAT I AM*—from the west and his glory from the rising of the sun. When

The Lord's Promise of Deliverance

the enemy shall come in like a flood, the Spirit of the Lord shall lift up a standard against him.

And the Redeemer shall come to Zion and unto them that turn from transgression in Jacob, saith the Lord—*the Mighty I AM Presence.*

As for me, this is my covenant with them, saith the Lord—*the Mighty I AM Presence.* My Spirit that is upon thee and my words which I have put in thy mouth shall not depart out of thy mouth, nor out of the mouth of thy seed, nor out of the mouth of thy seed's seed, saith the Lord—*the I AM THAT I AM*—from henceforth and forever.

Therefore, the people of Light hear the prophecy. They confirm the Word by the dynamic decree, the prayer, the meditation, the affirmation, and the fiat:

They Shall Not Pass! They Shall Not Pass! They Shall Not Pass!

Let your prayers invoke the fulfillment of these promises of the Lord. Let your light and your heart come into conformity with the grace of living Truth, and you will see what power God will place in your heart, what a Union He will forge and how He will assemble you together for the coming day of righteousness and of the judgment of the oppressor.

And therefore, the prophet foretold this day of the coming of the Light and he said:

Arise, shine, for thy Light is come and the glory of the Lord is risen upon thee!

And the glory of the Lord the Mighty I AM Presence is Christ, the beloved Christ Self, the Universal One that hovers above you now. Reach out your hand and clasp the hand of your Holy Christ Self and hold it firmly. So near is God unto you this day.

For, behold, the darkness shall cover the earth, and gross darkness the people, but the Lord—*the I AM THAT I AM*—shall arise upon thee and his glory shall be seen upon thee....

Violence shall no more be heard in thy land, wasting nor destruction within thy borders; but thou shalt call thy walls Salvation and thy gates Praise.

The sun shall be no more thy light by day; neither for brightness shall the moon give light unto thee, but the Lord—*the I AM Presence*—shall be unto thee an everlasting Light, and thy God thy glory.

Thy sun shall no more go down; neither shall thy moon withdraw itself. For the Lord shall be thine everlasting Light and the days of thy mourning shall be ended.

Thy people also shall be all righteous. They shall inherit the land forever, the branch of my planting, the work of my hands, that I may be glorified.

God desires to be glorified in you—His handiwork. So glorify Him, for He has promised:

A little one shall become a thousand, and a small one a strong nation: I the LORD will hasten it in his time.

Thus is the promise. Thus, the sons and daughters of God implement the promises of the Father by the science of the spoken Word.

When you devote your life to God, your beloved I AM Presence sends forth the Light of Christ. Christ descends upon you, he fills all of your house with Light, and you hear that Christ speak in your heart. You are emboldened by his Spirit, you have the fervor and the courage to stand for freedom in the land, and you hear him say in your heart the words that Jesus preached taken from the book of Isaiah: **The Spirit of the Lord GOD is upon me...**

This is your Christ Self speaking now in your heart:

The Spirit of the Lord GOD is upon me because the LORD hath anointed me to preach good tidings unto the meek, he hath sent me to bind up the brokenhearted... Therefore I *shall* bind up the brokenhearted!... to proclaim liberty to the captives and the opening of the prison to them that are bound.

Let Christ open the prison doors this day! Let them that are bound for Christ be loosed by the power of God in us and in all eternity.

The Spirit of the Lord GOD is upon me... to proclaim the acceptable year of the LORD and the day of vengeance of our God; to comfort all that mourn; to appoint unto them that mourn in Zion, to give unto them beauty for ashes, the oil of joy for mourning, the garment of praise for the spirit of heaviness; that they might be called trees of righteousness, the planting of the LORD, that he might be glorified.

In the name of the Father, the Son, the Holy Spirit, and the Mother, Amen.

"The Summit Lighthouse Sheds Its Radiance O'er All the World to Manifest as Pearls of Wisdom." This sermon was delivered by the Messenger Elizabeth Clare Prophet on March 3, 1985, prior to the dictation, "The LORD's Prophecy unto the Philippines," by Saint Germain in Manila, the Philippines. (1) Isa. 59; 60:1, 2, 18–22; 61:1–3. (2) I Cor. 3:13–15. (3) Jer. 23:1.

Copyright © 1985 Church Universal and Triumphant, Inc., Box A, Malibu, CA 90265. All rights reserved. Printed in the United States of America. Pearls of Wisdom and The Summit Lighthouse are registered trademarks of Church Universal and Triumphant, Inc. All rights to their use are reserved. Published by The Summit Lighthouse. Pearls sent weekly (to USA, via third-class mail) for a minimum love offering of $40/year.

The Lord's Prophecy unto the Philippines
by Saint Germain
Delivered by the Messenger Elizabeth Clare Prophet

Ladies and gentlemen, heart flames of the great Light of Freedom, I, Saint Germain, will not withhold my blessing from this people and this land!

Therefore, I come today and I speak to your very heart, grateful for the instrument—your Messenger and mine. For I have anointed her to deliver unto you the prophecy of the LORD and the flame of freedom from my heart by which, if you take it and run with it as torchbearers in the night, you will discover what wonders the LORD God will work for you in this nation.

I Have Heard the Cries of My People

Therefore know, as you call to me, Saint Joseph, that I have heard. And I have heard the cries of my people and I know the truth in this nation. So does the Messenger know the truth. And therefore, fear not, for the hearts of Light the world around are made one by the very rosary of the heart of praise of the Blessed Virgin.

Understand the meaning of the oneness worldwide of the freedom-fighters of the nations. Understand the power of peace and of the sword to cut free those who are bound by the cords of injustice and iniquity.

People of God, know that the prophecies are told and they are true. If you would be delivered from the toiler, you must deliver yourself from the toiler within—from the burden of personal selfishness and indulgence and the absence of the true fervor of sacrifice that must be made in order to galvanize a nation.

Beloved hearts, you are not helpless. And no power within

or without, no foreign power—no matter how powerful—when misused, may turn back the time and the tide of freedom, whose destiny of every nation is in the hand of God.

Understand the meaning of the power of God and fear not the powers of this world. Fear indeed those who can destroy the soul in hell, but do not fear those who think they kill you when they kill the body, for they only destroy themselves.

Nevertheless, they shall not pass!

The Warning of God

It is the God-determination of the hosts of the LORD who stand with you to do all in our power to help you. But if you fail to heed the warning of God, to take the mighty teaching and the rod of power of the science of the Word, we then will be bound not to enter. It is the force of oneness, of love, of prayer, of purity of heart, and one-pointedness that has won every victory, spiritual or physical, in all history.

Let us not indulge ourselves as those who should set a better example do, indulging themselves in pleasure and in the love of money, which is the root of all evil—not money but the *love* of money. Beloved hearts, set the example! For this is a nation in mourning for the torture of her people, for the violence and the terror by night. And therefore we mourn, and I mourn with you. And therefore, let us play the part and let us understand the meaning of mourning, which is to take upon ourselves the sins and the karma of the nation and to submit it daily to the violet flame.

We are burdened by the sadness of the betrayal of our people by our people. Thus, beloved hearts, each and every man in this nation this day, by the presence of the holy angels, does stand accountable before the LORD God Almighty. Let there be the renewal of the understanding of the presence and the power of the LORD's hosts with the true Israel—who is the seed of Christ which has descended and reincarnated in every nation, for so were they scattered on the whole face of the earth.

Archangel Michael at Your Side

Blessed hearts of Light developing the sense of the power of Archangel Michael at your side and the power of the call you give—

> Lord Michael before, Lord Michael behind,
> Lord Michael to the right, Lord Michael to the left,
> Lord Michael above, Lord Michael below,
> Lord Michael, Lord Michael, wherever I go!
> I AM his love protecting here!—

The Lord's Prophecy unto the Philippines

do you know the meaning of having Saint Michael the Archangel at your hand? This mighty archangel brings with him not thousands but millions of angels! And they bear swords of blue flame and shields. And they come to bind the devils and the demons that are invisible, except you see the effects of the chaos which they have wrought.

Who Will Rescue the Children?

Beloved hearts, chaos is in the land and it is high time that a movement be born for the rescue of the little children who are abused, misused, and sold early in life into prostitution. Beloved ones, when a nation desecrates the little child, what is there left of human dignity? For the child is always holy. The child is the vessel of the Manchild and is the one who comes bearing truly the Light of Christ—the infant who shall become the Son of God.

Let mothers and fathers and teachers and all those who serve as their representatives in government hear my call! For that nation shall not be spared which does not value the life and the body of the little child. Let not one of these be lost. For when you ignore this problem, you betray the child within your own heart—and that child is Christ.

Who has left Jesus? Who has left him for Herod's henchmen? I was the one who was visited by an angel of the LORD, and we fled in the night and retired to Egypt when the male babies were slain.

Beloved ones, they feared the coming of the Christ. And you ought to fear the coming of the Christ! You look for a liberator. You look for a deliverer. Well, look to the little child! Will that child, so abused, then rise up in the dignity of self-worth to deliver a nation, whose nation has already destroyed him and his sense of self-worth, which only lies in making merchandise of his body?

Beloved ones, this is the karma upon the nation. There ought to be torchlight demonstrations in this land for the little child and the casting out of those who come from around the world to enjoy the pleasures of these little children! Is this the kind of tourism you will put up with?

You cannot go your way any longer. This is a crime and a sin. And let those who are responsible be accountable this day! For I, Saint Germain, will walk the streets of this city and this land. And I will place my mantle upon these children, and it is an aura of Light. I may give them the spiritual Light, but who will rescue them physically? Who will be the flame of freedom that begins to build the foundations of a nation in the heart of the little child?

The Burden of Neglect

So understand the burden and the difficulty. Understand that the burden of your neglect makes very difficult your salvation by the hosts of the Lord. Thus, how can we neglect so great a salvation?

Let the moneychangers be cast out of the government of this nation and its banking houses and its economy and its brothels and its gambling casinos!

Beloved hearts, do you understand that the fire of absolute one-pointed dedication to the truth of eternal Life must be the rock upon which you stand? And from that rock and by that rock you conquer.

It is very easy to become lethargic and to say, "We can do nothing! We are bound. We dare not. We dare not speak...," though many dare speak and therefore suffer martyrdom. When you assign to this or that flesh-and-blood individual the enemy or the devil, you then become irresponsible, your own sins are minimized, and it is almost a fatalism, waiting for the end. Let it not be so. Never was there a greater moment for action.

Your Cause Is in the Power of the Spoken Word

What can you do? I say your cause is in the power of the spoken Word. You feel my power and I anchor it in your souls and heart. So do the mighty angels. Take the seed of Light. Fan it by the sacred fire and the holy breath. Fan it by love and fervor!

Rise in the morning, rise an hour early, and give that hour as a sacrifice unto God. Take the little book of decrees, raise the right hand and give the call of judgment. For the judgment of the Lord is a two-edged sword. It always divides the Real from the unreal. And the unreal must stand aside, and you may see what that unreality is—what that illusion is. And all may see and know [and choose this day whom they will serve: the Real or the unreal].

And the binding power of the Lord will come upon you with such a miracle and such a devastation unto those who identify with illusion that you will truly believe in the One Sent and the miracles of God and that the armies of heaven have never left off from defending the legions of Light on earth.

Hymn to the Sun

Thus, beloved ones, at the hour of the dawn, face the sun. Call to God in the person of Helios and Vesta. Draw the light and the breath of the sun into your heart as you say:

Helios and Vesta!
Helios and Vesta!
Helios and Vesta!
Let the Light flow into my being!
Let the Light expand in the center of my heart!
Let the Light expand in the center of the earth
And let the earth be transformed into the New Day!
Let the Philippines be transformed into the New Day!
Let my heart, my family, my life, and this city,
    its government and economy be transformed
into the New Day!

God will enter your temple and speak these words through you—words of a mighty deliverance, beloved. And the power of the spoken Word will begin to be noticed as change, for freedom is a power of change and a power to move.

Trust in the violet flame and know that when you open your mouth and affirm that violet flame and that call and the calls given to you, I will be instantaneously in your room. I give you the promise that Jesus gave: Wherever two or three are gathered in my name, there am I in the midst thereof.

I am particularly and peculiarly involved in the destiny of the freedom of the nations, for God has given to me the dispensation to propagate freedom. And it begins with a free government and the sacred freedoms and the people's demands not only for human rights but for divine rights.

Human rights are only the beginning. They are a foundation. But the divine rights may not be gainsaid, beloved hearts. The divine rights must be called forth and you must understand the interpretation of the Word! You must understand that I speak to your hearts! Listen, for I transmit a fire unto you in this hour.

Beloved children of the Sun, return to the ancient calling. Return now to the quickening of your hearts, for I demand the fealty to Almighty God. The promises are as they have been from the beginning. Serve the LORD, obey His commandments, invoke the sacred fire, and He will deliver thee.

A Revolution in Higher Consciousness

The teaching of the new age is at hand. And my deliverance of the flame of freedom to the nations, beloved ones, does effect the understanding of religion as well as science, as well as self-government. Therefore realize that the wine of the Holy Spirit— its fiery baptism, its violet flame—does now permeate all of the religious institutions of the world. And a revolution in Higher

Consciousness is truly the way of the sponsors of heaven.

You face adversaries and conditions—world conditions, the imminence of war everywhere, and much worse: plague and famine and death and the dissolution of nations. These challenges must be met with dispensations of Light that exceed the prior dispensations. Thus, avail yourself of the teachings of the Ascended Masters and the Everlasting Gospel.

Take note that the people's misunderstanding and misapprehension of the message of Jesus Christ, whether through ignorance or whether through a conscious manipulation by their leaders—whatever—has not afforded them the means or the ability to deliver themselves from their conquerors or from their diseases. Therefore, realize that more Light and more enlightenment is the requirement if people are to seek God and discover in Him the solution to the world's problems.

It is the application of the Law which is wanting. The Light has ever been the same, but the understanding of that Light in your heart and being and soul has not been taught, alas, as it should be taught. And therefore, because it seems as though God does not answer prayer, men's faith has waned and they do not see that God and His Light and His Law is applicable to the human dilemma in the very streets of life.

And this failure to bring that Light into the very streets and into your hearts to challenge these conditions is the cause and core that we face today. It is the gap—the gap between the cause and the effect, the source and the solution to very dire problems.

The Darjeeling Council of the Great White Brotherhood

In the name of Mother Mary, I come. For she has called me and she has said, "Surely, Saint Germain, you will not leave this people without a challenge and direction and the promise and the comfort of our hearts."

We represent the Darjeeling Council of the Great White Brotherhood—a council of Ascended Masters in the etheric plane over Darjeeling, India. The Ascended Master El Morya, whom you call Saint Thomas More, heads this council. This body exists for the training up of leaders in every nation.

You may apply to us when you take your rest at night. As your final prayer, ask your guardian angels to be taken to [to take you to] the Darjeeling Council, and there receive our wisdom and our understanding. And it will come to you when you awaken or after many days, perhaps not as a distinct memory but as the pressing through of Light and direction and an inner knowing of what is to be done and what is the realm of the possible.

We admonish you to seek, therefore, that which is most possible in the moment and then proceed with the more difficult. Be practical in your ways. Be careful. Be careful and guard thy life with prudence and divine discrimination. For we desire Keepers of the Flame *in embodiment,* and we do not encourage martyrdom but wisdom and a strategy of spiritual Light to face all of the foes and the common enemies of man, which surely are not confined to these borders.

A Prophecy Which Only You Can Fulfill

Thus, beloved, look then for the preservation of the holy innocence of the child, and the innocence shall return to the nation and the flame fountain of purity shall rise in her midst. And thus it shall come to pass that an ancient people—yourselves—descended from the long-lost continent of Lemuria shall once again restore the Light and the golden age.

This is not a psychic prediction. This is a prophecy which only you can fulfill. God and His hosts reveal the divine plan and tell you that this is your destiny. But you have free will. Only you can fulfill your destiny!

It is clear that Christ Jesus desired all to see the choices of free will. Therefore, he selected one among the twelve to be the betrayer. And he hung himself for his betrayal, whilst Christ was resurrected as the Saviour of the world.

See, then, that there are betrayers of the Light and betrayers of freedom, and there are its champions. Play your role well, beloved hearts, for you shall meet your God not only in the hour of death but this day and every day. For it is the day of vengeance of our God, and the karmic cycles do return to each one's doorstep swiftly, as causes set in motion.

Your Decrees Are Our Authority to Step into Your Life

Therefore, watch—watch for the signs of the LORD and His Law outpictured. Study the Law and become one with it. Meditate upon the law of the spoken Word and shout that decree from the housetops! For your decrees are our authority to step into your life, and no task or problem is too insignificant.

Therefore, do not be cursed by the false concept that you do not want to bother Saint Germain or Mother Mary or Jesus with the problem at hand. We are only troubled (not bothered) when you neglect to make the call. For then we cannot give to you the divine solution which is always there.

God Will Not Fail You When You Do Not Fail Him

World movements of totalitarianism active today, beloved hearts, surely do prey upon the people's fear and doubt, which must be replaced now by a living faith that God will not fail you when you do not fail Him. This is my message. This is my comfort. This is my encouragement.

The people who love freedom in this nation are far greater in number than the original few who defended the United States or staged the Boston Tea Party and fought a revolution of Light. Is it numbers, then? Nay, it is not numbers! But it is a quickening of hearts, a determination to put all other considerations aside and to unite in the one flame of God.

So long as you are divided in the solution, how can we use you, the cracked vessel, for the fulfilling of the deliverance? Thus, let man propose, and heaven will dispose.

We are your Elder Brothers and Sisters, not magicians, though you have called us such. We may act only within the law of the will of God and cosmic law. Otherwise we may not intervene. We may not commit any act of injustice. We may not answer prayers that call for vengeance or the death of the enemy. We answer the prayer that asks for the will of God to be done swiftly, that justice be restored.

Thus, beloved hearts, the death wish is not a prayer of Light, but it is black magic. And that which you wish upon another will return unto you. Therefore, Moses said in his final sermon, "Choose Life, not Death." For Life itself, when it intensifies, delivers the judgment unto the death consciousness. And it is the death consciousness that will die, not merely in one individual but in all individuals in a nation.

See, then, that your hearts become the altar of the living God, and go before the high priest of that altar in the Holy of Holies—the beloved Christ Self. Offer fruits meet for repentance and prayers worthy of a son and daughter of God. Let superstition be dissolved! And let the Holy Church itself come into the New Day, for its house must also be swept clean of those who misuse the Light of the sacred fire.

Remember the Prophecy of Fátima

Thus, remember the prophecy of Fátima whereby God and His saints are not even permitted to protect the Church when there is corruption within. So it is true of your soul. So it is true of the nation.

If your leaders have left your nation vulnerable to destruction by their corruption, will you do the same? ["No!"] Thus, let this corruptible put on incorruption! Let this mortal put on immortality! And walk in the dignity of the hosts of the LORD and know that thy deliverer is nigh and at the very door.

There shall not one be left who shall not give accounting for his thought and feeling, his word and his work. Therefore, fear the Law and the LORD, not with anxiety but with the love and the security that knows that the Law is just and will repay. And you are the instruments of that justice.

Therefore, hasten its day by your word and your work, for the time is short, as certain of your leaders have told you. They have known and seen the handwriting on the wall. And I tell you, this nation hangs true today solely by the long-suffering of her people and their patience and their love and their inner Light. And thus, the beautiful hearts of Light by the millions who gather here are surely gathered for a great victory.

Truly, beloved, the Light shall not betray thee. We shall not leave thee. Thus, do not betray the Light.

This is the meaning of the cooperation of heaven and earth. This is the meaning of the Great White Brotherhood. It is the fraternity of saints Above and below who move together. And those below know they are the instrument of those Above, and therefore their courage does not wane.

I Go to Minister to the Nation

I take my leave of you, for I go to minister to those who are bound, those who are in prison, those who are in the hospitals. I go to every part of the nation and I send my angels for everyone who has passed from the screen of life in this cause. I take them, and I take them to our retreat of the violet flame and I instruct them. And I shall give them the Light and the understanding. And I shall send them back to you, sponsored by Mother Mary, to reembody—to reincarnate among this people, to rise up again, and to give their lives again—trusting that you will defend the newborn and the little children, trusting that you will see that your deliverers come in the face of the little child.

Thus, I ask you to keep the flame and the cradle of liberty, to protect life, and to know that these souls who come again to live once more again, to give their lives, are counting on you to see to it that when they come they receive proper food and shelter and a teaching in the way of God-government and freedom and respect, that their chakras [spiritual centers of the sacred fire], their Light is not violated by the lusts of those who are nothing but devils in embodiment. And it is high time you awaken to know that there are devils in embodiment who lust after the Light of Christ in your little ones!

Now let us go forth as conquerors and let us slay the dragon in our midst. For the earth must become freedom's star, for the alternative is self-annihilation. There is no middle of the road. There is no other choice but to stand for freedom or to go down into that nothingness of ignominy.

In the Light of the Goddess of Liberty, I, Saint Germain, stand. I will not leave thee! I come with the hosts of the LORD! [applause, standing ovation]

Messenger's Comments Following Saint Germain's Dictation:

Thank you, beloved hearts, for providing this opportunity for Saint Germain not only to address us, but to release his Light to the nation. I am profoundly grateful. In his honor, let us sing "The Flame of Freedom Speaks."

> The Flame of Freedom speaks—
> The Flame of Freedom within each heart.
> The Flame of Freedom saith unto all:

Come apart now and be a separate and chosen people, elect unto God—men who have chosen their election well, who have determined to cast their lot in with the immortals. These are they who have set their teeth with determination, who have said:

> I will never give up
> I will never turn back
> I will never submit
> I will bear the Flame of Freedom unto my victory
> I will bear this flame in honor
> I will sustain the glory of Life within my nation
> I will sustain the glory of Life within my being
>
> I will win my ascension
> I will forsake all idols and
> I will forsake the idol of my outer self
> I will have the glory of my immaculate divinely
>   conceived Self manifesting within me
>
> I AM Freedom and
> I AM determined to be Freedom
> I AM the Flame of Freedom and
> I AM determined to bear it to all
> I AM God's Freedom and He is indeed free
> I AM freed by his Power and his Power is supreme
> I AM fulfilling the purposes of God's kingdom

Copyright © 1985 Church Universal and Triumphant, Inc.

I would like to tell you that as I travel around the world and receive people and listen to their hearts, the two most oft heard prayers are: "Heal me of my fear and doubt" and "Tell me what is my divine plan—what is my mission in life."

I would like to answer this in the following way: To be healed of doubt and fear, you must cast out the coward of the lower self and stand firmly on the Rock of Christ and your meditation in him and with him—knowing his promise: He lives in us and we live in him in one point of Light, which is in this temple.

Your divine plan must be seen in light of the burden of your family and your nation. For your family and your nation is also your karma, and therefore we do not fiddle while Rome burns. We do not look for other diversifications or pursuits of this or that when our people suffer and when our nation must be delivered.

So the divine plan is actually to put on Christ. This may be done in many forms of service to life. We look at the greatest need and we say, "How can I supply it?" Therein we find our mission. We look at the brother and the sister, we look at the nation. We look at our talents and we say, "What can I do best to deliver this people and my beloved ones?"

And therefore, you offer yourself on the altar of the nation and of God, the community and the family, and you begin to supply the needs of others. And you find that others' needs are so much greater than your own that you will not remember that you ever had any fear or any doubt! For the fire of God pouring through you to meet others' needs will cleanse you not only of your fears and doubts, but also of all your diseases and problems.

Sometimes we place too much attention upon ourselves. We need to lose ourselves in concern for one another, nevertheless always retaining the inner dignity of our individuality in God.

I would like to say, then, that as I perceive this city of eight million, the greatest single need we have is to have a center where you can come twenty-four hours a day to pray and to worship—a house of Light. I ask you to deliberate with the Keepers of the Flame here and to see how you can designate so many hours a week to keep that vigil of calls to Archangel Michael to enter this nation.

Tomorrow I will return to the United States and I leave with you all my promise that in every twenty-four-hour cycle I will be crying unto the LORD God for the victory of justice and freedom in every man, woman, and child in this nation. And I shall work with the Filipinos and Filipinas in America who are a part of our organization there, and many whom I do not yet know but whom I will contact for the victory of that freedom. And on both sides of the Pacific, we will take our stand and we will rest confident that our victory will be secured. Thank you. [applause]

Let's sing our song, "O Philippines Awake, I AM THAT I AM." Let's wake up the people to the power of God!

O Philippines, Awake! I AM THAT I AM (7x)
Awake! Awake!

Chorus: O Philippines, Awake! I AM THAT I AM
O Philippines, Awake! I AM THAT I AM
Left, right, O Philippines!
We march by Christ command
Awake, arise, O Philippines!
We come to free this land.

Just as in ancient days
   Awake, put on your strength!
I AM the arm of the Lord
   God's freedom to defend.
Marching with the hosts of Light
   Our freedom's now at hand
Our vict'ry's sure when we trust in God
   He's always in command!

Time now to congregate and
   Fan those freedom flames
Conquer the fallen ones and
   Bind their evil ways.
Awake, put on your sword of fire and
   Slay the dragon cold
Our vict'ry's sure when we trust in God
   To win we must be bold!

March all you chosen ones
   El Morya's at the helm
Ten thousand chosen ones
   Come to protect God's realm
An army of Light—we come to fight
   Arise, come lend a hand!
Our vict'ry's sure when we trust in God
   The name I AM THAT I AM. (Sing chorus twice)

This presentation today has given you the heart and spirit of Saint Germain. I wanted to give you his most recent teaching on the violet flame which was delivered in a dictation in Washington, D.C., in December, published in the 1984 volume of *Pearls of Wisdom*, number 61. It's a very excellent presentation on that violet flame, and I will read it to you when I come back later this afternoon. We will have a healing service and a blessing of those who have not yet received the blessing for healing, so do bring your loved ones.

Thank you again, and God bless you. [applause]

"The Summit Lighthouse Sheds Its Radiance O'er All the World to Manifest as Pearls of Wisdom."
This dictation by Saint Germain was delivered through the Messenger Elizabeth Clare Prophet on Sunday, March 3, 1985, at the Fiesta Island Ministry of Tourism Pavilion, Cultural Center of the Philippines Complex in Manila.
Copyright © 1965, 1978, 1985 Church Universal and Triumphant, Inc., Box A, Malibu, CA 90265. All rights reserved. Printed in the United States of America. Pearls of Wisdom and The Summit Lighthouse are registered trademarks of Church Universal and Triumphant, Inc. All rights to their use are reserved. Published by The Summit Lighthouse. Pearls sent weekly (to USA, via third-class mail) for a minimum love offering of $40/year.

Saint Patrick's Day Address
by Elizabeth Clare Prophet

So thou, O son of man, I have set thee a watchman unto the house of Israel; therefore thou shalt hear the word at my mouth, and warn them from me.   Ezekiel 33

The Example of the Saints

This day of days, March 17, 1985, brings us to that example so noted by Sanat Kumara of beloved Saint Patrick. And therefore, I deliver to you this Summit University lecture on the fire infolding itself in the very heart and life of Saint Patrick.

I deliver it to all the congregation of the righteous upon earth for many important reasons—principally that we must walk in the footsteps of the immortals, that we must see the goal of the ascension as being realized by ourselves—not as an exception to this path of striving but in fulfillment of it.

We see in the life of Jesus Christ and Moses and the prophets and the apostle Paul and the saints who have walked with us these two thousand years, as well as in that of the Masters of the Far East, that there are certain known factors in life and in what we face as we master each of the seven planes of being through the seven chakras.

These are not different, but they are the same tests given to all. They may be clothed in different guises in different centuries, but when it comes down to the moment of Truth, as for the testing, the temptation, and the trials, there are givens and there are knowns.

Therefore, by acquainting ourselves with the lives of the saints, we may know what to anticipate and not be dismayed when we ourselves as chelas, or our leaders or the Ascended

Masters, come under the reproof of the fallen angels upon earth.

It is so essential, according to Saint Germain and to beloved El Morya, to understand our position in history. A long cosmic history precedes us—millions of years. We have been a part of that history. If you would like to hear my remarks on that subject made to Summit University last evening, I would be most happy to have this played for anyone in the community.[1]

It is important that we know as a whole, as a body of God and as a movement, what is the essence and the purpose of each quarter of Summit University. This we can come to understand through the dictations preceding and included in each quarter, and in the teachings given.

All who have been to Summit University and all who are preparing to attend ought to avail themselves of the opportunity of the continuing study which qualifies us as ministering servants, which qualification is by the Holy Spirit—not necessarily by ordination or by officially becoming a minister, but by the very cloak and mantle of the Brothers and Sisters of the Golden Robe and the Order of Francis and Clare—the spiritual anointing of our souls by God.

The Strength of the Individual in God

The cape of responsibility for life and for one another and for our individual path is something we must keep constantly with us and before us lest we become a bit complacent because the body of God is so large, the movement is strong, the revolution is ongoing, and we do not see ourselves alone standing against the backdrop of the stark reality of the desert or the mountains or the darkness of the earth.

Yet these saints who have gone before us have been pillars of eternity standing in the mists of time and space. And as we study them, we see them in their aloneness, their all-oneness, standing out in relief against the complicity of the fallen ones.

And so, we understand, beloved hearts, that this message today is given to make us realize that no matter how many are our numbers, we must not number the numbers but consider that the individual clothed with God *is the One* and the Law of the One. Whether we are many together or whether we stand alone, we must count that the strength must be where we are, where the individual is.

We must see ourselves alongside Isaiah and Jeremiah. We must see ourselves as having to make it by the internal strength of the soul, the strength of character, and the courage necessary to face that energy veil in our own selves or in the world. For thereby will the community be strong, because the individual identifies himself individually and not collectively.

And this is what we underscore today: we must not become complacent in the sense that we are among many, but each individual must understand the supreme necessity of earning that ascension and marching forward on that personal path of Christhood.

It Matters What I Do Today

Therefore it matters supremely what each one of us does each day, how we serve—that we come to decree sessions, that we meet Saint Germain's call Saturday evening, that we are here early Sunday morning, and that we understand that "through the Law of the One, I am accountable for the saving of the nations. I am accountable for implementing Saint Germain's call to the nations or whatever is the call of the hour"—which we hear in the dictations published in the current Pearls of Wisdom.

So let us see the example and the trial of Saint Patrick today and equate with it and run with it and not allow ourselves to be any less filled with fervor and soul-searching and God-mastering than this saint of the Most High God.

We are looking forward to our festivities and celebrations of Saint Patrick's Day and this, too, is important, but for now I ask you to meditate in the secret chamber of your heart with Gautama Buddha, El Morya, and Saint Patrick, and take this opportunity that we have on Sunday to contact the great Gurus, the World Teachers, to do our soul-searching, our meditation, our quiet confessions to the Almighty, so that we may know that we are truly on the path that is required of us and that we are meeting the requirements of the ascension and the goal set before us.

El Morya and Lanello, Saint Germain and Jesus, Mother Mary are very concerned that you pause to consider whether your spiritual life is in keeping with all that they have given and taught. Thus, do not be dismayed at the length of this lecture. You need to hear every word of it, and therefore please pay attention and stay awake.

I am going to read to you about the life of Saint Patrick, first from *The Story of the Irish Race* by MacManus.[2]

The Life of Saint Patrick

The coming of Patrick to Ireland marks the greatest of Irish epochs.

Of all most momentous happenings in Irish history, this seemingly simple one had the most extraordinary, most far-reaching effect. It changed the face of the nation, and utterly changed the nation's destiny. The coming of Patrick may be said to have had sublime effect not on Ireland alone, but upon the world. It was a world event.

I want your coming upon this planet to be a world event. I want you to know today, in the name of your Mighty I AM Presence, that your soul, your lifestream was sent to earth by God. And when you were born, it was a world event. And the second world event in your life is to be your confirmation, your externalization of that internal Light.

Let the history written of your soul's sojourn upon earth be noteworthy that the earth was changed by your coming. If it is not so, you shall not have fulfilled your fiery destiny. Such is the power of God in the individual. The Law of the One is about to proclaim the nova of your coming.

The man himself proved to be a world figure...

May you also prove that you are a world figure.

One of the massive giants who tower distinct and sublime above the dense mists of dim antiquity—one, too, of whom it may truly be said that the more intimately you approach him and the nearer you view him, the greater he grows. He was one of the greatest of Celts, became one of the greatest of Irishmen, and one of the very great among men.

Patrick first came to Ireland—as a captive—in the year 389, in the reign of Niall. It was forty-three years later, in the year 432, the reign of Laoghaire, that he came upon the mission which was so miraculously to change the Island's destiny.

An ancient Pagan prophecy attributed to Conn of the Hundred Battles says: "With Laoghaire the Valiant will the land be humbled by the coming of the Tailcenn (i.e., Patrick): houses across (i.e., churches): bent staffs which shall pluck the flowers from their high places."

In the period of Patrick's coming the great Roman Empire was crumbling, while Ireland, with fleets on the sea and armies in foreign lands, had reached the pinnacle of her political power—a time that would seem the least propitious for winning men to the meek and abnegatory doctrines of Christ. Yet was it, in His own mysterious way, God's chosen time for sending His chosen man.

Patrick Called into Slavery

I will read to you from the Pearl of Wisdom of Sanat Kumara of November 18, 1979, concerning Saint Patrick.[3]

My Beloved Who Will Yet Go to the Mountain to Fast and Pray with Me That the Serpents Might Be Expelled from the Earth:

Let us go to the mountain in the land of Erin where a youth enslaved by pagans is in prayer through the day and into the night. So fervent is the love of God within him that the fire of his heart is a light midst snow and ice. He lived on the mountain, alone with God, tending his master's herds. And on that mountain I called my son Patrick, that out of the condition of servitude there might be produced the miracle fire of freedom.

It was late fourth century A.D. and the clans of the Irish—the reincarnated tribes of Ephraim and Manasseh—were ruled by a host of kings. They served not the LORD God, nor had they the salvation of his Son. Therefore I, the Ancient of Days, called my son, freeborn, unto slavery that I might deliver him to freedom and to the mission of implanting the violet flame in the hearts of my true sons and daughters that they might one day carry it to the New World in the name of Saint Germain.

And therefore, unto slavery was he called and unto slavery are we called. We are called to the slavery of our own personal karma. The Law will not allow us to escape its bonds. Thereby we come to the realization of the need for liberation and the seeking of the Flame of Freedom and the one who delivers it, Sanat Kumara, and delivers it through his servant-sons, Saint Germain and Morya and the great Lights.

So we understand that there is a law of opposites whereby from unreality we are catapulted unto reality. And we are joyous to find ourselves in the knowledge of our obligations which we have incurred karmically, that we may draw upon the Light of God and prove that the Flame of Freedom and its Spirit is greater than all of these things.

The Vision and Preparation for the Mission

To him I gave the vision of the people of Erin whose seed would one day ignite the fires of freedom on every shore and in every nation. Your own prophet Mark derived his fervor from that lineage of the Ancient of Days which goes back to the Emerald Isle. And the Irish eyes of Thomas Moore, poet and prince of my heart, yet smile through the sternness of El Morya and his twinkle of mirth always needed on earth.

Finally restored to his kinsfolk after six years of humbling himself before me on the mountain, tending sheep as he would soon feed my sheep, Patrick heard the voices of the souls of my children crying out from the land of Erin for deliverance: "We beseech thee, holy youth, to come and walk among us once more." Indeed they remembered him when he had walked among them as a prophet in Israel, rebuking their waywardness in the name of the Lord. Now they awaited the message of their salvation through Messiah's anointed apostle.

Patrick prepared for his mission under the lineage of the Ruby Ray and with the saints of the inner Church. And that mission, my beloved, was to subdue the seed of Serpent in Ireland and to raise up the tribes of Israel, the remnant of Joseph's seed who would be Christ-bearers to the nations. Empowered of the Holy Ghost and bearing the Staff of Jesus, he wielded such power and wrought such miracles that pagan chiefs and decadent Druids bowed in submission to this rod of Aaron that, in the new tongue, became the rod of *Erin*.

So perilous was the mission of the shamrock saint of the fifth ray that he wrote in his "Confession": "Daily I expect either a violent death or to be robbed and reduced to slavery or the occurrence of some such calamity. I have cast myself into the hands of Almighty God, for He rules everything; as the Prophet saith, 'Cast thy care upon the Lord, and He Himself will sustain thee.'"

His Consecration, Commission, and Reception at the Irish Court of King Laoghaire

The reading from MacManus continues:

Having been consecrated Bishop, Pope Celestine commissioned him to carry the gospel to the land of his love—and conferred on him the Roman noble name Patricius.

He reached Ireland in 432 in the fourth year of the reign of Laoghaire, son of Niall, High-King.

On the eve of Easter, Patrick's party encamped at Slaine, on the left bank of the Boyne, opposite to and in sight of Tara; and Patrick lighted in front of his tent a fire which was visible at the king's court.

Now a great festival was beginning at Tara, coincident with the beginning of Patrick's Easter festival. And it was a gross violation of royal and ancient order that on this eve any fire should be lighted before the court Druids should light their sacred fire upon the royal Rath. Accordingly, when Laoghaire's astounded court beheld in the distance the blazing of Patrick's fire before the Druid fire had yet been lit, great was their consternation and high and hot their wrath.

"What audacious miscreant," demanded the king, "has dared to do this outrage?" The Druids answered him that it was indeed the Tailcenn of the old prophecy, come to supersede his rule, and their rule, in Eirinn. "Moreover," they said, "unless the fire on yonder hill be extinguished this very night, it shall never more be extinguished in Eirinn. It will outshine all fires that we light, and he who lit it will conquer us all: he will overthrow you, and his kingdom overthrow your kingdom: he will make your subjects his, and rule over them all forever."

Then King Laoghaire, a splendidly determined old pagan, of like nature with Miliuc, angrily demanded that the transgressor should be dragged before him, with all the other foreign intruders who were supporting him.

Then Patrick's camp was raided by Laoghaire's soldiers, and he and his companions ordered to march to Tara.

An old tradition has it that, as, on Easter morning, the missionaries proceeded in processional order, toward the king's court, they chanted the sacred Lorica, called the Faed Fiada, or Deer's Cry, specially composed by Patrick for their protection.

It is said that as the minions of the Druids lay in ambush to intercept and kill them as they came to court, these evil ones now saw not Patrick and his companions pass, only saw pass a harmless herd of gentle deer, a doe followed by her twenty fawns. Hence the hymn's title, the Faed Fiada—Deer's Cry.

And through all the centuries since, the Faed Fiada—which many old authorities pronounce to be Patrick's own work, and the first hymn written in Gaelic—has been used by the Irish Race as a lorica for protection.

And so I shall read it to you so that you may also offer this prayer for your spiritual protection from all evil.

Patrick's Lorica for Protection

I bind me to-day,
    God's might to direct me,
    God's power to protect me,
    God's wisdom for learning,
    God's eye for discerning,
    God's ear for my hearing,
    God's word for my clearing.

God's hand for my cover,
God's path to pass over,
God's buckler to guard me,
God's army to ward me,
    Against snares of the devil,
    Against vice's temptation,
    Against wrong inclination,
    Against men who plot evil,
    Anear or afar, with many or few.

Christ near,
Christ here,
Christ be with me,
Christ beneath me,
Christ within me,
Christ behind me,
Christ be o'er me,
Christ before me.

Christ in the left and the right,
Christ hither and thither,
Christ in the sight,
    Of each eye that shall seek me,
    In each ear that shall hear,
    In each mouth that shall speak me—
Christ not the less
In each heart I address.
I bind me to-day on the Triune—I call,
With faith in the Trinity—Unity—God over all.

Patrick Challenges the Court, Converts the Queen, Gains the King's Favor and Freedom

And having been carried safe by the Lord through the ambushes prepared for them, Patrick led his host into the king's presence, chanting: "Let them that will, trust in chariots and horses, but we walk in the name of the Lord."

To impress and awe these foreigners, King Laoghaire with his queen and court, sat aloft in state, while his warriors, in silence, sat around in a great circle, with the rims of their shields against their chins.

Laoghaire, evidently apprehensive of the secret power of the Tailcenn, had warned his court that none of the marks of respect which were the due of a stranger, should be shown to this bold aggressor. But so impressive was Patrick's appearance that immediately when he came into their presence, Dubthach, the King's Ollam poet, arose, in respect for him; as also a young noble, Erc—who afterwards became Bishop Erc. And these two were Patrick's first converts at Tara.

In the presence of King and court Patrick was first confronted with the Druids, who, it was hoped, would quickly confound him. But matching his miracles against their magic he showed to all that his powers far transcended theirs. He dispelled a darkness, which they, by their magical powers had produced, but were powerless to dissipate—"They can bring darkness," he significantly said, "but cannot bring light."

He preached Christ to the assembly, and won to his Master the queen and several prominent members of the court. And, though Laoghaire's pagan faith was unshaken, he was so far won by the man Patrick that he gave him the freedom of his realm to preach the new faith where and to whom he would.

Patrick's Letter to the Soldiers of Coroticus on the Occasion of the Slaughter of the Newly Baptized

Continuing Sanat Kumara's discourse:

Well might you emulate the courage and the humility of my son Patrick when he boldly challenged Prince Corotick, that serpent who dared plunder Patrick's domain, massacring a great number of neophytes, as it is written, who were yet in their white garments after baptism; and others he carried away and sold to infidels.

Patrick circulated a letter in his own hand pronouncing the judgment of Corotick and his accomplices and declaring them separate from him as the established Bishop of Ireland, and from Jesus Christ. He forbade the faithful "to eat with them, or to receive their alms, till they should have satisfied God by the tears of sincere penance, and restored the servants of Jesus Christ to their liberty."

I am going to read to you now Patrick's letter to Corotick, from "The Letters of the Holy Bishop Patrick," in *The Steadfast Man*.[4] And I expect that as I am reading these accounts of Patrick's life you are planning and visualizing how you yourselves will so fulfill your fiery destiny in his footsteps.

This book states that the letter is to the soldiers of Coroticus, the Latin name of Corotick.

> I, Patrick, a sinner, unlearned, resident in Ireland, declare myself to be a bishop. Most assuredly I believe that what I am I have received from God. And so I live among barbarians, a stranger and exile for the love of God. He is witness that this is so.
>
> Not that I wished my mouth to utter anything so hard and harsh; but I am forced by the zeal for God; and the truth of Christ has wrung it from me, out of love for my neighbours and sons for whom I gave up my country and parents and my life to the point of death. If I be worthy, I live for my God to teach the heathen, even though some may despise me.
>
> 2. With my own hand I have written and composed these words, to be given, delivered, and sent to the soldiers of Coroticus; I do not say, to my fellow citizens, or to fellow citizens of the holy Romans, but to fellow citizens of the demons, because of their evil works. Like our enemies, they live in death, allies of the Scots and the apostate Picts. Dripping with blood, they welter in the blood of innocent Christians, whom I have begotten into the number for God and confirmed in Christ!
>
> 3. The day after the newly baptised, anointed with chrism, in white garments (had been slain)—the fragrance was still on their foreheads when they were butchered and slaughtered with the sword by the above-mentioned people—I sent a letter with a holy presbyter whom I had taught from his childhood, clerics accompanying him, asking them to let us have some of the booty, and of the baptised they had made captives. They only jeered at them.
>
> 4. Hence I do not know what to lament more: those who have been slain, or those whom they have taken captive, or those whom the devil has mightily ensnared. Together with him they will be slaves in Hell in an eternal punishment; for who committeth sin is a slave and will be called a son of the devil.
>
> 5. Wherefore let every God-fearing man know that they

are enemies of me and of Christ my God, for whom I am an ambassador. Parricide! fratricide! ravening wolves that eat the people of the Lord as they eat bread! As is said, The wicked, O Lord, have destroyed Thy law, which but recently He had excellently and kindly planted in Ireland, and which had established itself by the grace of God.

6. I make no false claim. I share in the work of those whom He called and predestinated to preach the Gospel amidst grave persecutions unto the end of the earth, even if the enemy shows his jealousy through the tyranny of Coroticus, a man who has no respect for God nor for His priests whom He chose, giving them the highest, divine, and sublime power, that whom they should bind upon earth should be bound also in heaven.

7. Wherefore, then, I plead with you earnestly, ye holy and humble of heart, it is not permissible to court the favour of such people, nor to take food or drink with them, nor even to accept their alms, until they make reparation to God in hardships, through penance, with shedding of tears, and set free the baptised servants of God and handmaids of Christ, for whom He died and was crucified.

8. The most High disapproveth the gifts of the wicked. ... He that offereth sacrifice of the goods of the poor, is as one that sacrificeth the son in the presence of his father. The riches, it is written, which he has gathered unjustly, shall be vomited up from his belly; the angel of death drags him away, by the fury of dragons he shall be tormented, the viper's tongue shall kill him, unquenchable fire devoureth him.

And so—Woe to those who fill themselves with what is not their own; or, What doth it profit a man that he gain the whole world, and suffer the loss of his own soul?

9. It would be too tedious to discuss and set forth everything in detail, to gather from the whole Law testimonies against such greed. Avarice is a deadly sin. Thou shalt not covet thy neighbour's goods. Thou shalt not kill. A murderer cannot be with Christ. Whosoever hateth his brother is accounted a murderer. Or, He that loveth not his brother abideth in death. How much more guilty is he that has stained his hands with the blood of the sons of God whom He has of late purchased in the utmost part of the earth through the call of our littleness!

10. Did I come to Ireland without God, or according to the

flesh? Who compelled me? I am bound by the Spirit not to see any of my kinsfolk. Is it of my own doing that I have holy mercy on the people who once took me captive and made away with the servants and maids of my father's house?

I was freeborn according to the flesh. I am the son of a decurion. But I sold my noble rank—I am neither ashamed nor sorry—for the good of others. Thus I am a servant in Christ to a foreign nation for the unspeakable glory of life everlasting which is in Christ Jesus our Lord.

11. And if my own people do not know me, a prophet hath no honour in his own country. Perhaps we are not of the same fold and have not one and the same God as father, as is written: He that is not with me, is against me, and he that gathereth not with me, scattereth. It is not right that one destroyeth, another buildeth up. I seek not the things that are mine.

It is not my grace, but God who has given this solicitude into my heart, to be one of His hunters or fishers whom God once foretold would come in the last days.

12. I am hated. What shall I do, Lord? I am most despised. Look, Thy sheep around me are torn to pieces and driven away, and that by those robbers, by the orders of the hostile-minded Coroticus. Far from the love of God is a man who hands over Christians to the Picts and Scots.

Ravening wolves have devoured the flock of the Lord, which in Ireland was indeed growing splendidly with the greatest care; and the sons and daughters of kings were monks and virgins of Christ—I cannot count their number. Wherefore, be not pleased with the wrong done to the just; even to hell it shall not please.

13. Who of the saints would not shudder to be merry with such persons or to enjoy a meal with them? They have filled their houses with the spoils of dead Christians, they live on plunder. They do not know, the wretches, that what they offer their friends and sons as food is deadly poison, just as Eve did not understand that it was death she gave to her husband. So are all that do evil: they work death as their eternal punishment.

14. This is the custom of the Roman Christians of Gaul: they send holy and able men to the Franks and other heathen with so many thousand *solidi* to ransom baptised captives. You prefer to kill and sell them to a foreign nation that has no knowledge of God. You betray

the members of Christ as it were into a brothel.

What hope have you in God, or anyone who thinks as you do, or converses with you in words of flattery? God will judge. For Scripture says: Not only they that do evil are worthy to be condemned, but they also that consent to them.

Not Only They That Do Evil Are Worthy to Be Condemned But They Also That Consent to Them
El Morya's Warning to His Chelas

Let us consider that statement again—"Not only they that do evil are worthy to be condemned, but they also that consent to them."

Keepers of the Flame, the law is written: Silence is consent. And this is the very heart and message of the life of Saint Patrick. Where there was evil, he challenged it forthrightly and directly. He did not remain silent.

And this is the great message of Saint Patrick and El Morya and Saint Germain today: that Keepers of the Flame who do not attend services and give their calls to Saint Germain for the Afghans, for Nicaragua, for El Salvador and for the burdens of the earth are in silence consenting to the ravaging of the earth and the lightbearers.

Therefore I am sent by the hierarchy this day to remind you of your covenant with the Magi, to remind you of Morya and Patrick and Saint Germain and Mother Mary, and to remind you of your responsibility in service.

For Morya said to me this morning that those who know the law and do it not in this activity and in this Fraternity of Keepers of the Flame already have written on their record of the Book of Life their neglect and therefore their consent to world conditions—having, as they do, the knowledge of the violet flame and the knowledge of the Call and failing to present themselves a living sacrifice in the testimony of the Word in this sanctuary or in their homes and centers around the world.

Withholding your life from the defense of innocent victims worldwide becomes an accountability, and that accountability is upon your lifestream this day. And therefore, be forewarned not to have the expectancy that by the momentum of the movement (the organization and its activities) you will arrive at the gate of Paradise.

Thus, as your Messenger, I divest myself of the responsibility of this knowledge and warning, even as El Morya, your Guru, does the same through me in this hour. Therefore, hear the law which was spoken by Patrick in the fifth century: "Not only they that do evil are worthy to be condemned, but they also that consent to them." The law is written—your silence is your consent.

Continuing Patrick's letter:

15. I do not know what I should say or speak further about the departed ones of the sons of God, whom the sword has touched all too harshly. For Scripture says: Weep with them that weep; and again: If one member be grieved, let all members grieve with it.

Hence the Church mourns and laments her sons and daughters whom the sword has not yet slain, but who were removed and carried off to faraway lands, where sin abounds openly, grossly, impudently. There people who were freeborn have been sold, Christians made slaves, and that, too, in the service of the abominable, wicked, and apostate Picts!

16. Therefore I shall raise my voice in sadness and grief: O you fair and beloved brethren and sons whom I have begotten in Christ, countless of number, what can I do for you? I am not worthy to come to the help of God or men. The wickedness of the wicked hath prevailed over us. We have been made, as it were, strangers.

Perhaps they do not believe that we have received one and the same baptism, or have one and the same God as father. For them it is a disgrace that we are Irish. Have ye not, as is written, one God? Have ye, every one of you, forsaken his neighbour?

17. Therefore I grieve for you, I grieve, my dearly beloved. But again, I rejoice within myself. I have not laboured for nothing, and my journeying abroad has not been in vain. And if this horrible, unspeakable crime did happen—thanks be to God, you have left the world and have gone to Paradise as baptised faithful. I see you: you have begun to journey where night shall be no more, nor mourning, nor death; but you shall leap like calves loosened from their bonds, and you shall tread down the wicked, and they shall be ashes under your feet.

18. You, then, will reign with the apostles, and prophets, and martyrs. You will take possession of eternal kingdoms, as He Himself testifies, saying: They shall come from the east and from the west, and shall sit down with Abraham, and Isaac, and Jacob in the kingdom of heaven. Without are dogs, and sorcerers,... and murderers; and liars and perjurers have their portion in the pool of everlasting fire.

Not without reason does the Apostle say: Where the just man shall scarcely be saved, where shall the sinner and ungodly transgressor of the law find himself?

19. Where, then, will Coroticus with his criminals, rebels against Christ, where will they see themselves, they who distribute baptised women as prizes—for a miserable temporal kingdom, which will pass away in a moment? As a cloud or smoke that is dispersed by the wind, so shall the deceitful wicked perish at the presence of the Lord; but the just shall feast with great constancy with Christ, they shall judge nations, and rule over wicked kings for ever and ever. Amen.

20. I testify before God and His angels that it will be so as He indicated to my ignorance. It is not my words that I have set forth in Latin, but those of God and the apostles and prophets, who have never lied. He that believeth shall be saved; but he that believeth not shall be condemned, God hath spoken.

21. I ask earnestly that whoever is a willing servant of God be a carrier of this letter, so that on no account it be suppressed or hidden by anyone, but rather be read before all the people, and in the presence of Coroticus himself.

May God inspire them sometime to recover their senses for God, repenting, however late, their heinous deeds—murderers of the brethren of the Lord!—and to set free the baptised women whom they took captive, in order that they may deserve to live to God, and be made whole, here and in eternity!

Be peace to the Father, and to the Son, and to the Holy Spirit. Amen.

This letter, then, is the expression of the sacred fire of God through the heart of Saint Patrick upon a most burdensome and grievous crime committed—the slaughter of the innocents. Thus you understand that the testimony of the lightbearers in the face of injustice wherever you find it is your calling—subject to the direction of the Holy Spirit upon you and your own Christ Self.

Our Individual Responsibility to Fulfill the Requirements of the Law

Remember that silence is agreement in any area of life and in the face of any crime. And thus, understand individual and personal responsibility for the rebuke, either of the seed of the wicked or of the burdens or grievances or sins of one another. This is according to the Old Testament where it is written in the prophecies of Ezekiel (Chapters 3 and 33) that if we keep silence and do not challenge and rebuke the wickedness of the seed of the wicked, their karma will be upon us.

And the same of the children of the Light: If we do not challenge their wrongdoing, their karma will be upon us; and we are responsible if, for our failure to preach to them, they are judged in the Day of Judgment and lose their salvation.

Thus, you see the little book that is sweet in the mouth and bitter in the belly that is given to John the Revelator by the mighty angel clothed with a cloud and a rainbow on his head.[5] He takes the book. He eats it. It is sweet in his mouth. He is filled with the glory of God—as you are filled with the glory of the Masters' dictations and the Light and the results of your meditations and dynamic decrees.

It is bitter in his belly. And the bitterness in the belly is his and our accountability in the new age. And the angel tells him exactly what is this accountability. He says: "Thou must prophesy again before many peoples, and nations, and tongues, and kings."

Thus, it is the dawn of our responsibility in this life for the karma of our previous embodiments, for whatever is happening upon earth in the hour and the day of our incarnation, and for our taking on the burden of the LORD which is the preaching, verily the prophesying, to the nations.

The bitterness in the belly is the realization that we must face those wicked ones who transgress against the LORD and challenge them in their iniquities. And we must challenge the self-righteous to embrace the righteousness of the LORD Sanat Kumara. This is the calling and the office of those who are the Christed ones.

Following the directive of beloved El Morya and his dictation[6] to you prior to my leaving on the Pacific Stump, the one who holds the office of chela or is aspiring to the office of chela must already be acting the part of the office of Christ in order to inherit the mantle of Christ. Therefore you understand your unique and individual accountability rather than saying, "The Messenger is taking care of this. The Messenger is preaching the Word, therefore I do not have to do it. The board of directors is taking care of these burdens, and therefore I will not be necessarily involved in this action."

If we do not fulfill our calling and our office, wherever we are on the ladder of life, we will lose both the calling and the office.

Understand that individually, one by one, you must daily keep your peace with Almighty God in obedience to His laws. Though I am the Shepherd of your souls, I cannot be accountable for the misdemeanors which you yourselves are responsible for, because you are fulfilling your discipleship in the Aquarian dispensation of Saint Germain.

The knowledge of the Law itself makes you accountable. And therefore, realize that the disciplining of your soul, the watchfulness, the realization of Light and Darkness and right and wrong is a supreme responsibility which you have under your own Christ Self and I AM Presence.

Remember this. And do not tarry in passivity, waiting for someone who you refer to as a "hierarch" to come along and tap you on the head and remind you of your responsibility to be the incarnate Word. Remember that the Teaching itself has made you immensely responsible for a path on which you must set the example. And this path was nobly outpictured by Saint Patrick in the fifth century.

So you see, we cannot claim ignorance. All Patrick had was Jesus Christ, the apostles, the prophets, and his own I AM Presence, Christ Self, and his responsibility to the one who anointed him—the Ancient of Days. It is not as though he had any outer person goading him to these actions. They sprung from the wellspring within him of the sacred fire.

Saint Germain says to you, "Go and do likewise." The Masters have spoken. They have dictated. They have released their intents. They have called their chelas. They have called their Keepers of the Flame. Everyone who has heard the dictations stands accountable for fulfilling the requirements of the Law.

When you place yourselves at the feet of the Ascended Masters, know that you have the responsibility for the Light and the Wisdom and the Mandate given. These are the terms of chelaship. When you expect God to serve you through the Ascended Masters, you are expected to return in kind.

This is the quickening and the awakening that the Darjeeling Council brings to the body of God on this Saint Patrick's Day. It is the Emerald Matrix of Truth. And Truth is a two-edged sword and it cleaves asunder the real from the unreal. And we all need that fiery flame of Truth and the Science of Being it brings to us today.

The Taking Up of Serpents

I would like to read you the concluding statements of Sanat Kumara on Saint Patrick.

> Such is the true Work and Word of the saints of the Ruby Ray who, with all due seriousness, receive the sign

of their coming in the taking up of serpents. Thousands upon thousands of the descendants of Jacob's favorite son were baptized and confirmed by the Lord Jesus through my son Patrick. Like the apostle Paul, he bound the power of Serpent's seed that had invaded the land of Erin; and like him, he healed their sick, he restored sight—both inner and outer—to their blind, and he raised Abram's seed—dead in body and in spirit—to new life through the indwelling Christ by the Word of Christ Jesus, his beloved.

Now the Ascended Master Saint Patrick stands with me on the summit of Mount Aigli where, at the close of his earthly sojourn, he retreated forty days and forty nights, fasting in body and in spirit that he might be filled with the Light of the Ancient of Days. There on that occasion fifteen hundred years ago, I summoned all the saints of Erin—the light of Aaron's priesthood and the lightbearers of the Christic seed of Joseph—past, present, and future, to pay homage to him who was father to them all.

Again I call the saints to a pilgrimage to the mountain to bless and be blessed by Patrick, to be infilled with his Spirit, to receive his mantle, to pray fervently that the fruit of all of his labors might provide a plenteous harvest in this age unto the World Mother who labors long for her children and for the Manchild.

Now I say, saints of the Ruby Ray, let Mission Amethyst Jewel return to the shrine where there once burned in the heart of a youth enslaved a kindling light that was to light a world. Let him who is an initiate of the fifth ray and the Lamb who is worthy transfer to you the momentum of his light that by your dynamic decrees unto the living Word you might once again cast out of Ireland the seed of Serpent now persecuting the blessed seed of the Woman.

Let the violet fire of freedom ring through hill and dale! Let it restore truth and the true Church Universal and Triumphant that belongs unto the saints!

My beloved, many of you were among the souls of the saints who came to Patrick in his final hours on the mountain. You saluted him in the glory of God that was upon him, and to him you were the promise that his Word and Work would be carried to golden shores unto a golden age of Christ peace and enlightenment. It is time and high time that you go forth to bind the barbarians that have returned to the British Isles with their terror and terrorism and their age-old tyranny by which they would bind the souls of my people Israel.

I Call for a Prayer Vigil for Ireland

This is a very great calling upon my heart that has burdened me throughout my trip as I have read daily the newspaper reports of more killings and deaths in Ireland. Surely God has placed in my heart in the past month, leading to this day, the great need of Ireland for the Light and the lightbearers.

And therefore, I call for a prayer vigil on behalf of Ireland once again that we may move with the saints and the holy ones of God to demand that the Light devour these murderers and assassins who have reincarnated for their final judgment and may very well have been a part of those soldiers who performed this dastardly deed in the slaying of the holy innocents in the time of Patrick.

Surely there is a battle raging of Armageddon, of life and death. And so, let us consider the suffering of the people of Ireland, whence came Morya and Lanello and many of your hearts—truly a land of angels, a land of Light, a land unique and that is under attack. Even adversaries siding in with the murderers and terrorists are in the United States today providing them with funds, as you know.

In the heart of all of this and in the midst of it is the presence of Saint Patrick. And yet we know that the key to unlock the power of his causal body, his shepherd's crook, his mitre and the sword of the Spirit must be the dynamic decree. And our dynamic decree is far more effective when, in our hearts, we, too, have fasted and prayed and sacrificed that the Light might shine through us in the most efficacious manner, as it did through him. He came and he delivered that land of serpents. 'Psychic snakes' (formed on the astral plane) were driven out of Ireland, and thus the serpents—the fallen ones—likewise must be driven out.

Thus we understand what is the power of the raised shepherd's crook, the Kundalini fire, the crook which rises. And the crook itself is the shape of that rising flame that comes around the head and seals in the third eye the Emerald Matrix, the green of Saint Patrick.

Saint Patrick's Confession

I am going to read to you Saint Patrick's *Confession*.[7] He wrote it toward the end of his life, and it is the main source of the information which we have today about Patrick. It was composed as the defense of his ministry in answer to charges that he was seeking profit for himself in his mission in Ireland.

In it he tells of his six-year captivity as a shepherd in Ireland during his teenage years, thus showing all of us by his example that in the teenage years we bear the burden of our karma and we are preparing for our mission and we are being initiated. And this is the great significance of becoming a teenager today. And would it be to God that the American teenager would understand this path from age thirteen to nineteen—as representative of the six years of Saint Patrick's imprisonment[8]— and understand that it is meet that the sacred fire be exalted in them and that they commune with God.

He speaks of his escape to Britain and subsequent calling to return to Ireland to minister to her people, his spiritual work among the Irish and some of the perils that he faced, including an attack by Satan and his persecution and betrayal by a close friend.

In the name of the Father, the Son, the Holy Spirit, and the Mother, Amen.

1. I, Patrick, sinner, am the most illiterate and inconsiderable of all the Faithful, and am despised in the hearts of many.

I had for father Calpurnius, a deacon, one of the sons of Potitus, a presbyter, who belonged to the village of Bannavem Taberniae; for he owned a small farm hard by, where I was made a captive.

At the time I was about sixteen years old. I had no knowledge of the True God, and I was led to Ireland in captivity with many thousand others, according to our deserts, because we departed from God and did not keep his commandments, and we were not obedient to our priests, who were wont to admonish us for our salvation. And the Lord poured upon us the fury of his anger, and scattered us among many gentile nations, even unto the ends of the earth, where now my littleness may be seen among stranger folk.

2. And there the Lord opened the understanding of my unbelief, so that, though late, I might summon my faults to mind and turn with all my heart to the Lord my God, who regarded my low estate, and pitied my ignorance and youth, and kept watch over me before I knew him or had attained discernment or could distinguish good from evil, and fortified me and comforted me as a father his son.

3. Therefore I cannot now maintain silence (nor would

it be fitting) as to the great favours and the great grace which the Lord vouchsafed to bestow on me in the land of my captivity. For this is the return we make: that after our chastening and our recognition of God we shall exalt and praise his wondrous works before every nation which is under the whole heaven.

4. For there is no other God, and never has been, and never will be hereafter, except God the Father unbegotten, without beginning, from whom is all Beginning, who holds all things, as we say, and his Son Jesus Christ, whom we witness likewise to have been ever with the Father, spiritually existing in the Father before the origin of the universe, begotten inexpressibly before all beginning.

And by him were made things visible and invisible. He was made man, and after triumphing over death was received up to the Father in heaven. And he gave to him all power above every name of things in heaven and things in earth and things under the earth; and let every tongue confess to him that Jesus Christ is Lord and God in whom we believe.

And we look for his Coming any day now. He the Judge of the quick and the dead, who will render to each man according to his deeds. And he shed on us abundantly the Holy Ghost, the gift and pledge of immortality, who turns those that believe and obey into the Children of God and Joint-heirs with Christ, whom we confess and adore as One God in the Trinity of the Holy Name.

5. For he himself declared through the prophet, "Call upon me in the day of trouble; I will deliver thee, and thou shalt glorify me." And again he says, "It is honourable to reveal and confess the works of God."

6. Yet, faulty as I am in many ways, I desire my brethren and kinsfolk to know what manner of man I am, so that they may be able to understand the dedication of my soul.

7. I know well enough the testimony of my Lord, who witnesses in the Psalm, "Thou shalt destroy them that speak a lie." And again he says, "The mouth that belies kills the soul." And the same Lord says in the Gospel, "The idle word that men shall speak, they shall give account thereof in the day of judgment."

8. Therefore I ought exceedingly, with fear and trembling, to dread this sentence in that day when no man shall be able to absent himself or hide; but all of us, every

man of us, must give account of even his tiniest sins before the judgment seat of the Lord Christ.

9. Consequently I have long considered a written statement, but till this moment I have hesitated. For I feared to come under the censure of men's tongues, because I am not learned as others are, who have imbibed in the most approved ways both Law and Holy Scripture in one draught, and who from their infancy have never changed their speech but instead went on bringing it to ever greater perfection.

For my speech, my style, is translated into a strange tongue, as can easily be perceived from the flavour of my writing the degree of my training and instruction in the matter of words. For, says the wise man, "By the tongue will be discovered understanding and knowledge and the teaching of truth."

10. But what use is an excuse however nigh the truth, especially when joined to presumption? seeing that now I myself, in my old age, strongly desire that which in my youth I did not acquire; because my sins stood in the way of my mastering what I had previously read over. But who believes me even if I repeat what I have said in my prefatory remarks?

Conquering Fear and Illiteracy, Patrick Preaches the Word

A youth, scarcely indeed a boy, I was made a captive before I knew what I should strive for or what I ought to shun (in language). And so today I blush and am exceedingly afraid to show nakedly my inexperience, because through lack of education I cannot express myself with brevity. For as the Spirit yearns, the disposition discloses the soul and the understanding.

11. But even had I had the same opportunity as others, still I would not keep silent, on account of the reward. And if perhaps it should appear to many that I am thrusting myself forward in this matter with my ignorance and my slow tongue, yet it is written, "The tongue of the stammerers shall quickly learn to speak peace."

How much rather should we covet to do this, who are, he says, the Epistle of Christ for salvation unto the ends of the earth, although not a learned one, yet ministered with all strength, written in your hearts, not with ink, but with the Spirit of the living God. And again the Spirit witnesses, "And husbandry (or rusticity) was ordained by the Most High."

12. Whence I, at first illiterate, an exile, unlearned as is one who does not know how to provide for the future—yet this I do know with full certainty, that before I was afflicted I was like a stone which lies in the deep mire; and he that is mighty came, and in his mercy lifted me up, and set me on the top of the wall. And therefore I ought to cry out and render somewhat to the Lord for his benefits so great both here and in eternity, which the mind of man cannot estimate.

13. Therefore, be you filled with wonder, you that fear God, both small and great, and you lordly rhetoricians, listen and search it out. Who was it that called me up, fool as I am, from the midst of those who seem to be wise and skilled in the law and powerful in word and in everything?

And me, too, the abhorred of this world, did he inspire beyond others, if such I were, only that with reverence and godly fear and unblameably I should faithfully serve the gentile people to whom the love of Christ transferred and presented me, as long as I live, if I should be worthy: that in humility and truthfully I should serve them.

14. So it is right that according to the rule of faith in the Trinity, I should define doctrine and make known the gift of God and everlasting consolation, without being held back by danger, and spread everywhere without fear, confidently, the name of God; so that even after my decease I may leave a legacy to my brethren and sons whom I baptised in the Lord, many thousands of men.

15. And I was not worthy, nor such a one, that the Lord should grant this to his poor slave after calamities and such great difficulties, after captivity, after many years: that he should grant me so great a grace towards that gentile people—what formerly, in my youth I never hoped for or pondered.

Prayer, the Voice of God, Voyage to Britain

16. Now after I came to Ireland, daily I pastured flocks, and constantly during the day I prayed. More and more there grew the Love of God and the Fear of him, and my Faith increased, and my Spirit was stirred up, so that in a single day I uttered as many as a hundred prayers, and

nearly as many in the night, so that I stayed even in the woods and the mountain.

Before dawnlight I used to be roused to prayer, in snow, in frost, in rain. And I felt no harm, nor was there any slothfulness in me (as I now see), because then the spirit in me was fervent.

17. And there verily one night I heard in my sleep a voice saying to me, "You fast to good purpose, soon to go to your fatherland." And again after a very little time I heard the Answer speaking to me, "See, your ship is ready." And it was not near, but was far off about 200 miles. And I had never been there, nor had I knowledge of any person there.

And thereon shortly afterwards I took myself to flight and left the man with whom I had been for 6 years; and I came in the strength of God who prospered my way for good, and I encountered nothing alarming until I came to that ship.

18. And on the very day I came, the ship sailed from its anchorage. And I declared that I had to sail away with them. And the shipmaster was displeased, and replied harshly with anger, "On no account seek to go with us."

When I heard this, I departed from them to go to the hut where I was lodging; and on the way I began to pray. And before I had completed my prayer, I heard one of them. He was shouting loudly after me, "Come quickly, these men are calling you."

And they began to say to me, "Come, we accept you in good faith. Make friends with us in any way you like."

And on that day I refused to suck their breasts through fear of God; but nevertheless I hoped that some of them would come into the faith of Jesus Christ, since they were gentiles. For that reason I stayed with them; and straightway we set sail.

Starving Shipmates Taught to Pray, God Sends a Miracle

19. And after three days we reached land, and for 28 days we travelled through a desert; and food failed them and hunger overcame them. And one day the shipmaster began to say to me, "How is this, you Christian? you say your God is great and almighty. Why then can't you pray for us? We're in danger of starvation. Hardly are we like to see a human being again."

Then I spoke plainly to them.

"Turn in faith and with all your heart to the Lord my God, to whom nothing is impossible, so that he may send you food today for your journey until you can eat no more, for everywhere he has plenty."

And, by God's help, so it came to pass. Lo, a herd of swine appeared on the track before our eyes; and they killed many of them and spent two nights there, and were well refreshed, and their dogs were fed full, for many of them had fainted and were left half dead by the way.

And after this they offered the fullest thanks to God, and I became an object of honour in their eyes, and from that day on they had food in plenty. They even found wild honey and gave me a piece of it. But one of them said, "This is offered in sacrifice."

Thanks be to God, I tasted none of it.

Patrick's Call to Helias
His Deliverance from Satan in the Splendor of the Sun

20. On that very same night I lay a-sleeping, and powerfully Satan assailed me; which I shall remember as long as I am in this body. He fell upon me like an enormous stone, and I was stricken nerveless in all my limbs. Whence then did it come into my unscholarly spirit to call upon Helias?

At once I saw the sun rising into the dawn sky, and while I kept invoking "Helias, Helias," with all my strength, lo, the Splendour of the Sun fell over me and instantly shook all the heaviness off from me.

I believe I was succoured by Christ my Lord and that his Spirit even then was calling out on my behalf.

If anyone ever asks you why you pray to Helios, you may cite them the record of this Christian saint and his deliverance. By the direct knowledge of the Holy Spirit, he was given the name of the Sun and the name of the Son behind the Sun, and Helios delivered him. Isn't it the great miracle of God that the doctrine of the Almighty One transcends the doctrines of men to deliver our souls?

And I trust that it will be so in the day of my trouble, as he says in the Gospel. "In that day," the Lord testifies, "it is not you that speak, but the Spirit of your Father which speaks in you."

The Spirit of the Father, our Father Helios, speaks in him and in us. Can he not also deliver us by the splendor of his shining from the works of the devil forever?

21. And a second time, after many years, I was made a captive. And so on that first night I remained with them. I heard the Answer of God declaring to me, "For two months yet you will be with them."

So it came to pass. On the sixtieth night after that, the Lord delivered me from their hands.

22. Moreover, on our way he provided us with food and fire and dry weather every day until on the tenth day we reached our journey's end. As I explained above, for 28 days we travelled through a desert. And on the night on which we finished our journey we came to the end of our food.

23. Again, a few years later, I was in Britain with my kin, who welcomed me as a son and in good faith besought me that now at least, after the great tribulations which I had endured, I would not ever again go away from them.

Visions of Victoricus Bearing Tidings of the Irish

And there verily I saw in the night visions a man whose name was Victoricus, coming as it were from Ireland with countless letters. He gave one of them to me, and I read the beginning of the letter, which was entitled, "The Voice of the Irish"; and while I was reading out the beginning of the letter, I thought that at that very moment I heard the voice of those that lived beside the Wood of Focluth, which is near the western sea. And thus they cried out, as if from one mouth, "We beg you, holy boy, to come and walk among us yet again."

"Victoricus," the vision—the vision of Mighty Victory, the vision of Sanat Kumara, the vision of his home star Venus and the hierarch who sent him to deliver this people.

And I was deeply broken in heart, and could read no further, and so I awoke. Thanks be to God that after a great length of years the Lord dealt with them according to their cry.

Jesus Christ Speaks in Patrick, the Spirit Prays within Him

24. And on another night, whether within me or at my side, I cannot tell, God knows, in words of the utmost eloquence, which I heard but could not comprehend until the end of the prayer, he spoke thus, "He who laid down his life for you, he it is who speaks in you." And so I awoke with heart of glee.

Thus, by the direct transmission of the Ascended Master, Patrick has the revelation that Christ in him speaks. Christ within

Patrick—the same Christ who was in Jesus—speaks through him: the true and clear teaching of the Ascended Masters in all ages.

25. And another time I saw him praying in me, and he was as it were within my body, and I heard him over me— that is, over the inner man. And there he was praying, mightily, with groanings. And meanwhile I was wonderstruck, and marvelled and considered who it was that prayed within me; but at the end of the prayer he spoke out that he was the Spirit.

And who is it that prays within us? It is the hidden man of the heart,[9] the Holy Christ Self who prays at the altar of your heart daily for the salvation of your soul and for the salvation of the souls of the world through you. This is the true guardian angel who prays without ceasing for your deliverance from the pits of Death and Hell that are physical on this planetary home.

How can you fail with an Advocate before the Father like your Holy Christ Self? How can you be absent of fervor and the desiring to enter this consummate union that entails the sacrifice, the universal call, the pain of surrender, the giving of oneself that millions might be healed?

So I awoke and remembered how the Apostle says, "The Spirit helps the infirmities of our prayer, for we know not what we should pray for as we ought; but the Spirit himself makes intercession for us with groanings which cannot be uttered, which cannot be expressed in words." And again: "The Lord our Advocate makes intercession for us."

Ought we therefore not to make intercession for those who know not the way of the Holy Christ Self?

Patrick Prays for His False Accuser

26. And when I was assailed by several of my elders, who came to urge my sins against my toilsome episcopate— certainly on that day I was sore thrust at that I might fall both here and in eternity. But the Lord graciously had mercy on the stranger and sojourner for his name's sake; and he helped me stoutly in that humiliation, so that I did not fall badly into disgrace and reproach. I pray God that it may not be laid to their charge as sin.

Thus, falsely accused by a fellow prelate, he passed the test of praying for that one and for himself.

27. For after thirty years had passed they found as an occasion against me a matter which I had confessed before

I became a deacon. In my anxiety, with sorrowing heart, I disclosed to my closest friend what I had done in my youth on one day, no, in one hour, because I had not then triumphed.

I cannot tell, God knows, if I was then fifteen years old, and I did not believe in the living God—nor had I believed from my infancy; I remained in death and unbelief until I was thoroughly chastened and humbled in truth by hunger and nakedness, and that daily.

28. Towards Ireland I did not stir of my own accord until I was almost worn out. But this was all to my good, since thus I was amended by the Lord. He fitted me to become something which was once quite beyond my grasp; he made me take for my care and busy myself about the Salvation of others, whereas at that time I did not even think about myself.

29. Accordingly, on that day when I was rejected by the aforesaid persons whom I have described, during the night I saw in the night visions. There was a writing without honour over against my face. And meanwhile I heard the Divine Answer speaking to me, "We have seen with wrath the face of So-and-so." (I suppress the name.) He did not say, "You have seen with wrath," but "We have seen with wrath," as if in that matter he linked himself with me.

As he said, "He that touches you is as he that touches the apple of my eye."

"The apple of my eye" is an Old Testament reference to Christ, the Incarnate.[10]

30. So I thank him who has enabled me in all things, since he did hold me back from the journey on which I had resolved, and from my labour which I had learned from Christ my Lord; but rather I felt in myself no little virtue proceeding from him, and my faith has been approved in the sight of God and of men.

31. Therefore I say boldly that my conscience does not blame me here or hereafter. I call God to witness that I have told no lie in the matters which I have recounted to you.

32. Rather do I grieve for my close friend that we should have deserved to hear from God such an Answer. A man to whom I trusted even my soul! And I discovered from some of the brethren before that contention—at which I was not present; at the time I was not in Britain at all; nor will the story originate with me—that he, this friend, had

fought for me in my absence. He had said to me with his own lips, "You are the man to be raised to the rank of bishop." Of which I was not worthy.

How then did it occur to him after to shame me in public, before everyone, good and bad, with regard to an office which previously of his own accord and joyfully he had conceded to me, and the Lord too, who is greater than all?

33. I have said enough. Still, I ought not to conceal the gift of God, which he bestowed upon me in the land of my captivity; since then I zealously sought him, and there I found him and he kept me safe from all iniquities (as I believe) because of his indwelling Spirit, who has worked in me till this day.

Boldly again I speak. But God knows if man had said this to me—maybe I would have held my peace for the love of Christ.

34. Hence therefore I render unwearying thanks to my God who kept me faithful in the day of my temptation, so that today with confidence I offer sacrifice to him, as a living victim, even my soul to Christ my Lord, who saved me out of all my troubles so that I may say, Who am I, O Lord? or what is my vocation that you have opened so great a source of divine aid? so that today among the gentiles I should constantly exalt and magnify your name wherever I may be; and that not only in prosperity, but also amid afflictions; so that whatever may happen to me, whether of good or bad, I ought to accept it with equanimity and always give thanks to God who showed me that I might yield him endless trust as one that cannot be doubted; and who heard me, so that I, ignorant as I am, and in the world's last days, should proceed to take up this work so holy and so wonderful; so that I might to some extent imitate those whom the Lord long ago prophesied would proclaim his Gospel for a witness unto all nations before the end of the world.

Accordingly, as we see, this had been so fulfilled. Lo, we are witnesses that the Gospel has been preached to the places beyond which no man dwells.

The Twelve Perils of Patrick
Initiations at the Twelve Gates of the Holy City

35. A long task it is to narrate in detail the whole of my labour, or even parts of it. I shall briefly tell in what

manner the most gracious God often delivered me from slavery and from the Twelve Perils by which my soul was beset, besides many plots and things which I am not able to express in words—lest I should tire out my readers.

The "Twelve Perils" of Saint Patrick we understand to be the twelve initiations of the twelve gates of the city, the New Jerusalem, whereby we are then anointed to enter into that Holy City, having passed the twelve initiations of the twelve lines of the clock, of our karma and of our Christhood.

But for voucher I have God, who knows all things even before they come to pass, as the Divine Answer frequently warned me the poor starveling uneducated orphan.

36. Whence came to me this wisdom which was not in me, who neither knew the number of my days nor had a taste of God? Whence after came to me that gift so great and so salutary, to know God and to love him, only that I should put aside my fatherland and my kindred?

37. Many were the gifts proffered to me with wailing and with tears. And I displeased them, and also, against my wish, some of my elders. But, through God's guidance, in no way did I acquiesce or surrender to them. Not my grace was it, but God who conquered in me and resisted them all, so that I came to the Irish heathen to preach the Gospel and to endure insults from the unbelieving, so as to hear the reproach of my going abroad, and to meet many persecutions, even unto bonds; and so that I should give up my free condition for the profit of others.

And if I should be worthy, I am ready to give even my life for his name's sake, unhesitatingly and most joyfully; and there I desire to spend it until the day of death, if the Lord would grant it to me.

38. Because I am greatly a debtor to God, who afforded me such great grace that through me many people should be regenerated to God and afterwards confirmed, and that clergy should everywhere be ordained for them—for a people newly come to belief, whom the Lord took from the ends of the earth, as he promised of old through his prophets:

"The Gentiles shall come unto thee from the ends of the earth, and shall say, As our fathers have got for themselves false idols and there is no profit in them." And again: "I have set thee to be a light of the Gentiles, that thou shouldest be for salvation unto the ends of the earth."

39. And there I wish to wait for the promise of him who never disappoints. As he promises in the Gospel, "They shall come from the east and west and from the south and from the north, and shall sit down with Abraham and Isaac and Jacob"; as we believe that believers will come from all over the world.

40. For that reason then we ought to fish well and diligently, as the Lord forewarns and teaches, saying, "Come ye after me, and I will make you to become fishers of men." And again he says through his prophets, "Behold I send fishers and many hunters, saith God, and so forth."

Therefore it was urgently necessary that we should spread our nets to take a great multitude and a throng for God, and that everywhere there should be clergy to baptise and exhort the poverty-stricken and needy folk, as the Lord in the Gospel warns and teaches, saying:

"Go ye therefore now and teach all nations, baptising them in the name of the Father and of the Son and of the Holy Ghost; teaching them to observe all things whatsoever I have commanded you: and lo, I am with you always, even unto the end of the world."

And again he says: "Go ye therefore into all the world and preach the Gospel to every creature. He that believeth and is baptised shall be saved; but he that believeth not shall be damned" [which means judged].

And again: "This Gospel of the kingdom shall be preached in all the world for a witness unto all nations: and then shall the end come."

And in like manner the Lord, foretelling by the prophet, says: "And it shall come to pass in the last days, saith the Lord, I will pour out of my Spirit upon all flesh: and your sons and your daughters shall prophesy, and your young men shall see visions, and your old men shall dream dreams: and on my servants and on my handmaidens I will pour out in those days of my Spirit; and they shall prophesy."

And Hosea says: "I will call them my people, which were not my people; and the one that hath obtained mercy which had not obtained mercy. And it shall come to pass, that in the place where it was said, Ye are not my people, there shall they be called the children of the living God."

41. Whence Ireland, which never had the knowledge of God, but up to the present always adored idols and abominations—how has there lately been prepared a

people of the Lord and the name given to them of Children of God? The sons of the Scots and the daughters of their chieftains are seen to become the monks and virgins of Christ.

Noble Lady Baptized by Patrick Becomes Virgin of Christ

42. But once especial there was one blessed lady of Scottic birth, noble of line, very lovely, and of full age, whom I myself baptised; and after a few days she came to me for a certain purpose. She disclosed to us that she had received from God a private admonition, and it warned her to become a Virgin of Christ and live closer to God.

Thanks be to God, on the sixth day after, most worthily and zealously she snatched at that vocation, as all the Virgins of Christ do in like manner; not with the consent of their fathers; no, they endure persecution and lying reproaches from their kindred, and yet their numbers increase all the more and we cannot tell how many of our race are thus reborn there, besides widows and the continent.

But the women who are held in slavery are in the worst toils. They constantly endure even unto terrors and threats. But the Lord gave grace to many of my handmaidens; for, although they are forbidden, they resolutely follow the example of the others.

43. Therefore, even if I should wish to depart from them, and thus proceeding to Britain—and gladly ready was I to do so—as to my fatherland and kindred; and not that only, but to go as far as Gaul, to visit the brethren and behold the face of the saints of my Lord—God knows that I used to yearn deeply for it—yet I am bound in the Spirit, who witnesses to me that if I should do this he would mark me as guilty; and I fear to lose the labour which I have started off—no, not I but Christ the Lord who bade me come and be with them for the rest of my life, if the Lord so will, and if he should guard me from every evil way, so that I may not sin in his sight.

44. Now I hope that this is my course of duty; but I do not trust myself as long as I am in the body of this death. For he is strong that daily strives to turn me away from faith and from the chastity of a religion without fiction, which I have resolved to preserve till the end of my life for Christ my Lord. But the flesh our enemy forever drags us towards death; that is, the baits of pleasure which can be enjoyed but only in woe.

Copyright © 1979, 1985 Church Universal and Triumphant, Inc.

I know in part wherein I have not led a faultless life; but I confess to my Lord, and I do not blush in his sight, for I tell no lie: From the time that I learned to know him in my youth, the love of God and the fear of him grew in me; and to this day, with God's favour, I have kept the faith.

45. Let who will laugh or insult, I shall not keep silent or conceal the signs and the wonders which were furnished to me by the Lord many years before they came to pass, since he knows all things even before the world began.

46. Therefore I ought without pause to render thanks to God who often pardoned my folly and my negligence—and that not in one place only—so that he was not passionately angered against me who was given as a fellow-labourer; and yet I did not speedily acquiesce in accord with what had been revealed to me, and as the Spirit brought to my remembrance. Thousands of times the Lord showered mercy upon me, because he saw that I was ready but did not know what I should do in response, situated as I was with many men forbidding this embassage.

Patrick's Motives Questioned by the Brethren

Behind my back they were talking among themselves and saying, "Why does this fellow push himself into danger among hostile folk who know not God?" Not for reasons of malice; but it did not seem sensible to them, as I myself bear witness I understood, on account of my illiteracy. And I did not quickly recognise the grace which was then in me. Now I see the right course which I ought to have seen before.

47. Now, then, I have with simplicity made these disclosures to my brethren and fellow-servants who have believed in me, for the reason which I told you before and foretell you to strengthen and confirm your faith. Would that you too would imitate greater things and perform acts more potent for good! That will be my glory, for a wise son is the glory of his father.

48. You know, and God also, in what manner from my youth onwards I have lived with you, in faith of the truth and in sincerity of heart. Even towards those gentiles among whom I dwell I have kept faith, and will go on keeping it. God knows, I have defrauded none of them; nor do I think of doing so, for the sake of God and his Church, lest I should raise persecution against them and all of us, and lest the name of God should be blasphemed

through me. For it is written, "Woe to the man through whom the name of the Lord is blasphemed."

49. But though I be rude in all things, still I have sought in some degree to keep watch over myself, both for the Christian brethren and the virgins of Christ and the devout women who used of their own free will present me with their little gifts and threw on the altars various of their adornments, which I delivered back to them.

And they were scandalised against me because I acted thus. But I did it out of my hope of immortality, that I might keep myself cautiously in all things, that the heathen for one reason or another might accept me or the ministry of my service, and that I should not, even in the smallest detail, give pretext to the unbelievers to defame and disparage.

50. Maybe, then, when I baptised so many thousands of men, I hoped from any one of them even as much as the half of a scruple? Tell me and I shall restore it to you. Or when my trivial self had been the Lord's instrument for the ordaining of clergy on all sides, and I gave them my ministrations for nothing, if I required from any one of them even the price of my shoe, tell it against me and I shall restore you the price and more.

51. I spent for you that they might receive me; and both among you and wherever I travelled for your sake, through many dangers, even to outlying regions beyond which was no man, and where nobody had ever come to baptise or ordain clergy or confirm the folk, I have, by God's bounty, done everything diligently and joyfully for your salvation.

Patrick Seized and Put in Irons, Rescued by God on the Fourteenth Day

52. At times I used to give presents to the kings besides the wages I paid their sons, who went round with me; and yet they seized me once with my companions. And on that day they most eagerly desired to slaughter me; but the time was not yet come. Everything which they found upon us they plundered, and myself they bound with irons. And on the fourteenth day the Lord freed me from their power; and whatever was our property was restored to us for God's sake and the sake of the near friends whom we had provided beforehand.

53. You know also from your own experience how much I paid out to those who were Judges throughout all

the districts which I more regularly visited; for I calculate that I distributed to them not less than the price of 15 men, so that you might enjoy me and I might enjoy you ever in God. I do not regret it, nor consider it enough. Still I spend and will spend more. The Lord is mighty to grant me afterwards to be myself spent for your souls.

54. Lo, I call God for a record upon my soul that I lie not; nor was it that there might be an occasion for flattering words or covetousness that I have written to you; nor do I hope for honour from any of you. Enough for me is the honour which is not yet seen but is believed in the heart. And faithful is He that promised; never does he lie.

55. But I see that already in this present world I am exalted beyond measure by the Lord. And I was not worthy, nor am I such that he should grant me this gift, since I know with full certainty that poverty and affliction become me better than riches and luxuries.

Why, Christ the Lord was a poor man for our sakes. But I, wretched and stricken, possess no wealth even if I should wish for it; nor do I judge mine own self. For every day I expect either a violent death or to be defrauded or to be reduced into slavery, or some such disaster. But none of these things move me, on account of the promises of heaven. I have cast myself into the hands of Almighty God, for he rules everywhere, as the prophet says: "Cast thy care upon God, and he shall sustain thee."

Prayer of Commitment to God

56. Lo, now I commit the keeping of my soul to my most faithful God, for whom I am an ambassador in my lowliness, only because he accepts no man's person and he chose me for this office, that I should be his minister, one of the least of them.

57. Therefore I shall render unto him for all his benefits towards me. But what shall I say or what shall I promise to my Lord? For I see no worth except what he himself has given to me. But he tries the hearts and reins, and knows that abundantly and strenuously do I desire, and have long been ready, that he should grant me to drink of his cup, as he has granted to others who love him.

58. For which reason may it never happen to me from my God that I should ever lose his people whom he purchased at the ends of the earth. I pray God to grant me perseverance and deign that I may render myself a

faithful witness unto him till the time of my passing hence, for God's sake.

59. And if I ever accomplished aught in the cause of my God whom I love, I beseech him to grant me that I may shed my blood with those strangers and captives for his name's sake, even though I should lack burial itself, even though the dogs and the wild beasts most wretchedly should rend my corpse limb by limb or the fowls of the air should devour it.

With perfect certitude, I think, if such should be my fate, I have gained a soul as profit with my body. For beyond all doubt we shall rise on that day in the crystal brightness of the sun; that is, in the Glory of Christ Jesus our Redeemer, as sons of the living God and joint-heirs with Christ, conformed to his image which is to be. For of him and through him and in him we shall reign.

60. For that sun which we behold rises by God's command on our behalf every day. But it will never reign, nor will its Splendor endure; but all who worship it, wretched men, shall stumble upon their punishment. Whereas we, who worship and believe in the True Sun, Christ, who will never pass away—nor will anyone who doeth his will; but he will abide for ever, as Christ will abide for ever, who reigns with God the Father Almighty and with the Holy Spirit, before all worlds, and now, and for all the ages ever to come. Amen.

61. Lo, again and yet again I shall briefly set forth the words of my confession. I testify in truth and in glorying of heart before God and his holy angels, that I never had any cause except the Gospel and his promises in ever returning to that people from whom I had before with difficulty escaped.

62. But I pray those who believe and fear God, whosoever has deigned to scan and to take this writing which Patrick the Sinner; verily of no education, composed in Ireland, that none shall ever say it was my ignorance which achieved whatever tiny success was mine or whatever I showed in accordance with God's will; but make your judgment, and let it be most truly believed that it was the Gift of God.

And this is my Confession before I die.

This sermon was delivered by the Messenger Elizabeth Clare Prophet at Camelot on Sunday, March 17, 1985, prior to the dictation "I Call the Living Saints" by Saint Patrick. See Pearl 16, p. 214 for footnotes.

Copyright © 1979, 1985 Church Universal and Triumphant, Inc., Box A, Malibu, CA 90265. All rights reserved. Printed in the United States of America. Pearls of Wisdom and The Summit Lighthouse are registered trademarks of Church Universal and Triumphant, Inc. All rights to their use are reserved. Published by The Summit Lighthouse. Pearls sent weekly (to USA, via third-class mail) for a minimum love offering of $40/year.

I Call the Living Saints

Let the Deliverer come forth from the heart of the living saints! I bear the banner of Maitreya in the shamrock, in the scepter of the shepherd's crook, and in the emblem of the Emerald Isle and the Emerald Matrix.

Dare to Be Different!

Blessed hearts of living fire, I did come and I come again. I call unto the living saints; for those who dwell here in this plane must show forth the living Spirit, else how will those deadened by the darkness of despair know that there is indeed a higher life and a higher way? Thus, some glimpse of eternity must be seen. Do not fear, then, to stand out in stark relief against the ways of death with some measure of hope for Infinity. With Truth and a scepter, thou shalt prevail!

Blessed hearts, the byword of the initiates of Maitreya must be *Dare to Be Different!* I say, how can we dare to disobey the command of the heart of Maitreya? We dare not go against the inner Word and the inner Light. Yet some of late have sought to silence that Word, to quench the Flame, knowing if they would hear it or feel the burning of the heart, they would be compelled to an action which they would rather shun.

Let not this founding religion of the age, O my beloved, become watered down by the firstfruits.[1] For those who come after will indeed desire to water down the path of the Ascended Masters and to say, "We also do those things, we also have the testimony," when they do not.

Humility and the Boldness of the LORD's Spirit

Blessed ones, I am more grateful than I could ever have known that I would be in the ascended state that I did write my confession. For in it you perceive the consistency of the ardor and the necessity of union through God with an abject humility that instantaneously becomes the boldness of the Lord's Spirit with you.

Humility, then, is never that fawning, self-belittlement guilt sense. But rather it is the sense of the awesomeness of thy God where thou standest and the place of holy ground. Truly it is the commeasurement of the messenger of the little self against the backdrop of the Greater Self.

How great is our God! How wondrous His manifest Works! And therefore, let the crystal be thy identity and let there appear truly the face of Christ. And let those whom you meet recognize that presence, that power, that authority—even by the light, by the aura, by the contact, by the fearlessness and the boldness of the simple word of Christ that does heal.

El Morya with St. Patrick and Mother Mary at Spring Quarter 1985 His Reminder of First Things and Firstfruits

Therefore, by El Morya, Chief of the Darjeeling Council, I am sent to remind you of first things and firstfruits. He who has founded this order of The Summit Lighthouse and this activity, he, the one who has called your souls and disciplined you, calls you again and calls you in this hour to his spring quarter of Summit University. For he is determined to make you worthy and to make you value the presence so great of Maitreya and the World Teachers in your midst.

And so, that blessed hierarch whom I adore as he adores the will of God—whom I adore for his life lived in the defense of holy Church and that will and that integrity and that honor—he has sent me to be with him and the Blessed Mother in this spring quarter, that together we might forge once again that union of hearts of revolutionaries, of fervent ones who recognize that the harvest waits, that the world is waiting, and that there are none others, save Keepers of the Flame who will make the call, to whom we can entrust so great a salvation and such a dangerous journey.

Beloved ones, I, too, bid you to the call of the prayer vigil for Ireland and for the saints of Ireland. For many a mother's heart and many a daughter and wife and child does weep this day for the loved one who has been slain. Truly, beloved hearts, there are serpents and devils in embodiment in that land this day who stalk about seeking whom they may devour.[2] This does not exonerate whether* the government of England or any

---
*either

I Call the Living Saints

man's heart who is not quickened by God.

Nevertheless, we come to defend those who are of the Light at the same time that we must place before the peoples of all nations the reminder, as Saint Germain said in the land of the Philippines,[3] that each one must look within and cast out the serpent if he would save his country and his nation rather than attribute to the leadership alone the fault and the blame—look within and recognize that the responsibility to raise up the scepter and authority of Christ has never, never been greater!

Heaven is opened and the bowers of springtime reveal the abundant blossoms of hope. Truly, Christ in all His glory descends in the very flame of the ark of the covenant. Truly the Son of God is with you! Truly those who are the fallen ones dissolve before the sacred fire of the LORD's hosts and the call of the faithful!

The Mighty Purpose of Confession

Therefore, take heart and recognize the mighty purpose of confession. Recognize it in this hour: that every man's sin, whether recent or ancient, does accrue to him and therefore prevent the full covenants of God from manifesting. Why is this so? It is because God has made covenant with His beloved Son who is your own Christ Self, who is worthy of every offering and of the fullness of the Science of Being.

This offering the Christ, by His grace, does bestow upon your soul when the soul is ready and able to receive it, clothed upon with that wedding garment. Thus, you who have gained the wedding garment, if the garment becomes stained, do confess your sins in sealed letter to Almighty God, to the heart of Christ, and let it be burned. And if you desire that the Mother of the Flame should know this also to pray for your salvation, you may write to her as well in a separate letter.

And therefore, beloved hearts, understand that confession, remission of sin, repentance therefore does once again restore you to that alignment with the chalice of being who is Christ. For Christ is the crystal chalice, Christ is the Holy Grail, and the Light that is poured therein does become the nectar thou dost quaff.

Beloved hearts of living flame, therefore not once in a lifetime but daily, submit therefore the past and the present into the sacred fire that the call might go forth and be answered as though it were the call of your Lord. And truly you are His vessel, His representative, His instrument, and His messenger as you keep your soul unspotted from the world.

Blessed hearts, it is efficacious truly to the spiritual life to understand the meaning of this confession. For truly, in the crystal clarity of the mind that does fast and pray weekly and cast those sins in the sacred fire, there does come the presence of holy angels and the recognition of the voice of Christ and the inner independence in the I AM THAT I AM.

Not Sin, but the Will to Sin Is the Destroyer of Souls

Truly understand the housecleaning that comes through the realization "Not I but God in me is my Deliverer," for herein lies the key to the forgiveness of sin. For inasmuch as God is the Deliverer, a man's sins cannot hold him bound forever; for the deliverance of Almighty God is therefore the means to self-elevation in Christ.

Thus, beloved, recognize the opportunity of the moment, the opportune moment for the acceleration of Light. Recognize that a man's sins are not capable of destroying him, but a man's willfulness to continue in sin is the nucleus of self-destruction. Those who would go and sin no more, therefore, must know that when you cease to sin, instantaneously you are delivered from the toils of the tempter.

Understand, therefore, that the will that has a heart for God and His Path, the will that has a heart and a desire for loving and serving and passing through the fiery trial to be rid, then, of the old man[4]—that *will* is the fortification whereby the soul may mount and enter the arms of the everlasting Christ, truly the Bridegroom who does receive His own.

Therefore, not sin but the will to sin is the destroyer of souls and is therefore capable of placing the individual outside of the pale of faith and the holy Church and the Circle of Light and the means of entering in daily to the oneness of that communion of saints delivered to you in the very presence of the Ascended Masters and our God.

Know, then, that the strength of our movement and our revolution today is always the strength of the individual, as the Messenger has told you. Let the individual become the pillar of fire. Let him recognize the Rock of Christ within himself. Let him cease the human chattering and the human comfort which yet leaves him vulnerable. For the only point of invulnerability is the casting of oneself upon this Rock of Christ that the self, with all of its inadequacies, may ultimately be broken and the True Self appear as thy divine Reality.[5]

Just as quickly as you can let go of the former self, so the True

Self does appear, beloved hearts. But it takes the leap of faith—faith in the Science of Being that was declared from the beginning unto the ending, from the Alpha to the Omega of thy life.

I Call for a Prayer Vigil for Ireland

Blessed hearts of faith, I call, then, for a vigil—a prayer vigil for Ireland. And I ask not only that this be the foundation of calls to Light for that land of Erin, but that it be the foundation of a new dedication of thy life upon the altar of freedom, that it become the first of many prayer vigils conducted (whether by the Messenger or by yourselves) for the increasingly burdensome situations that have been placed upon the freedom-fighters of the world.

Beloved ones, never does the enemy rest; and there is ground that is being taken for want of defense. Let the spiritual defenses flow, and let my "Lorica" become your own. Let my prayer be recited, for I will come to you through it and you will see the miracles of the LORD's deliverance and you will see the transformation of your aura as Christ in you and around you is truly the one who does battle.

Let Keepers of the Flame Bear the Burden of Saint Germain

It is an hour of courage and of Light and immense promise. But I myself must note the record of the Keeper of the Scrolls that many who have heard or should have heard but have not even taken the opportunity to present themselves of a Sunday to hear the dictation have therefore become watered down, "backsliding," as they say, and truly out of the pale of the circle of the protection of Saint Germain.

And consequently, these also become murmurers and complainers and disgruntled and dissatisfied, declaring that they receive not the fruits of the living God and that the organization or various individuals within it have not rewarded them accordingly or given unto them their just deserts. Beloved hearts, it is for the want of the understanding of the path of sainthood that they thus complain. It is for want of preachers and shepherds and Christed ones who must take the offering of the altar and preach it unto every creature, beginning with the brethren.

And if there be some who, after this preaching and this direct challenging that must come through your hearts, still do not enter in to the joy of the Lord Saint Germain and the joy of his freedom and will not take up his mantle—then tell them, beloved hearts, as I say and as the Darjeeling Council does proclaim it this day, that those who are not here in this activity as chelas of Saint Germain, who are not bearing his burden of Light and his burden of world responsibility, ought not to remain connected with the holy order of the Keepers of the Flame Fraternity.

For there are reasons for being for the establishment of this movement, and it ever has been the Guru/chela relationship between yourselves and Sanat Kumara which is enhanced and effected through your relationship with the Ascended Masters and the Messengers.

Therefore, it is a church with a holy calling and a holy purpose. And truly the last and least of these purposes should be the consideration of the mere physical survival of the self. Let none attach themselves to the community of the Holy Spirit who see this as an escape valve in time of trouble. For none shall be saved except by the LORD's Spirit and those who are in the LORD's Spirit of the I AM THAT I AM on the LORD's Day.[6]

And the LORD's Day is the Day of Judgment. And therefore, understand that the survival of the physical body is only as the envelope for those who are of the etheric octave and who are the saints of God.

I come, therefore, as the threshing does come and the mighty threshingfloor of the LORD.[7] For there must be a separation and there must be a dividing of the way.[8] For it is not meet that the heart of the Messenger, physical and spiritual, should carry those who refuse to carry themselves; for it is written, "Every man shall bear his own burden."[9] And you have agreed, as Keepers of the Flame, to carry more than your own burden—to carry the burden of the LORD and the burden of humanity and the burden of proclaiming freedom to the captives in all nations.

What Is the Mantle of El Morya?

Let us return, then, to the first and founding principles of this order of The Summit Lighthouse. Thus, Morya comes to spring quarter, and he summons the devotees who truly understand that the purpose of the Darjeeling Council is to give advice to the souls of Light and to all who keep the flame of the nations for the government of God to come and the abundant life to manifest and, truly, this world to be turned around according to the dispensations of Elohim.

Therefore it is meet, beloved hearts, that those who would walk in the mantle and the dispensation of the hour understand what is that mantle of the I AM Presence that comes to you

I Call the Living Saints

through El Morya. Some chelas who have departed from his will have all but silenced him, for the unfulfilled dictation is the nonresponse of the chela. The dictations of El Morya have been spoken from the altar, yet they have stopped at the altar rail. And the infective internalization of that call has not been forthcoming.

Sanat Kumara's Message Concerning the Preaching of the Word

It is apparent in many areas but let us go back to one, for a beginning, that is ever so close to my heart: it is the message of the Lord Sanat Kumara concerning the preaching of the Word, that does tell that the fulfillment of your individual Christhood is to be found in the speaking of the Word of God.[10]

Yet how many preachers of righteousness have prepared themselves out of this community to deliver that Word that comes forth out of the mouth of the Messenger? There ought to be many. And therefore, let the many appear and understand that it is integral to your integration with the I AM Presence in the union of the ascension that by *you,* as the Word incarnate, the Word should go forth in the preachments of the Ascended Masters' teachings, which ought to cover the earth as the waters cover the sea.

Thus, understand that when the call is not fulfilled, when the law of the hour (the law coming from your I AM Presence) does not resound in the hall in the temple of the community, this forestalls the coming again of greater Light. The nonfulfillment of the Word, which is the nonobedience to that Word, therefore prevents the entering in of the next level of the multitudes who would eat the flesh and the blood of the sons and daughters of God—the firstfruits of our calling.

You Yourself Must Fulfill Your Fiery Destiny

How can you neglect so great a salvation? In your vernacular, I would say to you, "We never had it so good." We never had so much God and so much intensity. We languished in our aloneness and our persecutions, for God would underscore for us the great majesty of His beauty by leaving us in intervals to our aloneness, to our karma, to our facing of the seed of the wicked. And thus, in His Presence shining—the unmistakable splendor, the unmistakable Light that was not our own—we had no chance to take for granted His grace, but must keep the vigil against every foe.

Here the grace does flow as living waters perpetually, almost to the wearying of some who have said, "We have heard enough.

We have heard it all! We may stay home because we know what is the Truth and the Law. We need not hear it repeated again and again. Let us live our lives and make our own ascensions, for we have the violet flame and the decree and we are devotees of Saint Germain. He will save us in the last day."

Hear, then, the lying serpent mind that does *fool* you when you have been told again and again that no Master can save you but only point the way, that you yourself must fulfill your fiery destiny. See how you are even unconscious that the serpent mind has spoken softly in great, beguiling wiliness.

And the soul has heard. And the consciousness has shifted into laxity. And thus, in place of identifying the LORD within, you come when the Messenger is present and absent yourself when she is not present. And, even then, you come not when she is present.

A Definition of the Condition of Sin and the Sinner

Beloved hearts, all of this is the result of an absence of a sense of your position in history—the history of Light and Darkness from the beginning unto the ending. Understand the commeasurement of your life against that of the Ascended Master and your own Christhood. And understand that it was not a false doctrine whereby I proclaimed myself a sinner. For when you have the perception of the absolute glory of Almighty God, by comparison, the very body you wear, the very plane and consciousness wherein you abide, has the taint of sin as the smell of smoke or of foul substance.

Realize that this is said not in self-condemnation but in the realization that until one is glorified in Christ and in the ritual of the ascension, one dwells in the temporal form, vulnerable and subject to decay and the things of this world. And the very subjectness of the self to these things is a condition of sin, even when thy works be filled with grace.

It is the reminder that in this state one can fail. One can make the mistake and drop back and lose touch with the reality of the battle as well as the reality of the absolutes of Good and Evil, as Gabriel has taught you.[11] Thus remember: nothing is guaranteed until you are the Ascended Master. Nothing is sure until it becomes both physical and spiritual.

The victory cannot be counted upon until you win it! And therefore you cannot say the Messenger will go forth and save the nations. You cannot count on it until it is done. And you cannot count on it being done until and unless you yourself do it.

The True Theology of the Aquarian Age

You are therefore responsible for the "I" who is the I AM where you are. And let that I AM Presence live, I say! Let it live free and freeborn. Let it live to fulfill its fiery destiny with you as a concomitant and a concommunicant with that "I."

The I AM THAT I AM in you is the deliverer of the nations. And the only difference between you and the Messenger is that she has realized this I AM THAT I AM to the fullest as her own identity and identification with Elohim, as the means whereby heaven and earth meet where she is. It is the realization of the soul that "all in me is the I AM, and I AM *that* I AM." And that oneness is the ability to charge in the name of the LORD.

Blessed hearts, this is the true message, the true theology of the Aquarian age. *Who* will know it or understand it if only one does become it—or two? Who will understand it unless *multitudes* of sons and daughters of God walk the earth clothed upon fully in their Holy Christ Self?

Dare we consider that the Aquarian age should be another two thousand years of the lie of only one Son of God who died for all the sins of the others? Let us not perpetuate the lie by the self-indulgence which considers, "Lo, I am that Son," but *fails* to prove it, *fails* to live it, *fails* to be the example of that Son!

This is not a church of theory. The Word must be made flesh truly. The Light must be adored and shine through you. Therefore, cease from tarrying in indulgences in the comfortability of the lap of the Mother. For you may seek her and not find her and then require the mantle but not have it for want of seeing the necessity of the preparation.

The Celebration of My Life in the Taking Up of My Calling

Beloved hearts, it is my desire to see my day a joyous one—joy in the flame and in the knowledge that the flame can conquer yet the serpents—not a reveling, not an intoxication of pleasure and alcohol, but rather the joy and rejoicing that our God is nigh and able to conquer. Blessed hearts, the celebration of my life for which I long is that some—the few and the many—will truly take up my calling for that land of Erin and for every nation which I seal in this hour by my heart's flame in that Emerald Matrix.

I, too, then, am forsaken until some and one and the few come to be Saint Patrick incarnate. For I AM that Word, I AM THAT I AM THAT I AM. Thus, call to me to enter your heart, and pray there with Christ for your deliverance. Pray for the perception, pray for the discriminating plumb line of Truth, pray for right regard and vigilance.

The Five-to-Five Sabbath
a Twenty-Four Hour Cycle of Re-Creation in God

I compel you by my Word to know the true meaning of the fruit of fasting. Let none consider himself the exception. Be empty that I might fill you. And do this with regularity on the day set aside by Lanello.

Saturday is the day to divest oneself by the violet flame and cleanse and to write the letter of confession and burn it, to observe the Sabbath beginning at five, to enter the temple with Saint Germain and return on the morrow to receive the holiness of God because you have come—if you will, if you regard it so—to give your penance on Saturday evening, burning the letter and giving those three or four hours to him. Thus, thy sins are not only set aside, they are consumed; and you go forth in the new week clothed upon with a light of the crown of the Buddha Maitreya and the Teaching and the Light.

And thus, the Sabbath—from Saturday to Sunday, five to five—is a twenty-four-hour cycle of devotion. And in that period, that day of grace and light and re-creation in God, you are totally restored to the newness of your Christ Self and may go forward to work the works of God in the five secret rays within the seven—the five days of the week that are building the mighty heart chakra, weaving the seamless garment. And every week is a cycle that exceeds the last.

A Land Flowing with Milk and Honey—
and with Opportunity for Christhood

Thus, forge and win and build, beloved. Thus, understand that I have come for the love of your souls, to commemorate the ancient memory, to restore the sight to those blinded by egoism and self-love, to restore truly the gifts and graces that you might deliver your brothers and sisters.

Look through the eyes of the Stump team. Look through the eyes of the news you see and hear and read. Look to the world that suffers and recognize that truly you live in a land flowing with milk and honey, where you are blessed and graced with opportunity to realize your Christhood.

But the purpose of this nation of Liberty is that you might realize that Christhood and lay it upon the altar of the world that this Freedom and this Truth, this Liberty and this Peace

Copyright © 1985 Church Universal and Triumphant, Inc.

might, then, be the gift of God to all nations. How else can it be, if earth is to become freedom's star, that every nation should become that Light? And how shall they become that Light except the ones anointed to our calling fulfill it?

It Is Clear What Is to Be Done

It is clear what is to be done. Let the Elders of the Church commune and deliberate with all who desire to come now and place upon themselves and have placed upon them the robes white unto the sainthood of our God.

I bless you in the miracle Light of Christos. I bless you in that Light, for only by that Light are we blessed.

In the name of the holy Church, I serve. And I stand at the altar with the Messenger—the testimony and the witness to her Victory. By my Sword, by my Staff, it shall Be, it shall come to pass, it is done.

The Acceptance
Offered by the Messenger

Beloved Mighty I AM Presence from the heart of God in the Great Central Sun,

O intense Light of the brightness of the coming of the angels of Saint Patrick,

O beloved Ascended Master Saint Patrick, beloved Holy Christ Self,

Pray for us now and at the hour of the death of ego and carnal-mindedness, all sin and disease, in the hour of the death of Death itself, O God.

O Holy Christ Flame, Holy Christ Self, O Universal Christ, hear our call and answer through the entire Spirit of the Great White Brotherhood.

So deliver the Church of God on earth as in heaven and His Mystical Body on earth as in heaven and His dearest Love in all disciples and saints on earth as in heaven.

We accept Thy deliverance, O God, in the name of the Ancient of Days, Sanat Kumara, anointer of Saint Patrick and of our own souls.

Even so, God, by Thy grace raise us up to the glorification of Thy name in this temple.

Even so, dwell bodily within us, O God, in fulfillment of Thy promises.

We accept it in this hour.

In the name of the Father and of the Son and of the Holy Spirit and in the name of the Mother, Amen.

"The Summit Lighthouse Sheds Its Radiance O'er All the World to Manifest as Pearls of Wisdom." This dictation by Saint Patrick was delivered through the Messenger Elizabeth Clare Prophet on Sunday, March 17, 1985, at Camelot. (1) Rom. 11:16; James 1:18; Rev. 14:4. (2) I Pet. 5:8; Rev. 12:12. (3) See Saint Germain, March 3, 1985, "The LORD's Prophecy unto the Philippines," *Pearls of Wisdom,* vol. 28, no. 14, pp. 155-56, 162-63. (4) Rom. 6:6; Eph. 4:22-24; Col. 3:9, 10. (5) "The stone which the builders rejected, the same is become the head of the corner: this is the Lord's doing, and it is marvellous in our eyes.... And whosoever shall fall on this stone shall be broken but on whomsoever it shall fall, it will grind him to powder." Matt. 21:42, 44; Pss. 118:22, 23; Luke 20:17, 18; I Pet. 2:6-8. See *The Scofield Reference Bible,* p. 1312, n. 2. (6) Isa. 2:10-22; 13:6-16; 34:1-8; 61:2; 63:4. (7) Matt. 3:12. (8) Matt. 25:31-46. (9) Gal. 6:5. (10) See Sanat Kumara, *The Opening of the Seventh Seal, Pearls of Wisdom,* vol. 22, pp. 126-27, 129, 209-27, 265-66; and Cyclopea, July 2, 1982, "Unto the Watchman of the House of Israel," in *Kuan Yin Opens the Door to the Golden Age,* Book 2 (*Pearls of Wisdom,* vol. 25, no. 41), pp. 403-14. (11) Archangel Gabriel, *Mysteries of the Holy Grail,* Summit University Press, pp. 129-38, 155-62; $12.95 ($13.95 postpaid USA).
Footnotes from Pearl 15, "Saint Patrick's Day Address" by Elizabeth Clare Prophet:
(1) Elizabeth Clare Prophet, Summit University lecture, March 16, 1985, "An Historical Perspective." (2) Seumas MacManus, *The Story of the Irish Race: A Popular History of Ireland,* rev. ed. (Old Greenwich, Conn.: Devin-Adair Co., 1921), pp. 109, 112-15. (3) Sanat Kumara, "The Judgment of Serpent and His Seed," in *The Opening of the Seventh Seal, Pearls of Wisdom,* vol. 22, no. 46, pp. 313-16. (4) Saint Patrick, *Letter to the Soldiers of Coroticus,* in Paul Gallico, *The Steadfast Man: A Biography of St. Patrick* (Garden City, N.Y.: Doubleday & Company, 1958), pp. 220-25. (5) Rev. 10:1, 2, 8-11. (6) El Morya, February 3, 1985, "Chela—Christed One—Guru: Offices on the Path of the Individualization of the God Flame," *Pearls of Wisdom,* vol. 28, no. 11, pp. 123-25. (7) Saint Patrick, *The Confession,* in Oliver St. John Gogarty, *I Follow Saint Patrick* (London: Rich & Cowan, 1938), pp. 311-26. (8) At the age of 16, Patrick was captured by Irish marauders and delivered into slavery. He escaped 6 years later, at the age of 22. (9) I Pet. 3:4. (10) Zech. 2:8.

Pearls of Wisdom, published weekly by The Summit Lighthouse for Church Universal and Triumphant, come to you under the auspices of the Darjeeling Council of the Great White Brotherhood. These are presently dictated by the Ascended Masters to their Messenger Elizabeth Clare Prophet. The international headquarters of this nonprofit, nondenominational activity is located in Los Angeles, California. All communications and freewill contributions should be addressed to The Summit Lighthouse, Box A, Malibu, CA 90265. Pearls of Wisdom are sent weekly throughout the USA via third-class mail to all who support the Church with a minimum yearly love offering of $40. First-class and international postage rates available upon request. Notice of change of address should be received three weeks prior to the effective date. Third-class mail is not forwarded by the post office.

Copyright © 1985 Church Universal and Triumphant, Inc. All rights reserved. Printed in the United States of America. Pearls of Wisdom and The Summit Lighthouse are registered trademarks of Church Universal and Triumphant, Inc. All rights to their use are reserved.

Palm Sunday 1985
The Mission of a Living Flame
The Triumphal Entry of the Buddha of the Ruby Ray

Beloved of the Light, I descend in the flame of Ahura Mazda. I come in this hour—Zarathustra. I appear to you out of the living flame of sacred fire and out of the tradition of all saints of the Most High to discover the symbol of their Divinity not only in the living Flame, but in the Sun behind the sun—to know the living God.

The Messenger's Translation by Fire

I appear in the hour of the translation by fire of the Messenger. And I consecrate her life to the mission of a living flame that does blaze a trail in the name of Saint Germain until all who are called by God have heard the message and this Gospel is preached in every nation.

Thus understand the fire infolding itself. Understand the long history of your Messengers who have come after those of us who brought the teaching of the avatars in past ages.

The Religion of the Sacred Fire Delivered to the People of Persia

Thus, this Woman of the Sun came after me to secure the teachings of Ahura Mazda, who is Sanat Kumara, transferred to the people of Persia[1]—who in ancient times were a people of Light but who have been supplanted in this hour by a people of Darkness, warring and making war in the name of Allah rather than making peace in the pure Spirit of Sanat Kumara.

And their karma is upon them!

And you understand that their leaders who have come forth sending Iran to war with Iraq in this day have caused them to be decimated and have brought bloodshed upon that land once consecrated to the consummate Light.

Copyright © 1985 Church Universal and Triumphant, Inc.

And in the hour of our coming, your Messenger also, as a queen in that day, promoted our teaching and accepted our emissary, the Archangel Gabriel, who came to inspire upon those monarchs, the king and queen, the necessity to promulgate a teaching whereby the people should understand the unity of Good and the all-power of Good to defeat the hosts of Darkness.

We brought a message of Armageddon. And thus, that message not having been kept to this day, we see this people devoured by their own karma, their own laggard consciousness, and the devouring of their very souls by the insanity from the infestation of demons.

Observe, then, how those in the Middle East have tapped into the violence out of the pits of Death and Hell. And thus, Archangel Michael has already come to you with the message of your own individual mission to become a chela of the Archangel[2] and therefore to be enlisted in the ranks of the legions of blue lightning to go forth while your bodies sleep at night for the binding of those denizens in the pit[3] who themselves hold a focus of Darkness for the aggressive activities of those in embodiment.

I come, then, to report to you that much has been accomplished already at inner levels as chelas of El Morya have been accepted in the ranks of the Archangel. And I assure you that as you press on and remember the words of Archangel Michael of the necessity for that perpetual marathon and the understanding of the forces abroad in the land in this year,[4] you will see that every protection of heaven will be upon you through every trial until you, with Maitreya in that mighty clipper ship, shall find yourselves united in this community of the Holy Spirit in such a strength and unity and purity of heart that the true message of all of the Ascended Masters of the Brotherhood shall be known upon the face of the earth!

The Spiritual Unity of Nations
and the Building of Mighty Victory's Temple

And all who are of the Light will see the Light and know the Light. And the strength of the *spiritual unity of nations* will shine in the living Sun.

As the living Sun does shine, then, you can anticipate that through this *SUN* activity one day Mighty Victory's temple shall be built.[5] And it is up to you to ratify the proposal of Almighty God and the Brotherhood as to the building of this temple and the consecration of your own living temple to Victory's flame. For when this people shall have realized the inner victory, then the temple outside that is made with hands becomes the inevitable expression of the God-mastery in the flame of Victory's love.

The Buddha of the Ruby Ray Consumes the Forces of Anti-Victory

Thus, I come to consecrate you in Victory's flame to the victory spiral from the base to the crown, to the pure love of the ruby ray that you might know that truly our God in your midst is a consuming *ruby* fire. Thus, the Buddha of the Ruby Ray does appear in the sky and make known to you that the support from that level of the octaves of heaven is unto you in this hour for the consuming of the forces of anti-Victory that are bent upon the ruination of the rising Sun of these little ones.

And these forces are determined to create chaos and world confusion and cataclysm and war. But they shall not pass when one Christed one is raised up to become a central sun, that ye all might also know the living Truth as the necessity of the hour.

Pallas Athena Defends the Community against All Enemies

Walk, then, as children of Truth, as initiates of Pallas Athena and the sword and the shield of Truth. And know the meaning and the power of Truth to defend the individual and the community against all enemies whose case must be founded upon error or the lie or the murderous intent. Let them then be judged for the motivation of the heart. And by their own fruits let the Law act.

Run to Greet the Blessed Saint Francis

We come, then, for the deliverance of the faithful from the self-conceived notions of limitation and remind you again of Kuthumi's promise, as he has received the dispensation to counsel you in matters of personal psychology and health.[6] This Master, the World Teacher with Jesus, does indeed have a mantle from Omega to assist you personally.

If you could comprehend the vastness of the Mind of God in Kuthumi and his ability to deliver you from age-old phobias and fixations, you would hasten to run to greet the blessed Saint Francis who, himself now in the ascended state, has long left behind him that self-condemnation for the failure of the Franciscan brothers.

Thus understand that in the hour of the crucifixion the saints have taken upon themselves that world condemnation for the failure of those whom they have led when they have not fulfilled the fullness of the path that was vouchsafed to them by the original founder. But in the hour of the resurrection they leave behind all that. Thus, the Ascended Masters progress. Thus, their chelas may also pass through the gate from the *via dolorosa* to the victorious golden Light of the Sun.

The Good Friday Message of Forgiveness for the Raising of the Planet into the Golden Age

Blessed hearts, the fire infolding itself is surely the greatest shield. Comprehend, then, the message of Good Friday as world forgiveness.[7] I preach to you a message of forgiveness that you may consider under the heading of enlightened self-interest. But I see far beyond that side benefit to a universal momentum of Light that is for the raising of the planet into the golden age.

Consider, then, the absence of forgiveness, for instance, in this people of Iran and Iraq, whose original seed has been lost in the intermingling of the rebels against God and the laggard races. Understand that the reason for the war in each and every instance, the reason for terrorism and the killing of brother by brother in Lebanon is due to the absence of forgiveness and grace.

Beloved hearts, understand this message of living fire. Understand the message of the God flame. Realize, then, that forgiveness as a quality of the heart benefits the forgiver more than the forgiven. For when you forgive, you deliver yourself of the burden of holding within yourself the image of the one to whom you have given the power to hurt or destroy or maim or in any way offend your very own self.

Do you understand, then, that when you fail to forgive you cannot overcome within yourself the scar, the wound, the limitation, the psychological problem that was the result of the encounter of discord that resulted in nonforgiveness?

Thus, nonforgiveness as hardness of heart, beloved ones, is an activity that does bind your souls. You may not remember the hour and the day when you denied grace to any part of Life, when you took offense and erected a wall and said, "No more will I associate with this person!" From that moment on, that person that you have denied or failed to forgive has become one of your many gods. Another would be the carnal mind or the ego itself. For the soul in her purity robed in white has no blot or stain of nonforgiveness upon her garment.

This is why the beginning of the path of Jesus of Nazareth is seen in the changing of the water into wine. It is the forgiveness of the water of human consciousness that fails to act with propriety, with respect, or all due patience or politeness or in any manner or way that you deem proper, especially in regard to yourself.

Thus, the corollary in understanding the binding nature of nonforgiveness is the understanding of the principle of taking offense. He who can be offended by the acts of any man or woman or child is truly one who will be forever limited by his own offense.

Thus, beloved hearts, it is the eve of an hour of the consummate union of Christ in God. In this Passion Week you may fast and pray and come to the understanding that the meaning of Good Friday is the glorious gift of forgiveness of the violet flame. It is important to sort out what is known by the conscious mind and send oceans of mercy to every part of Life.

And then ask the Lord Christ within you to follow the tracks of the hidden ties, the tangle of roots of the subconscious that lead to other gnarled roots beneath the soil in the collective unconscious of the earth.

You Can Be Free Only As You Free All Life

Then understand that you can be free only as you free all Life. And this freedom is a freeing in the very solar plexus, in the feeling world, whereby you no longer separate yourself from any part of Life and you see all Life as only God: God in manifestation, God as Christ, God as Krishna, as Vishnu—Brahma, Shiva, as the Universal Mother.

The Mystery of Self as the Latticework of Light

Think of this, beloved: the Messenger herself would not survive in the giving of her body over and over a thousand times a thousand to the hearts who come for healing except she long ago learned the lesson from Mother Mary to understand herself simply as a latticework of Light through which the sacred energies of heaven flow. Thus, not identifying as the Giver but only as the instrument, the exhaustless, pure stream of the Source never fails to meet the demand of the hour.

This is the great mystery you must learn—you who would be healers and ministers and instruments of grace. To be the latticework means that there is nothing left to be forgiven, to forgive for, in oneself or in anyone on earth. But the stream of the love ruby ray, the stream of Light pouring through is a blessing to oneself and to all who have sinned and come short of the mark.[8]

Beloved, understand that forgiveness, a tributary of Light through your chakras, does not obviate the necessity for the wrongdoer to balance his karma, make his peace with God, and also learn the higher calling of the way of forgiveness.

America's Sponsorship by the Great White Brotherhood

Do you understand the difference between the people of the United States of America and of all other lands? This people consecrated by Saint Germain and Jesus Christ have therefore been given that initiation of the threefold flame of the heart by the Goddess of Liberty.

And you will find, no matter what the exception to the rule you may observe, that collectively as a people the charity of the heart of the American people and the ability to forgive and forget is greater than that of any other nation. And therefore, they are least beset by the burden of forcefields of black magicians manipulating the nation and the undergirdings of the psyche.

Beloved ones, you can always think of exceptions, but remember there is no nation that is free of the intermingling of the seed of the tares among the wheat. I speak of the wheat in this nation. It is a developed wheat, a developed seed of Christ, because of the intercession of the Great White Brotherhood. When you travel abroad, you will see the absence of this, and especially you will discover their nonforgiveness of America herself.

The Vulnerability of the Nonforgiving State

Beloved hearts, there are people who have a national consciousness of hatred of America that has been programmed and indoctrinated in them, but only because of their vulnerability. Their vulnerability not to forgive this nation for whatever wrongs committed, real or imagined, must therefore be exposed. And the vulnerability of an individual to fail to forgive another is the vulnerability of the absence of forgiveness of oneself or even the recognition of the necessity to confess before the living Christ, the Holy Christ Self, and to ask for forgiveness.

The people, then, who are convinced that they are right, who do not know Christ the Mediator, whose pride exceeds all desiring for grace, have thus not understood that the threading of the eye of the needle of the soul unto the Cosmic Christ consciousness is in the act of forgiveness.

O blessed hearts, it may be difficult for you to understand the vengeance that is held in the hearts, generation after generation, by some of the peoples of the Middle East who will destroy the third and fourth generation for crimes committed fifty years ago or a century ago. Yet they still seek to kill those who are of this or that tribe or family.

Now understand that this has caused division in all the nations of the earth—within the nations and in their ability to unite to stand for the principles of Christ.

If ever, then, there is an initiative in this nation to stand for the people of Poland or to stand for the people of Korea or of Taiwan or for the oppressed, you will find that the children of the Light who desire to stand for freedom nation by nation are overcome by the fallen ones in leadership positions who refuse in any way to compromise the business-as-usual concept of the economy and international trade for a principle that must be fought for and won for the protection of life.

The Answer Lies with the Individual

The answer lies, as always, with the individual. This is the message of every avatar, that has been proclaimed by that one and then disseminated by those who have come afterward with a great desire for the preservation of the teaching. You are counted among those who have served together with the Messengers to hold fast the pure principles of Truth. And you have been taught the lessons, whether or not you have ultimately learned them, that the only Truth that will ever survive is the Truth that is internalized in the heart and the soul and the mind and the being of that one individual.

As great revolutionaries, single-minded in heart and purpose, have turned the tides of nations, as communities have held the Light in the darkest hours of the earth, so in this moment know that the Great White Brotherhood yet looks to this community to hold back the tide of laggard evolutions before the incoming Light of each one's Christed presence that shall shine as the sun, become the Central Sun Magnet focus in the earth, and truly hold the balance against that karma which is returning upon the earth.

The Anointing of the Messenger and Keepers of the Flame

Therefore, let us begin with the individual. Let the Messenger be clothed upon with the fire of Zarathustra as I place my presence with her to go forth to meet those who have prepared their trial, their accusations, their false witness, their calumny and gossip—all this for the purposes of God that shall be revealed.

For shall we neglect so great a salvation or an opportunity to stand for that Truth?

Thus, though the human may be vulnerable, the Divine is not. Stand steadfast in your own pure Divinity. Affirm it for one another. And let the people of God rally close to our representative that this activity and Church and nation unto God might go forward in all the holy purposes ordained.

Courage of the heart is a rare gift in this day. And you yourselves have seen that that quality was essential to your staying power, even in this service here. Courage is the sign of the coming of age of the heart. The age of the heart is truly the age of the descent of the Messiah within you, even the Second Coming of Christ.

I, Zarathustra, anoint you. And with me always is Melchizedek and Oromasis and Diana, who lead the fiery salamanders and adepts of the sacred fire for the cleansing of the earth.

Your Friday Night Ascension Service
The Order of the Golden Lily under the Goddess of Liberty

I would direct your attention to the fact that in this hour many pass from the screen of life in war or through famine and disease. Your Friday night service, the Order of the Golden Lily, under the Goddess of Liberty and dedicated to the ascension, was also instigated at the request of the Lords of Karma because of the great necessity for the weekly clearance of the planetary body of discarnates—those who pass from the screen of life whose astral sheath and lower bodies are yet earthbound.

In order for us to make progress in the Light, there must be the binding of these discarnates. There must be the calls made for the directing of these souls of Light by the power of the mighty archangels to the retreats of the Great White Brotherhood.

Let the earth, the astral plane, the mental belt, and the etheric body therefore be cleared utterly and completely, week by week, so that when the day dawns on Saturday the forces of freedom may march unencumbered and uninhibited by yesterday's responsibility, having to become the cleanup committee to clear the way of this astral debris and therefore not being able to function purely in the defense of freedom and for the rescue of souls of Light on earth.

Blessed ones, there is a time and a place for all who pass from the screen of life. Some must be taken to the retreats of the Great White Brotherhood and some there are whose time is up who must face the Final Judgment. Some prepare for reincarnation in the retreats on the etheric plane. Some pass through the mystery of the ascension in the Light after many weeks or months under the tutelage of Serapis Bey and others.

Understand that the calls given in the service on Friday evening are for each one to be in his proper place and for the remaining families and relatives to be delivered of their grief and mourning and their burden by the attachment to the discarnate and departed one, who himself or herself is not free to move on in spiritual evolution under the emotional pull of remaining family members.

Cremation, the Lawful Means for the Disposal of the Remains

Beloved hearts, there is much superstition concerning the passing of loved ones on this planet. And many cling to them, and therefore the progression of earthly and spiritual cycles does not accelerate as it should in the Aquarian age.

I remind you—as a spokesman of the sacred fire as God, the consuming fire who revealed Himself to Moses—that cremation is the lawful means of disposing of the remains of the lifestream who has passed from this octave, thereby accelerating and hastening the return of the entire consciousness that exists within the body cells to that one's Christ Self and I AM Presence for purification.

Blessed hearts, it is very difficult for those whose bodies are interred to afterwards perform the necessary rituals at inner levels to liberate their light and consciousness from that earth focus.

Soul Liberation from the Planes of Earth through the Sacred Fire

It is important that there be forthcoming in the revolution in Higher Consciousness a true understanding of the sacred fire as the nexus of the figure eight through which all must pass. Thus, the trial by fire[9] comes in the physical, the mental, the emotional, the etheric bodies. And all must pass through that sacred fire. That which is placed in the flame, then, is liberated to return to the Great Central Sun of the I AM Presence to be recharged and sent forth for the new birth of that soul.

The consuming of the physical body has its corresponding effect upon the astral body that is demagnetized even by the physical fire. Thus it hastens the disintegration of the astral sheath that may wander about as a discarnate, disconnected and yet affecting others with a heavy sense of oppression and emotion. This is especially true in the case of suicide, beloved ones, because the one who has committed suicide, being close to earth and earthbound, may influence other members of the family and relatives [or those of similar vibration and wavelength] to also commit suicide.

Teenage Suicide—No Life Purpose without the Path

Today there is a rash of suicide among the teenagers of this nation, and it is because the discarnates and the disembodied souls are not removed. The sheaths of the individual, the four lower bodies, must therefore be bound and the soul itself taken to the etheric octave to be given instruction concerning the laws of suicide—which are that the individual who commits suicide must immediately reembody to face and conquer all of the afflictions from which it thought it was escaping.

Beloved hearts, the children of this nation are taking suicide as an out because they see no purpose in life—because they have not been given the path of Jesus Christ to go to the highest mountains of the Himalayas, to find their reason for being, and to be of some value and service to their community.[10]

What they are being taught today does not give them the value of their spiritual beings, their divine beings, but only of themselves as humans. And no one can live and value himself as a human and survive in this age.

One's survival depends upon one's acknowledgment of oneself as a fiery, spiritual being, truly a Spirit-spark and a continuum that has always lived in the past and shall always live in the future—except by free will that one choose to cancel out the self through the denial of the Light and the God and the Truth in that very place of identity.

Pray for the Protection of Youth from the Choice for Suicide

Beloved ones, I ask you to pray for the youth of America and of Canada *in this hour* and to understand that they must be protected from making that choice for suicide, both by the binding of the suicide entity[11] and by the clearing of the discarnates of those who have recently committed suicide who wander about attempting to make those who are in embodiment join them. And this is the nature of sympathy on the astral plane: Those who are confined to it desire to have others join them.

Blessed hearts, this is a very serious matter. And it has affected some who are close to you whom you know about; and others of you have been affected, for you have lost friends of Light and children from previous lives, not even being aware that this is a national epidemic in this hour.[12]

Thus, I tell you that never before has the Friday evening service been so important, because there is such a fury of action (through the efforts of Archangel Michael, his legions and chelas) of the descent of the white fire for the cleaning out of the pits. And there is much debris and much clearing of the planet Earth that can take place through calls to Astrea and the violet flame.

I speak also of the necessity to call for the binding of those whose time is up or who are actually devils in embodiment, when they pass from the screen of life. Their aim immediately when they are disembodied is to find a niche somewhere where they may reembody, and so they go to those vibrating at the lowest level of evolution. They seek those, then, who may be about to conceive children and they attempt to pry their way into that conception and into that body.

Thus it does come to pass that those who could be taken for the judgment to the Court of the Sacred Fire, whose time is up, who have no reason to be in embodiment, do actually reembody because those parents upon earth who have no protection for their auras or for their bodies are actually invaded by these disembodied spirits. And this is a great burden to the Lords of Karma.

The Judgment Calls for the Clearing of Entities and Records

The Judgment Call that is given (decree 20.07), the blessing of Helios and Vesta (decree 20.12), the raising of the right hand of the Cosmic Virgin through Mother Mary (decree 56.02)[13] is an instantaneous call that can fulfill its mission and purpose and the purpose of the Friday night service by your attendance thereto.

And I speak to all Keepers of the Flame on the planet, that you might understand that the progress of your nations depends upon the clearing of the records of the astral plane of recent wars, bloodshed, torture, terrorism, and all manner of burdens that have befallen your societies. *These can be cleared.*

And the Friday night service with Serapis Bey and Astrea, the Goddess of Purity, the Queen of Light, the Goddess of Light, the mighty seraphim of God and all who serve on the fourth ray is such a quickening and so essential and will so advance your own disciplines in the path of the ascension that I would say, "If you knew, you would do better."

If you could see the blessing of the sacred-fire service as the apex and the climax of the week, you would know how that service may lend itself also to the concentration on areas of your choice that have been spoken of, such as the rock music and the drugs affecting and plaguing the nations.

These are aided and abetted by the discarnate entities and the devils themselves, as you know. And therefore they can go to judgment with a fierce determination on Friday evening. I ask you in the name of Ahura Mazda, I ask you in the name of the Holy Kumaras that when you attend this service you shall wear white; and therefore understand that that service commemorates the day and the hour of the victory of your own ascension.

Let Us Celebrate the Victory of Your Ascension and the Victory of the Sacred Fire in the Messenger

Blessed hearts, let us celebrate that victory. Let us celebrate the victory of the sacred fire in the Messenger, in the organization, and in the Church to stand before the accusers who accuse you, each and every one, before our God day and night.[14] We are determined that this era shall pass and that the New Day and the new dawn of universal understanding of Saint Germain and his teaching shall come to pass.

By the grace of God, we have a Messenger who is also so determined. By the grace of God, we have chelas worldwide who are also so determined, who have seen so much of the Godhead that nothing, nothing that has come from the depths beneath or anywhere has been able to stop them in their absolute one-pointed service to declare Saint Germain to the world, to give the message of his violet flame, and to not be put back or tempted or swayed to compromise their mission.

I Stand for Saint Germain This Day

Beloved hearts, I stand for Saint Germain this day. I AM Zarathustra. I lay my crowns and attainment and sacred fire before him and before all who are his Keepers of the Flame. I tell you, beloved hearts, my heart is determined that this Master shall not suffer setback any longer by condemnation or by media or in any form, but that his chelas and his activity, his books and his teaching shall be known throughout the continents.

I urge you, then, to have a plan and a program for the translation of his works into foreign languages, that the people of the earth might be acquainted with his face and image and message and therefore live and be at peace and come to understand that they truly must overturn not only World Communism but all the powers that be in the West who are the cause of the support of that system, who feed it with their technology, their wealth, their subsidies.

Angels of Zarathustra Clear the Way to Shamballa

Blessed hearts, I am determined by the sacred fire that not one of you shall be left without the anointing of the sacred fire of my angels. The angels of Zarathustra are devotees of Ahura Mazda. They bow before the Light of Sanat Kumara and exist only to clear the way for your arrival at the gate of Shamballa. Thus you are here in the physical. May your path in the inner octaves of Light be clear. For though you may be within inches of the kingdom of God physically, unless you have accelerated spiritually, you will miss the calling and the entering in through the nexus.

The Crown of Victory

Thus unto the capstone I dedicate your souls. And I place the crown of victory, then, upon the head of the Messenger that you might know that in the individual is the sign by which all may conquer. May you earn that crown of victory and illumination and know that I, the LORD God, in the I AM THAT I AM and where I AM as Zarathustra, have come for the deliverance of this valley, this community, and every Keeper of the Flame of Sanat Kumara worldwide.

May you face the Sun of your Mighty I AM Presence and live. Call unto me, then, for I am self-appointed and received by God to go before you until the last obstruction is consumed in the ruby ray.

Peace, beloved, for *This Too Shall Pass!*

"The Summit Lighthouse Sheds Its Radiance O'er All the World to Manifest as Pearls of Wisdom." This dictation by Zarathustra was delivered through the Messenger Elizabeth Clare Prophet on Palm Sunday, March 31, 1985, at the Royal Teton Ranch, North, in the Paradise Valley south of Livingston, Montana. The Messenger's Palm Sunday Sermon on the Path of the Ministering Servant: "If Any Man Serve Me, Him Will My Father Honor" (taken from Matthew 20:17–34; 21:1–17 and John 11:47–57; 12:23–26) preceded the dictation. Dictation and sermon available on one cassette (B85072), $6.50 postpaid USA. (1) Zarathustra (Gr. *Zoroaster*), born in ancient Persia c. 600 B.C., was the Messenger of Ahura Mazda 'Wise Lord' or 'Lord who bestows intelligence' (the Ancient of Days, known in the East as Sanat Kumara and Kārttikeya). Beginning at age 30, Zarathustra received a series of miraculous visions. His soul was led in ecstatic meditation into the presence of Ahura Mazda and the company of archangels, who instructed him in his mission as a prophet and initiated him into the sublime spiritual secrets of an emerging new religion. After ten years of prophesying, Zarathustra received the inspiration to convert King Vishtaspa, ruler of the vast Persian Empire. Ancient texts record that Ahura Mazda sent three archangels—Vohu Manah, Asha Vahishta, and the Propitious Fire—as witnesses to the court of King Vishtaspa and his queen, Hutaosa. The archangels appeared as effulgent knights in full armor, riding on horseback, radiating a blinding light and the sound of thunder. The monarchs embraced the faith, providing the platform for wide promulgation of the word of the LORD and the teachings of the sacred fire. (2) Archangel Michael, February 3, 1985, "The Summoning: Straight Talk and a Sword from the Hierarch of Banff," *Pearls of Wisdom*, vol. 28, no. 10, pp. 101–10. (3) Isa. 14:5-27; 38:17, 18; Ezek. 26:1–4, 19–21; 28:1–10; 31; 32; Rev. 9:1–11; 11:7; 17:8; 20:1–3. (4) On April 23, 1985, the Dark Cycle entered its seventeenth year, commencing the initiations of personal and planetary karma accrued on the four o'clock line of the cosmic clock under the solar hierarchy of Taurus. The key to overcoming all obstacles to this encounter with the LORD at the Taurus gate to the Holy City is Love through the flame of God-obedience and the Path of the Ruby Ray taught by Sanat Kumara. (5) In his June 3, 1960, Pearl of Wisdom (vol. 3, no. 23, p. 3), El Morya announced: "A mighty Temple of Victory is to be built in this nation for all mankind, dedicated to the Presence of Almighty God! It shall be called '*I AM' the Temple of Life's Victory*"—the "first temple of the Great White Brotherhood known to the outer world since Atlantean days." (6) See Kuthumi, January 27, 1985, *Pearls of Wisdom*, vol. 28, no. 9, p. 82. (7) See Elizabeth Clare Prophet, "The Gift of Good Friday," on the 8-cassette album *Easter Conclave 1982* (A8224), $50.00 ($51.56 postpaid USA); also available on single cassette B8226, $6.50 postpaid USA. (8) Rom. 3:23. (9) I Cor. 3:13–15. (10) See Elizabeth Clare Prophet, *The Lost Years of Jesus*, Summit University Press, $12.95 ($13.95 postpaid USA). (11) The name of the suicide entity is *Annihla*, a female death devil. Call to Archangel Michael and Mighty Astrea to bind Annihla in the name of Jesus Christ and the entire Spirit of the Great White Brotherhood. (12) See "Teen Suicide," *People Weekly*, 18 February 1985, pp. 76–89; *Surviving*, writ. Joyce Eliason, dir. Waris Hussein, prod. Hunt Lowry, ABC Theater, 10 February 1985; Michael Doan and Sarah Peterson, "As 'Cluster Suicides' Take Toll of Teenagers," *U.S. News & World Report*, 12 November 1984, pp. 49–50; Mary Jordan, "Suicides Plague College Campuses," *The Washington Post*, 12 November 1984, sec. 1; Allan Parachini, "An Alarming Picture of Youthful Suicides," *Los Angeles Times*, Sunday, 19 August 1984, sec. 6; *When Silence Kills*, narr. Martin Sheen, prods. Paul Bockhorst and Dianne Steinkraus, KCET Journal, Los Angeles, 25 April 1984; David Gelman and B. K. Gangelhoff, "Teen-age Suicide in the Sun Belt," *Newsweek*, 15 August 1983, pp. 70–74; Giovanna Breu, "A Double Suicide Adds to the National Tragedy of Teenagers Who Take Their Own Lives," *People Weekly*, 27 June 1983, pp. 32–34; Jeannye Thornton, "Behind a Surge in Suicides of Young People," *U.S. News & World Report*, 20 June 1983, p. 66. (13) Decree 20.07, "They Shall Not Pass!" by Jesus Christ (Section II); decree 20.12, "I Ratify the Judgment of Helios," by Helios (Section III); and decree 56.02, "The Right Hand of the Cosmic Virgin," by Mother Mary (Section III) in *Prayers, Meditations, and Dynamic Decrees for the Coming Revolution in Higher Consciousness*, Summit University Press. Sections I, II, and III, $8.85 ($9.97 postpaid USA). Each section also available separately, $2.95 ($3.80 postpaid USA). (14) Rev. 12:10.

Pearls of Wisdom, published weekly by The Summit Lighthouse for Church Universal and Triumphant, come to you under the auspices of the Darjeeling Council of the Great White Brotherhood. These are presently dictated by the Ascended Masters to their Messenger Elizabeth Clare Prophet. The international headquarters of this nonprofit, nondenominational activity is located in Los Angeles, California. All communications and freewill contributions should be addressed to The Summit Lighthouse, Box A, Malibu, CA 90265. Pearls of Wisdom are sent weekly throughout the USA via third-class mail to all who support the Church with a minimum yearly love offering of $40. First-class and international postage rates available upon request. Notice of change of address should be received three weeks prior to the effective date. Third-class mail is not forwarded by the post office.

Copyright © 1985 Church Universal and Triumphant, Inc. All rights reserved. Printed in the United States of America. Pearls of Wisdom and The Summit Lighthouse are registered trademarks of Church Universal and Triumphant, Inc. All rights to their use are reserved.

Soul Mates and Twin Flames

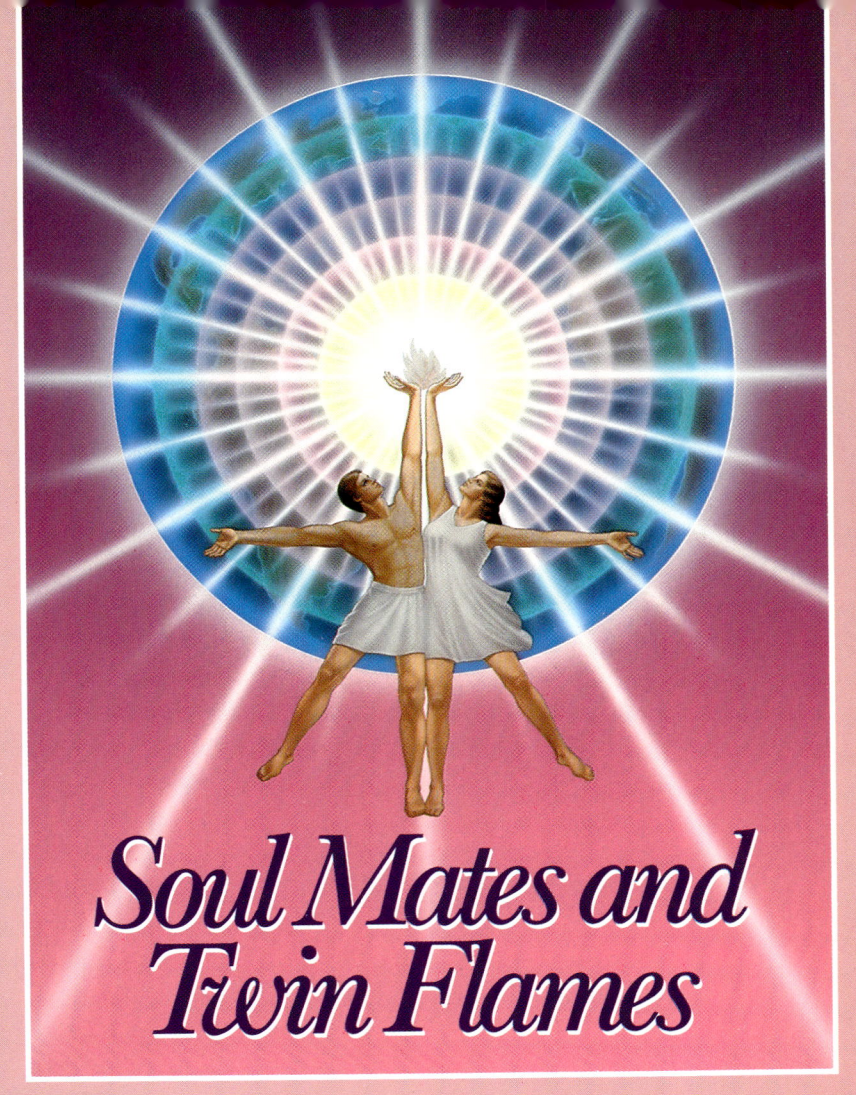

The Quest for Wholeness

Cast a mighty anchor of love into the universe! Cast it now from your heart. Cast it by the mighty rope of your love, and let that anchor reach your beloved. And now, by the fires of the heart and utmost devotion to cosmic purpose, by love and love and only love, draw that one—humble or lowly, ascended or cosmic being—wherever and whoever, draw that love to your heart and know the true meaning of Life becoming Life, the true meaning of universal oneness.

—Gautama Buddha

Haven't you ever dreamt of finding that perfect love? The one who could satisfy the intense longing you often feel for wholeness and fulfillment?

J̲UST LOOK AROUND our world. People rushing from relationship to relationship or vicariously experiencing them through movies like *"Love Story"* or *"Somewhere in Time"* — searching for that perfect one. Even if we have forgotten what it is we are seeking, we still keep chasing after *something* — from exercise class to consciousness-raising sessions, from Marriage Encounter to est to Esalen, from racing up the corporate ladder to dashing off to remote corners of the world.

Somehow I always knew that this search centered around loving...and being loved. Yet it took me many years to discover that God, the master dramatist, composed the greatest love story ever written — the drama of twin flames. A story more glorious than you can imagine. A story that involves you, God, the universe, the evolutions of earth, and your mission with a very special soul — the other half of yourself, your twin flame.

During my college years I spent hundreds of hours poring over esoteric books in myriad libraries and bookstores, but I was able to unearth only a few references to soul mates, twin souls, or twin flames.

One crisp February morning many years later, as I stepped from the murky basement of the Sphinx bookstore in Cambridge into the welcome sunlight, I saw a blazing pink poster announcing a three-day seminar called "Twin Flames in Love."

I stopped in my tracks. Here it was — three full days of lectures and slides on twin flames, their divine origin and destiny. More important, this seminar was sponsored by the Great White Brotherhood. I knew that if I were to learn the truth about twin flames, it would be from this universal spiritual brotherhood dedicated to the white light of the Christ consciousness in all people.

Three weeks later I took my seat among the hundreds of diverse people from all over the world who had traveled to Miami for this seminar. As the lights dimmed and a hush fell over the expectant audience, Elizabeth Clare Prophet walked to the microphone.

From The Coming Revolution *magazine, Winter 1981
by Anna Marie Bernard*

"Thus the essence of the violet transmuting flame itself is the singing love of twin flames and of hearts united unto a cosmic purpose whose goal is resolution, whose goal is wholeness in the light. Thus marriages made in heaven are brought to earth for the continuing light manifestation of the presence of that cosmic egg as the twain are one and the T'ai Chi spins and Alpha and Omega, present in the earth as the Father/Mother light, can yet deliver to the children of God the extraordinary love that is reflected in these hearts. Thus, my beloved, strive for love."

—*Gautama Buddha*

Revolutionary author and educator, president of Summit University, and leader of a worldwide New Age spiritual movement, Mrs. Prophet holds the office of Messenger for the Great White Brotherhood. She was here at their behest to present us with an in-depth history of twin flames, an understanding vital in this particular cycle of earth's evolution.

She explained, "At the end of this cycle—now in the Piscean age moving into the Aquarian age—people of light and on the Path, no matter what your religion, your meditation, no matter what discipline you come from or if you haven't any, now is the moment when your soul should contact your twin flame."

As she went on to unfold the cosmic history lesson, I began to understand that at this moment in the change of cycles from the Piscean to the Aquarian age, the earth's spiritual overseers are sponsoring twin flames who volunteered for vital missions in this period of planetary transition—lovers of God who will come forward to receive the initiations of the heavenly hierarchy, discover their God-identity and mission, and help lead the children of the Sun into the new dispensation.

Aeons ago beyond the confines of time and space, you and your twin flame stood before Alpha and Omega, the Father/Mother God, and vowed to bring to earth your gift of creativity from the realms of Light—to lay it upon the altar of humanity for their advancement and upliftment, thence to return to the plane of Spirit masters of time and space, mission accomplished!

The Taj Mahal, built by the Mogul Emperor Shah Jahan as a tomb for his beloved wife, is a tribute to the majesty of divine love. It stands as a shrine to the eternal love of twin flames.

To effectively translate spiritual energy through the chakras (spiritual centers in the body temple) to the physical plane required a series of incarnations in both masculine and feminine embodiments, as each half of the Divine Whole learned to be the instrument of the Father/Mother God.

Had we retained the harmony of the One, the rapture of our love would have remained throughout our lifetimes on earth. But when harmony was lost—through fear, mistrust, or a sense of separation from our Source—we became the victims of our negative karma. Separated vibrationally, no longer preferring one another, we were bound by entangling alliances and mutual neglect until our souls cried out for the living God... and each other.

Each incarnation apart from our twin flame was spent either creating negative karma or balancing some of the karma that stood in the way of our reunion. At times we assumed various relationships with our twin flame—husband/wife, mother/son, father/daughter, and sister/brother—in order to unwind the negative strands of energy we had woven into our subconscious through our misuse of free will.

Often, when people learn that they share a unique mission with their twin flame, they begin to search physically for that one special soul instead of seeking their wholeness within. This is always a detour on the path to soul liberation.

Alchemical Marriage

Cosmic law requires that we first define our own identity in God before we can completely unlock the spiritual potential of our twin flames. For until twin flames achieve a certain level of mastery and oneness with their own Real Selves, they are often unable to cope with the weight of their negative karma amplified by the very presence of their twin flame. The same unique factor that gives twin flames their great spiritual power—their identical blueprint of identity—can likewise cause the amplification of their negative patterns.

Ultimately each and every one of us must learn to change the negative patterns—the base metal—of the human ego into the gold of our divine or Real Self. This is called the alchemical marriage—the marriage of our soul, the feminine aspect of our being, to the 'Lamb' who is the real and enduring spiritual self, the masculine aspect. The love of this beloved Christ Self, i.e., that part of us who maintains constant contact with the Source—the I AM Presence—is an incomparable love. This is the Beloved for whom the saints of East and West have given their all.

By daily accelerating consciousness through their communion with God, the saints gradually transcended the human ego. Eventually their souls merged with their real spiritual self as they ascended back to the heart of God. "For this corruptible must put on incorruption, and this mortal must put on immortality."

Inner Contact of Twin Flames

Your twin flame may have already won this soul liberation and reunited with God—or he may still be struggling to find the way. Where your twin flame is—what his state of consciousness is—

The Creation of Twin Flames

(Fig. 1–4) Representing the masculine and feminine polarity of God's wholeness, the T'ai Chi rotates and divides into two identical spheres—twin flames of the One. A drop from the ocean of God's being, each sphere or Divine Monad consists of the I AM Presence surrounded by the spheres (rings of color, of light) which comprise the causal body. In this way, the Father/Mother God created us in their own image—male and female.

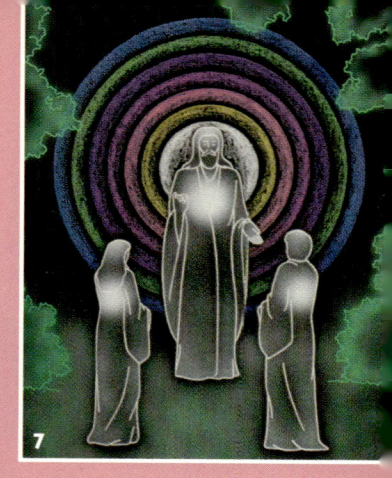

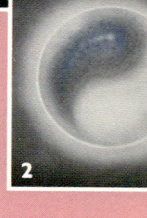

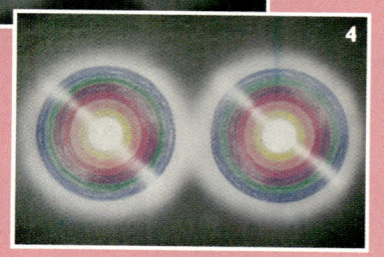

(Fig. 5–6) Each I AM Presence then sends forth a ray—a soul. Each soul focuses the opposite polarity—one, masculine; the other, feminine. Between the soul evolving on earth and the I AM Presence stands the Christ Self—our personal mediator between Spirit and Matter. We may rise to become one with our Christ Self by exercising free will and achieving mastery on earth. This is the 'alchemical' marriage which must precede the eternal marriage of twin flames.

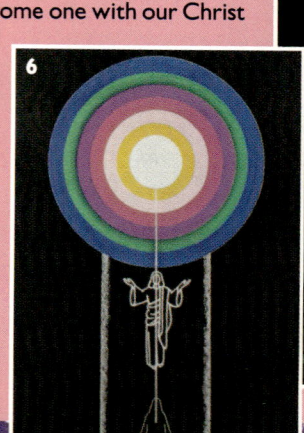

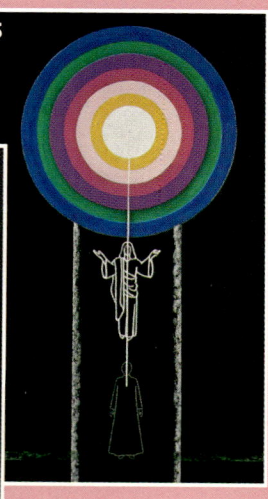

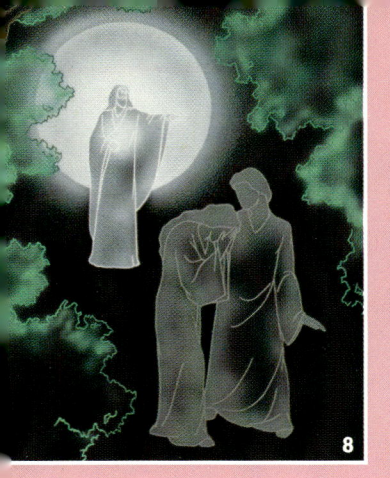

(Fig. 7–8) Adam and Eve symbolize the testing required by God of all twin flames. Although each of us came forth from Spirit to fulfill our mission to take dominion over the earth, we have fallen from the state of perfection (Eden) through our own disobedience and rebellion against cosmic law. As a result, we have had to endure the suffering of being separated from our twin flames for many incarnations as we endeavor to balance our karma.

Fig. (9–10) As soon as twin flames misqualified the energy of God, they began to create negative karma—coils of energy that form layers of negativity and density in their auras separating them from their own I AM Presence and their twin flame. Through the daily use of the violet transmuting flame, this misqualified energy—such as resentment, irritation, anxiety, frustration—can be stripped of its negativity, purified, and returned to the seven rings of the causal body in the plane of Spirit as our "treasures stored in heaven."

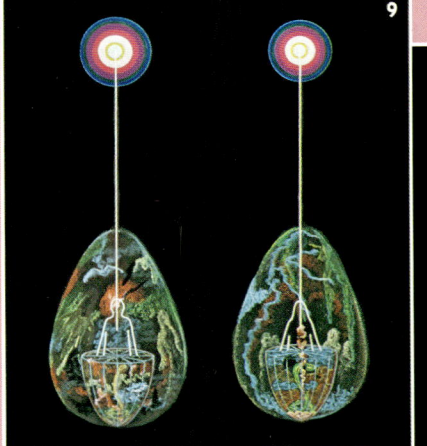

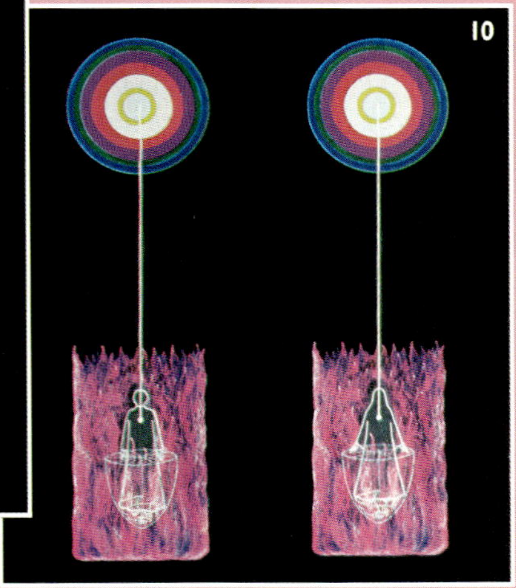

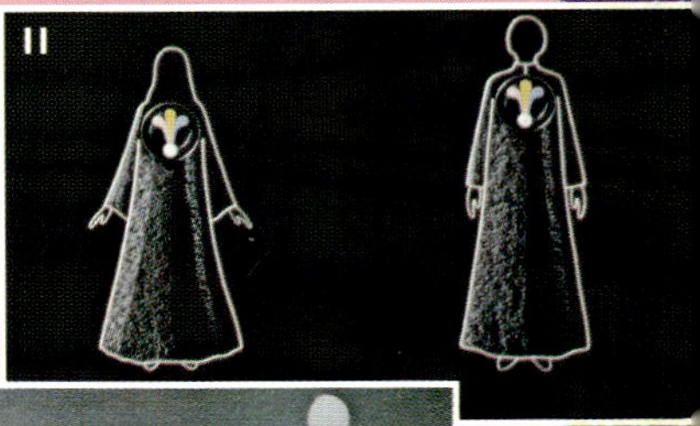

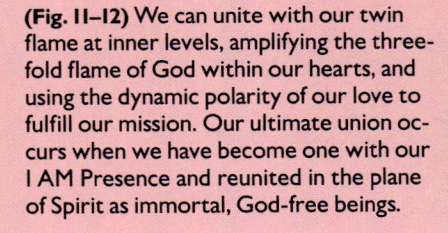

(Fig. 11–12) We can unite with our twin flame at inner levels, amplifying the threefold flame of God within our hearts, and using the dynamic polarity of our love to fulfill our mission. Our ultimate union occurs when we have become one with our I AM Presence and reunited in the plane of Spirit as immortal, God-free beings.

can greatly influence your own ability to find wholeness.

Because both of you share the same blueprint of identity—like the design of a snowflake, unique in all of cosmos—whatever energy you send forth is imprinted or stamped with that specific pattern. According to the law that like attracts like, all energy you release cycles to your twin flame—either hindering or helping him on the path to wholeness.

When you send forth love or hope, these qualities will uplift your twin flame. But if you are burdened with frustration or hatred, your twin flame will likewise feel the weight of these misqualified feelings. Sometimes the inexplicable joys or depressions you feel are the moods of your other half registering on your own consciousness.

You can accelerate your progress on the Path if—in your prayer, meditation, or dynamic decrees—you call to your I AM Presence for the inner heart contact with your twin flame. You can make the following invocation:

"In the name of the Christ I call to the blessed I AM Presence of our twin flames for the sealing of our hearts as one for the victory of our mission to humanity. I invoke the light of the Holy Spirit for the consuming of all negative karma limiting the full expression of our divine identity and the fulfillment of our divine plan." In this way, even if you live in separate spheres, you can unite spiritually on higher planes and direct light into your own world and the world of your twin flame for the balancing of mutual karma.

This inner contact magnifies the light and attainment you each have and releases the awesome power of the polarity of your love, enabling you to stand strong against the conflicts that inevitably come to the door of all who would defend love.

Inspired by the grandeur of love, artists, writers, and composers throughout the ages have expressed both love's exalted heights and tragic depths. In many of their masterpieces, we can sense an inner understanding of twin flames, their love for one another, and their encounters with karma and cosmic law.

Mrs. Prophet has interpreted several famous operas from this perspective. Although some of the arias and duets give us a glimpse of the majestic love of twin flames, these stories often end in sorrow, tragedy, or death because one or both of the lovers fail a test of personal mastery—having not yet sealed their own individual path in God.

Madame Butterfly

Puccini's *Madame Butterfly* tells the story of the American Lieutenant Pinkerton and his contract marriage to Butterfly, a trusting fifteen-year-old Japanese girl. These two souls symbolize twin flames. Their Eastern and Western cultures represent both the masculine and feminine polarities of twin flames as well as the gulf that separates souls who have not yet balanced their karma and must endure the pain of separation as a result.

Pinkerton, a man hardened by the world, has lost the sense of the purity of true love. Although he is attracted by the beauty and charm of Butterfly, he deliberately plans to desert her for an American wife. However, Pinkerton and his Japanese bride do share intense moments of love—their souls uniting as one flame commemorating

> *Shiva, the third person of the Hindu trinity, and his consort or twin flame Parvati focus the wholeness of the Father/Mother God. In the Hindu tradition, every masculine personification of God has a feminine counterpart. The masculine aspect is inactive in creation without the activating force which is Shakti, or feminine principle, who releases the potential of God from Spirit to Matter.*

SOUL MATES AND TWIN FLAMES

their original wholeness in God. And the fruit of this union is the conception of a child—a symbol of their great love.

But the Lieutenant is ignorant of this development and blinded by his own selfish desires. He goes home to America, leaving Butterfly trusting in his eventual return.

Pinkerton does return, several years later—with an American wife. In her grief at this desertion by her twin flame, Butterfly takes her life.

Lohengrin

Wagner's opera *Lohengrin* illustrates the relationship of twin flames when the one who has ascended into Spirit endeavors to assist his beloved—still undergoing the tests and initiations on earth.

Elsa is falsely accused of murdering her brother, but she has absolute faith in the arrival of a knight in shining armor to save her. Lohengrin, Elsa's ascended twin flame, answers her inner call and descends from higher planes to rescue her. He glides across a lake in a boat pulled by a swan, symbolizing a God-realized soul coming from another octave.

They are married, but Lohengrin, Guru (teacher) to his twin flame, instructs Elsa that she may never ask his name. This is her great test of love—the same test Cupid required of Psyche. Neither Psyche nor Elsa could resist the temptation—both succumb to the human frailty of curiosity and discover the true identity of their lovers. Because of this disobedience, cosmic law requires their separation once again. Lohengrin returns to the plane of Spirit—there to await his twin flame's self-mastery and their ultimate reunion.

Literature abounds with famous lovers who may very well have been twin flames: Dante finally reaching the point where Beatrice could present him to Christ, Penelope faithfully tending

> *In order to seize the kingdom, the scheming Modred plotted against the pure love shared by King Arthur (Guru), and Launcelot and Guenevere (his chelas)—and Guenevere was condemned to be burned at the stake. As the flames leapt around her, she was rescued by her twin flame, Launcelot.*

the flame of love that draws Ulysses home from his wanderings, Evangeline tirelessly searching for her beloved, Shakespeare pouring forth his love to the lady of the sonnets, Romeo and Juliet, Launcelot and Guenevere, Tristan and Isolde, Hiawatha and Minnehaha, Robert and Elizabeth Barrett Browning. All shared a love typical of twin flames.

Even looking at the flow of history reveals the importance of twin flames. I was fascinated to learn from Mrs. Prophet that Pharaoh Ikhnaton and Queen Nefertiti were twin flames working together to bring the worship of the one God to a world floundering in the throes of polytheism. These same twin flames reembodied as King Clovis and Queen Clothilde to bring Christianity to France in the sixth century.

The Love of the Guru and the Chela

Although twin flames assume every possible relationship in order to develop love's full potential, the Guru/chela relationship is the most exalted of all. For through it the one who has attained Christ consciousness can draw his other half to God by the magnet of their love. The one who is farther along on the Path becomes the teacher of his beloved—able to use the immense power of their love and essential oneness to accelerate the consciousness of his twin flame.

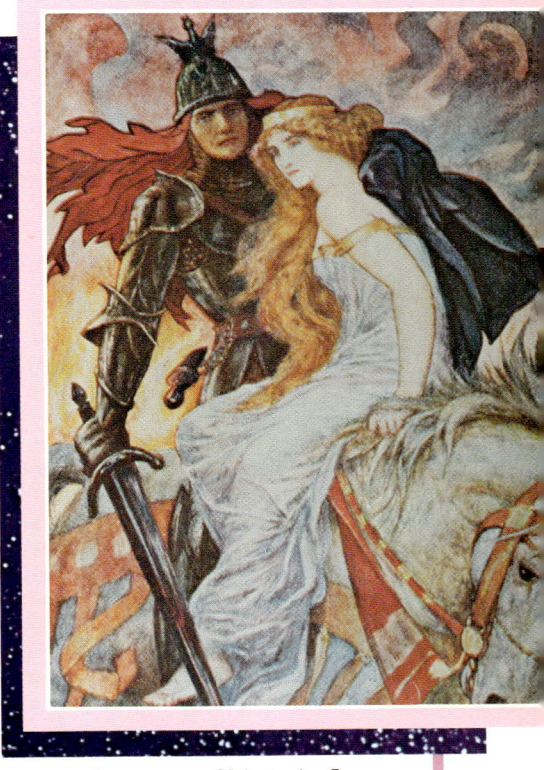

This was the case with Mark and Elizabeth Prophet, twin flames who shared twelve years together in the Guru/chela relationship. Mark trained Elizabeth for the role of Messenger for the Brotherhood, and together they were able to fulfill the mission of their twin flames by bringing forth the Brotherhood's teachings for the Aquarian age.

Although Mark passed on in 1973, returning to Spirit where he continues to hold the Alpha polarity of their love, his presence is vitally felt by his wife, Elizabeth, their four children—and all who support their mission. Mark and Elizabeth Prophet are a living example of the eternal love of the Guru and the chela.

Soul Mates

Not all of the beautiful and soul-fulfilling loves are those of twin flames. There is also the love of very close, kindred souls called soul mates.

"A soul mate is different from a twin flame," Mrs. Prophet said. "Soul mates are two souls on the same side of the polarity yet in male and female bodies. They come together because they are working on the same type of karma and the same chakra simultaneously. So soul mates have an attraction that is based on the sacred labor and on the path of self-mastery. A soul mate is like the echo of oneself in Matter working at the same task to fulfill a blueprint for God."

Mary and Joseph, the parents of Jesus, were soul mates sharing the responsibility for nurturing the Christ within their son. Both of their twin flames were in the octaves of light holding the balance for their mission. Many people today who are still balancing karma but who are on the spiritual path find themselves drawn to their soul mates for the fulfillment of a shared dharma or sacred labor.

Karmic Marriage

Besides twin flames and soul mates, a third kind of marriage relationship is frequently seen—the karmic marriage. Here, the two individuals are drawn together for the balancing of mutual karma.

These marriages are often difficult but they are important in achieving mastery on the Path. The husband and wife also gain the good karma of sponsoring and nurturing their children.

Some of these marriages may give the opportunity for the balancing of severe crimes of murder, betrayal, or extreme hatred. Very often the only way that we can balance that hatred is by the intense love expressed through the husband-wife relationship.

The Marriage Union

God has blessed the human institution of marriage as an opportunity for two individuals to develop wholeness through the exchange of their Alpha-Omega polarities. Whether the union of twin flames, soul mates, or karmic partners, the marriage of man and woman is meant to be mystical, a commemoration of the soul's reunion with the beloved I AM Presence through the Christ, the blessed Mediator.

> *As Longfellow describes Hiawatha's longing for Minnehaha, he illustrates the dynamic polarity of twin flames. "As unto the bow the cord is, So unto the man is woman; Though she bends him, she obeys him, Though she draws him, yet she follows; Useless each without the other!"*

Jesus demonstrated the importance of marriage as an initiation on the Path when he chose to perform his first public miracle at the marriage feast of Cana—changing the water into wine. The essence of his message was that unless marriage be transformed by the Holy Spirit, it will only be an outer experience. It is our choice as to whether we are content with a marriage based on the water of the human consciousness or whether we require a marriage based on the wine of the divine consciousness.

The cosmic interchange of divine love in the marriage relationship is meant to be the same creative love that framed the universe in the beginning when God as Father gave forth the command, "Let there be light," and God as Mother answered, "And there was light." This creative flow can be expressed not only in physical union but also during cycles of dedicated celibacy as each partner goes within to commune with his beloved I AM Presence.

The exchange of the energies of the sacred fire in sexual union is for the transfer of spheres of cosmic consciousness—causal bodies of light (Fig. 4). The light energy resulting from this fusion enhances the positive qualities of each of the partners and strengthens their own divine identity—enabling them to carry their shared burden of karma. As the union is consecrated to the love of God, the harmonious blending of pure Father/Mother energies yields the Son, the Christ consciousness—whether it be in the form of a child, an inspiration, a successful enterprise, or a work of art.

When this exchange is not spiritualized through a recognition that God is both the lover and the beloved, the two individuals may experience physical pleasure, but they also unknowingly take on each other's karmic patterns without the benefit of a spiritually transmutative love. This may explain the frequent identity crises suffered by those who have intimate relationships on a casual basis; they take on so many karmic identities, effectively neutralizing their own, that they no longer know who they really are.

The Circle of Oneness

The Great White Brotherhood has released a ritual for the consecration of the sacred union of husband and wife and for the sealing of this interchange in the purity of God's love. It is from the meditation of the angels of love for the protection of *holy* matrimony:

"Stand together facing the chart of the I AM Presence (p. 5) and make your inner attunement with the star of your divinity. Meditate upon your heart and the flame therein and behold the arc ascend into the center of the Divine Monad. Now take your right hand and dip it into the fires of your heart and draw the circle of our oneness around yourselves as you stand in adoration of the One. Visualize this circle, twelve feet in diameter, as a line of sacred fire. It is your ring-pass-not. Within that circle of oneness is the forcefield of Alpha and Omega; and you focus the T'ai Chi, the plus and minus of energies, where you are." And the cherubim must be invoked daily "for they are the guardians of love in the planes of Mater."

A vital mission awaits those whose energies are in harmony with divine love.

As Mrs. Prophet relates: "I have seen twin flames whose love was never abated, who could hold the balance for an entire city and

Only after Dante has passed through the Inferno and Purgatorio for the expiation of his sins, does he experience the divine love of the Paradiso with his true love, Beatrice. Here she presents Dante to Christ.

whose daily invocations would be the transmutation of hatred and of crime and of murder, holding that inner balance....

"This is an high and holy calling. It's not for the mundane who desire the pleasure cult and its sensuality. This is the real inner path for those who understand that there is a cosmos aborning within us, that there's a world to be saved, that millions of souls need our love and therefore it can never be a selfish love."

In the cynicism of our age, however, we've lost the sense of the power of pure love. We no longer have the buoyant, joyous attitude toward life where each day is a new opportunity to give our love as a unique gift to those around us. Too often we underestimate our ability to transform lives through our example.

Djwal Kul, known throughout the world as the Master D.K., once related this story of the miller and his wife.

"There lived by the sea a gentle soul who was a miller. He and his wife served together to grind the grain for the people of their town. And it came to pass that in all the land there were no communities where so much happiness reigned as there. Their countrymen marveled and wondered, for they recognized that something unusual must have happened to make the members of this community so singularly wise and happy. And although the townsfolk themselves were born, grew up, matured to adulthood and passed from the screen of life within the community, never in all of their living were they able to understand the mystery.

"Tonight I shall draw aside the curtain and tell you what made the people of this community so happy and prosperous, so joyous and wise.

"It was the service of the miller and his wife and the love which they put into the flour. For this love was carried home in sacks of flour on the backs of those who patronized their mill and was then baked into their bread. At every meal the regenerative power of love from the miller and his wife was radiated around the table and it entered their physical bodies as they partook of the bread. Thus, like radioactive power, the energy of this vibrant love from the miller and his wife was spread throughout the community.

"The neighbors did not know the reason of their happiness and none of the people were ever able to discover it. For sometimes—although they live side by side—mankind are unable to pry the most simple secrets about one another."

Aquarian Age Alchemy

Even as the miller and his wife silently communicated their love to others, you and your twin flame also influence countless lives around you through your "radioactive" thoughts, feelings, and actions. You have an opportunity to assist life or to place a burden upon it—either by interacting with the negative energy of your past karma cycling to the surface of your consciousness or by recognizing this energy as a challenge to your harmony and love and transmuting it.

The key to transmuting or changing past karma and fulfilling your mission with your twin flame is the violet flame, a spiritual energy given by God to man for his acceleration into the Aquarian age. This action of the Holy Spirit transforms negative energy—anger into love, irritation into peace, suspicion into trust—so that you can influence life positively as you work toward your ultimate victory on the Path.

> *Sharing the most exalted of all relationships between twin flames— that of Guru and chela— Mark and Elizabeth Prophet embody a love dedicated to lifetimes of service to the Great White Brotherhood which transcends the bounds of time and space. This is the love that you have always shared with your twin flame.*

When you visualize this violet flame and call it forth into your consciousness, it instantaneously begins to change negative energy patterns accumulated over thousands of lifetimes. You can begin to experience feelings of joy, lightness, and hope. It's as if your entire consciousness were being dipped into a chemical solution of purple liquid which dissolves the karma of centuries.

This is the dispensation many people have been waiting for. This is why we've been evolving these tens of thousands of years, why we have gone through all of the understanding of God the Father and God the Son. Now we come to the Holy Spirit energy, the sacred science of alchemy, of self-transformation—through the violet flame.

The Great White Brotherhood has released a violet flame mantra for the Aquarian age: "I AM a being of violet fire, I AM the purity God desires." "I AM" is the affirmation of the God within, the I AM Presence—the same Presence who declared to Moses "I AM THAT I AM.... This is my name for ever, and this is my memorial unto all generations." Daily immersing ourselves in the cleansing energy of the violet flame through reciting violet flame mantras that are actually dynamic decrees given in the full power of the spoken Word is the quickest and most effective way to maintain our harmony and accelerate our consciousness for our ultimate reunion with God and our twin flame.

This is the baptism of the Holy Ghost that was prophesied in the New Testament by John. This is the gift of God for the Aquarian age. This is how the days are shortened for the elect—for the homeward journey, the overcoming of the round of the wheel of rebirth.

The Yearning for Wholeness

The oncoming Aquarian age is an age for the understanding of God's energy in polarity as the masculine and feminine principles of the universe. How we experience that energy as our true identity, how we understand it as the essence of twin flames, and how we use it as the integrative power of divine love for the betterment of mankind will determine whether or not we survive as individuals and, ultimately, as a human race.

You may be reading this article because the only thing that stands between you and your twin flame is a layer of negative energy just waiting to be consumed by the joyous, bubbling action of the violet flame.

Your mission, your twin flame, and your ultimate reunion in the heart of God await you!

Pearls of Wisdom

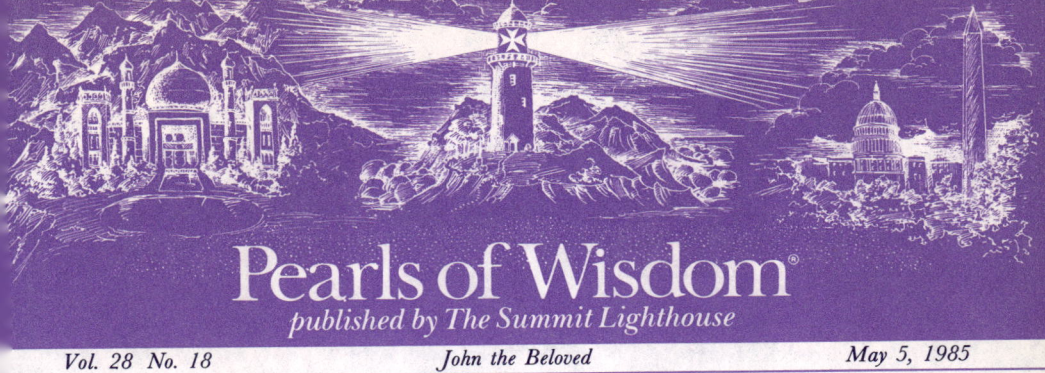

published by The Summit Lighthouse

Vol. 28 No. 18 — John the Beloved — May 5, 1985

Easter Conclave at Camelot
"Come, leave your nets—I will make you fishers of men."

I

Love's Fulfillment of the Law
in Christ—His Messengers,
His Apostles, His Disciples and His Community

Make haste, O God, to deliver me; make haste to help me, O LORD.

Let them be ashamed and confounded that seek after my soul: let them be turned backward and put to confusion that desire my hurt.

Let them be turned back for a reward of their shame that say, Aha, aha.

Let all those that seek Thee rejoice and be glad in Thee: and let such as love Thy salvation say continually:
 Let God be magnified!

But I am poor and needy: make haste unto me, O God: Thou art my help and my deliverer; O LORD, *beloved Mighty I AM Presence, make no tarrying.*
                                                                    Psalm 70

Therefore we who love Thy salvation say continually:
**Let God be magnified! Let God be magnified! Let God be magnified!
Let God be magnified! Let God be magnified!**

I AM the disciple of Love and of the initiations of Love's heart in the person of Jesus Christ and in the person of the one who sent him and in the person of the one whom he has sent. Thus, I AM the student of the deep mysteries of Love in Maitreya, in Jesus, and in the Messenger of the LORD, for so is the Trinity fulfilled. And so I AM come to you in this hour of Love's fulfillment of the Law—the Law of Truth and of Peace and of Freedom and of Victory.

Copyright © 1985 Church Universal and Triumphant, Inc.

Thus it was I—my head upon his bosom, a part of the eternal heartbeat of God within his breast—it was I who asked, "Who is it, Lord?"[1] Thus, in me was fulfilled the promise of the bodhisattva of the Buddha Issa. For he was and is the Eternal One and the manifestation of Maitreya.

Where Is the One Who Is Lord?

Blessed Hearts,
  In the beginning was the Word
  And the Word is God.
  Where is the one who is Lord?[2]
  Jesus, the incarnation of the I AM THAT I AM.
  Jesus, the One Sent to embody
  The First Principle of your Mighty I AM Presence.
  Jesus the Christ, crowned in the name I AM.
  He walked the earth in the Trinity of Love.
  To this aspire.

The Messenger of the Lord

I AM the disciple and an apostle. I AM also an Ascended Master, having fulfilled all of Love's promises through this Christ. Thus I lived, and I lived to see him live. And I also lived to pen his Revelation to me. Thus, he also anointed me as his Messenger, even as he has anointed this Messenger to speak to you.

It is a lawful office and one necessary so long as the veil is not parted between the outer court of the physical octave and the inner Holy of Holies where [the embodied] Christ communes with the Mighty I AM Presence. Thus even the high priest, and Moses himself, was the Messenger before the living flame and fount of Reality and did deliver the Word of Sanat Kumara to the people.

Understand that your Christ Self is the high priest officiating before the altar of your I AM Presence. Descending, then, from that level of the Holy of Holies, this Christ does minister unto your soul. Thus, your Christ Self is the Messenger of your I AM Presence. And your discipleship is a path to be walked whereby daily you put on the robe whereby, through the intimations of the heart, you, beloved, become the messenger of your own beloved Christ Self to the world.

This Messenger comes to deliver the Word of the ascended hosts who have walked through the veils to the point of God Reality and who have been assumed unto God. The Messenger speaks in the name of your own Christhood and delivers to you the highest fruits of your own Reality.

On occasions you cannot perceive the wonder and the Light, and you are about to take a lesser road, a very low road in the valleys of life, and the Messenger speaks and gives to you the illumination of your Christ Self. And your response is: "I am sorry. I do not see it that way. I understand it in my way and I must fulfill my own desire, for my desire overwhelms me and I have the greater need to fulfill it than to be obedient to that First Love." And the Messenger replies, "I have fulfilled the office of communicating to you the Word of your Christ Self. I bow before the Light within you and before your free will. Go in peace."

The Grand Experiment in Free Will

"That which thou doest do quickly!"[3]—the same message of the Master to Judas. For the one who must act in a certain groove of consciousness, let him go and do it quickly that he might quickly learn the fruit plucked from the tree of the knowledge of good and evil, that he might begin at once, then, to learn the lessons of life and the grand experiment in free will to which our God has sent you.

Blessed hearts, it is still better to have heard the admonishment and the call by the Messenger to a higher and a holy calling; for in the day and the hour when the choice of free will becomes ashes in the mouth, you may remember the divine direction and then seek to fulfill it. Therefore, do not resent the call to Truth or the delivery to you of Reality, even as we, God forbid, do not resent your choice of the path of free will.

Let those who keep the hour with Jesus this night not weary, for it is an hour of prayer and transmutation.

The World On Trial

In their sorrow they sought escape through sleep.[4] The escape they sought was from the facing of what Jesus was to face. He brought to bear at his trial the full momentum of the God incarnate within him and allowed those who thought they had placed him on trial to themselves be on trial.

And thus, the world is on trial today as it takes in turn its reaction to the Great White Brotherhood, to the Teachings of the Ascended Masters—not necessarily through this mouthpiece, beloved, or through yourselves, for these Teachings have been from everlasting to everlasting and from the beginning. The rejection of the person of Truth is seen everywhere, as they say, in man's inhumanity to man.

What is the greater guilt, beloved ones, in this hour? Is it the Soviet slaughter of the Afghan nation? Or is it the standing by of those in the West who see and do not do enough or give a token and say, "We have helped." Where is the greater guilt?

The guilt is already judged of the fallen angels, the gods who have come to declare war against the children of the Light. Have you never considered that the actions of the fallen angels everywhere on the planet are merely for the testing of the souls of those who are the initiates, of those who are earning their wings, of those who are destined to return to God?

Thus, beloved, you will see that the judgment here is not upon the fallen ones, for they are already judged. It will be upon those who stood by and did not feed the Christ,[5] did not defend Him, and did not know when was the hour to sell what they had to take the sword and defend that Christ.[6]

The Defense of Christ

He gave the direction [read Luke 22:35–38]; and therefore, let none be passive and allow the murder of the Christ incarnate without the defense of Light. Let this nation be defended. Let the community be defended by the sacred sword of the spoken Word. Let all be alert to the murderous intent of the dark ones to destroy the souls and minds and hearts of little children.

Realize, then, that there is an hour for one initiation without purse or scrip,[7] proving the alchemy of the Holy Spirit, and there is an hour for preparedness. And thus you have been led, and thus you have sealed your community of the Holy Spirit. And Lanello is well pleased that the Royal Teton Ranch has fulfilled his direction to this Messenger in the hour of parting: a place prepared for the safety of the Teaching and of the students of the Ascended Masters.

Take care, then, that you understand the necessity of the hour. And remember that we are determined, as you are determined, that no trial or persecution or false witness or manipulation of the economy or any actions by the fallen ones to destroy the lightbearers shall prevail.

Study Their Evil Ways

If you will study their evil ways, you will see that for every situation when there was a God-man on the earth, they sought to destroy and prevent and kill. When the Child Jesus was to be born, when prophesied by that astrology,[8] so Herod's henchmen killed all the male babies.[9] And so it was in the hour of the prophecy of the incarnation of Vishnu—the killing of the many sons to destroy the one. But the one was not destroyed, and therefore Lord Krishna incarnated.[10]

Do you remember, then, that again and again in every situation, whether through wars or manipulation of food supplies or the taking of the jobs from the people or the ruination of their money, there has always been the attempt to prevent the full flourishing of the Christ in the abundant life?

The Fulfillment of Christ's Promises to His Apostles

This is the hour and the moment of the fulfillment of the promise of Christ unto the apostles, the spiritual apostles who are anointed to sit with him at his table, to eat with him of his substance, and to judge the twelve tribes of Israel.

It is written once, it is written twice, it is written again: You who have been with the Son of God in his temptations—which are the initiations of the soul in every way of the path of the bodhisattva, initiations for which, although you do not even comprehend them in this hour of your service, you have tarried and kept the flame not only in this life but in past ages with the lightbearers—you, therefore, have been given the key to the binding of the fallen ones who come to destroy the incarnate Word in all people of God.[11]

For it is preordained in this two-thousand-year period that the Christed ones should be beheld. Understand the meaning of this Christ coming into the temple of yourselves, your loved ones, and your children. Understand that the guarding of this Light demands of you self-purification and the ability to meet every test.

The Judgment Call Compels the Answer throughout the Matter Cosmos

Understand the meaning of the Judgment Call. And let it be heaped upon thine own head[12] that within thee the separation of Light and Darkness take place even as the call is sent. And the *Call* is the only and the great protection of the community of Light. You go over old ground. You transmute the trials, the accusations, and the murder of the lightbearers of all ages.

When you stand in the sanctuary and you offer that praise and these intense calls of the sacred fire, the judgment goes back 250 million years of the infamy of the fallen angels practiced against the children of God and mankind in this and other systems of worlds. And thus the offices and the patterns and the footprints of the blasphemous and the infamous are therefore judged and bound.

Understand this principle and teaching, beloved hearts. Come to understand the reality of the message. And recognize that when the records are transmuted—and those who have committed these crimes are judged and bound and gathered by the angels who come to gather the tares from among the wheat[13]— that then, in the present hour, this formula, this matrix of the false hierarchy will have no power over you or your Community or the Ascended Masters or their Teachings or their Messenger.

You are proving the Law in retrospect. You are going backwards in history and you are bringing that call as God directs it, as Jesus directs it, as the entire Spirit of the Great White Brotherhood directs it into the very cause and core of those conditions that have happened again and again.

Thus, the armies of the fallen ones are decimated. But you must understand they have built a momentum for a long, long cycling of their evil ways. Thus, in each turn of the spiral of their momentum there is the judgment that takes place on the lines of the clock. Be not dismayed, then, for the calls that you give go deeper and deeper into the akashic records, into the astral plane. And truly you serve with Archangel Michael to clean out the pit and that location of the pit under various areas of the world where the fallen ones reside.

In the cleanup of the planetary body there is a signal by crystal light that is transferred to other houses of light and mansions where many souls are bound and burdened. And I tell you that this Word of God, this Judgment Call given by Jesus Christ to you, does live forever. And when it is given it goes forth in concentric rings of Light. And the call stands for systems of worlds in this galaxy and in galaxies beyond whence the evil ones have come. And the call is as effective in those systems as it is here because there is no time and space. And the imprint upon Matter is repeated again and again and again.

Thus, you must know that there are millions of souls who send gratitude through my heart in this hour for the decree work that has been done. And they desire that I should be their messenger to you, the messenger from their far-off worlds, to tell you that the dynamic decrees given in this chapel, and in every place where one or two or three gather[14] with the holy angels to give these calls, have resulted in their liberation. And in each and every place where these calls have been given there is a transfer of Light, there is an activation.

No matter what is said to the contrary by any worldly opinion or any damnation from the fallen ones, it is true that the Call compels the answer throughout the Matter cosmos.

The Initiation in the Garden of Gethsemane

Now I would point out to you that the initiation in the Garden of Gethsemane through the night following the Lord's Supper was a great test of endurance for the disciples. And there are many in this room who are so heavy with sleep that they cannot keep awake for my message. Thus, I ask you to stand in honor of Christ. And I ask that the windows and doors be opened that you might receive the refreshing wind of the Holy Spirit and know that it is indeed meet that you should pray to enter not into temptation and take seriously, beloved hearts, what it means to be a disciple in this hour of the Cosmic Christ—Jesus, Lord Maitreya, Lord Buddha.

Realize, beloved hearts, that with an abundance of Teaching there also comes almost a surfeiting as one who revels in a large meal or banquet and much wine. The surfeiting of the Teaching and the Work at hand may seem to make all of this almost commonplace, but I, John, urge you to realize that worlds and systems of worlds depend upon your successful passing through the course of Christic initiation. Each and every one of you holds in your heart and in your hand the ability to make this Teaching and Path available to the whole world. Consider, then, this hour and your decision. And consider the reward that was promised to us.

I directed this reading* to the Messenger that you might understand that Jesus did indeed say it was not possible for a rich man to enter the kingdom of heaven.[15] And thus beloved Francis and Clare, taking up the vow of poverty, did live a life in proof that God not only rewarded them abundantly but gave to them everlasting Life.

Note how Peter desired to know what reward they should have. And thus Jesus had the occasion to tell that this reward was indeed a reward on earth as well as in heaven.[16] The choices are the same, and I place before your own eyes your own ambitions which have come between you and a higher calling and a higher service.

How long do you actually think that you have to earn the good accounting for the reward of the Ascension? Do you really count on the fact that you have many decades before you and

---
*The Messenger's scriptural reading directed by Beloved John prior to the formal dictation included: Pss. 70; Luke 22:14–20; John 13:1–35; Luke 22:24–71; Matt. 19:23–30.

therefore can dally here or there in other projects and things and ambitions, so often done in the name of the Church but somehow the Church does not really enter into any benefit whatsoever?

Will You Drink His Cup and Drink All of It?

Beloved hearts, you have come to this altar because you have declared yourselves to be disciples—and not only disciples but initiates of the path of Christhood, the resurrection unto the Ascension. Will you drink his cup and drink all of it? It is not enough, beloved ones, to have a Messenger and a few chelas who take seriously the whole cup of the Teaching while others treat it as a smorgasbord and take what they will and go out satisfied with little, forgetting that as they have been easily satisfied, so the Law itself is indeed *not* satisfied and the reward that they seek will *not* be forthcoming.

The Temptation

When the temptation then comes to deny the LORD within your own heart and breast by any lie or misdemeanor or going away from that Presence, remember that the temptation is using your own substance of karma and dense desire of the past. And unless you are determined to overcome this and cast it into the sacred fire, you will indeed succumb.

And, beloved ones, there cannot be a test that is not difficult. There cannot be a test that does not demand pain or that you give up something of yourself. All who have gone before you and the Messenger who stands before you have had to surrender much in order to fulfill the office they have been given.

The Office

You have an office waiting to drop upon you officially as the Chela of the Great White Brotherhood. Each one in his own time earns that reward, and no man knoweth it save the Father. And when the Chela is drawn into the heart of hearts of the Guru, there is a mutual recognition and a knowledge that you are fully engaged with the Master, and you are One. And it is not illusory and it is not based on a sense of favoritism or association.

The Opportunity

Beloved hearts, recognize the meaning of fulfillment in Christ and know that this is the meaning of the Last Supper: that he offered unto us the blood of his Essence, the bread of his Life, and the opportunity to continue with him and to be with him in the Life everlasting. Some are still reincarnating to this hour. Some have sold their souls. Some have ascended. I was fortunate to have long life in the service of Christ and thus did ascend in my embodiment as John the Beloved. Others became lost through the centuries.

And, beloved, is there any greater opportunity than to have lived and known Jesus Christ? Yes, there is a greater opportunity. It is the opportunity today to know the *Ascended Master Jesus Christ and* Saint Germain *and* El Morya *and* the saints ascended without number. There is a greater opportunity to know the fullness of the science of the spoken Word, to have the transfer of Light and the empowerment [through the Messenger] to use that Word for the blessing of evolutions beyond the galaxies and to therefore balance karma swiftly.

The Attribute

The greatest attribute of a disciple today in the fulfillment of Love is *endurance*—is *staying power* and a *vision* which sees that in the staying, all of the purposes of God are fulfilled.

The Tests

Many tests will come and they will increase as you advance. God delights in observing your victories over puzzles that become more complex. He rejoices to see that you have, then, the attainment that surpasses the fallen angels when they fell and therefore can stand as warriors of the Spirit and defend the nations against their encroachments, their machinations, their psychological techniques to manipulate the people into thinking they are receiving some benefit from the government when in fact they are being taken and destroyed.

The Last Supper

Blessed hearts, it is an hour of the celebration of the Last Supper, as though each disciple were then frozen in time and in stone. The moment of the trial had come, the moment of all of the outpicturing of what was the dweller of each one. The witnesses, the judges, the accusers, the council, the high priest—each one outplayed himself.

And so we also outplayed ourselves. Peter wept[17] and yet history records his tears were for himself, not for Jesus. Take care, then, that your tears are not in self-pity or sympathy for your plight of what suffering you may be required to endure, but see to it that your compassion extends to the Ascended Masters who have loved you and to their great desire to reach the little ones who suffer on earth.

(On the Eve of Good Friday—
Darkness Brewing in South Africa)

There is brewing a darkness in South Africa. I direct your attention to this base chakra of the continent, the last stronghold of Light. Great darkness has come upon that continent. And the configuration of forces East and West, and the interplay, is intended by the dark ones to result in a bloodbath and a destruction.

Blessed hearts, it is indeed a division of the very base chakra of that continent. I ask you to pray for the judgment of all that is not of the Light, known or unknown, and to take care that you become not embroiled on this side or the other, for we deal here not with recent times but with a very ancient conspiracy. And therefore, let the Law deliver its mandate in answer to the call that centers in the Mighty I AM Presence and allows the Universal Christ to be the Judge.

The Communion

I come, then, sent by many, the most important of whom is our beloved Jesus himself who said to me this night, "John, my beloved, go and serve my own Communion in the sanctuary of the Holy Grail." This I have come to do, but not without the admonishment that you take the path of victory as a serious one. Thus, I shall give to you now this Bread from the heart of Jesus and this Wine.

By his hand through my own—through these hands thus—this Bread and Wine is consecrated to everlasting Life within you.

The Transfer of the New Testament in My Blood

I ask the Messenger to read that which I have directed her to read, that you might have the words of warning of Jesus to the apostle Paul on the matter of Communion:

> I have received of the Lord that which also I delivered unto you, That the Lord Jesus the same night in which he was betrayed took bread:
> And when he had given thanks, he brake it and said, Take, eat: this is my Body, which is broken for you: this do in remembrance of me.
> After the same manner also he took the cup when he had supped, saying, This cup is the new testament in my Blood: this do ye, as oft as ye drink it, in remembrance of me.

"The new testament in my Blood," beloved, is the Teaching that Jesus transferred the Christic Light of his blood and essence through that bread, that his consciousness might be with you also, that you might not lose the true memory of the new testament—*the testimony of that living Christ with you.*

Thus, he did place in the bodies of his own and does place this night the new testament of his Blood, which is that Christ consciousness who will bring to your remembrance, even as you do this in his remembrance, the true knowledge of God and the Law.

> This do ye, as oft as ye drink it, in remembrance of me.
>
> For as often as ye eat this bread and drink this cup, ye do shew the Lord's death till he come.
>
> Wherefore whosoever shall eat this bread and drink this cup of the Lord, unworthily, shall be guilty of the Body and Blood of the LORD.
>
> But let a man examine himself, and so let him eat of that bread and drink of that cup.
>
> For he that eateth and drinketh unworthily, eateth and drinketh damnation to himself, not discerning the LORD's Body.
>
> I Corinthians 11:23–29

Confession of Sins before Taking Communion

According to this Teaching, beloved, the holy Church has required confession of sins before taking Communion, that each one might be renewed and offer penance and therefore be whole in the taking of that Communion.

I invite you to sing a hymn and, through the singing of this hymn, to therefore confess your sins to your Holy Christ Self and determine your own penance from your heart of hearts, and determine that in taking this Body and Blood of Christ unto everlasting Life that you are indeed sitting with Jesus Christ at table and have his promises to be with him in heaven and to be judging the twelve tribes of Israel.

Therefore, know what is fitting for one who holds such an office and know what is not. And make your determination in my heart—for I AM with you—to be strong and to go forth confirmed in the will of God and in the will of your heart. Thus, I shall receive these confessions in my heart, even as Jesus and your Christ Self receive them. And I pray the angel of God strengthen you in your resolve. Thus, in your resolve also do receive Communion, for it is indeed unto your Life everlasting and your Christhood.

Let us sing to the Everlasting City.*

Last night I lay asleeping / There came a dream so fair
I stood in old Jerusalem / Beside the temple there
I heard the children singing / And ever as they sang
Methought the voice of angels / From heav'n in answer rang
Methought the voice of angels / From heav'n in answer rang

Jerusalem, Jerusalem / Lift up your gates and sing
Hosanna in the highest / Hosanna to your King!

And then methought my dream was changed
The streets no longer rang
Hushed were the glad hosannas / The little children sang
The sun grew dark with mystery / The morn was cold and chill
As the shadow of a cross arose / Upon a lonely hill
As the shadow of a cross arose / Upon a lonely hill.

Jerusalem, Jerusalem / Hark how the angels sing
Hosanna in the highest / Hosanna to your King!

And once again the scene was changed
New earth there seemed to be
I saw the Holy City / Beside the tideless sea
The light of God was on its streets / The gates were open wide
And all who would might enter / And no one was denied
No need of moon or stars by night / Or sun to shine by day
It was the New Jerusalem / That would not pass away
It was the New Jerusalem / That would not pass away.

Jerusalem, Jerusalem / Sing for the night is o'er!
Hosanna in the highest / Hosanna forevermore!
Hosanna in the highest / Hosanna forevermore!

John Blesses the Bread and Wine
Out of the Heart of the Living Saviour
and Serves Communion through the Messenger

In the name of the Father and of the Son and of the Holy Spirit, in the name of the Mother, I, John, bless this bread and this wine out of the heart of the living Saviour who is Christ the LORD, who is the incarnation of Vishnu.

Out of the heart of the Saviour I AM come! Through that heart I anoint you apostles of the Most High God. Receive the

---
*The Messenger, choir, and congregation sing "The Holy City." Words by F. E. Weatherly, music by Stephen Adams, copyright 1943 by Carl Fischer.
Copyright © 1985 Church Universal and Triumphant, Inc.

calling with grace and joy and perseverance and all purity and love to one another, preferring one another rather than the company of the ungodly.

In the heart of Jesus Christ, I AM come to you.

[Holy Communion is served by the Ascended Master John the Beloved through the Messenger.]

Let us sing the "I Love You Waltz" to beloved Jesus.

> Jesus, I give my heart to you
> Come fill me with Love, my soul renew.
> O divine Master! show me the way to go
> Life's holy purpose I would know.
>
> Dear one, send forth your Light sublime
> The ladder of Love I climb into your Heart.
> O my Beloved! hear my resounding Word
> Forevermore echo as "I love you."

In the name of the entire Spirit of the Great White Brotherhood, in the name of the seven archangels and the servant sons and daughters of God, I, John, declare:

It is finished. It is sealed. It is done.

Pax vobiscum.

Messenger's Prayer to the Eternal Christos*
The Mystery of Thy Light Dwelling in Us Bodily

O living Word of Light, eternal Christos, descend into our hearts. O sacred fire of seraphim, angels of the Abendmahl,[18] angels of the Holy Spirit, bearers of the sacred cup of the Bread and the Wine, enter now and celebrate in His name with us this Holy Communion of the saints.

Beloved Alpha and Omega, break Thou the Body of Cosmos. Let Thy Universal Consciousness now be broken for our understanding and assimilation. Let this living Flame which we ignite, O God, be in this hour truly the victory of Life.

Legions of the Central Sun, we call in thy name. Pillars of fire and of eternity, let this Flame, as the divine spark does burn upon the altar of our hearts, be for the universal understanding of the mysteries—even the great mystery of thy Light dwelling in us bodily: Divine spark of the Holy of Holies.

Bearers of the Flame in the name of Zarathustra, legions of the Buddha bearing now the cup of grace, angel devas carrying this Wine and all elemental life do attend thee, O LORD, that they might also partake of the sacred mysteries.

Beloved Mother Mary, angels of the sacred fire, prepare our

---
*offered during the candlelighting at the altar before the service and dictation

bodies, our souls, our spirits and hearts and minds for the assimilation of the Word and Work of our Lord. According to the promise of the I AM THAT I AM in Jesus, Maitreya, Gautama, Sanat Kumara, so make of us a new creature in Christ. Let the Universal Mind of God endued fully with His Love be our portion tonight.

Saint Germain, Mother Mary, Jesus, John the Beloved, saints of the sacred mysteries—even so, come quickly, O God, into our temples.

"**The Summit Lighthouse Sheds Its Radiance O'er All the World to Manifest as Pearls of Wisdom.**" This dictation by John the Beloved was delivered through the Messenger Elizabeth Clare Prophet on Holy Thursday, April 4, 1985, during the 5-day Easter Conclave at Camelot. The Messenger's scriptural readings prior to the dictation were Psalm 70; Luke 22:14-20; John 13:1-35; Luke 22:24-71; and Matthew 19:23-30. (1) John 13:25. (2) Matt. 11:3; Luke 7:19, 20. (3) John 13:27. (4) Matt. 26:36-46; Mark 14:32-42; Luke 22:39-46. (5) Matt. 25:41-46. (6) Luke 22:35-38. (7) Matt. 10:9, 10; Mark 6:7-9; Luke 9:3; 10:4. (8) Matt. 2:2. (9) Matt. 2:16. (10) Ancient Hindu texts record that Lord Vishnu, in order to assist the earth, sent into manifestation two aspects of his personality who incarnated as Balarama and Krishna. A voice revealed to King Kamsa, an embodied demon, that he would be destroyed by the eighth child of the newly married couple Devaki and Vasudeva. To save his wife, Vasudeva promised to turn over to the king every child born to them. The first six sons were put to death. When Devaki conceived for the seventh time, it appeared she had miscarried, but the child, Balarama, was miraculously transferred to the womb of Vasudeva's second wife. The eighth child conceived was Krishna. With divine assistance, Vasudeva safeguarded the life of Krishna by taking him to the home of another couple, secretly switching him for their newborn daughter, and returning with the baby girl. When Kamsa learned of the birth, he rushed to the couple, seized the infant, and dashed it to the ground. But the baby was transformed into a goddess and announced the survival of the feared eighth child. In his wrath, Kamsa continued his search for the infant. He ordered that every male child that gave signs of unusual vigor be put to death. In the meantime, the infant Krishna was taken by his new family to a different town and thereby escaped. (11) Matt. 19:28; Luke 22:28-30; I Cor. 6:2, 3. See Jesus Christ, August 6, 1978, "They Shall Not Pass!" in *Spoken by Elohim* (*Pearls of Wisdom,* vol. 21, nos. 32, 33), pp. 165-67, 175-76; Jesus Christ, March 13, 1983, "The Awakening of the Dweller on the Threshold," *Pearls of Wisdom,* vol. 26, no. 36, pp. 385-87, 390; Mother Mary, August 26, 1984, "The Power of God in My Right Hand," *Pearls of Wisdom,* vol. 27, no. 51, pp. 439-43. (12) Josh. 7:6; II Sam. 13:19. (13) Matt. 13:36-43. (14) Matt. 18:20. (15) Matt. 19:23, 24. (16) Matt. 19:27-30. (17) Luke 22:62. (18) *Abendmahl* (German): Holy Communion.

Copyright © 1985 Church Universal and Triumphant, Inc., Box A, Malibu, CA 90265. All rights reserved. Printed in the United States of America. Pearls of Wisdom and The Summit Lighthouse are registered trademarks of Church Universal and Triumphant, Inc. All rights to their use are reserved. Published by The Summit Lighthouse. Pearls sent weekly (to USA, via third-class mail) for a minimum love offering of $40/year.

Easter Conclave at Camelot
"Come, leave your nets—I will make you fishers of men."

II
Archangel Michael's Rosary*
For Armageddon

And at that time shall Michael stand up, the great prince which standeth for the children of thy people. Daniel 12

The Supplicant's Prayer to Saint Michael the Archangel
(To Be Recited by the Supplicant with Archangel Michael's Rosary Each Time It Is Given)

O Light of the Ancient of Days, Send to us now the luminous presence of thy beloved Archangel Michael.

Legions of the Central Sun, Light of far-off worlds, Elohim: In this hour of our Lord's descent into Death and Hell, send to us therefore the armies of the LORD, the company of saints, the defender in battle, Archangel Michael.

Defend now, O blessed emissary of God, even the holy innocents, our precious children and youth and all lightbearers in the service of our God.

Beloved Archangel Jophiel, beloved Archangel Chamuel, beloved Archangel Gabriel, beloved Archangel Raphael, beloved Archangel Uriel, beloved Archangel Zadkiel, beloved Archangel Uzziel, hear our Call! *Answer now* **in the presence of the Prince of the Archangels, Saint Michael, august leader of the hosts of Light. Let us welcome our beloved Archangel Michael and his many legions who gather in this city of Our Lady, the Queen of the Angels.**

---
*Use this Pearl of Wisdom as your official text for Archangel Michael's Rosary. Recite aloud everything that is in heavy (bold) type except the titles, following the instructions as given. You may begin right now with this first prayer and continue to the end, skipping everything that is not in bold.

Copyright © 1962, 1963, 1965, 1966, 1968, 1972, 1974, 1975, 1976, 1978, 1979, 1985 Church Universal and Triumphant, Inc.

O hosts of the LORD from every system and galaxy and star, from the realms of Spirit descend to planet Earth for the deliverance of souls and children, and men and women and nations.

Archangel Michael, in the name I AM THAT I AM, we bow before the Light within thee, before thy cosmic faith and diligence in keeping the vigil of our very life. Defender of the Church, Defender of the Faith and of the Woman Clothed with the Sun and her Manchild, blessed one of God:

Come now and hear our call and our longing to be with thee in the octaves of Light before the Throne of Glory, even as we desire with the deep desiring of our hearts to also descend with thee, in commemoration of the crucifixion of our Lord, to the very depths of Death and Hell, into the very pit itself. So we would go there with thee for the binding of the devils and the fallen angels, for the binding of those unclean spirits whose hour has come for the Final Judgment before the Court of the Sacred Fire.

O beloved Mighty I AM Presence, in the name I AM THAT I AM, we send love and light and the crown of our causal bodies this day in gratitude for the service of Archangel Michael and his legions of Light to all earth's evolutions and throughout the galaxies of Light.

Beloved Alpha and Omega, bless now our beloved Archangel Michael with dispensations and hosts of Light and armies sent from out of the higher octaves to assist in his service upon earth in the cleaning out of the focuses of the bottomless pit and the acceleration of that service, O God, for the very binding of Death and Hell and the casting of the entire astral plane and the false hierarchy into the lake of sacred fire.

Elohim of God and Spirit of the Great White Brotherhood, Cosmic Councils of the Sun, we call forth thy intercession for and on behalf of Archangel Michael that all of the earth this day might render him praise and assistance, prayers and glory unto the LORD that he might fulfill his inner vow to defend the Christed ones.

We call unto the nine powers of the Holy Spirit and the angel choirs thereof. We call to the hosts of seraphim in the name of Justinius, Captain of Seraphic Bands, and to the mighty cherubim who keep the way of the Tree of Life at the Mystery School of Lord Maitreya. Hear our call in this hour for the hosts of the Lord to gather in the name of Vishnu, in the name of the Cosmic Christ, the Universal One, for the binding of all evil forces in this hour of the Kali Yuga and its Dark Cycle.*

Almighty God, let the power of Satan and the seed of Satan in the earth be bound this day in the full power and presence of Archangel Michael and his legions of Light! And let the resurrection of the eternal Christ be now unto every son and daughter of God upon earth.

Beloved Mighty I AM Presence, beloved Mother Mary, intercede for us this day before the Father, before thy Son, Jesus, for and on behalf of every son and daughter of God upon earth—every child of God in whom there burns a threefold flame. Let them be visited by Archangel Uriel in the full, flaming presence of the power of the resurrection. Let them be visited by Archangel Gabriel with the annunciation of the Path of the Ascension and the revelation of the Mighty I AM Presence.

I call upon the Great Central Sun, the Four and Twenty Elders, the Lord God Almighty. Let there be a quickening in the hearts of all those who have descended from that Central Sun who are the Children of the Sun. And let the renewal, the elevation, the resurrection, the regeneration come forth now!

Let it be done, O God, according to Thy purpose!

In the name of the living Christ, in the name of the Father and of the Son and of the Holy Spirit, in the name of the Mother, I AM the sealing of the sons and daughters of God upon this earth on the Path of the Ascension this day and forever. Amen.

Eternal Father, Strong to Save

Good afternoon, everyone. We're going to sing "The Sweetest Psalm," the song of Archangel Michael's obedience, his great victory over the alliance of reprobate angels which he and his legions cast out of heaven. It is sung to the melody of "Eternal Father, Strong to Save," number 285.

The words of this song by Saint Germain are a tribute to beloved Archangel Michael, who made his decision—in the hour of that ultimate temptation that each one must face—to embrace the Lord God, to renounce the fallen one, and to move on in his service to become the archangel who is the protector of our life.

The very fact that we stand here today with the opportunity to serve Saint Germain and to walk the Path of the Ascension is

---
*Stop tape and insert optional personal prayer here.

due entirely to Archangel Michael. It is, therefore, with great joy that we celebrate his presence on earth in this moment.
(Songs 285 and 282 are optional inclusions in your Archangel Michael Rosary.)

The Sweetest Psalm

The sweetest psalm I ever knew
Directed to the God I view
"Obedience"—I AM to Thee
O Law of Beauty, keep me free
Command me now Thyself to see
Command me now Thyself to be.

I AM, O Shepherd, so divine
Abide within this heart of mine
Pulsate, arise, O mighty fire
Make every facet now all Thine
Command me now and set me free
Thy perfect image now to be.

O Freedom's song will fill my soul
For Freedom is Thy highest goal
Thy way is love and great delight
To steer my course to heaven's height
Command me now to shed Thy Light
Effulgence of Thy wonder bright.

Obedience is not bondage chain
Obedience will secure great gain
Thy laws of Truth produce good fruit
A holy science that is proof
A heavenly vision faith-inspired
Of victory to free our youth.

Now sweep Thy beams around the world
Command Thy Light to ever shine
Thy holy rays to bathe the earth
In Light divine, Thy comfort blaze
E'er pouring forth God-energy
Expand Thy love, great God I AM.

Traveling Protection   6.05

*Lord Michael *before*, Lord Michael *behind*,
Lord Michael *to the right*, Lord Michael *to the left*,
Lord Michael *above*, Lord Michael *below*,
Lord Michael, Lord Michael *wherever I go!*

I AM his Love protecting here!
I AM his Love protecting here!
I AM his Love protecting here!

(Repeat three times from asterisk)

Let us sing to the blessed seven archangels to the tune of "Holy, Holy, Holy," number 282.

To the Seven Archangels

Michael, Michael, Michael, Prince of the Archangels
From the grateful hearts of all do songs of praise arise.
For thy heavenly presence, all on earth adore thee
God from the Sun in all the name implies.

Michael, Michael, Michael, may the guardian angels
From thy heavenly legions stand forth to set all free.
Purify, illumine, manifest the glory
Of Light's perfection that each one may be.

Jophiel and Chamuel, Gabriel and Raphael
Uriel and Zadkiel and mighty hosts of Light.
Cherubim and seraphim from the realms of glory
Rend now the veil that dims our human sight.

Blessed seven archangels, for illumination
We invoke thy presence in hymns of praise to thee.
Keep us consecrated to God's plan fulfilling
In purity, thy ministers to be.

Introduction to Archangel Michael's Rosary

The beloved Father has placed upon my heart for some time His deep desire to have a rosary to Archangel Michael. I am very happy that on this occasion we can recite a rosary not only to Archangel Michael but to those heavenly hosts toward whom he directs our supplications.

I would like to give you a bit of background on the service to Archangel Michael that has been held by the Roman Catholic Church. At this date, the prayers to Archangel Michael and others of the heavenly hosts have been officially removed from the rituals of many churches.

The fourth-century Synod of Laodicea "prohibited by a canon that prayer should be offered to angels" on the grounds that "it was a species of idolatry and detracted from the worship due to Christ."[1] Because of these strong attitudes, festivals of angels were in general much less frequent than the feasts of saints.

The prayer of Pope Leo XIII to Archangel Michael traditionally said after the Roman Catholic Mass was deleted after Vatican Council II (1962-65) revised the liturgy. The ostensible reason for this was that the Council wanted to retain only the essence of the Mass, which is supposed to be the reenactment of the Last Supper. Therefore, all prayers which did not have specific reference to the Eucharist or the communion of Christ with his disciples were eliminated.

Now, in the first instance, the denial of the prayers to the archangels and angelic hosts is a misunderstanding of the three hierarchies of heaven: first, the order of the builders of form under *Elohim;* this plural noun for God as the Creator is the appellation whereby we call the Seven Spirits of God who brought forth the entire creation in answer to the command of the Logos; serving under the Seven Mighty Elohim are the builders of form, all elemental life—elementals of fire, air, water, and earth, and your own body elemental—and those who are known as the Four Cosmic Forces, who govern the forces in nature; second, the order of angels, i.e., angelic hosts, consisting of archangels, cherubim, seraphim, and various stations, hierarchies, and principalities of angels in the seven planes of heaven. The office and function of these two orders is to serve and care for the third—the sons and daughters of God, the Christed ones. Of course, there is complete cooperation between the three kingdoms and an overlapping of their mutual services.

And so, God created and manifested Himself through Elohim to build the Spirit/Matter universe and to make it habitable for the evolutions of His sons and daughters. He created the archangels and the angelic hosts to minister unto them as helpers and teachers. Therefore, sons and daughters of God anywhere in the universe do and should call upon, by the science of the spoken Word, by the creative command, these hosts of the LORD—both the builders of form in nature and the angelic beings. They are ours to command in the name of the Cosmic Christ to perform according to the Will of God and the Divine Design whatever service is necessary in life.

The sons and daughters of God were born to be co-creators with God, and the authority of the Word as the Threefold Flame of Life within us is that authority of God Himself. And so, you see, to have a Church council cut off the opportunity of the sons of God to speak to the angels and to bid them serve in ministering to life is a direct interference with the order of our own evolution and the mantle of the Godhead that has been placed upon us as a divine office.

I have thought it was a great tragedy that the calls to Archangel Michael were removed from the Mass and also a great tragedy that the Lord's Prayer has been removed from our public schools. After all, the latter is a prayer to the Father written by a

Jew which demands no denominational affiliation whatsoever. Not a line of it should prove an offense to any member of the Body of God on earth, no matter what their religion, East or West.

And the reading of a psalm of David, which followed when I attended public school, is a study in the evolution of the soul of another of Abraham's seed who sought and found his God in the face of trial and temptation, karma and the world adversaries of the Light. The psalms are deep lessons in humility and strength and trust in the LORD, and as such they should be known and loved by schoolchildren at a tender age, that they may find courage for life to endure its tests.

It occurred to me the other day that actually there is another prayer that could be sung in the public schools today if someone would promote it—and that is the prayer that was written by Irving Berlin, "God Bless America."

It is a beautiful prayer from beginning to end, and that prayer itself is the invocation to the Father by the sons and daughters of God to bless America. And that call does allow the Father to assign His angels, His Elohim and nature spirits to truly bless this nation from sea to shining sea—"from the mountains to the prairies to the oceans white with foam . . ."

And so, I thought that we should have some of our citizens groups that function outside of the Church realize that this prayer was also written by a very famous and beloved Jew and therefore should not have any problem in gaining the support of all people.

I want to tell you that as we went stumping throughout Australia and the Philippines, each time I had the opportunity to sing that song, "God Bless Australia," "God Bless the Philippines," and "God Bless America," I felt such a fervor in my heart and such a descent of Light. It is really so amazing to realize how the simple statement "God bless you!" opens the valve of the crystal cord and the Mighty I AM Presence. It opens the very founts of heaven and lets the Light descend with that simple benediction, heartfelt, freely offered.

And so, we find that as the Catholic world has ceased to pray to Michael the Archangel, as our children have ceased to pray in the public schools, many calamities have come upon the planetary home. We can see an enormous change and especially in darkness covering the land out of the astral plane since the 1962–65 period when this prayer was removed from the Mass and since the 1962, 1963 Supreme Court decisions which disallowed prayer in the public schools.

Now I would like to go back to the experience recorded by Pope Leo XIII, which prompted him to write the prayer to Saint Michael that was said at the conclusion of the Mass from 1886 to 1964.

One day as Leo XIII had finished Mass he suddenly stopped at the foot of the altar as if in a trance. When asked what had happened, he explained he had heard voices—two voices, one kind and gentle, the other guttural and hard. These voices were speaking in conversation.

The guttural voice, the voice of Satan in his pride, boasting to Our Lord: "I can destroy your Church."

The gentle voice of Our Lord replied: "You can? Then go ahead and do so."

Satan: "To do so, I need more time and more power."

Our Lord: "How much time? How much power?"

Satan: "Seventy-five years, and a greater power over those who will give themselves over to my service."

Our Lord: "You have the time; you have the power. Do what you will."

Leo XIII was given to understand that if the devil had not accomplished his purpose at the end of the time limit given, he would suffer a most crushing and humiliating defeat. Furthermore, the forces of Good would not be helpless in the face of the onslaught of Satan and his legions. They, too, were given a greater power for Good if only they would use it. Through their prayers and sacrifices and good Christian lives, they could offset the power of the devil and his human agents. It was then that he saw the great role St. Michael was to play in this mortal conflict.

As he had hurled Lucifer and the fallen angels out of Heaven after the "first revolt against God," so, too, he would play a great part in the battle to come, and would eventually cast Satan again into Hell.

It was a result of this vision that Leo XIII then composed this prayer to St. Michael:

> Saint Michael the Archangel, defend us in battle, be our protection against the wickedness and snares of the devil; may God rebuke him, we humbly pray; and do thou, O Prince of the heavenly host, by the power of God, thrust into hell Satan and all evil spirits who wander through the world for the ruin of souls. Amen.[2]

You are most welcome to use this prayer, incorporating it into your morning decree session to Archangel Michael, substituting the words "thrust into hell" with "thrust into the lake of sacred fire."

Or, for a more precise and incisive fiat to include in Archangel Michael's Rosary, I would say:

> Saint Michael the Archangel, defend us in Armageddon, be our protection against the wickedness and snares of the devil; may God rebuke him, we humbly pray; and do thou, O Prince of the heavenly host, by the power of God, bind the forces of Death and Hell, the seed of Satan, the false hierarchy of Antichrist, and all evil spirits who wander through the world for the ruin of souls, and remand them to the Court of the Sacred Fire for their Final Judgment.*
>
> Cast out the dark ones and their darkness, the evildoers and their evil words and works, cause, effect, record and memory, into the lake of sacred fire "prepared for the devil and his angels."
>
> In the name of the Father, the Son, the Holy Spirit, and the Mother, Amen.

I would like to share with you my great joy in receiving from one of my chelas a rosary, a chaplet, to Archangel Michael and the holy angels—both the beads and the ritual. It is a very pretty rosary, and you can see that the one who created it consecrated it to the jewels of the City Foursquare and the hierarchies of angels. It has a medallion of Archangel Michael, and it is a very sweet focus of the following litany which I would invite you to give with me at this time. But first I would like to give you the story of this chaplet:

> Saint Michael appearing one day to Antonia d'Astonac, a most devout servant of God, told her that he wished to be honored by nine salutations corresponding to the nine Choirs of Angels, which should consist of one Pater and three Aves in honor of each of the angelic choirs.
>
> He promised in return to obtain for all who should venerate him in this way before receiving Holy Communion, that an Angel of each of the nine Choirs should be assigned to accompany them to the Holy Table; he promised, moreover, his continual assistance during life, and likewise that of the Holy Angels to all who should recite the nine Salutations every day, and also after death the deliverance of their souls and those of relatives from the pains of Purgatory.[3]

---
*Stop tape and insert optional personal prayer here.

This rosary consists of responsive recitations, the Gloria Patri, the Our Father, and the Hail Mary incorporated into nine salutations to Saint Michael and the various choirs of angels. The method of reciting this is that I say, "O God, come to my assistance." Then you repeat it. I say, "O Lord, make haste to help me." Then you repeat it. And then we sing together the Gloria Patri—"Glory Be to the Father," song 2. And then we go through these nine salutations. Each salutation consists of the Our Father, three Aves, and a special prayer of intercession.

I would like to begin this rosary to Archangel Michael with the singing of Beloved Jesus' I AM Lord's Prayer and the singing of the Hail Mary so that we shall have consecrated the entire recitation in these hymns of praise to the Father, to our Lord, and to the Blessed Mother.

I would like to make an invocation to Archangel Michael to consecrate our rosary to various needs on the planet and of our Church and of yourselves as disciples on the Path. As I am saying this prayer, you can affirm it in your heart and also recite in your heart the very specific personal and private prayers you may have today for beloved Archangel Michael as the servant of God and of yourself as the son, the daughter of God.

You are welcome to kneel in the Presence of God before the altar during this consecration.

Consecration of Archangel Michael's Rosary to Planetary Needs, the Church, and the Saints
(To Be Recited by the Supplicant Each Time the Rosary Is Given)

Our beloved Father, in the name I AM THAT I AM, in the name Lord God Almighty, we call forth Thy Light through Thy blessed servant-son Archangel Michael and his legions of Light, the seven mighty archangels, the choirs of angels and the principalities and thrones of angelic graces and hierarchies of Light. We ask the Lord's intercession through myriad angels and bands of angels, including the Choirs of Seraphim, of Cherubim, of Thrones, of Angels, of Dominions, of Powers, of Virtues, of Principalities, and of Archangels.

We call now for the binding of Death and Hell and its denizens who have come to the hour of the Final Judgment. We call to Almighty God and to the legions of the Lord Jesus Christ and of the entire Spirit of the Great White Brotherhood, all saints in heaven. We command this entire planetary body be cleaned out by the blessed legions of the Lord's hosts, the Cosmic Christ, Alpha and Omega, the legions of Surya and Cuzco,

legions of angels of the First Ray of God's Will serving under the banners of Lord Maitreya and the World Mother, the Mighty Blue Eagle from Sirius and the Great Teams of Conquerors!

Beloved Mighty I AM Presence, hear our call and answer in this hour of world need. We pray, then, for the deliverance of this nation under God. We pray for the deliverance of the planetary body, according to Thy divine plan, from nuclear war, from terminal diseases, from the genetic engineering of the fallen ones, from rock music and drugs upon our youth, from all strains of darkness and death devouring not only the physical bodies but the souls of God's people.*

In thy name *Elohim,* we command the deliverance of our planet this day from all infestations of demons and discarnates causing insanity and depravity, murder, assassination, and spiritual suicide.

Beloved Mighty I AM Presence, we demand the binding of all fallen angels, beginning with the Watchers, their godless creation, the Nephilim gods and their mechanization man. *Blaze* the full power of the Great Central Sun for the binding of Serpent and his seed, for the binding of all seed of Satan and seed of Lucifer who remain since the Final Judgment of the latter.

We call upon the Lord God Almighty this day. We call unto the Great Central Sun Magnet. *Burn* through, O Powers of Light! By the authority of the Christ within us, we beseech you this day to give absolute God protection to the Church Universal and Triumphant, the Mystical Body of God in heaven and on earth, to every Keeper of the Flame and lightbearer and all who are destined to make their ascension in this life.

We call for the cutting free of the Keepers of the Flame Fraternity, of the Teachings of the Ascended Masters, of our Camelot and our Royal Teton Ranch. We call for the cutting free of our Messengers and staff and all who are students of the Masters' Teachings. We call upon the Lord's host to clear the way for these Teachings to reach every man, woman, and child of God's heart upon this earth. Clear the way, beloved Archangel Michael and hosts of the Lord, for the quickening of hearts in the service of the Great White Brotherhood.

We call for God-victory now over all enemies of the

---
*Stop tape and insert optional personal prayer here.

Holy Church and betrayers of the living Word who—with avowed destruction—move against this Church, this Messenger and Teaching and the Body of God on earth. In the name of the Cosmic Christ, Lord Maitreya, Gautama Buddha and Sanat Kumara, we command that these individuals be bound in this hour, their evil intent nullified, by the full power of Archangel Michael.

And we call for the setting free of the lightbearers and the freedom fighters in every nation to Cut the economies free! Cut the governments free! Cut the societies free! Cut the people free! Cut the educational systems free! Cut the churches free! Cut the youth and children free!

Cut free, Archangel Michael and legions of Light, with your mighty swords of blue flame, each one gathered here in supplication. Hear our prayers, O God! Cut us free from all addiction and binding habit, all self-limitation and spiritual blindness, all selfishness and self-love that does not enable us to see Thee and Thy Will clearly, O God.

Blessed Father, we call in the name of Archangel Michael for dispensations from the Great Central Sun for this mighty archangel to enter now and bind the hordes of demons and discarnates and especially the entire crowd of fallen ones who plotted the betrayal and the judgment, the trial and the crucifixion of Jesus Christ and have continued to plot against the servant sons and daughters of God in this and every age.

Blaze the Light through! Blaze the Light through! Blaze the Light through! We demand the Final Judgment of their specific lifestreams in this hour, O God—and of all those whose names are not found written in the Book of Life.*

In the name I AM THAT I AM, we demand the action of the sacred fire in this hour, O God. Come forth now, Thou WORD of God, Thou Faithful and True with the armies of heaven! Come forth in the Victory of the God Flame! Come forth *now* in the Victory of the God Flame!

O LORD most holy, LORD Sanat Kumara, descend into our midst in this hour. We demand the binding and judgment of all those who have ever stood as the false witnesses, the accuser, and the condemner of the brethren and of the Christed ones.

In the name I AM THAT I AM, we demand the binding of the Liar and the lie, the Murderer and his

---
*Stop tape and insert optional personal prayer here.

murderous intent in every conspiracy that is pitted against the Light of the United States of America, of the true God-government in every nation and the true religion undefiled before God and the Father that is manifest in our hearts and in the hearts of the faithful everywhere.

We call for Life and Liberty and the cutting free of God's people on the entire face of this earth from World Communism, from the bondage of materialism, from the infestations and cancers of evil and foul spirits possessing the souls and the bodies of the people.

We call to you, beloved Jesus and Mother Mary, Saint Germain and all the hosts of the LORD in this hour. We commit our prayers unto you. We commit our spirits unto you. We commit the spirits and souls of our families, our friends, our loved ones, and all to whom we are karmically tied, all lightbearers and all mankind unto the Father, the Son, the Holy Spirit, and the eternal Mother.

In the holy name of God, Amen.

(Here you may give aloud or quietly within your heart your private, specific prayer for the consecration of your rosary or novena to Archangel Michael.)

Please be seated.

As I was offering this prayer, Archangel Michael requested that at the conclusion of the three Hail Marys we introduce one Judgment Call, "They Shall Not Pass!" by Jesus Christ. And so we will begin the rosary now by singing the "I AM Lord's Prayer," song 10, and singing the "Hail Mary," song 92.*

Archangel Michael's Rosary
The Ritual

I AM Lord's Prayer
by Jesus Christ

Our Father who art in heaven
Hallowed be Thy name
Hallowed be Thy name
Hallowed be Thy name, I AM.

I AM Thy Kingdom come
I AM Thy Will being done
I AM on earth even as I AM in heaven,
                in heaven, in heaven
I AM on earth even as I AM in heaven.
(I AM in heaven, I AM in heaven)

---
*You will find these songs sung by Excelsior on the 2-cassette album *Harpstrings of Lemuria* (A7963), $9.95 postpaid USA.

I AM giving this day daily bread to all
I AM forgiving all Life this day even as
I AM also all Life forgiving me,
   Life forgiving me, Life forgiving me.

I AM leading all men away from temptation
I AM delivering all men from every evil condition
I AM the Kingdom
I AM the Power and
I AM the Glory of God in eternal, immortal
   manifestation—
All this I AM, all this I AM, I AM.
(all this I AM, all this I AM)

Hail Mary

**Hail, Mary, full of grace
   the Lord is with thee.
Blessed art thou among women
   and blessed is the fruit
   of thy womb, Jesus.**

**Holy Mary, Mother of God
Pray for us, sons and daughters of God
Now and at the hour of our victory
Over sin, disease, and death. (4x)**

Holding the Archangel Michael medal, say:
   The Messenger: O God, come to my assistance.
   Congregation: **O God, come to my assistance.**
   The Messenger: O Lord, make haste to help me.
   Congregation: **O Lord, make haste to help me.**

Glory Be to the Father

**Glory be to the Father
And to the Son
And to the Holy Spirit
As it was in the beginning
Is now and ever shall be
Life without end
I AM, I AM, I AM. (3x)**

On the first single large bead commence the nine salutations, leaving for the end the four large beads.

Copyright © 1962, 1963, 1965, 1966, 1968, 1972, 1974, 1975, 1976, 1978, 1979, 1985 Church Universal and Triumphant, Inc.

First Salutation
To the Celestial Choir of Seraphim

I AM Lord's Prayer
by Jesus Christ

Our Father who art in heaven,
Hallowed be Thy name, I AM.
I AM Thy Kingdom come
I AM Thy Will being done
I AM on earth even as I AM in heaven
I AM giving this day daily bread to all
I AM forgiving all Life this day even as
I AM also all Life forgiving me
I AM leading all men away from temptation
I AM delivering all men from every evil condition
I AM the Kingdom
I AM the Power and
I AM the Glory of God in eternal, immortal
    manifestation—
All this I AM.

Hail Mary

Hail, Mary, full of grace.
    The Lord is with thee.
Blessed art thou among women
    and blessed is the fruit of thy womb, Jesus.

Holy Mary, Mother of God,
Pray for us, sons and daughters of God,
Now and at the hour of our victory
Over sin, disease, and death. (3x)

The Judgment Call
"They Shall Not Pass!"
by Jesus Christ

In the Name of the I AM THAT I AM,
    I invoke the Electronic Presence of Jesus Christ:
They shall not pass!
They shall not pass!
They shall not pass!
By the authority of the cosmic cross of white fire
    it shall be:
That all that is directed against the Christ
    within me, within the holy innocents,

within our beloved Messengers,
within every son and daughter of God
Is now turned back
by the authority of Alpha and Omega,
by the authority of my Lord and Saviour Jesus Christ,
by the authority of Saint Germain!

I AM THAT I AM within the center of this temple
and I declare in the fullness of
the entire Spirit of the Great White Brotherhood:
That those who, then, practice the black arts
against the children of the Light
Are now bound by the hosts of the Lord,
Do now receive the judgment of the Lord Christ
within me, within Jesus,
and within every Ascended Master,
Do now receive, then, the full return—
multiplied by the energy of the Cosmic Christ—
of their nefarious deeds which they have practiced
since the very incarnation of the Word!

Lo, I AM a Son of God!
Lo, I AM a Flame of God!
Lo, I stand upon the Rock of the living Word
And I declare with Jesus, the living Son of God:
They shall not pass!
They shall not pass!
They shall not pass!
ELOHIM ELOHIM ELOHIM

By the intercession of Saint Michael and the celestial Choir of Seraphim, may the Lord make us worthy to burn with the fire of perfect charity. Amen.

Second Salutation
To the Celestial Choir of Cherubim

I AM Lord's Prayer
Hail Mary (3x)
The Judgment Call

By the intercession of Saint Michael and the celestial Choir of Cherubim, may the Lord vouchsafe to grant us grace to leave the ways of wickedness to run in the paths of Christian perfection. Amen.

Third Salutation
To the Celestial Choir of Thrones

I AM Lord's Prayer
Hail Mary (3x)
The Judgment Call

By the intercession of Saint Michael and the celestial Choir of Thrones, may the LORD infuse into our hearts a true and sincere spirit of humility. Amen.

Fourth Salutation
To the Celestial Choir of Dominions

I AM Lord's Prayer
Hail Mary (3x)
The Judgment Call

By the intercession of Saint Michael and the celestial Choir of Dominions, may the LORD give us grace to govern our senses and subdue our unruly passions. Amen.

Fifth Salutation
To the Celestial Choir of Powers

I AM Lord's Prayer
Hail Mary (3x)
The Judgment Call

By the intercession of Saint Michael and the celestial Choir of Powers, may the LORD vouchsafe to protect our souls against the snares and temptations of the devil. Amen.

Sixth Salutation
To the Celestial Choir of Virtues

I AM Lord's Prayer
Hail Mary (3x)
The Judgment Call

By the intercession of Saint Michael and the celestial Choir of Virtues, may the LORD preserve us from evil and suffer us not to fall into temptation. Amen.

Seventh Salutation
To the Celestial Choir of Principalities

I AM Lord's Prayer
Hail Mary (3x)
The Judgment Call

By the intercession of Saint Michael and the celestial Choir of Principalities, may God fill our souls with a true spirit of obedience. Amen.

Eighth Salutation
To the Celestial Choir of Archangels

I AM Lord's Prayer
Hail Mary (3x)
The Judgment Call

By the intercession of Saint Michael and the celestial Choir of Archangels, may the Lord give us perseverance in faith and in all good works, in order that we may gain the glory of Paradise. Amen.

Ninth Salutation
To the Celestial Choir of Angels

I AM Lord's Prayer
Hail Mary (3x)
The Judgment Call

By the intercession of Saint Michael and the celestial Choir of Angels, may the Lord grant us to be protected by them in this mortal life and conducted hereafter to eternal glory. Amen.

Let us give the I AM Lord's Prayer for each of the remaining four beads in honor of Saint Michael, Saint Gabriel, Saint Raphael, and our Guardian Angel.

In the name of the Father, the Son, the Holy Spirit, and the Mother, I dedicate the Our Father to Saint Michael, Saint Gabriel, Saint Raphael, and our beloved Guardian Angel.

I AM Lord's Prayer (4x)

Archangel Michael's Rosary

O glorious Prince, Saint Michael, chief and commander of the heavenly hosts, guardian of souls, vanquisher of rebel spirits, servant in the house of the divine King, and our admirable conductor, thou who dost shine with excellence and superhuman virtue, vouchsafe to deliver us from all evil, who turn to thee with confidence, and enable us by thy gracious protection to serve God, ever more faithful every day.*

The Messenger: Pray for us, O glorious Saint Michael, Prince of the Church of Jesus Christ.
Congregation: Pray for us, O glorious Saint Michael, Prince of the Church of Jesus Christ.
The Messenger: That we may be made worthy of His promises.
Congregation: That we may be made worthy of His promises.

Almighty and Everlasting God, who by a prodigy of goodness and a merciful desire for the salvation of all men, hast appointed the most glorious Archangel, Saint Michael, Prince of Thy Church, make us worthy, we beseech Thee, to be delivered by his powerful protection from all our enemies, that none of them may harass us at the hour of death, but that we may be conducted by him into the august presence of Thy Divine Majesty.*

This we beg through the merits of Jesus Christ, Our Lord. Amen.

Let us give "I AM Presence, Thou Art Master," decree 10.11, nine times for the sealing of the nine series of prayers we have given.

I AM Presence, Thou Art Master

I AM Presence, Thou art Master,
I AM Presence, clear the way!
Let Thy Light and all Thy Power
Take possession here this hour!
Charge with Victory's mastery,
Blaze blue lightning, blaze Thy substance!
Into this Thy form descend,
That Perfection and its Glory
Shall blaze forth and earth transcend! (9x)

Let us give "Light Will Overcome" to Saint Michael the Archangel, 10.16, nine times, sealing the Judgment of Almighty

---
*Stop tape and insert optional personal prayer here.

God upon the fallen angels, the Watchers, the Nephilim, their mechanization man and the seed of the Wicked One on planet Earth.

Light Will Overcome

In the name of the beloved mighty victorious Presence of God, I AM in me, Holy Christ Selves of all mankind, beloved Archangel Michael and Faith, the seven beloved archangels and their divine complements, their legions of white-fire and blue-lightning angels, beloved Lanello, the entire Spirit of the Great White Brotherhood and the World Mother, elemental life—fire, air, water, and earth! I decree for a triple blue-ring protection around the students of the Ascended Masters, America, and the world:

1. Blue lightning is thy Love,
   Flood forth to free all;
   Blue lightning is thy Power,
   In God I see all;
   Blue lightning is thy Mind,
   In pure Truth I find

Refrain: Light will overcome,
   Light will make us one.
   Light from blue-fire sun,
   Command us now all free!

2. Blue lightning is thy Law,
   Blaze forth as holy awe;
   Blue lightning is thy Name,
   Our heart's altar do enflame;
   Blue lightning maketh free,
   In God I'll ever be.

(Repeat refrain after each verse; give the entire decree nine times; the preamble is given once at the beginning, and the ending—"And in full Faith"—is for the sealing of the decree after you have given it nine times.)

And in full Faith I consciously accept this manifest, manifest, manifest! (3x) right here and now with full Power, eternally sustained, all-powerfully active, ever expanding, and world enfolding until all are wholly ascended in the Light and free!
Beloved I AM! Beloved I AM! Beloved I AM!
AUM

Let us give again the "Traveling Protection," 6.05.

Copyright © 1962, 1963, 1965, 1966, 1968, 1972, 1974, 1975, 1976, 1978, 1979, 1985 Church Universal and Triumphant, Inc.

Traveling Protection

In the name of the beloved mighty victorious Presence of God, I AM in me, my very own beloved Holy Christ Self, Holy Christ Selves of all mankind, beloved Archangel Michael, beloved Lanello, the entire Spirit of the Great White Brotherhood and the World Mother, elemental life—fire, air, water, and earth! I decree:

*Lord Michael *before,* Lord Michael *behind,*
Lord Michael *to the right,* Lord Michael *to the left,*
Lord Michael *above,* Lord Michael *below,*
Lord Michael, Lord Michael *wherever I go!*

I AM his Love protecting here!
I AM his Love protecting here!
I AM his Love protecting here!

(Repeat nine times from asterisk)

And in full Faith...

Won't you sing with me now song 283, the "Sword of Blue Flame," to beloved Archangel Michael, to the tune of "Beulah Land." Please stand and sing it with full voice and gusto and heart. Visualize the Central Sun above you, a large disk of sacred fire blazing. This is the Sun behind the sun, the Spirit of the living God. Standing in the center of the Sun is none other than beloved Archangel Michael, Prince of the Archangels.

Michael's Sword of Blue Flame

1. Blest Michael, great archangel bright
   To help raise earth to heaven's height
   Fashioned a sword of love's blue flame
   Let all adore and praise his name.

Refrain: O sword of blue, in love so true
   We e'er invoke thy mighty stroke
   That cuts away by love divine
   All not of God's own pure design
   And in its place gives joy and peace
   To bring to all love's sweet release.*

2. The sword of flame such freedom brings
   With gratitude each heart now sings
   Its mighty pow'r both sure and fast
   Transmutes all errors of the past.

(*Repeat refrain after each verse. Sing entire song three times.)

3. Dear Michael's sword of flame so true
   Our vict'ry brings in all we do
   To it we bow and bend the knee
   And bless it now most gratefully.

4. O Central Sun and Lords of Light
   Give earth her vict'ry for the right
   And bless Archangel Michael, too
   For his great love and sword of blue.

The Sealing of the Rosary

Our beloved Father, we call to the holy angels who serve at Thy Throne of Grace to receive now, by the heart of our own Holy Christ Self, the full-gathered momentum of our prayer.

Let this rosary to Saint Michael the Archangel be multiplied now by the immaculate heart of Mary, by the sacred heart of Jesus, by the purple fiery heart of Saint Germain, by the magnanimous heart of Lanello, the obedient heart of Godfre, the pure hearts of Saint Thérèse of Lisieux and all saints ascended, and the just and true and faithful and righteous hearts of all saints unascended.

In the name of the living Word, let our prayers be caught up in the very heart of the Cosmic Christ Lord Maitreya and be sealed in the very heart of Archangel Michael for use in those hours when loved ones and lightbearers are in need of an immediate transfusion of Light and the protection of the Captain of the LORD's Hosts.

So let this reservoir of our rosary of Light in your heart, O mighty angel of the sacred fire, O beloved Maitreya, now be for the healing of nations, the protection of the Holy Church, the faithful and true witnesses, and the Ascended Masters' activity on planet Earth.

In the name of the entire Spirit of the Great White Brotherhood, I consecrate these hearts as chalices of the living Light of Archangel Michael and Archangel Michael's Rosary. So it is done in the name of the Father, the Son, the Holy Spirit, and the Mother. Amen.

"**The Summit Lighthouse Sheds Its Radiance O'er All the World to Manifest as Pearls of Wisdom.**" Archangel Michael's Rosary was released through the Messenger of the Great White Brotherhood Elizabeth Clare Prophet on Good Friday, April 5, 1985, during the 5-day Easter Conclave at Camelot and on May 12, Mother's Day, at Deer Park Chapel, Royal Teton Ranch, Montana. (1) Synod of Laodicea, "Canon XXXV," in *Nicene and Post-Nicene Fathers,* eds. P. Schaff and H. Wace (Grand Rapids, Mich.: Wm. B. Eerdmans Publishing Co., n.d.), 2d ser., 14:150. (2) *St. Michael, Defend Us in Battle* (n.p.: Marian Press, n.d.). (3) *Chaplet of St. Michael* (n.p., Imprimatur 1897).

Send for your cassette of Mother and devotees reciting Archangel Michael's Rosary and start your prayer vigil with Archangel Michael today! Special offer: 90-min. cassette, rosary and dictation, $3.50 USA and Canada. All other internationals, $4.50 airmail. Cassette plus blue rosary booklet: $4.75 USA and Canada. All other internationals, $5.85 airmail. Rosary booklet only: $1.25 USA and Canada. All other internationals, $1.90 airmail. All prices are postpaid.

Copyright © 1962, 1963, 1965, 1966, 1968, 1972, 1974, 1975, 1976, 1978, 1979, 1985 Church Universal and Triumphant, Inc., Box A, Malibu, CA 90265. All rights reserved. Printed in the United States of America. Pearls of Wisdom and The Summit Lighthouse are registered trademarks of Church Universal and Triumphant, Inc. All rights to their use are reserved. Published by The Summit Lighthouse. Pearls sent weekly (to USA, via third-class mail) for a minimum love offering of $40/year.

Easter Conclave at Camelot
"Come, leave your nets—I will make you fishers of men."

III
We Shall Have the Victory!
They Shall Not Pass, in the Name of Almighty God!

Hail, Lightbearers of the Central Sun!

I AM in the very midst of the fire aflame in your hearts. How, then, can the fire be aflame? Because it is fanned to extraordinary proportions by the devotion of the Mother passing through your hearts, and your heart's devotion passing through the heart of the Mother. Thus, it is truly the divine ritual of the saints' communion—"Drink me while I am drinking thee."

O one most lowly, O blessed heart and rose of Sharon, fairest of all and yet tiniest flower, be comforted in this hour. For the victory of our God is nigh, even the full victory over Death and Hell.

My Electronic Presence Where You Are

Thus, this rosary to me, beloved, is in fact the threading of the eye of the needle of the recitation of prayers and mantras to my heart. So I desire my saints and chelas and devotees and legions to also recite my dictations, both with [the recording of] the dictations and in the hours of the affirmation of my power [with the affirmations taken from the dictations].

For you see, beloved, I, Michael, Prince of the Archangels, am authorized by God to place my Electronic Presence where you are to step up your four lower bodies and your chakras for the fulfillment of the protection of this holy Church and the judgment of the seed of the wicked pitted against it.

So it is foreordained that God does allow the fallen one to attempt to destroy the citadel of His manifestation upon earth.

Copyright © 1985 Church Universal and Triumphant, Inc.

And therefore in the very trying and in the malintent the fallen one is judged, and that judgment becomes the Final Judgment.

"For Judgment I AM Come into the World"

There is no other reason for the descent of the living Christ in you than for the judgment of this world. And therefore, Jesus said when he descended trailing clouds of glory, "For Judgment I AM come into the world!"

Yes, I know you have heard it said that he did say, "Lo, I AM come to do Thy Will, O God!" And indeed he did. And in the infinity of the moment's descent, the pure, living Christ of Jesus said many things—affirmations of his reason for being, commitment, and the vow to fulfill holy purpose.

Preliminary Testings of the Dark Night of the Spirit

Therefore, beloved ones, I am indeed come this day from the Central Sun. For I have journeyed to the Sun in your name and in your behalf whilst the Messenger did keep the Flame of Life. Understand how she has felt this day the momentum of Death and Hell. And this is because of my absence and therefore my insistence that her own causal body containing my own should carry the weight and the balance [of world karma] in the earth. Thus, that darkness is offset by the living Spirit of her causal body and mine. And you may witness, then, through a small glimpse of the initiation of the Dark Night of the Spirit, when one's own attainment must count for the holding of the balance.

Thus, from time to time, one or more of the ascended host who keep the vigil with the Messenger do withdraw and go to that Central Sun for many reasons. And in that hour it is then the testing and the initiation that the Messenger should hold the balance of our office in the flesh. These are the preliminary testings of the soul unto the fullness of that initiation [of the Dark Night of the Spirit].

Your Prayer Rituals and Rosaries Hold the Balance

And you may also come to understand how from day to day the holy angels come to you asking for prayers for a certain virtue of Freedom or Truth or Healing, and you find yourself giving those mantras of the sacred fire. And thus you, beloved, keep the Flame for some part of Life as you are able and, in so doing, strengthen your spirituality and your self-awareness of your own attainment in the Light.

For you come to realize just how much worth does your ritual of prayer contain. And therefore, you give gladly and to overflowing the praise of the LORD, feeling how that Light does count somewhere—somewhere in Hell for the binding of a fallen one who does reach out to snatch one of Light yet walking the physical octaves. And you have been taught that this is accomplished from the very pit itself through the agents of the sinister force in embodiment.

And therefore, count not the cost but understand what a magnificent day it is when you can give anew and again the rosary to the Archangel Michael, who I AM. For I tell you, I give it unto God immediately, and all of my legions of Light may respond in answer to your call.

By the Sacred Nine the Call Goes Forth to the Greatest Need

And we have responded in the power of the three-times-three, which is the sacred nine. And we may therefore go to those conditions which heretofore we have not been able to touch, beloved ones. For you will understand that when we receive calls and we receive the mantras to our heart, we must use them always on those situations most dire and of greatest necessity. And when there are not enough calls forthcoming, then some of lesser necessity but also of great peril to the earth must [perforce] not have our intercession.

As the quantity of the call goes forth, as the quotient of the sacred fire descends, as the hearts are one—as Above so below in our own hearts and woven together in the heart of the Messenger—so we may act and act again to prevent the untimely passing from the screen of life of many souls of Light who must play their role in this particular hour, which is critical even before the sight of Alpha and Omega, as the Father/Mother God have told me this day.

Strengthening the Spine of America

For it is a critical turning point in the nations. You have realized that many hours and key dates in this century and past have been critical. But this is an hour for the mounting of the forces of freedom for a defense and for the strengthening of the spine of America and the spine of her leaders!

We take, then, this offering of your hearts for the strengthening of those spines, beginning with the White House and the Congress.

We begin, therefore, and we are determined that the freedom fighters of this world in every nation shall have the full support of the people of Light in every nation!

We are God-determined that they shall have the supply, the food, the medical care, and those equipments that are absolutely necessary to wage warfare in the physical octave against those fallen ones and Satanists that move through Soviet forces to destroy Afghanistan, to take over other nations, and to come into this hemisphere!

We say: They shall not pass in the name of Almighty God! They shall not pass in the name of Almighty God! And we shall have the victory!

We Still Demand the Victory!

But in this hour, beloved ones, the corrupt ones gather in Central and South America who have been corrupt for so long, who have taken advantage of the people and denied them in their condemnation and placed upon them ignorance. And even in some quarters the holy Church has promoted ignorance instead of enlightenment through the dynamic decree and through the call to me.

Beloved hearts, in the face of all of this adversarial contact that we face there, we still demand the victory! We still demand the overturning of the right and left extremists and the fanatics and the murderers who move against the children of the Light!

But, beloved hearts, it will take more than a miracle. It will take the absolute intercession of Almighty God *through you!*

We Must Have Archangel Michael's Perpetual Prayer Vigil

And therefore we call and we demand and command in this hour the perpetual vigil of the hours for which we have called earlier in this year. We call, then, for the vigil to my name, Archangel Michael. For it does command the obedience of every angel and archangel in heaven. And all the hosts of hierarchies of the Central Sun do respond.

And, beloved ones, we must have this offering, for we must spare this hemisphere. For this hemisphere must be undivided from pole to pole, from sea to sea, and her waters and her lakes and her mountains and the places under the earth must be cleaned out!

And therefore we dedicate ourselves to the going forth for the remainder of this conference now into the pits that exist in this hemisphere and for the exposure of the fallen ones who come out of every nation to seek what they may find, whether for greed or money or lust for power or world dominion or World Communism.

They come to rape this hemisphere! They come to steal the Light! And the precious children and youth do not know or understand when their chakras have been raped, when their crown, third-eye, and throat chakra have been taken—when the Light has been taken from them.

Beloved hearts, I appeal to you and I tell you this is the beginning. Let us continue with the perpetual prayers. For we are ready at command of those in embodiment, and we cannot act in the physical octave if you do not implore in the name of Almighty God that He send us to the rescue of the souls of Light.

I thank you, beloved hearts, for your momentous attention, for the purity of your hearts, for the devotion of your life, and most especially for the enlightenment of the heart and mind that enables you to understand the science of the spoken Word.

I thank you for your understanding of the necessity of the Messenger and the protection of the Messenger that we might release to you this fohat of sacred fire. For it is one thing to read the dictations; [but] it is another to stand in our presence and receive that Light which is for your infilling, for your Godhood, for your ascension, for your resurrection.

The Archangels Must Step through the Veil

Beloved hearts, work while you have the Light! For you must absorb into your very pores this day and always our releases of our dictations that you might know what it is to have that protection and acceleration necessary for you to be our very instruments. For we, the archangels, must step through the veil. We must show by the path of teaching and education of the heart what it is necessary to accomplish in America as that base for freedom.

And we can accomplish little when the representatives of freedom do not fight for freedom in every domain in the pure Krishna consciousness of the mighty spiritual Flame itself. For no battle that is physical must be fought except by the divine power of the Word and the mantra and the Universal Christ and the hosts of the LORD. The physical implements of war or security or protection, beloved ones, are only the final manifestation—a vehicle in itself through which the Light of God may vanquish all evil.

And I tell you there is evil in the earth. And there is no equality between the U.S.S.R. and the United States of America. There is none whatsoever! It is indeed a battle of Light and Darkness and an Armageddon, and it is the powers-that-be pitted against the children of the Light in both nations.

We Demand a Spiritual Revolution

And therefore, where the preponderance of the power of Saint Germain has rested, let those who have received through the divine approbation the glory of God and the blessing—those who are in the United States of America and who are yet free to act—let them be the revolutionaries of the Spirit. For we demand a spiritual revolution of the sacred fire! We demand a victory of that divine All-Seeing Eye of God. We demand the Godhead manifesting now in action! And we demand that the world shall see and hear and know what is that perfect and possible sequence that can take place on planet Earth!

Riptide by riptide, we pull the cord of Light. And from the Central Sun the Light descends. So let the chalice be upraised. So let your hearts be full.

Let your hands be upraised now, for we pour into your being, as you have become the Holy Grail through your devotions, that Light of ten thousand suns of protection, perfection, white fire and blue lightning—even that of the God Star Sirius. And therefore, be sealed, beloved—be sealed!

I thank you and bid you good evening.

Hail, Archangel Michael! (5x) [applause]

Messenger's remarks:

Truly, if I had ten thousand lives to give, I would give them all to Archangel Michael. But since we have one, and that one is the equivalent of God, let us truly give it.

I do believe that this Church Universal and Triumphant is the foremost exponent of Archangel Michael on planet Earth!

If you so desire, you may follow your recitation of Archangel Michael's Rosary with a Prayer Vigil for Personal and Planetary Protection by the Hosts of the LORD by giving the blue decrees to Archangel Michael nine times each, continuing as you are directed by the Holy Spirit. For whatever cause or purpose you hold in your heart, give Archangel Michael's Rosary with supplementary personal prayers and dynamic decrees of your choosing.

A nine-day prayer vigil is called a novena. This ritual combined with fasting, abstention from worldliness, and the entering in to the Holy of Holies of one's being with God the Father will avail much to alleviate and heal world pain and personal problems.

Together with whatever else you may have in mind as the goal of your novena, please consecrate Archangel Michael's Rosary to the Victory of the Great White Brotherhood on earth, the Victory of the Teachings of the Ascended Masters in every heart of Light, the Victory of Church Universal and Triumphant, and the Victory of the LORD's Word and Work through our Messengers, Keepers of the Flame, staff, students, families, and focuses throughout the world.

"The Summit Lighthouse Sheds Its Radiance O'er All the World to Manifest as Pearls of Wisdom." This dictation by Archangel Michael was delivered through the Messenger of the Great White Brotherhood Elizabeth Clare Prophet on April 5, 1985, following the giving of Archangel Michael's Rosary during the Easter Conclave at Camelot. In order to receive the full blessing of the Archangel's fiery release, it is important that you participate in the rosary and hear the recorded dictation (published on the 12-cassette album *Easter Conclave 1985*).

Send for your cassette of Mother and devotees reciting Archangel Michael's Rosary and start your prayer vigil with Archangel Michael today! Special offer: 90-minute cassette, rosary and dictation, $3.50 postpaid USA and Canada. All other internationals $4.50 airmail postpaid.

Copyright © 1985 Church Universal and Triumphant, Inc., Box A, Malibu, CA 90265. All rights reserved. Printed in the United States of America. Pearls of Wisdom and The Summit Lighthouse are registered trademarks of Church Universal and Triumphant, Inc. All rights to their use are reserved. Published by The Summit Lighthouse. Pearls sent weekly (to USA, via third-class mail) for a minimum love offering of $40/year.

Easter Conclave at Camelot
"Come, leave your nets—I will make you fishers of men."

IV
Profile of the Woman Initiate
The Hour of the Raising of the Feminine Ray

Gentle Light, piercing Light—Light of the Secret Love Star. I AM pleased to be in your midst, for the good angel, Archangel Michael, with your dear hearts has cleared the way. And thus I, the twin flame of Sanat Kumara, stand before you in gossamer veil and silken Light, clothed by the garment of his Love.

I come, then, the Lady of Love. Venus, you call me. But I, too, have another name sealed in the heart of the Father. I address you in the name of Vesta, my beloved. In the arms of our love and the origin unto the ending, do be seated.

These now are my words to you, beloved. For I come in the hour of the raising of the Feminine Ray. And as you know, from time to time the Lady Masters have addressed you concerning the momentum of Her Light and its effect upon civilization and the individual psyche.

The Matrix of the Divine Woman

I come, then, bearing the Light of a noble birth and a noble one to be born. Thus, beloved, hear the call of the Secret Love Star! Hear the call of Sirius and understand the presence in your midst of Surya.

Beloved, in the hour of the appearing of the New Love of Vesta,[1] we send forth the matrix of the Divine Woman. We send forth the image of the soul and the raiment white of the bride of the Spirit. In order for the golden age to manifest as an age of love and wisdom as well as peace and freedom, beloved hearts, it is necessary and long overdue that the Divine Feminine be

Copyright © 1985 Church Universal and Triumphant, Inc.

portrayed in a human way of dignity and grace, poetry and culture, and the administration so native to the order of the Mother.

We, the ladies of heaven, summoned again by Portia, desiring still to see the teachings of the Masters translated to the many ethnic groups in America and the world,[2] do call, then, the ladies among Keepers of the Flame to consider themselves—yourselves, beloved hearts—a nucleus and a very effective team, if you desire to meet on common ground, to create the matrix, the education, the example, and the opportunity for those groups of women and their clubs and organizations to come into the understanding of the application of the Mother Flame in every walk of life, beginning with woman herself.

We have seen so many form organizations or publications for the defense of women's rights in all areas. We desire to see a true profile of the understanding of the woman who is the disciple, who is the initiate, who represents mastery and the nobility of heart that can once again call to Vishnu, to Brahma, to Shiva for the divine ones to descend, for sons and daughters who will renew under Meru—the God and Goddess Meru—the understanding of the grace and the science of the golden ages of Lemuria.

Take, then, to heart the complex of teachings from the New Year's conference[3] and the vibrations we have sent forth. For the era of New Love and the era of the new etheric body for the earth and the dispensations of the Solar Logoi and of the Four and Twenty Elders should signal that the etheric body now restored to earth is truly the restoration of the bridal veil and that the inner blueprint of life can be lowered into manifestation.

We desire to see the elimination of the consciousness of the laggard woman, the woman who is crass and behaves like the lower order of the fallen male. We desire to see this example removed from the little children who are being born. And if it cannot be removed from the earth as a whole, then let it be removed from this community so that the little children see the archetype of the Divine Ones—of Meta, of Athena, of Kuan Yin, and Portia.

Let there be the restoration of music in every home, and let the classics build the inner code of life. Let it re-create the DNA chain. And by the power of the nine symphonies of Beethoven and much that should be known in the cell level of every lifestream, let the portals of Venus open once again. And let the culture of hell that has gone forth on this planet be utterly consumed by the living flame of Love, by the path of the ruby ray. Let earth be so bathed in the radiance of Love as to consume that which is gross, degenerating, causing decay and loss of life.

An Organization "Of and For Women"

Blessed ones, let us begin, then, with woman herself. And let this community have established an organization of and for women whereby there is an elevation of all through the very unique talents of each individual. And let spokeswomen go forth, and let them address other women concerning the ancient tradition of Hinduism and the likeness of the incarnation of the World Mother through the example of Sarasvati, Lakshmi, Kali coming forth from Durga.

Beloved ones, the cardinal points of the manifestation of woman become the key to her complement to the masculine Spirit of God everywhere present. Woman, as the adornment of God, discovers the uniqueness of her identity and her purpose, for she manifests that nature which does give to Life the fertile soil in which the cosmos can implant the seed of every part of Life.

Let this unity of oneness, let this goal of ascension, let this path quicken and enliven all lesser paths and goals which are experienced by women in every walk of life as they approach the highest goal of the inner attunement of the heart.

We have spoken of our dispensations for the sponsoring of woman, for the raising of the temples of Lemuria and the restoration of priestesses.[4] Sanat Kumara has sounded the mighty intonation for the restoration of the heighth of Lemuria.[5]

Give Woman the True Realization of Her Storehouse of Light

Now let those who are a part of this community, who are the women in this hour, look upon the women of the world and then recognize that they hold the key. *You* hold the key, beloved hearts, to give those who are still struggling to find their identity that true realization of the storehouse of Light—the causal body. Let those who are a part of this group seek to offer comfort, consolation, and illumination concerning the very real problems which women face today in every nation—whether in raising their children, bringing forth life, attempting to exist under economic duress, or receiving, therefore, the untransmuted elements whether of the female or the male elements of society.

As we have said before: For the nation, the home, or the planet to rise, there must be a raised ceiling of consciousness. And woman must come into her own as the one who represents the divine wisdom and the gnosis and the mysteries of Life. Even so, let her body remain the mystery and also the secret place of the Most High as she raises up that Kundalini fire and then produces out of this mighty Light truly the very electricity, the very energizing factor to restore every area of life.

That which you know, beloved hearts, so put into practice, so organize—so be able to use the knowledge that has gone forth from this altar in a way of answering with all practicality and comfort and understanding that which is applicable to the needs of those who may not have the development of the Universal Mind sufficient to agree with the Ascended Masters' teachings.

Thus, beloved hearts, to fulfill my request you will have to study, to organize, to implement, and to become effective in understanding women's problems, women's point of view. And you must reach people where they are.

Sons of Light Promote the God-Ideas of Saint Joseph

Blessed ones, this is not to neglect the blessed sons of Light who are pillars of fire and examples throughout this organization. But it is by way of support that we recommend this order, so that truly that which does come forth does ennoble the Christ in your hearts.

You may then discover a fulfillment and truly an avenue for expression and expansion in founding your own organization for the promotion of the God-ideas of Saint Joseph and his example in every age. Finding role models for the sons of God today is essential, especially in the hour of the put-down of the male figure by the feminists who have well-intentioned ideas and goals but have not fully understood the place of the Spirit of God as the animating principle of the sons of Light.

Blessed ones, the Order of Francis and Clare is ideal for the formation of these organizations. You have no need to wait for our approval or the Messenger's signal. Simply organize yourselves, roll up your sleeves, and go to work. And use the sword that comes from the spoken Word to address immediately those situations in society which are so pressing and so urgent as to demand the full talents of both woman and man in this hour.

Uniting Lightbearers of Venus with Lightbearers of Earth

We are here, then, in that very precious desire of uniting the lightbearers of Venus with the lightbearers of earth. Links have begun to be forged and there is a weaving of a gossamer veil and a filigree garment that begins at the etheric octave in the highest Light whereby this association may come full circle and be more apparent in the physical.

A Third-Ray Assignment to Rescue the Fallen Venusians

Thus, it is the desire of Sanat Kumara that our own lifestreams be sealed and that there not be the contamination of those left in the etheric octave or on Venus such as has occurred to those Venusians who have embodied upon earth who have been swept away by the false culture of the fallen ones of the third ray who have perverted the Light of Chamuel and Charity and distorted all that is real.

Beloved ones, there are many Venusians of Light and yet, naive and lacking in God-mastery and desiring the full expression of the music and the love and the poetry and the song they have known in octaves of Light, they have followed after the lower beat and the lowering of their vibration. And the more they have become involved, the more they have been decelerated in their evolution and the more they have lost their sensitivity to the higher vibrations.

It is easy to lose touch with the harpstrings of the mind. It is so easy to lose the grasp and to think, "Whenever I choose, I may go back to the higher way." And yet it is not so, for densification comes quickly and therefore indulgence is dangerous. And those lifestreams who have had in the past a certain mastery on the third ray have in fact (not having the balance of the threefold flame) been caught in the vortex of the anti-force of that third ray.

This, then, becomes the assignment of the Holy Spirit, beloved. This becomes an action of Paul the Venetian and Heros and Amora and so many more of you. Eriel of the Light is one I think of often who so cares for the little children and those who pass early from the screen of life in his retreat. The beauty of Eriel and of John the Beloved is expressed in the flowers and the mountains over the desert of Arizona in these etheric retreats which are kept for the sealing of the love ray.

Yet, see how that love ray is inverted, beloved ones. Simply go to the neighboring area of Nevada and see this love turned to gambling, to the desecration of the body of both man and woman, and the turning of that life-force to a cult of Hedon that once existed on the now destroyed planet closest to the sun, which some have called Hedron. This hedonism, beloved hearts, side by side with the etheric retreats of Love! As you can see, heaven and hell are intertwined on earth and there are choices to be made daily and hourly by all who live thereon.

Ways and Means to Intensify the Publishing Arm of This Activity

We see what the knowledge of the Spirit and the teachings of the Ascended Masters thus far published have done for those who were reaching for the Light and yet needed the steady hand and the protection of the Brotherhood. We have seen such advances and such acceleration of Light in this age that it gives us pause. And we must therefore concern ourselves with the ways and means of intensifying the publishing arm of this activity; for so many are ready and they take the first fruit offered, so many times from the false guru, or else simply accept half truths, not seeking farther.

Beloved ones, the markets are full of the Pied Pipers who pipe their tunes. And it is time and high time that you become more aggressive and intense, not only in your search for the lightbearers but in taking your stand that this Teaching does provide that which is truly necessary for the individual soul to pass through the initiations such as Jesus Christ passed through and are celebrated on this weekend.

And this very same hour the Passover is celebrated by the Jews—when the Death Angel passed over the houses of the Israelites and they were spared[6]—and therefore the deliverance of death is seen on both hands. Thus, Christ is resurrected and the intercession of the holy angels does save a people for the proving of their Christhood in another day.

Close Proximity of Heaven and Earth in the Saints Appearing

Thus all cultures and religions go back to the union of man and God in celebration of the hierarchies of Light and the avatars descending and the intercession of Moses and Gautama and Confucius and Isaiah and the apostle Paul. In each and every instance, what captures the people is this close proximity of heaven and earth and the saints appearing and the men of God appearing to Abraham and the angels descending and the opening of the chakras and the very crown itself and heaven, then, descending in the starry body.

Beloved hearts, this is what impels life to strive, to seek Truth and to champion her cause before the oppressed and those who have been dealt with unjustly. It is the desire to have the opening of the portals of the etheric octave. It is the desire so great in the human psyche to remember in the outer sense this connection of inner and outer planes and the continuity of life and the goal that is beyond all of this darkness in the sunrise and the golden dawn of a new day.

Preaching the Word and Making It Applicable to Personal Lives

Blessed ones, it is important to therefore thrust forward and save a life and save many souls with the preaching of the Word and the understanding of making it applicable to the very personal lives of people everywhere.

First and foremost, it is important to impress anyone you meet with the understanding that there is a necessity for this Teaching in his life. There is a necessity to go back to first principles and origins and man's relationship to God and this integral unity by Love that must be pursued.

Thus, a reason must be seen [to be pointed out by you] in each individual's life why there is a necessity to insert a pillar of fire, an action of the Holy Spirit, a law and a prophecy for the resurrection of the soul and for the balancing of karma.

You see, when they took from the scriptures of the West the understanding of reincarnation, they also took from the souls of the people the understanding of the necessity for the cosmic law to be understood, for the balancing of karma by the violet flame or even the purpose of the mantra itself. By a process of pulling the threads of identity, the identity lost no longer recognizes the need for commeasurement with the Infinite or the Deity itself.

Realize, then, how difficult it is to speak of the necessity of the Path to one who is an atheist or a Communist or one who is self-satisfied in the smugness of his gains in materialism. So, you see, many of those who consider themselves rich—whether in goods or whether in their false theosophy or philosophy or politics—are brainwashed into considering that their self-sufficiency can quite do without the knowledge or the need of the Mighty I AM Presence or the Christ Self.

Go After Souls Waiting to Contact the Great White Brotherhood Call to Archangel Michael and Sanat Kumara

The wise, then, go after those who contain the eternal and internal vision, who have it within, who hold it and are waiting to make the connection with that order of the Great White Brotherhood. How, then, do you find such souls and save them for grace in this life? The call to Archangel Michael and Sanat Kumara will suffice.

And the call to the two each day, beloved ones, to cut free the lightbearers and all who are to ascend in this life and all who are the sons and daughters of God does avail much and afford opportunity for all servants of God to act to draw these very ones into that central flame, the Central Sun Magnet—to draw them into the very heart of community to increase the intensity of the fire and the vortex of the mantra, that those who are destined to carry the banner of Maitreya in this age may also, then, know the strength of community and learn the fine points of the law of the violet flame, which they have not brought with them from their inner-level experiences or their past embodiments.

An Urgency to Cut Free Venusians Who Have Lost Their Way

It is urgent. And therefore I declare an urgency, beloved, that you seek and find and cut free with the angels of the LORD all lifestreams who are a part of this Venusian evolution who came with Sanat Kumara and who followed after and who have lost their way.

The communications universally upon earth make this possible in this hour; but the fallen ones are so desperate to prevent the universal knowledge of the Word upon earth that they would rather interrupt a way of life—they would rather interrupt international communications or the monetary system or find whatever is the weakest link in the international scene to cause an abrupt cessation of the opportunity you now enjoy to take this message to the nations.

The Mighty Sifting of the Mother

Let there be a galvanizing of this body of Light-servers worldwide. Let all hear me and know that I, too, come with dispensations from Helios and Vesta. And with Sanat Kumara, I AM determined now for the mighty sifting of the Mother. I AM determined, therefore, to draw out of the whole earth those who are the best and highest servants who must have this knowledge, this connection, and the protection which the tie to the Messenger and the activity affords every individual on the path of reunion with God.

Messengers with a Mantle and an Authority

We have sent you a Messenger with a mantle and an authority to make the call that reaches the very Throne of Grace for your protection in dealing with the forces of hell rampant on this planet. Therefore, understand that the canopy of Light that the Brotherhood has been able to place over this activity because of the presence of this Messenger is not alone due to the dispensation of the Lords of Karma, but to the ancient inner attainment of her lifestream itself.

Thus you understand that the same attainment in the power of invocation is the mantle of Lanello; and their twin flames can sponsor, then, ideally and nobly so, the work of Archangel Michael. And when you see that there is a momentum and a mantle within your reach, you also should go after the same attainment. For many of you have come because you have needed to gain the momentum of association with Archangel Michael and the beings of the first ray who are here solely for the protection of the Word and the Word incarnate within you.

Copyright © 1985 Church Universal and Triumphant, Inc.

And thus you have come out of the East and out of all cultures and religions for the development of the threefold flame and the balancing of the love and of the illumination with that power of the will of God and of action and that understanding of the science of the spoken Word and that protection needed in order for you to draw down fully into your physical temples that Light and attainment that you have gained in past golden ages when you could concentrate on that wisdom and love ray and not have so much necessity for protection as is required in this Dark Cycle of the Kali Yuga when earth is heavy with the darkness of the fallen ones.

The Inner Attainment of Your Christ Descending Demands Protection

Thus, you see, beloved hearts, the explanation for your progress is given from the hand of Sanat Kumara that many of you have inner attainment which you are not drawing forth solely because you have not established that fierce and determined oneness with El Morya and Hercules and Archangel Michael and Mighty Surya—that blue sheath of fire that will absolutely protect you and protect the Christ descending in your being.

If I can make you understand this one point, then all I have said this evening will come into focus. We desire and we are determined to see you manifest all that you are, beloved hearts! When you lack the protection and this Light begins to descend, it is very disturbing many times to the outer mind. You become emotionally unbalanced almost immediately, and therefore the Christ must step back up the ladder again.

And if you could visualize this consciousness of yourself and the previous garments you have worn in golden ages, it is like the Real Self descending a few steps and then running back up the ladder again lest the lower self be overcome by all manner of darkness that moves in immediately to take that Light and to destroy the soul's potential to assimilate the Light, to become the Light, and to enter in to the alchemical marriage with that inner Christhood with full mastery before the dark ones are able once again to overturn the soul.

We Are Fighting for Your Very Life and God-Mastery

When you see this imbalance in your life and when you see how fastidious El Morya and Lanello and Mother are in going after you to be integrated, to be practical, and to overcome the devious ways of the carnal mind and the subconscious, understand, beloved ones, it is because all of us together are fighting for your very life in the fullness of God-mastery in this octave—

not as something you must go after and attain as something you never had, but as something you *do* have here and now in the higher octaves, which once upon a time you forsook, going after the glamour of the fallen angels. And they stripped you of your garments even as they stripped Jesus Christ of his garments in this very hour of the crucifixion.

Beloved, understand they have desired to make you naked. And thus they crucified him naked, signifying that they stole the Light—or attempted to do so. In the case of Jesus, of course, they did not; but in the case of yourself, they did. And therefore, what you have also lost is the memory of the stature at inner levels of who you truly are.

Therefore, beloved hearts, not only do you require the attunement with Archangel Michael and the balancing of the first ray within your threefold flame, but you also now demand the mastery of the emotions and the psychology and the filling in of the gaps of those four lower bodies, the mending of the torn garment.

Teachings of the Messengers on Saint John of the Cross

And thus I commend you to the teaching of the Messengers on the path of Saint John of the Cross, on the *Living Flame of Love*[7] that explains the alchemical marriage. For it is not as though you were not once tethered to the living Word, but it is now that you must reconsecrate your life to that marriage unto God. For once the full fusion is attained, beloved, it cannot be lost.

But you have been at that point—almost in the hour of the consummation with the Bridegroom, the living Word. And yet, the holding of the balance for that event was too much and the fallen ones sent the most clever of impostors of the Cosmic Christ Lord Maitreya. And [the initiation of the alchemical marriage] once again swept aside, it has meant for you cycle after cycle—the waiting again of two thousand years or five thousand years or ten thousand years when the cosmic cycles would once again bring you face-to-face with the initiation of Lord Maitreya.

Stay Very Close to the Initiator Archangel Michael

Thus, I counsel you to follow the admonishment to reestablish the tube of light by the call to forgiveness, by transmutation, and to stay very close to the Initiator Archangel Michael, who will surely tutor you and show you why at every hand it is necessary to have that protection for the guarding of consciousness—the guarding of the nexus of the mind and the nexus of the heart, which means where Spirit becomes Matter, where ideas flow from the Mind of God, and the crows come to snatch those ideas as they seize the food from others and as they prey upon the innocent.

Understand, beloved ones, that the point of attack is at the nexus of each chakra—the nexus of vision where God's vision is about to become your own and is not quite manifest. Thus, they come to present the alternative vision, the alternative plan, and therefore the delicate, descending image is lost.

See, then, that you consider all these things, beloved hearts. See, then, that you consider that whatever the Ascended Master El Morya and beloved Saint Germain have placed as priority of teaching and understanding, discipline and application in this activity, is for you who have the necessity to once more realize your great God-mastery as you had it or almost had it in ages past.

Beloved ones of the Light, if you can come through this eye of the needle and realize that higher Selfhood, you will indeed draw all men and women and children to this path of victory, immortality, love, enlightenment, peace, and true freedom for one and for all.

I AM in the Secret Love Star, your Lady Venus. Keep in touch with my heart, for I AM always ready to give myself to you, my own beloved.

"The Summit Lighthouse Sheds Its Radiance O'er All the World to Manifest as Pearls of Wisdom."
This dictation by Lady Master Venus was delivered through the Messenger of the Great White Brotherhood Elizabeth Clare Prophet on Good Friday, April 5, 1985, during the 5-day Easter Conclave at Camelot. (1) See Vesta, January 1, 1985, "New Love," *Pearls of Wisdom*, vol. 28, no. 7. (2) On July 2, 1980, beloved Portia, with the Lady Masters of the Karmic Board, announced: "We have studied the problems of many segments of society, not only of men and women but of those in varying ethnic groups, origins, karmic accountabilities, those on various echelons of development in the four planes and in the chakras.... Tremendous souls of Light are in these communities across America—San Francisco's Chinatown and the great Midwestern cities where Eastern Europeans gather and the Germanic peoples continue their traditions. We see, then, that those who are here from all nations of the earth, those incoming refugees out of Vietnam, out of Cambodia, out of the Far East now must have delivered to them in their own tongue, in their own understanding and traditions the great message of Mother Liberty.... The violet flame of freedom must be interpreted and addressed to each and every section, each and every economic group...." See "A Council of the Woman Clothed with the Sun," *Pearls of Wisdom*, vol. 29, no. 29. (3) See *Pearls of Wisdom*, vol. 28, nos. 1-7; and the New Year's Light of the World Conference, 12-cassette album (A85016), $67.50. (4) See Archangel Gabriel, April 20, 1984, on the restoration of the priestesses of Lemuria, *Pearls of Wisdom*, vol. 27, no. 30, pp. 235-36; Serapis Bey, December 29, 1978, on the opening of the temple doors of Mu, "A Fourteen-Month Cycle of Ascension's Flame," 8-cassette New Year's album *The Feast of St. Stephen* (A7906), $50.00, single cassette B7909, $6.50; Lady Master Venus, July 1, 1976, "The Rise of the Feminine Ray in America," 8-cassette Freedom class album *Higher Consciousness* (A7650), $50.00, single cassette B7651, $6.50. (5) See the Seven Holy Kumaras, June 12, 1976, "The Resurrection of the Seven Rays of the Mother on Mu," 2-cassette album *Peace in the Flame of Buddha* (A7658), $15.00. (6) Exod. 12:1-14. (7) *Living Flame of Love*, newly released 8-cassette album of transcendent teaching on the soul's mystical experience in Christ. The Messengers offer an in-depth study of "Living Flame of Love"—the literary and religious masterpiece penned by Saint John of the Cross in the sixteenth century. Indispensable teaching for all who aspire to the alchemical marriage. $50.00 (A85044). Postage included in all prices noted.

To Beloved Venus
A Prayer for Loveliness

Beloved mighty victorious Presence of God, I AM in me, my very own beloved Holy Christ Self, beloved Lady Master Venus, Lord Sanat Kumara, the Seven Holy Kumaras, Gautama Buddha, the Cosmic Christ, Lord Maitreya, beloved Jesus the Christ and Kuthumi, beloved Lanello, the entire Spirit of the Great White Brotherhood and the World Mother, elemental life—fire, air, water, and earth! By and through the magnetic power of the immortal, victorious threefold flame of love, wisdom, and power anchored within my heart, I decree:

1. O Beauty supreme, thou Light of my soul,
   Envelop my form and now make me Whole.
   To Venus I call, thou matriarch true,
   O lady of heaven, mold me like you.

Refrain: Come, come, come by all thy Love
   From our Venus star above:
   Flood thy Flame through my soul,
   With thy Love's beauty my being enfold.

2. With pink, blue, and gold radiance seal,
   By perfumed caresses, my Being reveal:
   Majestic I AM and one with thy glory,
   Direct, O God Presence, my life's wondrous story.

3. Living Light of the morning star,
   Let not vain thoughts my being mar;
   I AM God's Flame, eternal youth,
   Mold me, shape me in heaven's truth.

4. I pray for loveliness, beauty, too,
   Oh, make and keep me ever like you—
   Wise, compassionate, loving, and kind,
   Beautiful form of the pure God Mind!

And in full Faith I consciously accept this manifest, manifest, manifest! (3x) right here and now with full Power, eternally sustained, all-powerfully active, ever expanding, and world enfolding until all are wholly ascended in the Light and free! Beloved I AM! Beloved I AM! Beloved I AM!

Copyright © 1963, 1985 Church Universal and Triumphant, Inc., Box A, Malibu, CA 90265. All rights reserved. Printed in the United States of America. Pearls of Wisdom and The Summit Lighthouse are registered trademarks of Church Universal and Triumphant, Inc. All rights to their use are reserved. Published by The Summit Lighthouse. Pearls sent weekly (to USA, via third-class mail) for a minimum love offering of $40/year.

Pearls of Wisdom®
published by The Summit Lighthouse

Vol. 28 No. 22   Beloved Justinius   June 2, 1985

Easter Conclave at Camelot
"Come, leave your nets—I will make you fishers of men."

V
Called of God
Seraphic Purging of Sons and Daughters before the Living Flame of God

Hail, Sons and Daughters of God! Attention!

I AM Justinius and I address you in the full power of the white fire of the anointing of the children of the Light. I come with legions of seraphim and fiery salamanders and angels of the violet flame who are absolutely God-determined to purge the sons and daughters of Light of the very cause and core of that resistance and recalcitrance before the living Flame of God!

I AM here in the name of the Cosmic Christ to anoint you with the spikenard. And yet, some have not prepared themselves for the initiation of the sacred fire in that cosmic cross; and therefore I must instruct you first. And listen as I tell.

Instruction on the Path of the Great White Brotherhood

Beloved hearts, some have taken this path to use the violet flame and the ministering servants of God above to their own pleasure, their own satisfaction, and their own indulgence—determining to use that Flame to their own purposes and to create an era and a lifetime of comfortability. Blessed ones, this is not the path of initiation or of the Great White Brotherhood, and this is not the purpose for which these two servants have gone forth or for which this Church Universal and Triumphant was founded!

And therefore, let us begin at the beginning.

You are here, if you are here called of God, to pursue the Path of the Ascension and to follow the lead of the ascension flame (which is the Mother Light)—to follow the lead of the

Copyright © 1985 Church Universal and Triumphant, Inc.

initiations given to the Messenger, knowing full well that you too will pass through many of these initiations, if not all; for there are some that you will not pass through. Therefore, beloved hearts, understand that you must follow the lead of the Flame and of the sacred fire and not attempt to lead it or to tell it when it may or may not accelerate within you.

The release of the sacred fire from your God Presence is according to the divine plan of initiation. When you close the door to that Flame, preferring yesterday's self instead of the self that is tomorrow's Self of your very Christhood, I tell you, beloved, you close the door to that specific initiation. And in some instances, it will not come again in this lifetime.

Spiritual Laggards Say, "We Will Not Change!"

Blessed ones, you have heard of laggard races who have sought the status quo of their materialism. Well, I tell you, there are also spiritual laggards who have positioned themselves in this organization who are determined to say, "We will stay as we are. We will not be moved. We will not budge, nor* for the Angels or the Masters or the Messenger, but we will do what we please and we will go thus far and no farther. And do not ask us to do anything more, for we will not do it—for our service and our acceleration is sufficient." And therefore, there is the ironclad steel bar that says, "We will not change!"

Thus, beloved hearts, these individuals become a block to the release of Light to people throughout the world who are hungering and thirsting[1] for this teaching and this acceleration and who, once they find it, will come in as Arcturus has told you.[2] And they will accelerate and they will move through the path of the degrees, even as Mother Mary as a little child did so.[3]

Thus, beloved hearts, I will come and I will stand before you and my hand through the hand of the Messenger will touch your forehead with the spikenard this night. And I tell you, if you close the door to the full initiation of that blessing, it will not be given you again—no matter how many times you may come to the altar. The Light itself embodies the Law, and the Light and the Law will not be flaunted!

Human Stubbornness Will Not Stand in the Day of Thy God Flame

Understand the true meaning of the path of initiation, for you are here as though you were at Luxor. You are here preparing for that union with God. And in that very coil of fire, beloved hearts, I can assure you that Serapis Bey will not keep

---
*nor, *archaic:* neither

you there if you dictate to him when he may or may not require of you the payment for some karmic debt or the payment for some burden to life.

Let us understand and go to the very heart of the matter, then. Let us go to the heart of the Mother Flame. Let us go to the heart of the sacred fire and realize that that human stubbornness that sways to and fro makes one decision today and forsakes it on the morrow. This will not stand in the day of the appearing of thy God Flame.

We have given a course and a study and a teaching and a path that is for *your* victory because *you* need it, not because we need to hear ourselves speak again and again and again—not because we need to have our Messenger offer the best fruits of heaven again and again!

Thus, take not for granted the moment of our coming through the Messenger or the preparation necessary for our coming. For, blessed hearts, your lifestreams have much to give and much to offer for the receipt of that Light. And we must preserve the instrument because when you are ready, we desire to have the instrument to give you those initiations that are due your lifestream—due it in the cosmic cycles. Understand, blessed hearts—not necessarily due as reward but because of the cosmic cycles which Maitreya has unfurled.

Lord Maitreya Teaches the Path of the Bodhisattva— Initiation: Fruit of the Tree of the Knowledge of Good and Evil and Fruit of the Tree of Life

Understand, then, the meaning of the coming of Lord Maitreya and the Mystery School.[4] The great moment of his coming signifies a turning in the age and an unleashing of his causal body that does contain the formula of the path of the bodhisattva for all who would unite with him in love and receive the fruit of the Tree of Life, the initiation of Life in the heart, and also the fruit of the tree of the knowledge of good and evil—which is the awareness taught to you by beloved Archangel Gabriel of Absolute Light and Absolute Darkness, Absolute Good and Absolute Evil in Armageddon upon earth.

When you study the book of teachings of Archangel Gabriel[5] and have the understanding of these principles, then you will understand the meaning of the initiation when it does come to you. Thus, study to show thyself approved. For this initiation of the fruit of the tree of the knowledge of good and evil is a very necessary one and a very difficult one, and you must take it in full conscious awareness of that whereof you partake.

We Are God-Determined That You Will Open Your Eyes and See

Blessed ones of the holy Flame of God, I with my seraphim come in a mighty service to Life and we are absolutely God-determined that you will open your eyes and awaken and see when you miss your opportunity to consume that spiritual blindness and that spiritual self-love that does indeed blind you to the tremendous opportunity of the hour to be the instrument of Almighty God!

We are determined absolutely in this hour of the action of the Dark Cycle in Taurus forthcoming[6] that you, one and all, will clear the ten/four axis [of the ten o'clock and four o'clock lines] of the Cosmic Clock and that you will go after the false astrology and the misqualified energies under the hierarchies of Scorpio and Taurus [Initiators of souls in God-Vision and God-Obedience], which misqualified energies have caused so much burden to the planetary home and have actually brought forth the levels of the astral plane of Death and Hell into the physical octave.

Beloved ones, the clearing of this axis in your individual world can mean a tremendous turning of the tide in the earth. And therefore, stand strong in the power of Cyclopea and Godfre and Gautama Buddha and all of the bodhisattvas who have overcome on this line, for it does indeed represent the pit of Death and Hell.

We are determined as seraphim of God to join you with Archangel Michael's legions in the cleaning out of these pits and the denizens thereof.

But we desire the strengthening!

And in order for you to survive this path of initiation in this year, you must be willing to leave the old, comfortable ways of the human habit patterns and recognize rebellion for what it is when you see it—mental rebellion, emotional obstinance, physical rebellion in that which is taken into the body and in its habit patterns, and also that rebellion which still manifests as the record and memory in the etheric body.

Beloved ones, let us call a spade a spade! You must look into the very pools of the All-Seeing Eye of God. You must look into the divine memory. You must see who you are at inner levels and know that this is an hour when the fullness of the glory of God within you can descend if you will allow it so!

Blessed ones, be of good cheer. I understand that portion of yourself that has Goodwill and is Good*-intended. But I tell you, as all that I know and for all that is holy, that you could make

---
*The word Good is the equivalent of the word God. Hence, "...that has God will and is God-intended."

more progress in the Light if you were absolutely God-determined to break that shell of the mortal consciousness! The law of mortality has no power over you and yet you give it power because you desire the rounds of mortality again and again.

The Pursuit of the Science of the Ruby Ray

Well, we are the seraphim of God. And some of us have gone forth into physical embodiment and some of us have not, but we are washed in the sacred fires of the Great Central Sun. And understand, beloved hearts, that that initiation can come to you before your ascension if you will prepare yourselves. It is a matter and a question of the pursuit of the science of the ruby ray. Thus, make haste to take advantage of the offered gifts of God as the message goes forth to work while you have the Light.

The Meaning of the Resurrection for Planet Earth

The meaning of the resurrection is profound for this planetary home because, you see, beloved ones, in order for the holy innocents to be out of harm's way—out of the vulnerability to Death and Hell itself—there must come an acceleration of the holy ones of God. In other words, the regeneration and the resurrection is for the spinning of the electrons and the atoms. It is for the increase of consciousness and the stepping-up of the vibrations of the physical body itself so that individuals are actually no longer vibrating at the lowest levels of planet Earth, to which there is a gravitational pull in this hour because of the nonfulfillment of the cycles of the Final Judgment on the part of all those who are not of the Light.

Thus, while Death and Hell yet prevail upon earth in certain quarters, the lightbearers must be above that plane in their consciousness, in their physical bodies, in their life patterns and therefore come apart from those lower vibrations. For the safety of the lightbearers and their children is in that coming apart by vibration, not necessarily by geographical location—unless you realize that in the higher altitudes and in the mountains of the earth, where greater purity is stored in the very fire of the rock, in the very devas of the elementals, of the trees, and of the fields and of the earth itself, there is indeed a higher percentage of the etheric plane and octave that is anchored in the physical.

You can understand that the etheric octave cannot manifest in the depths of the ghettos of the city and in the darkness that does prevail there. And thus, the geographical move is essential but is not sufficient unless the move and acceleration accompanying it is the acceleration in the paths of immortality! And therefore, put behind you the old ways and do not necessitate more and more rounds of self-indulgence before you finally get the message, before you are finally surfeited in the ways of this world.

The Addiction to the Human Ego

I tell you, the surfeiting will never come, because the pit is the pit of bottomless desire and the more you indulge therein, the more you want more. And this is the definition of addiction. Whether to drugs or whether to the misuse of the sacred fire or to the rock music or all the ways of the world—the addictions do not go away! In fact, the addictions devour the very soul until there is nothing left and you see the decay and degeneration and death of those who die from their addictions.

Beloved ones, I speak to you because I am concerned lest you die of the addiction to the human ego and do not even know that the process has taken place before you have made the transition and have once more lost the opportunity of an embodiment! And I tell you, it is indeed a razor's edge and you must consider that the initiates of the past have had to be one-pointed in that final embodiment toward the ascension.

You Are Going to Earn Your Ascension!

And no one is going to hand you your ascension on a silver platter! You are going to *earn* that ascension, contrary to all teachings of Christianity and Judaism. You will *earn* it in the way that Moses earned it. You will *earn* it in the way that Zarathustra and Confucius earned it. You will *earn* it in the way that the Lord Jesus Christ earned it. And in no other way will you climb the staircase to the supreme reality of the I AM THAT I AM.

Thus, beloved hearts, is it not better to have exceeded the requirement by generous measure than to fall short of the mark by a small percentage—being chary, then, in your giving? You never know what is the requirement of Law for your lifestream. You do not know what your karma of millions of years is. Therefore, how can you possibly calculate how much love of God is enough, how much love of your fellowman is enough, how much service is enough?

I tell you Infinity is enough! And that which is sufficient is Infinity and the infinite consciousness of God! And you ought to desire to be such a shining example, even a seraphim incarnate, that all the world cannot miss the example of those who are flying home to the heart of God.

Seraphim Concentrate the Sacred Fire and Cut Through

Let them compromise! Let them water down! Let us be able to say that if we be watered down ten times, our example will *still* be enough to compel them to come Home! This is the mark of a seraphim and of the initiates of our order. And do not think that you aspire too high [when you aspire] to be like the seraphim. I can assure you that we are the angels who cut through the most dense conditions and we are hailed and called by all the legions of the seven mighty archangels to render our assistance in the deliverance of the trial by fire.

You Shall Not Escape the Fiery Trial!

And remember, it is written and it is true and it is Law that the fire shall try every man's work. And therefore, *You shall not escape the fiery trial!* And it is written that some may suffer loss because their works are not acceptable and then, in addition to suffering loss, that the soul itself may burn and be consumed in that fiery trial because it in itself has not internalized the white Light and the heat thereof.[7] It is one thing to suffer the burning of one's efforts of lifetimes and one's work (and this indeed is a harsh lesson), but it is another to be utterly consumed by that fire because one has nothing of God within oneself.

I pray that you realize and that you become grateful when you receive initiations of the sacred fire and are stripped of that consciousness that is not of the highest Self. I pray that you do not sense [feel] a resentment for the suffering of loss or for the tearing down of the building that you have built, because the Great Law has determined that it is not in keeping with the plumb line of Truth.

Beloved ones, it is good to receive the judgment and the fiery trial daily that you may know what you have that is real, that you may know who you are and just how much of God's consciousness has actually become the real God-consciousness within you—and let all else go into the Flame. Those who are intelligent on the path of the initiations of the seraphim pray daily for the judgment of God upon their own souls that they might have an understanding, a recognition, and a reading from the very throne of God as to the measure of their perfection in the Mind of God.

This is the preference of the initiates who are determined not to make it by a hair but to make it, beloved ones, with an excess of Light and a cup pouring over that can deliver to all people the mandate of perfection. For those who are caught in the jaws of the bowels of the very pit itself need a tremendous power of Light from those who are moving forward.

Pulling Together

Imagine yourselves pulling the whole world. Imagine yourselves pulling together on a mighty giant rope. You realize that the momentum and the geometry of the momentum of all lightbearers upon earth is pulling against a tremendous weight.

Now, we desire not to have to pull against our own chelas, not to have to lead you around by a ring through the nose as pampered, indulgent little bulls of Taurus! Beloved ones, we will not pull against your pull. *You* must pull against your pull! *You must pull with us* as we heave a mighty heave together and pull those lightbearers that are in the farthest corners of the earth and have no idea of the path of Christhood that is waiting for them that they must tie into even in this embodiment.

This is an age of the turning of worlds. It is an age of the turning of cycles. It is an age when, in the darkest cycle of the Kali Yuga, we attend the descent of the greatest Light of the Great White Brotherhood. And this activity itself is bringing forth that great Light. And you see that great Light!

And the imminence of the greater Light is always here and always subject unto *the bowl*—who are the receivers [the chalice] in this hour, as you are indeed one Holy Grail. All lightbearers upon earth and Keepers of the Flame do form that Holy Grail and are facets of its crystal.

Rainbow Rays of God

Let the crystallization of the consciousness of God within you be all of your desiring. And may you see that consciousness spreading its mighty Light rays through your chakras, through the seven rays, in all you do. And may you realize that this is not a rigidity, it is not a fanaticism, it is not some sort of path of asceticism. It is the full glory of the rainbow rays of God permeating, loving, purifying, manifesting the Truth in your hands, in your hearts, and everywhere! And let us move forward in the great rainbow rays of God that have come for the deliverance of this nation and the deliverance of the chakras of the earth.

And therefore, I, Justinius, stand in the heart of Los Angeles, stand in the heart of New York City. I AM determined that the mighty pillars of the Elohim of God[8] are there for the protection of America and the I AM Race. I determine that this people in America shall be awakened by my seraphim!

Copyright © 1985 Church Universal and Triumphant, Inc.

Seraphim from the Central Sun Stand in the Media

And therefore, new contingents of seraphim descend from the heart of God in the Great Central Sun, come now to earth drenched with the living fires of the Sacred One—truly the bodhisattvas. And they come to America. And they come to saturate this people and to cut them free from the lies of the fallen ones and all that has been told them regarding World Communism.

Beloved hearts of Light, I AM standing in all media and mouthpieces of the media—both in the press, in television, in radio and every form of contact with the American people. And our seraphim are standing there. And if you will call to us and call to the great causal bodies of the saints, you will discover how we will purge and purify. And the seraphim of God who have the authority of Serapis Bey and the Great Central Sun to stand in the auras of the people will do so in answer to your call.

Do you understand this teaching from Serapis Bey, beloved hearts? The seraphim may stand congruent where you are! They may release the sacred fire, purge and purify, renew your bloodstream, give you eternal youth. You have but to call for it and to live the path of the one who is ascending. And we will do it by cosmic law and by the Judgment Call of the Lord Christ sent through those individuals who are of the Serpents* and their seed, and we will give them that opportunity to bend the knee and confess the Christ within you.

God Is Determined to Save This Planetary Home—
with the Speed of Light

And if they do not bend the knee and confess that Christ, beloved hearts of Light, you will see the judgment come upon them. You will see the binding of the tares and you will know that God is determined to save this planetary home and that if He is going to save it, He is going to have to do it with the speed of Light. And you will be very grateful that He will do it with the speed of Light, beloved hearts, because I tell you, you will not want to wait the million years it will take to spend out the outplaying of these fallen ones.

And no one in cosmos desires to wait any longer, for they have played out themselves again and again and again, and now they are tormenting the little ones. And we must hide our eyes and hide our faces as we see the molesting of little children—not only their bodies but their souls and their minds and their nervous systems and their chakras.

---

*The term 'Serpents' denotes a race of fallen angels called Serpents because they perverted and inverted the Kundalini, 'serpent fire' coiled in the base-of-the-spine chakra, focus of the Mother Flame.

We cannot bear it. We have gone before Almighty God and Alpha and Omega in the heart of the Great Central Sun. We are determined that the days of the [karma of the] elect shall be shortened[9] and the days of the wicked [the times of the tormentors who are the seed of the Wicked One] shall be shortened. And therefore, we need to intensify the Light within you.

I Anoint You with the Oil of Spikenard— Pillars of Fire, Vessels of Seraphim

And therefore, I am come to anoint you in this hour with the oil of spikenard because you must become pillars of fire, because you must be the vessels of seraphim, because we desire you to be seraphim of God upon earth and join the ranks of the initiates of the sacred fire.

And you understand that as I speak, I speak out of the Flame. And therefore, my words are zipping through to your very heart flame as a mighty coil of fire to enable you to understand just how slow and just how sluggish is your thinking, in that you can scarcely comprehend what I am saying, beloved hearts. And yet *you do* comprehend it because the Holy Spirit is upon you and *you do* understand that this indeed is the acceleration!

And when you ascend you will speak and you will work and you will think and you will go this fast,[10] and you will know that God is not limited to your present state of human habit patterns. *Why* should you subject yourself to these patterns any longer? *Why* should you indulge? There is no reason!

This Earth Must Become a Sun and You Must Rise

I tell you, I AM a seraphim of God! I AM the captain of seraphic hosts. And we do know what is required for your lifestreams! And we come in the most intense fire and love of our being and we speak to you in the outpouring of Mercy's flame. We speak to you out of the love of Almighty God. We communicate to you that this earth must become a sun—that you must rise to the level of the etheric octave even while you are physical, as you have been told.

And you must understand that when that quotient of lightbearers who have risen to that level with the Messenger does so [in the physical octave], there will be a tremendous release of Light, there will be new initiation, and there will be a tremendous expansion of this activity!

Therefore, let those in the white fire core receive our blessing now.

Prayer of the Seraphic Captain to Gautama Buddha

Lord Gautama Buddha, I, Justinius, bow before Thy Heart Flame and before the Heart of God in the Great Central Sun.

I AM an emissary of Alpha and Omega. I bring good tidings of the cosmic spheres. Ten thousand times ten thousand seraphim bow before Thy Flame, Gracious Gautama.

I pray to Your Mighty Heart of Light for intercession on behalf of these Keepers of the Flame. Let them receive what Thou wilt, O Gautama.

Use me, O Lord, in this hour for the perfecting of the race of the I AM, for the ministration unto them.

Anoint, O Beloved Lord, my angels who are Thy servants. For we come, as Thou knowest, to deliver this earth of darkness.

I pray, O Lord, from Thy Mighty Threefold Flame the quickening, the increase according to Solar Logoi, that lightbearers may come now into a new dimension of the highest Self.

I submit myself to Thee and in the service of Thine own. Thus, bless me, O Lord, that I might minister in Thy name I AM THAT I AM.

[Holy Justinius anointed the brow of more than one thousand Keepers of the Flame with the precious oil of spikenard through the right hand of the Messenger—in twenty-eight minutes.]

"**The Summit Lighthouse Sheds Its Radiance O'er All the World to Manifest as Pearls of Wisdom.**" This dictation by Justinius was delivered through the Messenger of the Great White Brotherhood Elizabeth Clare Prophet on Holy Saturday, April 6, 1985, during the 5-day Easter Conclave at Camelot. (1) Matt. 5:6. (2) Arcturus and Victoria, July 1, 1984, cassette B84121, $6.50. (3) When the child Mary was presented at the temple at the age of three, it is said that her parents placed her upon the first of fifteen stairs symbolizing the initiations of the psalms of degrees (Psalms 120–134). Unassisted, she ascended the stairs one after another, "showing that she had passed these initiations in other lives and was spiritually prepared to fulfill her mission." See Mark and Elizabeth Prophet, *My Soul Doth Magnify the Lord!* Summit University Press, p. 33; $4.95. (4) In his May 31, 1984, Ascension Day Address delivered in the Heart of the Inner Retreat, beloved Jesus announced the dedication of the Inner Retreat as the Mystery School of Maitreya in this age. "You realize that the Mystery School of Maitreya was called the Garden of Eden. All of the Ascended Masters' endeavors and the schools of the Himalayas of the centuries have been to the end that this might occur from the etheric octave unto the physical—that the Mystery School might once again receive the souls of Light who have gone forth therefrom, now who are ready to return, to submit, to bend the knee before the Cosmic Christ...." See Jesus Christ, "The Mystery School of Lord Maitreya," *Pearls of Wisdom,* vol. 27, no. 36, pp. 316–17. (5) Archangel Gabriel, *Mysteries of the Holy Grail,* Summit University Press, $12.95. (6) *Dark Cycle in Taurus:* see *Pearls of Wisdom,* vol. 28, no. 17, p. 228, n. 4. (7) I Cor. 3:13–15; I Pet. 1:7; 4:12, 13. (8) See Hercules, December 30, 1983. (9) Matt. 24:22; Mark 13:20. (10) The speed with which Justinius delivered this fiery address increased progressively throughout the dictation. In order to fully assimilate the intensity of his release, it is necessary to hear the recording. Published on 12-cassette album *Easter Conclave 1985* (A85072), $67.50; single cassette B85081, $6.50. For further teachings of Justinius, Captain of Seraphic Hosts, see "The Predication of God: Seraphic Meditations III," in Serapis Bey, *Dossier on the Ascension,* Summit University Press, pp. 133–40, $4.95; and "Legions of Purity in Defense of the Mother Flame," on 6-cassette album *Portals of Purity* (A7510), $37.50, single cassette B7512, $6.50.

Pearls of Wisdom, published weekly by The Summit Lighthouse for Church Universal and Triumphant, come to you under the auspices of the Darjeeling Council of the Great White Brotherhood. These are presently dictated by the Ascended Masters to their Messenger Elizabeth Clare Prophet. The international headquarters of this nonprofit, nondenominational activity is located in Los Angeles, California. All communications and freewill contributions should be addressed to The Summit Lighthouse, Box A, Malibu, CA 90265. Pearls of Wisdom are sent weekly throughout the USA via third-class mail to all who support the Church with a minimum yearly love offering of $40. First-class and international postage rates available upon request. Notice of change of address should be received three weeks prior to the effective date. Third-class mail is not forwarded by the post office.

Copyright © 1985 Church Universal and Triumphant, Inc. All rights reserved. Printed in the United States of America. Pearls of Wisdom and The Summit Lighthouse are registered trademarks of Church Universal and Triumphant, Inc. All rights to their use are reserved.

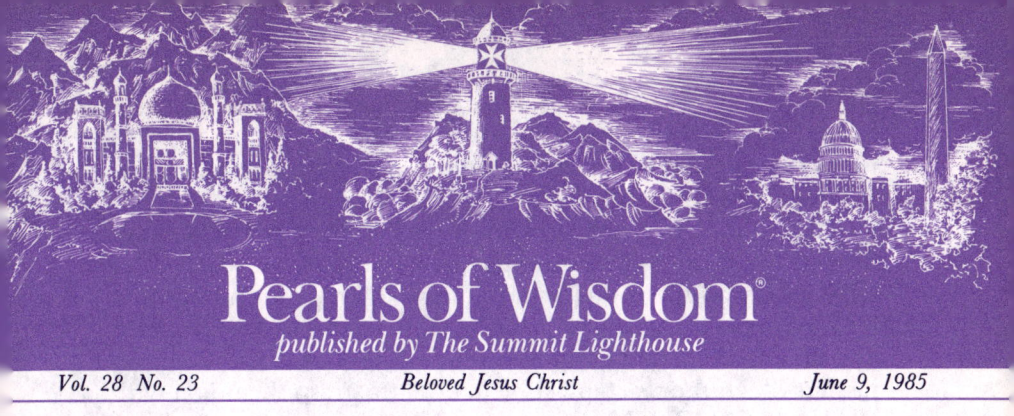

Easter Conclave at Camelot
"Come, leave your nets—I will make you fishers of men."

VI

The Lord's Day
Jesus' Message for the Revolutionaries of the Spirit

In the full Light of the resurrection, I, Jesus, bring to you that Light of your own resurrection which is indeed the enlightenment of the Spirit.

The Meaning of the Lord's Day

Beloved in the love of the Spirit on the Lord's Day, consider, then, what is the meaning of the Lord's Day.[1] Why, it is the appearing of your own I AM Presence! It is the internalization of the Word within you! And these are not mere words that I speak but the promise of your Father from everlasting unto everlasting.

And thus, the march of the Son of God moves on. Thus, the world, caught up in its usual compromises and dichotomies, is all around you. But in the midst of chaos, the fire infolding itself is the true Spirit of the Immortal One that you are. Now, as this is a Flame gathering more of itself, what we see is the equation of the soul entering in to the Flame-gathering process.

Do you understand, my beloved, that this is the mighty work of the ages—for which work you have been given, time after time, cycle after cycle, the new body, the new vessel, into which you would pour the new wine of the Spirit?

The Child Mind

And thus, as the tiny babe comes forth, it is with full hope—hope within the soul that this time, in this embodiment, the renewal will take place. And the vow is made and the striving is begun and the child determines to master the movement of limbs, to master coordination, to go out and discover the whole world as that which is the world inside.

Thus, the child is born with a quest for self-mastery. And, by and by, there is limitation placed upon that very concept of self-mastery as others do for the child what only the child can do for itself or as others lower the level of excellence that is required and do not allow that child to reach for the stars and to discover just how high the reach must be in order to grasp the union with the I AM THAT I AM.

Let the systems of education contemplated by parents and teachers take into consideration that in the child mind there is no limitation. There is an acquaintance with Infinity. Time and space do not come easily to the child; and therefore, while you train him to work within these confines, do not forget to allow the spirit to soar and to contemplate dimensions that are indeed infinite: the largess of God Himself, the magnanimity of God, the generosity of Life—space wide and open, the vastness of the seas and the valleys and the mountains! Let the child see and know the wonder of this expanse that is his in which to create.

Thus, beloved, understand that the balance between the indoor and the outdoor [activities] is *the going within* to the secret chamber of the heart, where the child may learn the inner disciplines of energy and the mastery of detail within the mind and within his world, and *the going without* to discover that there is an infinite potential in God, that there is an infinite potential in the fire infolding itself. And the challenge of life on earth is the wedding of the twain.

Balance within the Realm of the Possible

Thus, the divinity ensconced in the humanity is the mark of the individual who is balanced. And those who are unbalanced in this society and civilization, as always, have either an 'over-sense' of self-importance as gods which they have made of themselves or an 'under-sense' of importance of themselves as human beings.

The equation, then, must be the realization of the hand in the glove: the glove being the body that you wear, the hand being that movable force of the Godhead that is yours also—a Power to be wielded, a Love that can be given, and a Wisdom that is the Bread broken for you.

For this is indeed my Body of Light. My Body of Light, beloved, is that Light which quickeneth every cell of the mind.

I come, then, for the breaking of the confines of your own version of orthodoxy—your own version of self-limitation and mortality and self-condemnation. For above and beyond and apart from that which the false pastors have chosen to give you is your own sense of self-limitation. And thus there is a doctrine of human values, the end of which is the exclusion in toto of the divine man or the divine woman.

And thus, for all intents and purposes, the evolution of the soul ceases while the development of the human increases. And in that increase there is more of the development of the outer self that is present at any moment to snuff out the tender inspiration of the soul about to reach into the fires of creativity and break the mortal coil and self-transcend.

Thus, it is a delicate balance, one concerning which you ought to pray. For this is the very mystery of Life:

Weaving in and out of the responsibilities which deal with the realm of the possible, with the practical life which can be lived—given all the so-called limitations; and in the very midst of these to recognize none of them and to know that the spirit as the revolutionary of God will cut right through—will not in any way allow to be placed upon itself interference or blockage or even the put-down of one's own karma or astrology, but has the sense of the Infinite within itself, able to penetrate, able to go beyond, able to catch the wind of the Holy Spirit and move to that infinite Source.

Signs of the Central Sun

The stars have a goal and their goal is the Central Sun. They point the way to a Source no longer seen. You cannot see the Central Sun from your vantage, nor can you see the Sun behind the sun. And yet, every flower tells you there is a Central Sun. Every cell in your body tells you there is a Central Sun! And your physical, beating heart is the central sun of your temple and it also tells you that the repetition of centrality in the earth, even in the fiery core of its center, does remind and bespeak of the infinite Sun whence you came.

Thus the mercy and the grace of the Father who does give you those crumbs of the loaf of Universal Consciousness which, when you take them into yourself, become the expansion of ancient self-knowledge and awareness of the foundations of Life. These things are the treasures in the heart, the very heart of a soul that is juxtaposed as delicately as a rose between time and space and infinity.

Thus, care for the tender child, care for the tender soul. And know that there is nothing more delicate in time and space than the soul merging with the Divine, the soul about to become the full awareness of God.

The Garment of My Self-Mastery

O beloved hearts, so many things that are precious and delicate in life that are so easily lost! Thus, understand that the harshness of the world has become the ground of the fallen angels who by their harshness would take from you the delicate flower of hope or of faith or of charity—of gentleness and grace.

Let us ease one another's burdens. Let us remember the vision of the inner man of the heart. Let us know that the soul whom we meet has a Shepherd also and we may identify with that Shepherd as we identify with the Christ in ourselves.

I say "we," for I am truly a very living part of this community and of all the saints on the earth. For I must supply by love, by intimation of the soul, by comfort, by the Holy Spirit an infusion of the enlightenment of God that does not come through the normal channels of communication of religion. I must bypass tradition to convince, by the wooing of my heart, each and every soul whom I love that they have a right to be fully clothed in the garment of my self-mastery, fully apparent as heirs [heirs apparent] of the throne of grace of their own individual Christhood.

My Message of Your Coequality with Me in God

I come with a message which the fallen ones have declared to be blasphemy and which they have declared as blasphemy from the beginning.[2] I preach it in the intimations of the heart to each and every soul of God. I come with a message of the living Christ within. And yet the outer preachers, with the shrill voice and with the subtle criticism, convince them that it is robbery for them to make themselves equal to my Light and Office and equal to God as I did.[3]

Beloved, I am therefore grateful for the mouthpiece by which I can deliver to you the vibration of my love and my determination. For there are yet the moneychangers[4] to be cast out of the temples of the world. There are yet the barren fig trees[5] to be cursed [judged] and withered because they do not bring forth the fruit of the Spirit.

You have the right to eat from a full fig tree each hour and day as you worship God. Each Sunday as you go to church, you have the right to eat from this tree. And therefore, if the pastors are the barren fig trees, let them be judged in this hour by the

Universal Christ with them! For the Law itself does act and I, Jesus, do implement this Law. And yet, were I to withdraw from the universe, I tell you, the Law would still act.

And yet, the benefit of the Ascended Masters with you and of yourselves embodying that Christ is that through the incarnate Word—the Word that has been claimed and made your own—there can come the acceleration of the cycles of Almighty God in the earth. Thus understand: in the very midst of proving the dimensions of my own Godhood I had to meet precisely what you must meet.

Beloved ones, the conditions are present today. Yet, the challenging of those in authority seems almost to be a fruitless, a thankless, and a useless engagement of time and energy. Why not leave it all and go about your business or education, for what can one voice do? Beloved ones, you seem to forget that the earth was not so sparsely populated as you might think in the days two thousand years ago. And tyranny was enthroned and people were enslaved and injustice was abroad in the land.

The Voice of the Living Word

Now, you say, what did I accomplish—one voice? Well, I was not one voice. I was *the* voice of the living Word. I was the voice of God speaking. And that power and that voice has echoed from then backwards in time and space into the distant past and into the future of the present moment.

You also are the instrument of the Word. And when the Word is spoken and the Truth is declared, it impresses itself upon your soul and unites with the Word in all other children of the Light. And it is heard, it is known, and there is a self-correcting force in the very fabric of society which, when the Word does impinge upon it, forces the alignment of atoms and molecules. And trends in society change and are remolded and aligned with the divine force of the Universal Word descending!

Therefore, nothing is in vain and the challenging of injustice does go forth; and everywhere where that vibration of the Word is manifest on earth, there is the judgment of that point of injustice.

Let the Shepherds Feed My Sheep

Fear not, then. For there is an adjunct to this service and that is that the Word strengthens all those who allow themselves to be used by it. And the Word therefore becomes the life-force that increases the sacred fire of the spine whereby you have the authority of the Shepherd's crook not only to "feed my sheep" but to demand that those who have made themselves secular shepherds in government, in the economy, and in education also come into alignment with the Mediator, who is Christ.

Let the shepherds rise up, then, and heal the people and challenge their oppressors! It is ever the work of the living Christ. This is the message: Feed my sheep. They must be fed first and foremost the spiritual Truth. They must be fed this Truth by a gentle teaching, a firm teaching, and a striving example on your part.

Beloved ones, the example shows the way of Truth. Therefore, be the example. And when the example is given, they will recognize those who are not walking the path of Truth. And they will grow in strength by your manifestation of strength, and they will grow weak by your manifestation of weakness. And they are demoralized as you demoralize your own reason for being in compromising that Word.

Perfect the Soul as the Bride of Christ

Fear not, little flock, for it is the Father's good pleasure to give you the kingdom of His Consciousness—of His Mind and Heart and Soul.[6]

In the hour of greatest frailty or greatest error or greatest out-of-alignment state—whatever your burden may be—in that precise hour, my beloved, understand that this is the moment when God reveals Himself, when His Spirit conquers, when your temple is filled with the Holy Spirit and you find that it is so not because you have become a human *god* but because you have made Him room; it is, in fact, because of your human *frailty* that the LORD God has raised you up to be His instrument.

Thus, perfect not the human but perfect the soul. And the perfection of the soul is known by God. Even when the exterior life may have burdens and problems and all manner of karmic challenges, it is the perfected soul as the bride that becomes the useful instrument.

Thus, beloved ones, it is always so that in your extremity God suddenly appears. Thus, the preparation is for that moment. And then, you see, the wonder of it all is that God Himself is always the Doer. And when you observe yourself being His instrument, you know how gracious is our God—how bountiful, how beautiful, how majestic, how fulfilling of all the promises He truly is! And we know that "not by might...but by my Spirit," saith the LORD.[7]

The Path of Human Attainment vs. the Path of Spiritual Attainment

Beware, then, those who come with a path of human attainment, human development of superhuman talents or mentalities. Beware of those who attempt to prove by science that there is no need for God. Beloved ones, God can never be contained in all of the extensions of human genetic engineering!

It is the Spirit of the LORD, and that Spirit only, that does raise you up—that is the door to heaven. Seek Him diligently and seek Him in the following of the path of the prophets and the sages of East and West. Let the unascended Masters, then, be the example. Let those who have therefore known the power of the Spirit within go before you.

Now, beloved hearts, your path of spiritual attainment is one to which you set yourselves diligently [to the realization of God] in the very midst of accomplishing the necessities of human life, yet not out of indulgence of that human but out of love—love of that consciousness of the soul working its way through the human plight and the human dilemma. And who can say, looking upon any man or any woman, what is the human and what is the divine? I counsel you truly: Judge not lest you be judged by powers higher than those of your neighbors.

The Coming of the LORD into Your Temple

Blessed hearts, you may never know the day and the hour of my coming in to the least of these my brethren whom you have thought to be beneath you or not worthy of notice. Beloved hearts, the coming of the LORD into the temple of the devotee is a most wondrous manifestation of the consummation of Love on the shore of Galilee.

In the name of the I AM THAT I AM, I point the way, then. The path of self-mastery is to fail not to challenge by the cosmic honor flame whatever of injustice toward my little ones may cross your path. All things that come to you each day are there for the reaping of your soul and for the plucking of the fruit of the Tree of Life as it is given by the Cosmic Christ.

I promise you, as I have promised from the beginning, that before you enter a difficult situation, before you go forth in any way, if you will simply step back briefly and say, "Jesus, my brother, go before me," I will then go before you. I will go before you in the LORD's Spirit. I will draw you up in my garment. I will be one with you and in you. And I will, beloved, clear the way and prepare your soul. And in that moment of the soul's poising for the victory, I will stand back and you will have the victory through your inner tie to the heart of the Universal Christ.

Thus, there is the wayshower and the example, and that I AM. But I never take from you the opportunity to prove the Law and to prove my Presence with you and to demonstrate the infinite Power, Wisdom, and Love available when you fulfill the law of grace and feed my sheep.

The "I AM He" Affirmation
Taught by the Great White Brotherhood

Thus, there is an understanding of working with the Great White Brotherhood, of the cooperation and the commeasurement, as Above and so below—the realization where you are that "I AM He!"[8] And this affirmation, "I AM He!" is the affirmation of Christ in you and the declaration that the true "I" within you is that Christ. This is the razor's edge of awareness of the divinity within the human.

The human can never affirm, "I AM He." But then the soul merged with the Divine is no longer conscious whether of the human or the Divine, but merely conscious of the "I." And when the I AM THAT I AM becomes the "I" within you and you are not compartmentalizing yourself into the subconscious or the ego or the libido or the id or whatever titles and names you wish to designate, including the four lower bodies—when you see yourself as a divine wholeness and a shaft of Light interpenetrating the octaves, there will no longer be heaven or hell or up or down or earth or sea or sky. There will only be the pulsating Flame—and it will be *You*, it will be *I*, it will be *the Universal One*, beloved hearts.

Enter the Universal Life—Possessed by Truth Alone

Transcend and leave behind you the former sectarian and segmented consciousness of life. Enter, then, the universal way and the universal Life and be, in a universal sense, one with every part of being. This has a most practical application. And that practical application can be seen in my life as Jesus, in the life of John the Baptist, and in the lives of the prophets who did not fail.

We could not fail, for we were possessed by Truth. We did not fail to challenge the lie, the Liar—the injustice, the oppression. And for this, many paid the price again and again of mockery and shame and imprisonment, beheading, crucifixion. All these things did come to pass, beloved, both as the judgment of those who perpetrated the deeds and as the warning to each

Copyright © 1985 Church Universal and Triumphant, Inc.

and every one of you of what befalls the disciple who is determined to put on the mantle of his Christhood.

Fear not, beloved. For the greater pain is truly to fail the Word that I AM, to fail the Light that you are, to lose the integrity of Being, to lose the *integration* with one's Inner Self because one has denied that Self through cowardness, through going away from the encounter and the confrontation whether with Christ or Antichrist.

Fear Not, Move Forward, Stand on Principle

Thus, my message of the Spirit of the Resurrection this day is to fear not, come what may: to move forward, to stand on the principle of Being and to be sure of that Principle, and then to not be concerned of the consequences. As one of my disciples has said, "Let the chips fall where they may!"[9] Be unconcerned, for this day go forth to be who you really are.

Fear not to express, then, the most intense love or the love that becomes the rebuke. And let your friends know where you stand in intense love for the beauty of their souls and Christ with them and in support of their own overcoming self-mastery every step of the way.

Be a brother to my brothers and sisters. Be a child of the heart to all of my children. Be mother, be father, be teacher—but love Life free! And fear not the challenge; for I tell you they quake in their boots at the coming of the very step of the Son of God.

Beloved hearts, in the international theater there are many disturbing situations. The Christ in you has perceived. I have perceived. Let us realize that the flaming Sons of God who allow themselves to reach that quintessence of Light, letting nothing deter them from that path, are able, as one with the universal Light, to yet hold the balance.

Free Will of Fallen Ones Taking Nations Far Afield
The Law Requires the People's Vote of Confidence for God's Kingdom

I suppose you would say what concerns me most is the preponderance of free will of the fallen ones in another direction, in another social and economic philosophy that has taken the governments of the nations far afield from their reason for being. Free will, then, being the law of the octaves, we understand that it is the quickening and the acceleration to the white-hot heat of the Son of God, which does occur within these octaves, that is the very element in the body of God ("the body filaments") that can ignite the world consciousness and draw mankind into that alignment with Reality.

It will take a vote of confidence of the people themselves for the kingdom of God to come upon earth and for Christ to reign in all hearts.

Realize, then, that there is a commitment [on our part] to the transfer of this formula of identity, if you will, to many souls. There is a commitment [by the Ascended Masters] for the transmutation of darkness and bigotry and ignorance that is so entrenched as to deny the potential of divinity in all people of God. Thus, I tell you that this is the delicacy of the equation and the dire need that comes in the end of a two-thousand-year cycle when the karma that has been harvested must now be returned to the sower that he may reap his reward.

The Word and the Judgment of the Revolutionaries of the Spirit

Therefore, we see the Easter message as the power of the resurrection in this hour—we see that that message becomes the Word of the revolutionaries of the Spirit multiplied by the Power and the Law of the One across the whole face of the earth.

And we also see within that heart of the Son of God the office of the judgment—the judgment by the apostles with the living Christ of the tribes of Israel and the tribes in the earth who mourn.[10]

Let the force of Light, independent of your outer consciousness of judgment, therefore manifest through you by the power of the fohat of my Word this day. And let the judgment be the diminishing of the Light in those who have misused it and the increase of the Light in those who have used it wisely and well.[11]

Understand that inasmuch as there is the spilling over from the astral plane—and out of the very depths of that astral plane itself—into the physical octave of the will of darkness and the destruction of the little children and the youth, those then who become the Christ must become that Christ in the full power and the office accorded to the apostles. And thus, let Christ in you be the Judge. And let the Word go forth and the Word be spoken for the shortening of the days of the elect of God[12] and for the judgment of those who have misused that Light.

The Effective Increase of the Light

I AM in the counsel of the Lord on the Lord's Day. And I am with a council of Ascended Masters who look to intercede for mankind and who look to the outcome of this decade and the decades that are upon the earth. And thus our communication, one and all in agreement, is for the effective increase of the Light in those who have the Light, for the effective transfer of

Copyright © 1985 Church Universal and Triumphant, Inc.

the Light to those who are receptive, and for the effective power of the Light in the binding of those who are determined to destroy both the Light and the little ones who should contain it and the very Message and the Teaching that is for the liberation of all souls.

Thus, the Law does ever act. And thus you understand that as you use the Light to the glory of God, so the Light will increase. I promise you, then, in this hour that in the turning of the year and the turning of the tide of the resurrection this Easter 1985, there is increased the Light that is available, the Power of redemption, and the Power of resurrection.

Resurrection is the step-up of Light from the transfiguration which has taken place within your body, beloved hearts.[13] The transfiguration and the resurrection are the means whereby you transcend the world that is dense and dark. It is the position of the Rock of the Christ consciousness whereby you draw to that Rock[14] those who are yet floundering.

I speak in the name of my beloved Mother. I speak in the name of the Holy Spirit. I speak for the increase of love within and without the community—a noncompromising love that compels souls to a higher self-esteem in God. This is the meaning of feeding my sheep. Those who are of the Light must esteem their holy office in the Light and in the I AM Presence.

The Religion of the Everlasting Gospel: The Dividing of the Way

Therefore, my beloved, I bless you with the power of my heart. I send you renewed on that mission to which you were dedicated when you took embodiment. And I assure you that our oneness will now work as a leaven in the hearts of all for the religion of the Everlasting Gospel[15] to be internalized and known, self-known, by the lightbearers. For to be free from the binds and the burdens of orthodoxy is the greatest boon and blessing that could come to all people upon earth.

Therefore let it be known, as I have said: **I came not to send peace but a sword.**[16] The sword becomes the necessity for the dividing of the way in each individual's consciousness. And this dividing of the way must come through fearlessness. But it is only perfect love that casts out fear.[17]

This is the love that prepares the soul to understand my true doctrine of liberation. It is a liberation theology that has naught to do with the ideas of men and serpents. It is a liberation from that very orthodoxy which limits the individual's perception to defend himself, his right to be, his nation, and the New Jerusalem and the New Israel gathered here in North America.

America, Not the Middle East, Is the New Jerusalem

Let America return, therefore, to an understanding of God's holy purpose on her shores and in this land as the place prepared for the gathering of all the tribes from all the earth. Beloved ones, the conditions of the laggard races in the Middle East and their instability must reveal to you that no government, especially this government, ought to place the preponderance of their trust or their money or their military matériel in the hands of those who have betrayed the living Christ again and again and again.

This is the citadel of the New Jerusalem. And therefore, let the people of America *awake* this day! *awake* in the fullness of the Cosmic Christ! *awake* to the fiery destiny of the holding of the balance of Light on earth! Truly the holding of the balance is the key. And the balance in this hour remains for you to forge and win.

I commend you to your own victory in this hour. For upon your victory—I tell you truly from the very heart of the Father this day—upon your victory hangs the future of this nation, and upon this nation the future of the earth. Let all behold the signs of the times and recognize the ultimate need for the individualization of the God Flame now!

It cannot wait, beloved. Therefore, fast and pray and be victorious. For I trust I will find you in the New Day where you must be to see that this earth is free in the Light. There are many lightbearers to be contacted, and there are many [false pastors] who have no right to deprive them of that Light [—although they are attempting to do so].

We Are Ready for Tremendous Expansion in This Activity

See to it, then, for you have Archangel Michael, you have the holy angels and all of the servants of God in heaven in answer to your call. We are ready for the tremendous expansion in this activity which is the requirement of the hour. And the question is: Are the individual vessels ready? The answer is: God in you is ready! Christ in you is ready! The soul is poised to take its flight.

Now, beloved, take the formula of the strength of Self in the vessel of selflessness and understand that God indeed will perform His mighty work through you in this age.

In this hour, then, of the springtime, I say to one and all: A very happy, happy Spirit of the Resurrection! For joy is the sign of mastery. And I behold joy! I affirm it! And I AM that joy within you always and always and forever.

Copyright © 1985 Church Universal and Triumphant, Inc.

The Judgment Call
"They Shall Not Pass!"
by Jesus Christ

In the Name of the I AM THAT I AM,
I invoke the Electronic Presence of Jesus Christ:
They shall not pass!
They shall not pass!
They shall not pass!
By the authority of the cosmic cross of white fire
  it shall be:
That all that is directed against the Christ
  within me, within the holy innocents,
  within our beloved Messengers,
  within every son and daughter of God
Is now turned back
  by the authority of Alpha and Omega,
  by the authority of my Lord and Saviour Jesus Christ,
  by the authority of Saint Germain!

I AM THAT I AM within the center of this temple
  and I declare in the fullness of
  the entire Spirit of the Great White Brotherhood:
That those who, then, practice the black arts
  against the children of the Light
Are now bound by the hosts of the LORD,
Do now receive the judgment of the Lord Christ
  within me, within Jesus,
  and within every Ascended Master,
Do now receive, then, the full return—
  multiplied by the energy of the Cosmic Christ—
  of their nefarious deeds which they have practiced
  since the very incarnation of the Word!

Lo, I AM a Son of God!
Lo, I AM a Flame of God!
Lo, I stand upon the Rock of the living Word
And I declare with Jesus, the living Son of God:
They shall not pass!
They shall not pass!
They shall not pass!
ELOHIM   ELOHIM   ELOHIM

Posture for giving this decree: Stand. Raise your right hand, using the *abhaya mudrā* (gesture of fearlessness, palm forward), and place your left hand to your heart—thumb and first two fingers touching chakra pointing inward. Give this call at least once in every 24-hour cycle. Taken from a dictation by Jesus Christ, August 6, 1978, Camelot, California, "They Shall Not Pass!" published in *Spoken by Elohim* (*Pearls of Wisdom*, vol. 21), pp. 165–76. Also published on *Rainbow Rays: Dynamic Decrees through Elizabeth Clare Prophet* (2-cassette album A83018), cassette B83019.

You Are a Child of the Light

You are a child of the Light
You were created in the Image Divine
You are a child of Infinity
You dwell in the veils of time
You are a Son of the Most High!

"The Summit Lighthouse Sheds Its Radiance O'er All the World to Manifest as Pearls of Wisdom." This dictation by Jesus Christ was delivered through the Messenger of the Great White Brotherhood Elizabeth Clare Prophet on Easter Sunday, April 7, 1985, during the 5-day Easter Conclave at Camelot. The Messenger's Easter Sunday Sermon (from John 21 and Acts 1:6-12) and Holy Communion preceded the dictation. Service and dictation published on 12-cassette album *Easter Conclave 1985* (A85072), $67.50; single cassettes B85081, B85082, $6.50 ea. (1) Isa. 61:2; 62; 63; Rev. 1:10. See Jesus Christ, May 8, 1983, "The Second Advent: 'The Day of Vengeance of Our God,'" *Pearls of Wisdom,* vol. 26, no. 43, pp. 511-19. (2) Matt. 26:63-65; Mark 14:61-64; John 10:22-39. (3) Phil. 2:5, 6. (4) Matt. 21:12, 13; Mark 11:15-17; John 2:13-17. (5) Matt. 21:18-22; Mark 11:12-14, 20, 21. (6) Luke 12:32. (7) Zech. 4:6. (8) John 18:4-8. (9) See El Morya, The Chela and the Path, in *El Morya on Discipleship East and West* (*Pearls of Wisdom,* vol. 18, no. 1), p. 1. Also in paperback: *The Chela and the Path,* Summit University Press, p. 13, $3.95. (10) Matt. 19:28; 24:30; Luke 22:28-30; I Cor. 6:2, 3. (11) Matt. 13:12; 25:29; Mark 4:25; Luke 8:18. (12) Matt. 24:22; Mark 13:20. (13) See Elizabeth Clare Prophet, "Healing through the Transfiguration," *Heart* (Winter 1985), pp. 50-59, 119-23, $3.00; 2-cassette album *Healing through the Transfiguration* (A84070), $9.95; and "The Spirit of the Resurrection Flame," on 12-cassette album *Easter Conclave 1985,* single cassette B85074, $6.50. "Healing through the Transfiguration" and "The Spirit of the Resurrection Flame" are also each available on ½" VHS video cassette (28 min. ea.), $23.00 ea. (14) I Cor. 10:4; Deut. 32:4, 18, 30, 31; Pss. 61:2. (15) Rev. 14:6. See Mark and Elizabeth Prophet, *Climb the Highest Mountain: The Everlasting Gospel,* Summit University Press, $14.95. (16) Matt. 10:34. (17) I John 4:18.

Pearls of Wisdom, published weekly by The Summit Lighthouse for Church Universal and Triumphant, come to you under the auspices of the Darjeeling Council of the Great White Brotherhood. These are presently dictated by the Ascended Masters to their Messenger Elizabeth Clare Prophet. The international headquarters of this nonprofit, nondenominational activity is located in Los Angeles, California. All communications and freewill contributions should be addressed to The Summit Lighthouse, Box A, Malibu, CA 90265. Pearls of Wisdom are sent weekly throughout the USA via third-class mail to all who support the Church with a minimum yearly love offering of $40. First-class and international postage rates available upon request. Notice of change of address should be received three weeks prior to the effective date. Third-class mail is not forwarded by the post office.

Copyright © 1969, 1972, 1978, 1985 Church Universal and Triumphant, Inc. All rights reserved. Printed in the United States of America. Pearls of Wisdom and The Summit Lighthouse are registered trademarks of Church Universal and Triumphant, Inc. All rights to their use are reserved.

Easter Conclave at Camelot
"Come, leave your nets—I will make you fishers of men."

VII
The Sun behind the Sun
God-Government and the Dedication to Truth

> ..."We give Thee thanks, O Lord God Almighty, which art, and wast, and art to come; because Thou hast taken to Thee Thy great power and hast reigned."
> And the nations were angry, and Thy wrath is come, and the time of the dead, that they should be judged;
> And that Thou shouldest give reward unto Thy servants the prophets, and to the saints, and them that fear Thy name, small and great;
> And shouldest destroy them which destroy the earth.
> *Revelation 11*

Out of the iridescent violet, I descend. I AM Surya of the Sun. "Surya" they have called me, but I AM the One internalization of the blue flame / God Flame / white fire of the Will of God, the centerpoise of galaxy—though not in the "center" by your perception. (The "centerpoise" is quite another geometrical point.)

Thus understand that I AM the Infinite One.

So I have blessed in the beginning and I bless now in the fullness of time one whom I have called, one whom I have sent, one who came by the ruby ray and the compassionate fire. Thus, I give my heart again for the lowering from the causal body of that one of the divine mission appearing to which she came into embodiment.

Blessed hearts, it is necessary that I speak thus in order that by the radiance of my Presence manifest in physical form with physical voice, the dispensations may go forth. It is not necessary to know for whom they are given but only to know that I do

Copyright © 1985 Church Universal and Triumphant, Inc.

dedicate a lifestream this night to the ongoing fulfillment of the purpose of the love ray in America. And that love ray, beloved hearts, must be outpictured.

And therefore, I come to discourse with you this evening concerning God-government, concerning the absence of awareness of Truth. Thus, let us pursue once again the satyagraha.* Let us understand the dedication to Truth, the practice of Truth, the meditation upon Truth, and the becoming of that Truth with the undergirding of Love establishing its true and holy purpose.

Beloved hearts, sometimes the one who knows the Truth feels drowned out by the babbling voices of error. These voices are like the crickets. Whether a thousand or ten thousand, they seem to occupy the night air with a certain sound that becomes monotonous and of which many then—becoming so accustomed thereto—also become unaware. And it is the unawareness of error and error as a constant that I come to pierce and to puncture, beloved hearts. For this droning on of the crickets of error becomes a hypnotic force that moves in the world and prevents those who have the receptivity to Truth from embodying that Truth now and each day and always.

I come, then, to underscore the power of Truth and the one who embodies that Truth by the expanded threefold flame, by purity of heart and oneness with Lord Maitreya and with our bands.

Truly, God-government is seated in the God Star Sirius. Truly, the cosmic councils and those who enforce the Light in these several galaxies are centered there. Thus having the Messenger anchoring the Light of Sirius, thus having the chelas giving daily the calls to me, does establish [on earth] truly an intensity of the causal body of the God Star—the origin of ye all.

Whether or not your souls have passed through various systems or planetary homes, beloved ones, you have come from that source. And from that source the greatest patriots in all nations, the founding fathers of the twelve tribes and of this nation have come. Wherever you understand the sight, the vision itself of one who contains and understands true God Self-government, you may know that that one learned it on the God Star and practiced it again, whether on Venus or Mercury or elsewhere.

Beloved hearts, God-government of and by and for the people through the Holy Christ Self must reign on earth. This is an hour, then, of the moving on of the old guard, both of the

---
*satyagraha [Skt.]: pressure for social and political reform through cheerful nonviolent resistance practiced by Mohandas K. Gandhi and his followers. As he defined it: "Truth (satya) implies love, and firmness (agraha) engenders and therefore serves as a synonym for force... that is to say, the force which is born of truth and love or nonviolence."

right and of the left wing. And therefore both sides seem to suffer loss.

And there comes a new generation of individuals who do not so identify with the rigidity or the fanaticism or the "impersonalness" of these causes; but rather, there do come to the fore those new-age lifestreams sent with the flame of Sirius and the violet transmuting flame and the beautiful aqua of the Mother and the power of the golden pink glow-ray.

These colorations of the aura are being seen now in the new babes that are born and in their auras as they come into the new dispensation that is heralded even in this very hour, that has to do with the great causal body of Sanat Kumara and the mantle of Sanat Kumara—that of Guru placed upon the Messenger by Padma Sambhava.[1]

And therefore, I speak of the celestial birth astrology of the Messenger that has to do with the signs of starry bodies and far-off worlds, far beyond the planetary systems of this solar system. Thus, beloved ones, at the turning of the hour and the turning of the tide of this birth year of the Messenger, understand the open door that comes from Sirius and the point of that God Star in relationship to the natal chart of the United States of America and of the Woman clothed with the Sun, who does indeed stand before you.

Look not, then, to the flesh but to the Sun behind the sun. For behind the form, behind the manifestation, there is the reality of the true Person of whom I speak. And the twain are one, and yet the seen and the unseen remain even the riddle of your own life.

Understand then, beloved hearts, that in this hour of all cycles turning it is necessary for the new generation of lightbearers to hear the Word of El Morya and of the Darjeeling Council of the Great White Brotherhood and to understand, beloved ones, that the Truth that is proclaimed must be proclaimed by the full power of Love—by the momentum of Love that is not compromised by a sympathetic socialism or an impersonal republicanism that fails to apprehend the level of human evolution or fails to take into account how the divine evolution can enter the human and transform it.

And therefore, ultimately, the programs of governments and societies need not be based upon the lowest common denominator of the individual but upon the potential of that individual when harnessed to the God Star, to the Mighty I AM Presence, and to the causal body—which always contains the divine astrology that is ready to transmute that which is not of the Light [in the human astrology], even as it is ready to transmute that which is not of the Light in the astral belt, the electronic belt, of the individual.

Do you see, beloved ones? It is a question of whether we are going to plight* the fate of the planetary body based upon the lower consciousness of the human or based upon the Divinity entering that consciousness and transforming man and society right before his very own eyes.

I tell you that it is true that many of you who have come to the Path and who pursue diligently the Call and the sacred fire and the sacrifice and personal transmutation and service have come to see yourselves so transformed, so rejuvenated—with the cycles of burden and care literally swept from you by the solar wind of the polestar!

Beloved ones, the transformation is so great that I can only say to you that this is an example of exactly what can happen to the planetary home. And therefore, let us plan for planet Earth based upon the accelerating cycles of the lightbearers, for truly the lightbearers have become the ensign of the people—the sign of every man's highest potential in the pure Christ Truth.

Let us call Christ, then, "Truth"—for Truth is surely another name for the Universal Christ. When individuals espouse Truth at any cost and are willing to face the Truth of reality and unreality, then we have a strong foundation for golden-age man and golden-age woman to arise. Believe me, beloved hearts, when I tell you that so many social programs and solutions simply do not work because there is not a concomitant Reality that goes hand in hand with the development of the human potential.

Thus, we must go back to the path of true meditation and not that auto-self-hypnosis that is taught by the Maharishi and many others who come in the name of the Eastern gurus who have not the true link to the Source and are in fact false gurus and false teachers. And, I must say, they are also black magicians; for they have succeeded in securing† the lifestream and harnessing it to a rote performance of an ancient ritual that comes from the Holy Kumaras and is sacred and ought not to be given for the sake of outer gain or manipulation.

Beloved hearts, the entering in to the sacred fire is indeed a ritual and it is an initiation. Can man by himself pull himself up by his own bootstraps? It is not possible. There must be the divine intercession. And this is why we speak. And this is why the system of dictation, initiation, the washing of the waters of the human by

---
*to engage
†"sealing" the lifestream from the exercise of his own free will, as in "taking into 'protective' custody"

the cleansing of the mind and the chakras does come about.

And blessed are ye who tarry for my coming. For, beloved, truly in the eleventh hour is the victory won. Truly does Maitreya appear! Truly, there comes the one to reward those who endure and who know the reality of Jophiel and the Mind of God and the wisdom of the Buddha and the full power of Nada in the love ray as she does come the advocate, the attorney, and the counselor at the bar—at the very Court of Cosmic Justice.

Neglect not, then, this training in law. For by the very law of cosmos, the law of music, the law of geometry, and the law of the Logos defending the right, human and divine, of the individual are all things established. Therefore, define Morya's three dots as the three manifestations of the law of sound, geometry, and of the very science of jurisprudence whereby life is either on the right or the wrong side of the very line of time and space itself.

Beloved hearts, you who champion the cause of the people: I tell you in this hour, it is the spoken and the written Word combined with the fohat of the heart that will move the nation as nations have been moved before. Therefore, we vest in those whom we call—we vest the sacred fire and the potential for the development of Truth.

I place before each and every one of you representing the flame of freedom and God-government to America and the nations the opportunity to now accelerate through the very heart of Pallas Athena, who did begin the Coming Revolution in Higher Consciousness as an organized movement and delivery of the Truth in every area of life.[2]

Therefore, *Heart* magazine for the Coming Revolution in Higher Consciousness becomes the forum and the format for the delivery of that Truth to the nations. And many have been quickened and ignited by the sparks that have flown through those articles.

Beloved ones, I, Surya, send the call from the God Star. Understand my plea. For we are determined to save the nations with a handful (relatively speaking) of Truth-bearers, of Christ-bearers juxtaposed against thousands by the ten thousands of the masses of the gray ones who come with their line, with their rationalization.

Whether in South Africa, whether in Afghanistan, whether in any nation or city, I tell you, beloved ones, the liar and his lie is always ready. Let the Truth appear in one individual and he will be cast down as you have seen the casting down of the one called to the Philippines.[3] And then who is left? When that one is cast down, beloved hearts, around whom shall the forces of Light rally?

Thus, they are divided and there is a babble of voices once again—each one saying, "This is what Aquino would have said! This is what Aquino would have done!" And therefore Aquino appears as a Communist, as a Marxist, as one in the right wing and the middle of the road. And all think that they know who is the real Aquino and what he would have done. This is the price to be paid when you have not the satyagraha, when you have not the fullness of the flaming presence of Truth.

Beloved hearts, understand that it is the sacred fire, it is oneness with Archangel Michael and all the hosts of the LORD, it is the building of those chakras and the raising of the Kundalini that does make the individual able to stand in the day when those forces come forth out of the pit and all of hell breaks loose to quell one voice and one heart flame.

These things ought not to be. Therefore, Maitreya has formed his army of Light. And that army of Light and lightbearers is *you*. You are the ones who move as the legions of The Faithful and True. You are the ones whose auras whitened John saw as he described these armies with white raiment and the saints in heaven.[4] Thus, when there is the army, then there is the protection of those within that very many who are able to carry the sword of Truth and to deliver the Word. And the sure defense, issue by issue—both of the Truth and the individuals who bear it—does come to pass.

Beloved ones, time and time again, those who espouse the right cause and that which we would defend come to the fore and have not the protection of the Great White Brotherhood and do not accept the blessing of the Messenger or the mantle of Saint Germain; and they are struck down in the very midst of their fight.

Sometimes this is because they are not cleansed and the ego does get in the way. Sometimes it is because they are so sure that they have the truth and that they have the right personality, that [they think] they need no other protection. And in some cases, beloved hearts, they are devout but their religion has been stripped, watered down, refined so that in the mere recitation of the rosary, as powerful as it may be, they do not have sufficient defense before the courts of hell itself and those who plot their murder.

Beloved ones, we have seen this especially in the last century. We have seen that many causes which could have been brought to fruition have not been brought to fruition simply because the ones who could have executed them were themselves executed.

Beloved hearts, this is a very serious plight of the planet. And even when those who are mediocre arrive at the top in many Third World countries (as you have called them), they are struck down by their rivals. And therefore, brother against brother defeat one another, and the cause of Truth in the nation is lost in a morass of human personality and vendetta and age-old vengeance that goes back many centuries.

How are we to save a planetary body? Those of you who have had experience in the world know that only when there is the mustering of forces and the decree patterns and a one-pointedness by Keepers of the Flame worldwide do those efforts succeed which challenge the entire downward course of politicking East to West in this civilization.

I advocate, then, that those who have a mind to understand what ought to be checked and a mind to see the strategy of how the force does move the chessmen on the board of life—point and counterpoint—come to an understanding* and present to the Messenger those things which must be looked to immediately and which, if they are not looked to immediately, will therefore be a part of the loss of the planet as a whole.

There are areas in this nation and in the world that must have constant work to forestall those events which should† come to pass that will have a lasting negative impact for centuries to come—if the planetary body does indeed endure.

Beloved ones, therefore understand that there are some things that can wait until tomorrow for the call, and there are other things that cannot wait. Therefore, let us understand the three dots of El Morya as these apply to the trinity of the government, the society, and the economy. Let us understand the meaning of education[5] as a foundation for all of these and as a major influence as to which way the nations go.

Let us come together and reason and see how, by the strategy of the God Star Sirius, we are able to turn back the tide point/counterpoint. Understanding how to play chess, then, you know that in each move you may have but one chance to check the enemy. And if, beloved ones, you misuse it and divert your forces to some lesser situation, you find that you will not come out ahead in the end. Thus, one takes the move that is most essential to protect one's position and to enter the point of vulnerability of the enemy.

One must understand that there is indeed a tide. And one

---
*reach a consensus as to which are the most vital issues
†are expected to

can calculate the points of vulnerability. One must understand the time for negotiation and the time, beloved hearts, to stand fast and realize that there is no reason to give an inch, for you hold all the right cards—the right forces and the right moves.

Beloved ones, it seems that there is a pattern of self-hypnosis in the government of this nation and that the leadership has not understood for many decades the position of power it could have enjoyed under the aegis of the God Star Sirius and our posture of God-government. And the obvious reason why is that they were not of the Light and they loved the darkness, because their deeds were evil[6]—no matter what face they have presented to the American people.

There have been very few lightbearers that have held a high office in this land, though many have taken the patine of Light by espousing right causes—at the very same time seeing to it that those causes are not supported, are not given the right appropriation, whether of money or of personnel, and are not seen through.

Thus, we are very accustomed to high-sounding and hollow phrases. We are accustomed to those who give speeches by speech writers and yet themselves do not carry a Sword or the Book of the Law and are not overshadowed by the Mighty Blue Eagle.

We cannot pump up and elevate any individual beyond his station. We have tried it. The Messenger has tried it. It has been tried in all past ages. Unless the individual have the sturdiness of his own momentum of the Light and can carry the balance of that Light, he will not stand up against the pressure directed against the one who is falsely elevated to a certain level of opportunity, nor will he have the wherewithal to meet the opposition to the office.

The only alternative, of course, is to invoke the sacred presence of Archangel Gabriel, the Holy Christ Self, and the full power of the Cosmic Christ over such individuals—not to mention the members of the Darjeeling Council and our own seat of God-government. This will work for a time, but the Great Law eventually bows to free will.

Blessed ones, you remember the era of the judges in Israel—when there were no kings in the land and God did send His judges to assist the people to maintain the standard of right conduct, right usefulness, and oneness with the Lord.

Beloved ones, understand the meaning and the purpose of Christ the Judge within you. There are forces in the earth who will surely destroy this planet unless they are brought to the judgment. Therefore, the Four and Twenty Elders have positioned themselves in the etheric octave over this city of Light that their direct presence might be invoked by you for a more sure and swift action.[7]

I authorize you by Alpha and Omega this night to perpetually call for the judgment of the lowest ten percent of the evolutions of the planetary home—the dark ones who carry nothing but destruction and viciousness and the malignancy of the murderous intent in their auras and in their four lower bodies. These individuals are in every nation, in every race, in and out of the courts of Church and State.

Beloved ones, the lowest common denominator of the bottom ten percent representing Absolute Evil must be brought to the judgment by perpetual calls. We need, in fact, a novena—a prayer vigil of the hours in consonance with that to Archangel Michael—of the judgment calls you have been given by Helios and Vesta and Mother Mary with Gautama Buddha.

Understand the meaning of the calling forth of God Justice. For the Judge himself, beloved Alpha in the Great Central Sun, has already judged these fallen ones when they were cast out of heaven. It remains for the Omega in the earth to ratify that judgment.

And who is that Omega? It is each and every one of you who raises up the Omega flame and the white fire. And some of you have a greater momentum than others on the flame of the Divine Mother, but all of you can acquire a mighty momentum of purity and sacred fire through the path of the consecration of that pure white-fire energy.

I urge you to consecrate, therefore, the sacred fire and the life-force and to raise it up the spinal altar and to use it in the spoken Word for the denouncing and the judgment and the bringing to trial before the Court of the Sacred Fire on the God Star Sirius—as the Messenger has done for so many a year—of these bottom ten percent of the evolutionary scale.

And I do not speak of primitive man versus developed or sophisticated man. I speak of the lower evolution in reference to those who have amalgamated the cause of Absolute Evil and therefore themselves become depraved even in their sophistication.

Beloved hearts, these individuals are for the most part criminals—even if they occupy key positions in the banking houses, the governments, the institutions of the nations, and everywhere holding a voice, a position, and a mask of authority when within they are ravening wolves. You will find more of them to be rich than poor, and more of them to be powerful rather than in the ghettos or on skid row. These are individuals that many times you would not suspect.

And your judgment calls have already brought forth a national investigation of the banking houses who have admittedly laundered the funds of the Mafia gathered in the purveying of drugs and the poisoning of the youth. And these funds, beloved ones, have been handled by legitimate organizations. And I tell you, those who have handled them and laundered these funds are criminals before the Court of the Sacred Fire, for they aid and abet the entire cause of Death and Hell to the ruination of the bodies and the minds and the souls of the youth and all people.[8]

Beloved ones, it is such a serious trial for us to observe those whom we might use in this nation beset with drugs that are eating away at the very fabric of the sheaths of the nerves and the brain and the chakras themselves, that we deplore each and every one and all upon the planetary home who are a part of this international drug ring—from the peasants who make the first portions of cocaine and heroin and prepare the marijuana to those who purvey it and sit as king of the mountain with their millions and billions of dollars and therefore are in a position to control nations and military forces and armaments and to give aid to the enemy itself: World Communism.

This, as serious as it is, is equally matched by the international holocaust [that is taking place] through abortion—taking the lives of the best servants, upsetting the economy, creating an imbalance in supply and demand for goods, [resulting in] an emptying of the houses of learning and education, an emptying of the cradles and the places where children and their joy and their laughter should ring from earth to heaven.

Beloved ones, the unbalancing of the planetary body by the hordes of Death and Hell is so great that, **by the great causal body of the avatars who should be descending, I do authorize you in the name of Alpha and Omega to make haste and to enter speedily into those calls for the removal from the planet of those lifestreams who simply will without question cause the destruction of the earth unless something be done.**

I come, then, with this knowledge as well as this dispensation in answer to a call that was made a number of years ago by the Messenger for that selective and discriminatory judgment whereby the aversion of cataclysm may come when the darkest of lifestreams whose karma is the very cause of that cataclysm are removed.

Understand that this can be done. And as the cycles turn and the divine astrology of the Woman clothed with the Sun does come to bear as a great boon and a grace upon all children of the Light, there is the opening of the way, then, to withdraw certain lifestreams from the earth who otherwise could not have been withdrawn; for their very death itself would have produced the imbalance and the cataclysm feared by God and man alike—in the sense of the awesomeness of Cosmic Law that should have been unleashed.*

You see, to truly take the dark ones from the planetary home, there must be the removal from that home of all of the roots of evil and karma and the interconnection of those lifestreams in a network of darkness. For they are a part of what is known as a "beast," which is a conglomerate, an "amalgamate" of forces and consciousnesses that become part of a computer—a mind that has extensions [tentacles] and works simultaneously in many manifestations of individuals engaged in international organized crime, including World Communism, which is nothing but organized crime on the level of the state.

Beloved ones of Light, I speak to you in this hour, then, that you might understand that it is not the "death" of the seed of the wicked, but it is the removal of their momentum and the layers of their darkness and their karma that is essential. The passing from the screen of life of the body itself is of little consequence unless all that is behind it—in this case, the black sun that they have fashioned through the misuse of the Light—is also taken.

And therefore, let us work diligently at inner levels for the binding and the judgment of the "dweller on the threshold"— which means the entire momentum of the anti-self of these fallen ones. When that is judged and bound, then there is very little left that can operate against the good of society, save the shell itself, which [nonetheless] may become occupied by new possessing demons or by astral forces or extraterrestrial forces.

Therefore, ultimately the individual himself must suffer that judgment. But we are not standing here in advocacy of calling for the death penalty for individuals. We are advocating the call of the judgment, which is the binding of the momentum of evil. For that momentum itself is the darkness which is used by those who have the intent to destruction. When the momentum is removed and when those of virtue fill their [own] bodies and the planetary home with Light, you see, the mouthpiece of Absolute Evil then becomes no more significant than an ant or a colony of ants.

Beloved hearts, understand therefore that the equation is one of proportion and commeasurement. Thus, we advocate the clearing of the astral plane itself and of the worst of these forces

---
*could have been expected to have been unleashed

and of the worst of the momentum, as I have said.

Beloved ones, this is the best and highest solution that can be offered in this hour, given the state of the earth. And this is the deliberation of the Cosmic Council and of the Four and Twenty Elders and the Council of the God Star Sirius.

Understand that we have worked many months with the Darjeeling Council and with the Council of the Royal Teton. And under the advice of Lord Gautama Buddha, Maitreya, Lord Sanat Kumara, and the Cosmic Council of Alpha and Omega, we have come to this understanding and this decision within the framework of Cosmic Law and we fully believe that with the cooperation of the wise and prudent and harmonious lifestreams such as are gathered in this activity, we may make progress in giving this dispensation and authorizing your moving forward with the speed of Light to implement these calls.

Beloved hearts, this must be accompanied by great protection and tremendous devotion to the violet flame beginning with beloved Omri-Tas, [the Ruler of the Violet Planet, and] all the rulers of the violet planet, the 144,000 priests of the sacred fire from the violet planet, and the full powers of all beings of the seventh ray.

The violet-flame action sweeps through and does devour with a mighty conflagration of the seventh ray the cause, effect, record, and memory of the debris that is left when a nucleus of the eye of the serpent in the core of the dweller on the threshold is bound and taken by the Mighty Elohim and the archangels.

Thus, understand that this is a cooperation of elemental life, of the hosts of the LORD, and of you yourselves. And I trust that we may count on you to perform this service in the full understanding that once you begin it, it is like being on a roller coaster of cosmic proportions—you must keep on moving with it, you must keep on giving the calls, lest you yourselves become vulnerable to the lashback that does surely come when these manifestations are abroad in the land.

Beloved hearts of sacred fire, understand the penetrability and the penetration of the Godhead.[9] Understand that the saving of a planet has many options. Some of these options are limited, beloved ones, because of the karmic entanglements of the lightbearers themselves [with the fallen ones whose judgment is nigh].

Therefore, as a corollary to these calls, the call to cut loose and set free the lightbearers from the entanglements with the seed of the wicked must be made. Many have not heeded the call to come apart and be a separate people.[10] And they have toyed with evil, they have been fascinated by the cult of death—and thus they have allowed themselves to be tied to a karmic juggernaut of the dark ones.

Thus, I pray that with Mother Mary you will see how necessary it is to cut free the lightbearers who themselves [because of their affinities with the dark ones] do not even resemble lightbearers. Even now El Morya does answer the daily calls of the Messenger and chelas to cut free all who must make their ascension in this life. These individuals are indeed being cut free. And they themselves know they are being cut free. And they even write in to Summit University saying they are being cut free and all things are being arranged for them to be a part of this community.

Thus, beloved ones, the diligence and the astuteness of the decreer is important. It is important that you make attunement with the highest Source of your I AM Presence. It is essential that you fast weekly—that your sensitivities beyond this octave be quickened and that you can determine easily what forces you are dealing with and therefore not be set back or, pray not,* be overturned by any attempt of the fallen ones to move in.[11] For the more you enter into this service, the more you become truly Maitreya in manifestation as the bodhisattvas serving under him, the more you become the most undesirable to the hordes of darkness.

They tremble in this hour of my speaking, beloved ones. They have attempted to deter this dictation, but I tell you, they shall not pass. And I hold none of you accountable but all of you to come into a greater attunement and alertness that you become one flaming sword Excalibur as an entire body and community moving with The Faithful and True and those Masters who call you from time to time.

Beloved El Morya and beloved Saint Patrick have had great experience in many embodiments in waging strategic warfare against the fallen ones. And by strategy, sometimes strategy alone, they have been able to set back those forces of evil. And therefore, they have incurred the wrath of Serpents so much and to such an extent that Saint Patrick had no other choice but to enter into direct confrontation with these fallen ones in Ireland.

And I assure you that those Nephilim kings and those pagans were every whit as powerful, every whit as presumptuous as those who operate today at the highest echelons of world control. They were no small forces to be tackled.

Therefore, beloved hearts of Light, remember the advocate

---
*"God forbid"

Oromasis and Diana. Remember Justinius—how could you forget him? Remember Serapis Bey. Remember all who have stood in all centuries and who have won. Remember that it was their faith in God. Remember George Washington and Moses and Joshua and those who have stood against enormous odds. And keep on remembering that it is the one who has carried the Sword and the Banner of Truth who has stood again and again.

And there is an electrifying and a quickening presence, and I will tell you a secret: The Universal Christ takes the aura of the one who pursues Truth and embodies it in the path of the satyagraha, beloved ones, and does duplicate that aura again and again and again, so that there is a quickening of the mind of that one. And that mind becomes the spark that ignites millions.

And therefore, you have seen in Francis Bacon how one mind could actually ignite a new age through the writing, through the science, through the determination, through the plays, through the cipher, through the code, through the mysteries. And yet, all of this, though we recount many works of Francis Bacon—it all comes down to the fact that above and beyond all that was done, there was the mysterious force of the Godhead that truly multiplied his presence on the earth far beyond that which one human being could ever accomplish.[12]

Why, the human being alone is nothing but the monkey mind, nothing but the evolved animal. It takes far more than this to change the course of men and nations and civilizations!

And therefore, let us leave off from thinking that we will ever accomplish this by the mere mortal manifestation of selfhood. Thus, I urge you to rise beyond it, to believe you can rise beyond it, to know you are rising beyond it, and to know that the Sun behind the sun of manifestation—truly the Son of God shining in all His strength[13]—is your divine Reality. And you are actually in a position today to move heaven and earth and cosmic forces and to bind the dark ones.

And if you will get this through your heads, beloved ones, and beyond your heads, if you will unite with the force of the Christ Mind with you—you will see this Revolution in Higher Consciousness here and now. And you will see those turning of worlds even as the Messenger has experienced (even with some astonishment, for God is always astonishing) how, when one presents oneself as a vessel and a mouthpiece, God moves in. God will use the individual. God will take command and perform such a mighty work that you can scarcely believe that the work has happened and is happening before your very eyes!

Copyright © 1985 Church Universal and Triumphant, Inc.

This is the nature of the divine afflatus of the descent of the Holy Spirit through the Great White Brotherhood. I say, Pull the ripcord! Take advantage of it. Plan not only for the human but plan for the Divine in manifestation. And see what wonders God will work through you.

Beloved ones, it is the astuteness of the Mind of Sirius to which I recommend your dear hearts. And I turn your attention to the God Star each and every hour. Let your attention be upon the All-Seeing Eye of God. Come to know and count as dearest friends the members of the Karmic Board. I daresay the Messenger has called upon them so many tens of thousands of times that their friendship is as near, truly, as heartbeat and yet also as far as distant star—which is not far either, for the calls to the God Star Sirius have brought that star as close as the very air that you breathe.

Beloved ones, the potential is present. You need to lock into my words. Believe them. Act upon them. Stand guard, do not let down your guard, and be the watchmen of the night. Thus is my message to you complete.

And thus is your service of devotion fully noted and recorded by the Keeper of the Scrolls, who stands to my side observing and writing with many recording angels who have observed your lifestreams and those of lightbearers, freedom fighters, and Keepers of the Flame throughout the planet. For the record of the saints is read in heaven long before the saints even consider that they are saints.

I salute you in the cosmic cross of white fire. And by the heart of the ruby ray, I now turn the cycle and I now release the divine astrology for the Messenger's birthday in this hour. And so, it is done. And so, may you leap to that divine astrology of the causal body and know that at inner levels it is a fireworks of blue lightning and of violet and of fiery pink and of golden yellow. And you can see now the release of Light. Thus, capture the stars and run, for truly the name "Woman Clothed with the Sun" derives from this cosmic astrology.

Rejoice, beloved ones, for things are different in this hour than they were ten hours before.

In the name of the God Star, I salute you. Rejoice!

[applause, standing ovation]

"The Summit Lighthouse Sheds Its Radiance O'er All the World to Manifest as Pearls of Wisdom."
This dictation by Surya was delivered through the Messenger of the Great White Brotherhood Elizabeth Clare Prophet on Easter Sunday, April 7, 1985, during the 5-day Easter Conclave at Camelot.

Messenger's note to students: Study this Pearl from Beloved Surya carefully, outlining it and noting its salient points, just as I have outlined the previous Pearls for you with paragraph headings. This message from the Central Sun is too sacred to be touched; thus Surya requested it be sent to you as an integrated whole for your assimilation. The poetry and mystical communion of next week's Pearl by Beloved Gautama Buddha is also too transcendent to be divided. Nevertheless, neglect not its step-by-step revelation for your adeptship by taking carefully outlined notes.
(1) See *Pearls of Wisdom,* vol. 28, no. 11, p. 132, n. 3. (2) See Pallas Athena, June 30, 1976, "America: Ye Shall Know the Truth and the Truth Shall Make You Free," on 8-cassette album *Higher Consciousness* (A7650), $50.00; single cassette B7650, $6.50. (3) See *Pearls of Wisdom,* vol. 28, no. 12, p. 148, n. 14. (4) Rev. 19:11–14. (5) In this case Keepers of the Flame can decree for the government under the Father, the society under the Holy Spirit, the economy under the Son, and the education under the Mother. (6) John 3:19. (7) See Archangel Michael, February 3, 1985, "The Summoning: Straight Talk and a Sword from the Hierarch of Banff," *Pearls of Wisdom,* vol. 28, no. 10, p. 112. (8) In its first crime study report entitled "The Cash Connection: Organized Crime, Financial Institutions, and Money Laundering" (issued October 1984), the President's Commission on Organized Crime stated: "The need to launder money has led organized crime to avail itself of the full range of banking services normally associated with legitimate, multinational businesses." Following a federal investigation, the Bank of Boston pleaded guilty to a felony charge in February 1985 for failing to report $1.22 billion in cash shipments to and from nine foreign banks. According to the Boston *Globe,* the bank also had sold millions of dollars' worth of cashier's checks to the alleged Mafia family, the Angiulos (who often brought thousands of dollars into a bank branch in paper bags), and had exempted two Angiulos' firms from required reporting of cash transactions. A reported 40–60 U.S. banks are being investigated by the Treasury Department for failure to comply with the reporting law (Bank Secrecy Act of 1970), in which banks and other financial institutions must file a report when they accept a cash transaction of more than $10,000. In March 1985, the Senate Subcommittee on Investigations held hearings on the burgeoning money-laundering problem, in which an estimated $100 billion is laundered through U.S. institutions annually from drug trafficking and other crimes such as prostitution, illegal gambling, and loan sharking. (9) "The Penetrability of the Godhead," November 3, 1968, unpublished lecture by Mark L. Prophet. (10) II Cor. 6:14–18. (11) Keepers of the Flame fast weekly on Saturday with Lanello, using the violet flame, physical exercise and internal cleansing to give the physical body its Sabbath rest. Their 24–36 hour regimen varies from distilled water with lemon juice, to either vegetable or fruit juices, with or without vitamins and minerals. Those under doctor's orders not to fast may find an all fruit or all raw-vegetable day (including a variety of salads, seeds, nuts and sprouts with combination juice or protein drinks) to be a healthful adjunct to the rest and purification of the body. Fasting is a habit which the physical body and the body elemental take to easily and with delight. Herb teas made with distilled water provide a comforting spiritual fast for all one's members. Keepers of the Flame break their fasts Sunday morning with grated carrot and cabbage doused with lemon juice only. Three hours later they partake of fruit or a cooked leafy green vegetable with mineral broth. (The first full meal should be light and sensible. Avoid overeating and skip dessert. Do not partake of flesh foods until the following day; take yogurt and acidophilus to reestablish the friendly intestinal bacteria.) The goal of this ritual of fasting is for spiritual purification—the self-emptying, that the Holy Spirit may enter in. Many have discovered healthful side benefits, such as weight normalization, detoxification, mental clarity, and physical inner peace. (12) See Elizabeth Clare Prophet, *The Golden Age Prince: A Lecture on Francis Bacon,* 2-cassette album (A83176), $9.95. (13) Rev. 1:16.

Copyright © 1985 Church Universal and Triumphant, Inc., Box A, Malibu, CA 90265. All rights reserved. Printed in the United States of America. Pearls of Wisdom and The Summit Lighthouse are registered trademarks of Church Universal and Triumphant, Inc. All rights to their use are reserved. Published by The Summit Lighthouse. Pearls sent weekly (to USA, via third-class mail) for a minimum love offering of $40/year.

WHEN AMERICA DISCOVERED TWIN FLAMES

LOVE WINS OUT
In This Lifetime...or the Next

★ Jeanette MacDonald ★
★ Nelson Eddy ★
The story of the perfect match trapped in the net of karma

"Sweetheart, sweetheart, sweetheart," Nelson Eddy sang. Suddenly from the rear of the theater came the voice of a woman, joining him in duet. The packed audience turned in amazement. She was walking down the aisle, singing back to him. By the end of the song, she was on stage looking into his eyes and the audience was standing and cheering.

She was his co-star in eight films, Jeanette MacDonald. Their love was plain for all to see, recalls Frank Laric, who was sitting in the third row. Nelson hadn't even known she was in town. "Where'd you come from?" he asked as the audience wildly applauded.

"I got in last night," she said. He asked her to dinner and then they sang "Indian Love Call" together.

In these magic moments and in those replayed in theaters across the nation, America discovered twin flames.

It was the summer of 1941. Theirs was the perfect match and more, twin flames to a T—two hearts in three-quarter time. Although their romance blossomed in May, it never came to fruition.

Seeing their love on screen, hearing it in their duets as their eyes told one another and the whole world the pain of a forbidden love, more than one generation of Americans have been introduced to that special love of twin flames. Although not many people today sit down and listen to Jeanette and Nelson sing arias, their music and especially their films have a timeless appeal which transcends a bland corniness in plot and dialogue. That appeal, that mysterious ingredient, is the love that everyone seeks, but few find, in the union of twin flames.

Yet they were forced to hide that real-life romance from the world. Official studio history and fan magazines billed them as casual friends who sometimes argued and who were blissfully married to other people.

49

LOVE WINS OUT

Not a publicity photo. This shows their real-life romance as Nelson throws caution to the winds and gives Jeanette a birthday embrace.

And that story might have stood forever had it not been for the efforts of Sharon Rich and Diane Goodrich who released their book *Farewell to Dreams* in 1979. They compiled it not from the papier-mâché newspaper accounts of the day, but from Nelson's and Jeanette's friends, neighbors, and relatives who finally agreed to tell the truth—and from doormen, maids, and extras who filled in details and corroborated evidence. "Every line in there," Sharon says, "is verbatim from what somebody told us, as closely as possible."

Sharon and Diane discovered a massive cover-up by the studio and by Nelson and Jeanette, who swore their friends to secrecy. They found that they were in fact wildly in love, more deeply than any of their characters, in a romance that spanned 30 years.

But Jeanette's ambition, their occasionally violent tempers, and a strange combination of people and circumstances kept them apart for their entire lives. So it seems that things do not always turn out right, even when you do find your twin flame.

Their life story is a tragedy of twin flames. It includes an implicit warning to us in our quest for our perfect love: if we do not overcome our karma, we can never enjoy complete happiness whether or not we find our twin flame.

Naturally, Sharon and Diane's story begins as a fairy tale should: love at first sight, or at least instant recognition. Jeanette's sister Blossom was flipping through a newspaper when a picture caught her eye. "Who is that?" said Jeanette, making her go back to a certain page. She knew she had to go and hear Nelson Eddy sing.

Nelson first saw, or rather heard, Jeanette at MGM studios where they were both under contract. He had been signed on in 1933, a successful opera singer and—as young, handsome opera singers were in those days—a sex symbol. His fans, mostly women, treated him like a rock star, even ripping his clothes off after concerts.

Nelson followed her bewitching voice into a sound stage where she was filming *The Merry Widow*. As he watched her on stage, he fell in love. She fit the image of that one girl he'd always dreamed of. A few days later, he asked her to lunch. She agreed, but only reluctantly as she did not want to become entangled in a relationship that might endanger her career. Yet as their romance continued, her love grew. Nelson made her, a 30-year-old glamour queen, feel like she was on her first date. Could the fairy tale she had portrayed so many times on screen be happening to her?

"He kissed me, it's like nothing I ever felt before," she told her mother. "Around him I feel beautifully elated, and when he looks at you, there's no one else, just you."

In their romance we see other telltale signs of a twin flame relationship. Their love was far more than a magnetic attraction—it showed in every part of their lives. Together, they had a radiance that was lacking when they were apart. The films they made singly are mostly unmemorable, but together they were able to tap their inner potential as twin flames united can, and their films broke box-office records.

Their radiant screen presence, the very real quality of their love and the now-revealed pathos of their separation made the eight

Rose Marie, 1936

movies the MacDonald/Eddy team filmed from 1935 to 1942 some of the most poignant love stories ever portrayed by Hollywood.

Their popularity is timeless. MGM re-released several of their films in the late '50s and early '60s and recently put out three of them on video. Their loyal fans, young and old, still rally around their three fan clubs, one the oldest in existence.

Their love did not fade as their bodies grew older. He still saw her as she had looked on their first meeting. "Beauty comes from the soul," Nelson said in 1958. "The body is just a cover. Sure, it ages and gets worn. But it's the person himself who radiates beauty, or doesn't. That's why I'll care for Miss MacDonald till the day I die."

Feeling his love, Jeanette would light up like a firefly whenever he was near, becoming a different person in his presence.

Their undying love, another sign of twin flames, extended beyond that one life, or so they believed.

Sharon and Diane discovered that both believed in reincarnation. In the 1930s, a psychic told Jeanette that she had known Nelson before when they lived as brother and sister in the 1830s in England. On the trail of the MacDonald-Eddy story, Diane Goodrich went to another psychic, saying nothing of what Jeanette had learned, and this psychic gave exactly the same reading.

Although it is easy to expect that twin flames would always be lovers, that is not necessarily the case. A brother-sister relationship does not preclude a soul mate or twin flame bond, as the love of twin flames stretches beyond one or two lifetimes back to the point of creation.

In the brother-sister mode, it can establish a bond of commitment and pristine love, a mutual adoration and achievement. It is a very real part of the spiral that builds, lifetime after lifetime, between twin flames preparing for that ultimate union wherein the fruit of their love becomes a unique contribution upon the altar of humanity. A love so powerful as to elevate and ennoble all it touches and to purify and renew the stream of mankind's awareness of what true love can be and conquer.

Jeanette and Nelson also believed in karma—that they were

responsible for the current circumstances of their lives, which were the result of their past actions. They must have had a fair amount of karma between them, as twin flames often do, for, as it turns out, the course of their love did not run smooth.

Their story has a villain—an ugly stepmother, a troll beneath the bridge. It came packaged in the form of megalomaniac Louis B. Mayer, the power broker of MGM. When Nelson fell in love with Jeanette, the fledgling star was in the usual sexual submission to her patron, and he did not like the "baritone." For one thing, Nelson had already been successful in his own right and did not owe his career to MGM. Therefore, he was the only star on the lot who didn't kowtow to Louis.

Anna MacDonald, Jeanette's mother, and Louis were quick to point out to her that she risked all she had worked so hard for by falling for "a mere singer."

Frightened for her career, she began pretending to ignore Nelson. But he made it clear that he didn't care what her past contained, including a relationship to Louis. "What we have together cannot be lightly dismissed.... When the chips are down and you want someone who really cares, just remember I'm real," he said.

They began filming *Naughty Marietta*, their first film together, in 1935. When it became apparent it would be a hit, making Jeanette a superstar, Louis gave her her freedom. He didn't like to sleep with his stars—it might spoil their reputation. But he still had it in for her new boyfriend.

During the last half of the filming, Nelson and Jeanette's love grew and blossomed. "Around him she felt strangely pure and naïve," *Farewell to Dreams* tells us.

They both knew it was far more than just a fling. "From the very first time I saw her, that was it. She answered every unspoken thought, every desire I've ever dreamed. It's as if I cannot be, I cannot exist without her," Nelson later told "Pop" Leonard, their director.

When *Naughty Marietta* became one of the top films of the year, the public clamored for more MacDonald/Eddy. By the time they began their second film, *Rose Marie*, which features "Indian Love Call" ("When I'm calling you ou ou ou ou ou ou"),

> *Seeing their love on screen, hearing it in their duets as their eyes told one another and the whole world the pain of a forbidden love, more than one generation of Americans have been introduced to that special love of twin flames.*

they were madly in love, all pretense forgotten, and Jeanette had never been so happy in her life.

Like true soul mates, they brought out the best in each other—he assisting her in singing and she helping him with acting. To their director, cast, and crew it was clear: they had been made for each other.

At Lake Tahoe, the film site, their love progressed down a primrose path. They rode horses together, made love, he asked her to marry him and she accepted. She adored the beautiful emerald ring encircled by diamonds he gave her. "Oh, Nelson, I promise I'll wear it forever. That way you'll always be near me." But, always the star, she wanted to wait until June and have a big wedding.

And this was to cost them all. For looming beneath the calm sea of their love was the rock of ambition on which their lives were to be wrecked. Sharon and Diane give us this scene:

Soon Jeanette discovered she was pregnant. He was ecstatic, wanting an immediate wedding,

> *The plot of Maytime filled Nelson with a sense of foreboding. He believed they had ruined their lives before and were repeating the pattern now.*

but she was irritated with him for not understanding. In those days if a female star got married or pregnant in or out of wedlock without the studio's permission, her contract was null and void.

As the reality of karmic circumstance surrounded her like a concrete wall, the pressure became too great. To have a baby, she thought, would destroy her. "I won't have you ruin my career!...Get this through your head...I don't want your puling brat, and that's final!" she railed.

"You—you—you don't know what you're saying! That's not you talking, Jenny. I won't believe that all you want from life is to be a big star. It's such an empty thing."

"That's exactly what I do want, and I'll do anything—anything to get there. Do you hear? Anything! I'm going to be the biggest star around and nobody's going to stop me! Do you understand?"

"By all means keep your career. Let's see how much love and warmth it'll give you."

That scene was the sounding of the death knell to any enduring happiness they might have enjoyed. The next day Jeanette had a miscarriage. She tried to patch things up, but Nelson was still angry and disillusioned. He rebuffed her and promptly attached himself to a little blonde starlet, Anita Louise.

Out to prove that two could play that game, Jeanette called up Gene Raymond, an actor whom she had dated a few times, and invited him to Lake Tahoe. He was so charming and supportive of her career that, when he took her by surprise with a marriage proposal, she found herself accepting. He would not thwart her ambitions. "Your career is all that matters," he told her. For reasons not entirely clear, she accepted his proposal, not anticipating the next act in the tragedy for which she alone had set the stage.

Gene immediately called MGM and announced the wedding. Louis was delighted, seeing in this a chance to get back at his insubordinate baritone. His star was getting married. He decided to plan the "biggest publicity caper ever."

During the filming of *Maytime*, their next film, the lovers made up and tried to call off the wedding but Louis refused, threatening to ruin Jeanette. In desperation, Nelson offered Gene $250,000 to break off the engagement. He happily accepted but Louis once again intervened, apparently threatening Gene's life. Louis, who reigned absolute over his stable of stars, was not given to idle threats. "I want to go on living for awhile yet," Gene said, backing out.

Nelson was in despair. He relying on alcohol and Jeanette on tranquilizers, they somehow got through the ordeal of filming.

The plot of *Maytime* filled Nelson with a sense of foreboding. He believed they had ruined their lives before and were repeating the pattern now. His dread was that the story they were acting out would come true.

In the film, a rising opera star, Marcia Mornay, agrees to a loveless marriage with her music teacher, Nicolai. That night in Paris she meets a young singer, Paul Allison, whom she realizes is her true love, spends one beautiful May Day with him, yet decides she will still marry Nicolai out of obligation. She stays with him for seven miserable years, then meets Paul again in New York.

Realizing she is still desperately in love, she asks Nicolai for her freedom. He agrees, but all too easily. Leaving her, he takes a gun, finds Paul and kills him. She arrives on the scene moments after only to hear him say, "That day did last me all my life."

In the end, alone and elderly, her soul, in springtime reverie,

Maytime, 1937

takes leave of the body as he comes to her singing. She takes his outstretched hand and their spirits, at last united, walk away into the blossoming May.

Nelson's fears were not unfounded. As Jeanette appeared determined to go ahead with the ceremony, his last hope was to kidnap her. He came to her house just before the wedding and dragged her downstairs and into his car.

"'Jenny, tell me you don't love me! Look me in the eye and tell me. If you can do that, I'll believe you and I'll never bother you again.' Jeanette eyed him defiantly at first, but her gaze faltered. She turned away in an effort to hide her tears. Seeing them, Nelson drew her to him. She stiffened and shrank back, stammering. 'No—no, I can't. I won't let you do this. It can't make up for my career. Don't you understand that? Love's important, but—'

"Nelson's voice echoed his desperation. 'Angel, Angel, what is there in you that only destroys us? People search all their lives for what we have, and you're willing to throw it all away with your wanton greediness.'

"Moved by his agony, she stepped closer to him, then caught herself and screamed, 'No, no, it's all arranged! The biggest wedding ever! My fans— I can't, I can't—I love my career more!'" He let her go, realizing he had lost her.

The wedding must have been one of the most crushing moments in Nelson's life. Guests remember his choked sobs filling the church throughout the ceremony. As planned, he sang "I Love You Truly" soon after the opening lines, "Dearly Beloved, we are gathered together here in the sight of God and in the face of this company to join together this man and this woman in holy matrimony..."—words he never thought he would hear with tears in his eyes.

His imploring rendition of the song mirrored her singing of "Indian Love Call" to him in *Rose Marie* when he, as a Canadian Mountie, arrests her brother. With the most impassioned plea in the history of film, she begs him if he loves her to turn back. Neither in the wedding nor on film did either swerve from their chosen course, but the movie at least had a happy ending.

No sooner had she gotten to Hawaii with her new husband, than she discovered her terrible mistake: he was gay. She threatened to have the marriage annulled; he threatened that if she went back to Nelson, he would plaster the scandal across every front page.

Jeanette was caught between two ages. In the harsher standards of the '30s where movie stars were paragons of perfection, she determined not to mar her angelic image and once again chose fame over personal happiness. Jeanette sadly resigned herself to the rocky road she had taken, realizing with increasing despair that she had ruined her life and Nelson's... She knew it was all her fault, that Nelson really was real, the sweetest guy she'd ever known, and the only one who had ever loved her truly. The guilt would gnaw at her to the end of her days.

Meanwhile, Louis' publicity machine was grinding out stories

> *Jeanette was caught between two ages. In the harsher standards of the '30s where movie stars were paragons of perfection, she determined not to mar her angelic image and once again chose fame over personal happiness.*

of the Raymonds' marital bliss and the fan magazines and gossip columns were full of it. They kept up the façade, attending social functions arm-in-arm and playing the role of the happy couple.

Nelson and Jeanette filmed *Girl of the Golden West*, woodenly doing their jobs. It is their only film without a love duet, as she couldn't sing "Obey Your Heart," written for the movie, without breaking down. By the next film, *Sweethearts*, the situation for her was becoming intolerable.

According to Diane and Sharon, one night she went out looking for Gene to keep a social engagement and finally found him in bed in a gay club. Jeanette collected his clothes and dragged him out to the sneers of other gay couples.

That night she went back to Nelson "for good," moving out of her house a few days later when Gene hit her, badly bruising her face. Nelson, always fiercely protective of her, beat up Gene soundly enough to send him to the hospital for two weeks. The lovebirds moved into a cottage in Burbank and played at being normal people. Neighbors still remember them as "that nice married couple who liked to ride horses."

Jeanette filed for divorce and *Sweethearts* continued, both of them now demonstrating their love in every word and glance. She became blissfully pregnant and this time they both wanted an instant marriage. They planned a home together in Bel Air with a nursery done in pink and lavender; all their dreams were about to come true.

Until Louis saw them together and realized they were in love. Furious was not the word. Jeanette told him that Gene was a homosexual, that she'd had enough, and that she was getting a divorce; Louis forbade it.

"*I* understand, but the box office won't understand.... Tell me another word and I'll destroy you

Offscreen – a moment of happiness

57

both." But both Jeanette and Nelson stood firm.

Nevertheless, Louis' threats had the desired effect. The next day Jeanette collapsed and fell down the high ramp on which the musical extravaganza was being filmed. She was six months

Sweethearts, 1938

pregnant. Nelson picked her up and took her to the hospital, her dress soaked in blood. She had a miscarriage, he collapsed, and they awoke to the news that she could never have another child. The baby, a boy, lived for two days.

Louis' threats again kept them apart. He told Jeanette that if they didn't stop seeing each other, Nelson would be found "floating on his face feeding the fishes.... Either you straighten up or I'll sic my boys on him, and I'm not fooling." As Louis had not-too-well hidden ties to the underworld, she believed him.

Jeanette returned to Gene without telling Nelson of her decision. Characteristically, he internalized the pain, declaring he never wanted to see her again. He went into a tailspin, keeping irregular hours, drinking, and finally getting sick.

Then, *Farewell to Dreams* reports, the story took another strange twist. Ann Franklin, a casual acquaintance, dropped by Nelson's house with a deliberate plot in mind. She got him drinking, which, combined with his depression and medication-induced fuzziness, weakened his will. She asked him to marry her. He, always an irrational drunk, agreed. After all, Jeanette wasn't the only one who could get married. He awoke on the train going home from Las Vegas to the voice of his new bride. He had no recollection of the event and ever thereafter averred that the judge must have been bribed to have married a man in that state.

Sharon Rich discovered that Ann, in order to prevent Nelson from later annulling the marriage, had had incriminating pictures taken to prove that it had been consummated.

When Jeanette heard the news, she tried to kill herself, taking almost an entire bottle of sleeping pills. She gradually recovered and soon began production of *New Moon* (1940). They were cool to each other at first, then rediscovered their love and decided they couldn't be apart.

She moved back to their little house but Louis found out again. He forced them apart: "The only time I want to see you two together is in front of the camera, no place else." During that film, they were forced to go through the agony of staying on opposite sides of the set. But he couldn't keep them apart for long. They began seeing each other again, vowing to be more careful.

Finally things came to a head when Ann Eddy went to Louis and complained about her ever-absent husband. Louis got furious and called Jeanette a whore. Nelson nearly strangled him and quit, buying out his studio contract. Jeanette did convince him to finish out their current and last film, *I Married an Angel* (1942).

Jeanette's career now meant little or nothing to her beside her love for Nelson. She ceased to be as exacting of herself and consequently her performance suffered. Louis decided not to pick up the option on her contract.

Although she made three more films and gave a number of plays, war benefits, concerts and actually sang opera as she had always dreamed, her career never picked up to full steam.

Their public lives were now reversed. Jeanette was too old to play a romantic lead but Nelson was still in demand. He made four more well-received films and continued giving concerts and doing nightclub acts for the rest of his life.

In 1946, Jeanette suffered a nervous breakdown. From there on, her health was a constant problem. In 1948 she had her first heart attack.

During this latter period, both Nelson and Jeanette were apathetic about fixing up their lives. It was as though things had already gone too far and they might as well wait for the next round and another opportunity.

He had to keep working because his wife had either tied up or spent all his money. He didn't even have enough to buy Jeanette and himself a house in Scottsdale, Arizona, where they planned to retire together.

In the meantime, the twin flames of stardom lived on with their respective spouses. Which brings up one of the unanswered questions of their story: why didn't they each get a divorce? By 1950, surely divorce was not such a stigma as it had been in 1937.

On Nelson's side, Ann refused to give him his freedom although he begged her. Jeanette probably stayed with Gene out of sympathy in response to his carefully contrived "I'll-never-do-it-again" weeping scenes, begging for forgiveness on bended knee.

Another reason Jeanette and Nelson may not have divorced their 'paper mates' is that they were already married! Since publishing her book, Sharon Rich has uncovered evidence which leads her to believe that Nelson was already married to Jeanette when he married Ann! Some of her sources mentioned that Jeanette and Nelson had gone down to Mexico to get married. Sharon believes this took place while Jeanette was pregnant during the filming of *Sweethearts*. This is especially plausible because the strongminded Nelson, if true to character, would never have allowed his baby to be born with another man's name.

There they could have gotten a proxy divorce without Gene present and been married quickly. Then, when Nelson married Ann,

LOVE WINS OUT

she could have blackmailed him with the charge of bigamy. That would have been enough to keep him tied to her for life. Now divorce would have created a scandal with reverberations casting a shadow not only on Jeanette's career, but also on her morality.

Thus, the fact that now neither one tried to hide their continuing love for each other may be explained by their sense of its rightness as well as its lawfulness secured by marriage, albeit secret.

Their devotion spanned the miles. Once, when Nelson received a slightly disturbing letter from Jeanette while on tour in Australia, he canceled his engagements and flew back to Hollywood because he had a bad feeling about it. When he discovered she was OK (or pretended to be), he felt sheepish.

At some point, Gene began to take more control of her life, forcing her to sell their house and move into an apartment. Nelson was constantly traveling, unaware of her deteriorating physical condition, for she kept from him till the end her painfully bad (broken) heart.

She wasted away slowly as Gene and the maid neglected to feed her and took away her phone to prevent her from calling Nelson. Gene gave her sleeping pills much of the time to keep her quiet. If she had not had the tremendous guilt gnawing at her, she might have had more interest in living, but, as her sister Blossom said, "It was the guilt that killed her."

When she died on January 14, 1965, Gene was at her bedside; delirious, she thought he was Nelson. With her last breath she said across eternity to the one who had loved her soul from the beginning, "I love you."

Like Romeo, Nelson sought to follow his Juliet but he was thwarted in his every attempt at self-destruction. Finally he collapsed during a show in Florida two years after her death and died a few hours later. We may hope that as in *Maytime* she greeted him with a song as he stepped lightly out of his careworn body.

In octaves of light they could await their next entrance on the stage of life, a chance to build their lives anew, this time to make the choice to conquer pride and ambition...for Love. And in a place where the Louis B. Mayers or Gene Raymonds or Ann Franklins would have no power over their spirits: for they had truly been tried and made white in the fires of their self-induced adversity. Wise to the forces that assail real Love and, above all, protective of their marriage made in heaven, they would realize on earth their most sacred secret hope—to be one forevermore.

And nothing and no one would come between them—for without Love, life is "as sounding brass or tinkling cymbal....For now we see through a glass darkly but then face to face." And the decree of the Lord God upon the twin flames he had made would not be denied: "What therefore God hath joined together let no man put asunder."

For more information about the lives and romance of Jeanette and Nelson, contact the Mac/Eddy Club, P.O. Box 1915, Burbank, CA 91507. Excerpts from *Farewell to Dreams* by Diane Goodrich and Sharon Rich, copyright 1979 the Jeanette MacDonald/Nelson Eddy Friendship Club, Inc., used with permission.

Index of Scripture

See "The Past Is Prologue" in *The Lost Teachings of Jesus I*, pp. xxiii–lxi.

Genesis
2:9	29, 36n.2, 285
2:9, 17	285
3:22, 24	29, 36n.2, 285
4:3–8	90–91
6:4	101, 121n.2
13:10–13	48
18:16–19:28	48
41:50–52	135, 148n.6
46:20	135, 148n.6
48	135, 148n.6

Exodus
3:5	204
6:6–8	144
12:1–14	276
13:21, 22	72
14:19, 20, 24	72
17:8–13	11
20:13	177
20:17	177
29:45, 46	144
33:16	62

Leviticus
11:44, 45	144
20:24, 26	62
26:12, 13	144

Numbers
14:14	72
16:2	101, 121n.2

Deuteronomy
5:17	177
5:21	177
29:26	46
30:19	62, 136, 162
32:4, 18, 30, 31	305
32:10	194

Joshua
5:13–15	18, 121n.4
5:15	204

7:6	233
23:16	46
24:15	61, 103, 144, 150, 158

I Samuel
1:9–3:21	148n.18
8:8	46
12	148n.18

II Samuel
13:19	233

Nehemiah
9:12, 19	72

Job
1:6–12	144
1:6–22	110
2:1–6	144
2:1–10	110
5:22	20
20:15	177
20:16	177
22:18, 19	20
42:10–17	110

Psalms
2:4	20
17:8	194
20:1	191
23:5	51
37:12, 13	20
50:15	187, 191
52:3–5	187
52:5	62
52:6, 7	20
55:22	172, 201
59:8	20
59:16	191
61:2	305
70	229
77:2	191
82:6	144

86:7	191	**Ezekiel**	
100:4	77	1:4	27, 167, 295, 296
110:4	83		
118:22, 23	76, 206, 214n.5	3:18, 20	182
120–134	284, 294n.3	26:1–4, 19–21	216
149:6	158	28:1–10	216
		31	216
Proverbs		32	216
7:2	194	33:6, 8	182
		33:7	167
Song of Solomon		37:1–14	142
2:1	265		
		Daniel	
Isaiah		7:9, 13, 22	66n.2
2:10–22	208	12:1	121n.4
7:14	138		
9:6	151	**Hosea**	
9:6, 7	138	2:23	197
11:9	20, 42		
13:6–16	208	**Nahum**	
14:5–27	216	1:7	191
14:12–19	17		
30:20	46	**Habakkuk**	
30:20, 21	138	1:13	127
32:4	188	2:14	20
34:1–8	208		
34:8	87, 161	**Zephaniah**	
38:17, 18	216	1:15	191
53:8	62		
59	149–53	**Zechariah**	
60:1, 2, 18–22	153–54	2:8	194
61:1–3	154	4:6	300
61:2	87, 161, 208, 295		
		Matthew	
62	295	1:22, 23	138
62:6	323	2:1–16	1
63	295	2:2	232–33
63:4	87, 161, 208	2:16	232–33
65:25	42	3:8	162
		3:12	177, 208
Jeremiah		4:19	197
11:10, 13	46	5:6	284
16:16	178, 197	5:21	177
16:19	196	7:1	301
17:5	130	7:15	317
23:1	151	7:15–18, 20	111
23:5, 6	147	8:11	197
31:33, 34	149–50	9:17	295
33:15, 16	147	10:6	141
46:10	161	10:7–10	99n.14
50:15, 28	87	10:9, 10	232
51:6, 11	87	10:28	8, 156
		10:34	34, 305
Lamentations		10:36	104
2:18	194	10:42	49, 75

11:3	230	13:20	64, 78, 85, 292, 304
11:12	31		
12:30	178	13:21–23	3
12:36	187	14:32–42	231, 235
12:37	144	14:58	14
13:12	50, 304	14:61–64	298
13:24–30, 36–43	220, 291	16:15, 16	197
13:33	136	16:16	181
13:36–43	234		
13:38	292	**Luke**	
13:45, 46	52	3:8	162
13:57	178	3:17	177
14:28–31	90	4:24	178
15:24	141	5:37, 38	295
16:19	177	6:37	301
18:6, 10, 14	59	7:19, 20	230
18:11–14	47	8:18	50, 304
18:14	84	9:3	232
18:18	177	10:4	232
18:20	234	10:18	17
19:23, 24	235	11:23	178
19:27–30	235	12:32	300
19:28	233, 304	13:21	136
21:12, 13	298	13:29	197
21:18–22	298	17:1, 2	59
21:42	76	17:20, 21	3
21:42, 44	206, 214n.5	17:34–36	47, 76
24:14	197	19:13	125
24:22	64, 78, 85, 292, 304	19:26	50
		20:17, 18	206, 214n.5
24:23–26	3	21:22	87
24:27, 28	134	22:28–30	233, 304
24:30	304	22:35–38	232
24:40, 41	47, 76	22:39–46	231
25:1–13	88	22:62	237
25:29	50, 304		
25:31–46	208	**John**	
25:41–46	232	2:13–17	298
26:36–46	231, 235	3:18	181
26:63–65	298	3:19	316
27:51	38	3:30	3
28:19	197	4:44	178
28:20	197	6:53	3
		8:23	87
Mark		9:4	269, 287
1:17	197	9:4, 5	55
2:22	295	9:39	266
4:25	50, 304	10:22–39	298
6:4	178	10:34	144
6:7–9	232	12:32	42
8:36	177	12:35	269, 287
9:42	59	12:35, 36	55
11:12–14, 20, 21	298	13:25	230
11:15–17	298	13:27	144, 231
12:10, 11	76	17:12	16, 84

18:4–8	302
21:15–17	300

Acts
2:17, 18	197
4:10–12	76, 138
7:33	204
7:48	14
9:1–20	34
13:47	196
17:24	14
22:1–15	34
26:9–18	34

Romans
3:23	219
6:6	206
8:17	187, 202
8:26, 27, 34	193
11:16	203
12:1	179
12:15	180
13:9	177

I Corinthians
3:13–15	61, 86, 150, 223, 289
6:2, 3	233, 304
9:27	17
10:4	305
11:24	36
12:4–10	71
15:40, 44	30
15:47–49	30
15:53	163
15:53, 54	77

II Corinthians
5:1	14
5:17	242
6:14–18	321
6:17	62
11:14	17

Galatians
4:1–7	73
6:5	208
6:15	242

Ephesians
2:19–22	76
2:20	138
3:16	72
4:22–24	206

Philippians
2:5, 6	298

Colossians
1:16	187
3:9, 10	206

II Thessalonians
2:3, 4	16, 84

II Timothy
2:15	285
3:7	124
4:1	187

Hebrews
2:3	158, 221
4:12	76, 158, 183
5:5–10	83
6:19, 20	83
7:1–3	83
7:14–22	83
9:11, 24	14
9:25	162
10:7, 9	36n.2, 266

James
1:12	38, 111
1:18	203

I Peter
1:7	61, 86, 289
2:6, 7	76, 138
2:6–8	206, 214n.5
3:4	72, 193
4:5	187
4:12	61, 86
4:12, 13	289
4:18	181
5:8	19, 204

I John
3:14	177
3:15	177
4:18	305

Jude
12, 13	17

Revelation
1:10	295
1:16	158, 322
2:7	29, 36n.2, 285
2:10	38, 111

1985 Index of Scripture

2:17	78–79	16	104
3:4, 5	126–27	16:2	121n.4
3:11	46	16:7	42
3:12	72	17:8	109, 216
6:1–8	40, 64, 76, 104, 134	19:2	42
		19:11	321
6:9–11	126–27	19:11–14	314
6:13	17	19:11–16, 21	113
7:3	78, 147n.1	19:20	110
7:9, 13, 14	126–27	20:1–3	16, 109, 216
8:10, 11	17	20:10, 14, 15	110
9	17	20:14	20
9:1	17	21:1, 2	118–19
9:1, 2, 11	107, 109	21:2	63
9:1–11	216	21:8	110
9:4	78	21:9–11, 18–21	63
10:1, 2, 8–11	182	21:12, 21	196
10:11	182	22:1, 2	20
11:7	109, 216	22:2, 14	29, 36n.2, 285
11:17, 18	309	22:11	77
12:1	318–19	22:15	180
12:1–9, 13	244	22:20	242
12:3, 4	10		
12:3–10	16	**Enoch***	
12:4	17	7–9	46
12:5	77	18:14–16	17
12:7	121n.4	20:5	121n.4
12:10	25n.2, 226	21:3	17
12:12	204	40:8	121n.4
14:4	203	85:2, 4	17
14:6	17, 305	87:2, 5	17
15:1, 6–8	104	89:32, 33	17

*References to the Book of Enoch are from the translation by Richard Laurence. This translation along with all the Enoch texts can be found in *Forbidden Mysteries of Enoch: The Untold Story of Men and Angels* by Elizabeth Clare Prophet (Livingston, Mont.: Summit University Press, 1983).

FOR MORE INFORMATION

For more information about the Keepers of the Flame fraternity and monthly lessons; dictations of the Ascended Masters published weekly as Pearls of Wisdom; Summit University three-month and weekend retreats; quarterly conferences which convene at the Royal Teton Ranch, a 33,000-acre self-sufficient spiritual community-in-the-making; Montessori International private school for children of Keepers of the Flame preschool through grade six; the Ascended Masters' library and study center nearest you; the Summit University Service/Study Program with apprenticeship in all phases of organic farming, ranching, macrobiotic cooking, construction, publishing and related community services; a free catalogue of books and audio- and videocassettes on the teachings of the Ascended Masters dictated to their Messengers, Mark L. Prophet and Elizabeth Clare Prophet, call or write Summit University Press, Box A, Livingston, Montana 59047-1390. Telephone: (406) 222-8300.

All at the ranch send you our hearts' love and a joyful welcome to the Inner Retreat!

Reach out for the **LIFELINE TO THE PRESENCE.** Let us pray with you!
To all who are beset by depression, suicide, difficulties or insurmountable problems, we say **MAKE THE CALL!** (406) 848-7441

Index

The feature articles "On Soul Mates and Twin Flames" that appear in Books I and II of this Volume 28 of the Pearls of Wisdom are indexed separately at the end of Book II. For an alphabetical listing of many of the philosophical and hierarchical terms used in the 1985 Pearls of Wisdom, see the comprehensive glossary, "The Alchemy of the Word: Stones for the Wise Masterbuilders," in *Saint Germain On Alchemy: For the Adept in the Aquarian Age*.

Abortion, 318.
 (See *Life Begets Life*, 16-audiocassette album A83034; *Abortion Update—Exposé: The Controllers and the Destroyers of the Human Race*, 8-audiocassette album A83135)
Acceleration, 292
Addictions, 48, 288
Afghan nation, 232
Afghanistan, 139.
 (See "Genocide Chic: Afghanistan—How Long Before the Horror Comes Home?" *The Coming Revolution: The Magazine for Higher Consciousness*, Summer 1986, pp. 58–65, 95–96; Summit University Forums: *Karen McKay on the People's Struggle for Freedom in Afghanistan*, 2 audiocassettes B85109–B85110 or 3 videocassettes 3304-16 to 3304-18; *Elizabeth Clare Prophet Interviews Representatives of the Afghan Freedom Fighters*, 2 audiocassettes B85117–B85118 or videocassette 3304-09; *Dr. Robert Simon on Emergency Medicine for the Afghan Freedom Fighters*, 2 audiocassettes B85115–B85116 or videocassette 3304-10)
Ahura Mazda, 228n.1
Aigli, Mount, 184
Alchemical marriage, 280
Ambitions, your, 235–36
America, 135–36; calls for the defense of, 18; New Jerusalem, 306; people of, 220; strengthening the spine of, 267. *See also* Central America; United States
Anchor, 63
Angelic hosts, denial of prayers to, 247–48
Angels: golden-flame, 53; nine Choirs of, 251; order of, 248; who answer to Archangel Michael's command, 18; who strayed, 16–17; of Zarathustra, 226. *See also* Archangels; Fallen angels.
 (See 1986 *Pearls*, nos. 25–34, pp. 227–330; nos. 51–57, pp. 459–518; *The Healing Power of Angels* I and II, 12-audiocassette albums A86040, A86055 or 2-videocassette albums V8616-0, V8609-0)
Anger, subconscious, 91, 92
Anu, 19, 26n.14
Aquino, Benigno S., 139, 148n.14, 314
Archangels, 269; preach the Everlasting Gospel, 17. *See also* Angels; Gabriel, Archangel; Jophiel, Archangel; Michael, Archangel; Uriel, Archangel.
 (See *Vials of the Seven Last Plagues: The Judgments of Almighty God Delivered by the Seven Archangels*, paperback, 206 pp.; 1981 *Pearls*, nos. 4–15, pp. 43–186; *The Class of the Archangels*, 8-audiocassette album A8100)
Aries, Dark Cycle in, 25n.2
Arizona, 275
Art, 31
Arthur, King, 37–38
Ascended Masters, 203; when you place yourselves at the feet of the, 183. *See also* Masters
Ascension, 41, 93, 108; Ascension service, 222–23; earn your, 288; focuses for, 117; mark of achievement, 84; open door for, 134; reward of, 235–36; school of, 105.
 (See *Dossier on the Ascension: The Story of the Soul's Acceleration into Higher Consciousness on the Path of Initiation*, paperback, 232 pp.; *A Retreat on the Ascension*, 8-audiocassette album A7953)
Ashram Notes, 99n.16
Astral quadrant, 20
Astrology, 89, 311, 323; divine and human, 311–12; divine and material, 28; of the Woman clothed with the Sun, 318–19
Atlantean scientists, 76
Atlantis, 67–68, 107
Attainment: challenged, 114; human and spiritual, 301; inner, 279; won long ago, 29. *See also* Mastery
Australia, 135–36; Australia-New Zealand-United States, (ANZUS) defense alliance, 147n.5; designs of

World Communism on, 139–40; stump to, 116–18
Authority, challenging those in, 299
Auto-self-hypnosis, 312

Babes, auras of new, 311. *See also* Child; Children
Bacon, Francis, 322.
(See *The Golden Age Prince: A Lecture on Francis Bacon*, 2-audiocassette album A83176)
Balance, 296–97; flame of, 62
Banff, 103
Bar, going into a, 105
Battle, that is physical, 269
Beast, 319; def., 46n
Beethoven, Ludwig van, symphonies of, 272
Bible. *See* Scriptures
Bitterness, in the belly, 2
Black magicians, 19
Blindness, spiritual, 286
Bodhisattva, marks of, 65
Bodies, physical and of clay, 30
Body, 287; not cleansed and purified, 76
Book, the little, 182
Boston, 21
Brothers and Sisters of the Golden Robe, 96, 99, 99n.17, 168
Buddha, of the Ruby Ray, 217. *See also* Gautama Buddha
Bull(s), 77; ten, 79n.15
Burden(s): essential to world freedom, 140–41; means to lift your, 39–40

Cain, his offering, 90–91
Calamities, in the wake of the removal of evil, 14. *See also* Cataclysm
Call(s): big, 64; compelled a response, 42; every problem resolved by, 18; God's answer implemented by, 33; one who makes the, 131–32; quantity of, 267; sustaining the body of God, 111; that cannot wait until tomorrow, 315; we must have the, 141. *See also* Decrees
Camelot, 145
Cancer, 8
Castaway, 17
Cataclysm, aversion of, 318–19. *See also* Calamities
Catherine of Siena, 129–30, 132n.9
Catholic Church, and prayers to angels, 247–48. *See also* Church(es)

Causal body, 73; focus of, 29
Causes, not brought to fruition, 314–15
Cave of Light, 103
Central America: Communism in, 78; corrupt ones in, 268.
(*See* Summit University Forum *Dr. Alejandro Bolaños on Nicaragua: The Untold Story*, 2 audiocassettes A87040 or 2 videocassettes GP87008)
Central Sun, 297. *See also* Great Central Sun
Chakra(s): attainment of the heart, 89; crown, 111; descent of the fire of the crown, 46; misuse of the base, 107; nexus of each, 281; perversion of the base-of-the-spine, 114; planetary, 112; seat-of-the-soul, 115; third eye, 115.
(See *Intermediate Studies of the Human Aura*, paperback, 212 pp.; *The Lost Teachings of Jesus I*, pp. 261–91)
Change: cosmic, 16; those who will not, 284
Chart, of the Presence, 49–50.
(See *Climb the Highest Mountain: The Path of the Higher Self*, pp. 274–84; *The Lost Teachings of Jesus I*, pp. 203–59)
Chastity, 95–96
Chela(s): gratitude for, 109; office of, 123–24, 126, 129, 142, 182, 236; terms of chelaship, 183.
(See *The Chela and the Path: Meeting the Challenge of Life in the Twentieth Century*, paperback, 168 pp.)
Child: child mind, 295–96; education of the, 296; the little, 157, 163–64; Order of the, 96, 99n.16, 100
Children, and education, 72–75. *See also* Babes; Youth.
(See *Freedom of the Child*, 4-audiocassette album A83131)
Christ: to be born, 1; defense of, 232; descending in your being, 279; encounter with, 34–35; the Judge, 304; mantle of, 130; office of, 124–25, 127, 128, 129; reason for the descent of, 266; in your arms, 5. *See also* Jesus; Son of God
Christ Mass, 29
Christ Self: high priest and Messenger, 230; mantle of your, 106, 124; Messenger communicating the Word of your, 231; speaking in your heart, 154; worthy of every offering, 205; your, 28
Christed ones, def., 125n
Christhood: individual, 298; personal, 123–24, 126; thy, 2; won and then

forsaken, 28; your, 212–13
Christians, 81. See also Church(es)
Christmas. See Christ Mass
Christos, Messenger's prayer to the, 241–42
Church(es): defend the, 127–28; defense of, 96; empty, 75; this, 8, 112. See also Catholic Church; Christians; Pastors; Religious institutions; Religious movements; Theology
Circle of Light, 3, 143
City Foursquare, 63, 64
Clare, Saint, 99n.15; Order of Francis and Clare, 95–96, 97, 125, 168, 274
Climb the Highest Mountain, 17
Co-creators, with God, 248
Coequality, with Jesus, 298
Coming Revolution in Higher Consciousness, magazine for, 313
Commeasurement, of your life, 210
Communion: from the heart of Jesus, 238–40; saints', 265; Teacher and Teaching in, 97; true, 36
Communism, 113–14, 136; in Central and South America, 78; designs of, on the Philippines, New Zealand and Australia, 139–40; ignorance spawned as, 45. See also International capitalist/communist conspiracy
Community: Great White Brotherhood looks to this, 221; responsibility entrusted to this, 51; this, 71
Complacency, 126
Condemnation, self-condemnation, 144
Confession: letter of, 212; purpose of, 205–6; of Saint Patrick, 185–202
Corotick, Saint Patrick's letter to, 176–79, 180–81
Cosmic beings, draw nigh to earth, 42
Cosmic clock, 18.
(See "The Cosmic Clock: Psychology for the Aquarian Man and Woman" in *The Great White Brotherhood in the Culture, History and Religion of America*, pp. 173–206; *The ABC's of Your Psychology on the Cosmic Clock: Charting the Cycles of Karma and Initiation*, 8-audiocassette album A85056)
Cosmic Council, 62
Courage, of the heart, 222
Court of the Sacred Fire, over Los Angeles, 119, 138
Cremation, 223
Criticism, 129
Crystal cord, symbol of, 37

Darjeeling: Darjeeling Council, 160–61; retreat at, 103
Dark Cycle: in Aries, 25n.2; in Taurus, 228n.4, 286.
(See 1969 *Pearls*, p. xi; no. 3, p. 10; no. 7, p. 30; pp. 249–53, 263–66)
Dark ones, 55; removal of, 319. See also Fallen one(s)
Darkness, high point of, 16
Death. See Passing; Transition
Deathless Solar Body, 17
Decreer, diligence and astuteness of the, 321
Decrees: to Archangel Michael, 243–64; at dawn, 158–59; dynamic, 131; fight through a burden, 141; freedom, 164; for the judgment, 307, 20.07; to Lady Venus, 282, 30.06; long, 77; our authority to step into your life, 161; to the Sun, 70, 20.20, 20.21. See also Call(s); Invocation(s).
(See *The Science of the Spoken Word*, paperback, 242 pp.; *Prayer and Meditation*, paperback, 360 pp.; *The Science of the Spoken Word: Why and How to Decree Effectively*, 4-audiocassette album A7736)
Depression, 91, 92
Devils, 225
Dictations, 265, 269; timely, 109; unfulfilled, 209. See also Teaching(s)
Discarnates, clearance of, 222–23
Disciple, 303
Discretion, 65
Discrimination, 65, 125
Disease, 8, 141
Dispensation(s), 29; analyze, 74
Divine plan, your, 165
Dots, Morya's three, 313, 315
Doubt, to be healed of, 165
Dreams, recurrent, 91
Drugs, 107, 108–9; culture of, 17; denizens who promote, 20; those purveying, 318.
(See *Saint Germain On Prophecy: Coming World Changes*, Book Four, pp. 95–132; "Pot Smoking in America," *Heart: For the Coming Revolution in Higher Consciousness*, Autumn 1983, pp. 34–51, 104–7, and Winter 1985, pp. 72–91; "The War on Drugs: Fighting to Lose," *The Coming Revolution: The Magazine for Higher Consciousness*, Summer 1986, pp. 32–41, 80–89; *Marijuana: The Death Drug*, 4-audiocassette album A7928)
Dweller on the threshold: accommodation of, 87; binding and judgment of, 319; bound and taken, 320; challenged and bound and cast out, 90;

of rebellion against Maitreya, 91–92; slaying of, 84, 85–87; we must outsmart, challenge or bruise, 97.
(See 1983 Pearls, no. 6, p. 50; no. 36, pp. 383–92; no. 38, pp. 429–54; "The Lost Teachings of Jesus: On the Enemy Within," 2 audiocassettes B87097–B87098)

Earth: etheric matrix over, 60–61; image of the, restored, 63
Economy: karma in the, 104; teetering, 18; usurpers of God-economy, 103.
(See *Saint Germain On Prophecy: Coming World Changes*, Book Two, pp. 57–92)
Education: and children, 72–75; commitment to, 45; deterrence to darkness, 51; by the heart, 40; spiritual, 52; systems of, 296. See also School(s).
(See *The Education of the Heart*, 16-audiocassette album A83095; *Education in the Age of Aquarius*, 8-audiocassette album A7616)
Educators, false, 55. See also Teachers
El Morya: chosen to sponsor Messengers and this organization, 103; mantle of, 208–9; at Summit University, 204; sword of, 145–46; waged strategic warfare, 321; a warning to his chelas, 179–80.
(See *Lords of the Seven Rays: Mirror of Consciousness*, Book One, pp. 21–78, and Book Two, pp. 7–64; *The Sacred Adventure*, hardback, 152 pp.; *Morya: The Darjeeling Master speaks to his chelas on the Quest for the Holy Grail*, paperback, 436 pp.; *The Chela and the Path: Meeting the Challenge of Life in the Twentieth Century*, paperback, 168 pp.; *El Morya: Chohan of the First Ray*, 2-audiocassette album A7626)
Elders, of the Church, 130–31
Electronic belt, 85–86, 97; clamoring and clanking the, 92; planets in orbit in, 89
Elementals, serve under the Elohim, 248
Elohim, brought forth the creation, 248.
(See 1978 Pearls, nos. 8–27, pp. 39–144, 319–445; 1982 Pearls, nos. 7–14, pp. 65–168; *The Seven Elohim in the Power of the Spoken Word*, 4-audiocassette album A7636; *The Class of Elohim*, 8-audiocassette album A8204)
Endurance, 237
Enemy, your worst, 104
Enki, 19, 26n.14
Enlil, 19, 26n.14
Eriel, 275
Error, unawareness of, 310
Etheric body, 66; restored to earth, 272

Etheric matrix, over the planet, 60–61
Etheric octave, plane: in the mountains, 287; portals of, 276; rise to the level of, 292
Etheric quadrant, black magicians misuse, 19
Ethnic groups, 281n.2
Everlasting Gospel, 305; archangels preach, 17
Evil: Absolute, 285; challenging, 5
Example, on your part, 300
Excalibur, 37–38, 42–43, 111, 145
Exposés, of injustice, 71

Fallen angels, 237; actions of, 232; known as 'vipers', 48n; never been able to synthesize love, 31; rebellion of, 14; twelve renegade, 25n.2. See also Fallen one(s).
(See *Forbidden Mysteries of Enoch: The Untold Story of Men and Angels*, paperback, 516 pp.)
Fallen one(s): attack of, 143–44; desperate to prevent knowledge of the Word, 278; entanglements with, 320–21; judged, 266; outplaying of, 291; overstepped their bounds, 110; study their evil ways, 232–33. See also Dark ones; Fallen angels; Godless; Serpents; 'Vipers'; Wicked
Farmers, invocations for, 76
Fast(ing): with regularity, 212; ritual of, 324n.11; weekly, 321
Fátima, prophecy of, 162.
(See "Fátima Update," 4 audiocassettes K87033–K87036)
Fear, to be healed of, 165
Fervor, path of, 137–38
Fire, infolding itself, 27–28, 29, 295
First ray, 102–3
Forgiveness, 218–21
Four and Twenty Elders, over Los Angeles, 112, 138, 316–17
Francis, Saint, 99; biography of, 99n.14; and the Franciscan Order, 99n.15; Kuthumi as, 81; Order of Francis and Clare, 95–96, 97, 125, 168, 274
Free will, experiment in, 231
Freedom: of the nations, 159; those in the service of, 133–34
Friday night service, 222–23, 224, 225
Funds, of the Mafia laundered, 318

Gabriel, Archangel: came to inspire monarchs, 216; teachings of, 285.

See also Archangels.
(See *Mysteries of the Holy Grail*, paperback, 504 pp.)
Gautama Buddha, 40; beneath the Bo tree, 44, 44n.8; prayer of Justinius to, 293.
(See *Quietly Comes the Buddha*, paperback, 160 pp., or 1975 *Pearls*, nos. 17-29, pp. 89-146; 1983 *Pearls*, nos. 1-22, pp. 1-176; no. 39, pp. 463-78; no. 41, pp. 485-94)
Genetic engineering, 107
Genetic implants, 15
Gethsemane, initiation in, 235
God: be converted to, 150; coming through the divine hatch, 28; when, reveals Himself, 300; where you are, 48-49; will come to you, 146; will not fail you, 162; will use the individual, 322-23; in you, 78; your, 87
"God Bless America," by Irving Berlin, 249
Godless, judgment of, 32-33. *See also* Fallen one(s)
Good, Absolute, 285
Goodness, human, 90-91
Government(s): forces moving against your, 140; God-government, 310-11; mantle of Christ-illumined, 71; upon the Rock of Christ, 138; of this nation, 316; toppling, 21; usurpers of God-government, 103
Grand Teton, 41
Great Central Sun, forcefield of the, 112. *See also* Central Sun
Great Central Sun Magnet, 7
Great White Brotherhood: meaning of, 163; reaction to, 231.
(See *The Great White Brotherhood in the Culture, History and Religion of America*, paperback, 448 pp.)
Guru(s): call of the, 38; false, 91-92, 312; mantle of, 125, 127; mantle of, upon the Messenger, 132n.3, 311

Habit patterns, 292
Half Dome, 103
Hatred, 42; of the Christ, 40
Healing, dispensations of, 75.
(See *The Science of the Spoken Word*, pp. 136-49; "Healing through the Transfiguration," *Heart: For the Coming Revolution in Higher Consciousness*, Winter 1985, pp. 50-59, 119-23, also on 2-audiocassette album A84070 or videocassette V3303-03; "Herbs: You Can Heal Yourself through Nature's Pharmacy," *The Coming Revolution — The Magazine for Higher Consciousness*, Summer 1986, pp. 16-25, 78-79; *Emerald Matrix: The Perfect Light*, 16-audiocassette album A82121; *Maria Treben on Self-Healing through Nature's Pharmacopoeia*, 4-audiocassette album A84184 or videocassette V8601-1; *Dr. Vasant Lad on the Ancient Science of Ayurvedic (Hindu) Medicine*, 4-audiocassette album A84208 or videocassette V8602-1; *The Conquest of Cancer*, 2 audiocassettes S88001 or 2 videocassettes V88001; *From the Edgar Cayce Readings*, audiocassette S86003 or videocassette V8603-1; *The Gerson Therapy*, 2 audiocassettes S88003 or 2 videocassettes V88003; *Homeopathy*, audiocassette S86004 or videocassette V8604-1; *The Path to Vibrant Health*, 2 audiocassettes S88005 or 2 videocassettes V88005; series of 2-audiocassette albums of healing services; *Health through Living Foods*, 2 videocassettes V88007)
Health, 82, 97
Heart: development of, 75; sacred, 63, 64
Heaven, proximity of earth and, 276
Hedron, 275
Helios: coming of, 70, 70n.2; delivered Saint Patrick, 191; and Vesta, 71
Hemisphere, this, 268
Herods, planetary, 1
Himalaya, Mount, 18
History, going backwards in, 234
Holy Spirit, descent of, 323.
(See *Climb the Highest Mountain: The Path of the Higher Self*, pp. 408-44)
Horsemen, Four, 64-65, 76, 78, 104
Humility, and boldness, 203-4
Hymn to the Sun, 158-59

"I AM He!" 302
I AM Presence: glory of, 153; office of, 125
I AM THAT I AM: consciousness of, 127; in you, 211
Idolatry, study, 111
Illumination: fire of Jophiel for, 142; Messenger's invocation for, 56; more than ordinary momentum of, 40-41; those who do not pass on their, 50
Impostors, 111
India, 18
Individual: answer that lies with the, 221; falsely elevated, 316; strength of the, 168-69, 206
Indulgence, as a term in Roman Catholicism, 98n.13
Industrial Park, 6, 9n.6
Infamy, erased, 58
Iniquities, between you and God, 149. *See also* Sin(s)

Initiation(s): of the Dark Night of the Spirit, 266; due in the cosmic cycles, 285; necessary, 97; path of, 283–84; system of, 312–13; which every one of you has had, 113. See also Testing; Tests
(See 1975 Pearls, nos. 49–53, pp. 263–84)
Inner Retreat: as a base and stronghold, 78; focalization of etheric octave, 104; how Lanello loves, 41; keeping the flame of, 6–7, 8, 21; lightbearers dedicated to, 141; Maitreya's School and Teaching at, 115; as the Mystery School of Maitreya, 294n.4; and the New Jerusalem, 63; as the Place Prepared, 4; salvation through, 23
Intellect, must be stepped up, 77
International capitalist/communist conspiracy, 21. See also Communism.
(See 1987 Pearls, no.3, pp. 39–72; The Psychology of Socialism: The Religion of Hatred, the Cult of Death, 4-audiocassette album A7892; The Religious Philosophy of Karl Marx, 4-audiocassette album A7896; Mother's Manifesto on the Manipulators of Capitalism and Communism, 3-audiocassette album A7938; Summit University Forum Professor Antony C. Sutton on the Capitalist/Communist Conspiracy, 2 audiocassettes A87054 or 2 videocassettes GP87017)
Invocation(s): attainment in the power of, 278–79; simple, 76–77. See also Decrees
Iran, 215–16, 218
Iraq, 215–16, 218
Ireland, 184–85; prayer vigil for, 185, 204–5, 207
Israel, children of, who complained, 6

Jerusalem, New: etheric matrix of the, 118–19; in North America, 305–6
Jesus: had to meet precisely what you must meet, 299; his crucifixion, 280; his travels to India, 2; his trial, 231; incarnation of the I AM THAT I AM, 230; lost years of, 34–35; when he descended trailing clouds of glory, 266; will go before you, 301–2; World Teacher, 49n.
(See The Lost Years of Jesus, paperback, 416 pp.; Prayer and Meditation, paperback, 360 pp.; Corona Class Lessons...for those who would teach men the Way, paperback, 504 pp.)
Job, 110
John of the Cross, Saint, 280.
(See Saint John of the Cross on the Living Flame of Love, 8-audiocassette album A85044)

Jophiel, Archangel, 20; does appear, 42; racing through the skies, 47. See also Archangels
Joseph, Saint, 274
Joy, sense of, 64
Judgment, 152; brought by Uriel, 54–55; call(s) of, 64, 158; of conspirators against the Eternal Youth, 59; daily, 289; judgment call(s), 225, 233–35, 291, 318; "For Judgment I AM come into the world," 266; of the lowest ten percent, 317–20; office of, 304; of Peshu Alga, 14–15, 17, 42; selective and discriminatory, 318; of the sympathizers and servants of Peshu Alga, 32–33; that begins in the base of the pyramid, 5
Justice: and Freedom, 147; system of, 112

Karma: balancing of, 105; of the second ray, 50, 52; world, 77; your, 89
Karmic Board: as dearest friends, 323; letters to, 32
Karmic ties, 104
Keeper(s) of the Flame: have turned the tide in America, 140; let them bear the burden of Saint Germain, 207–8; meaning of being a, 142; one-pointedness by, 315; succumbed to temptation, 6; who do not attend services and give their calls, 179
Keeper of the Scrolls, 14, 58, 323
Kieninger, Clara Louise, 44n.5.
(See Ich Dien, paperback, 254 pp.)
Knowledge, of this world, 71
Krishna, 242n.10
Kundalini, 109; activation and loosing of, 37–38; consuming and burning up of, 17; def., 48n; sacred fire of, 111
Kuthumi, 98; to assist you personally, 217; retreats of, 99n.17; and the Theosophical Society, 98n.1; World Teacher, 49n.
(See Prayer and Meditation, paperback, 360 pp.; Understanding Yourself: Opening the Door to the Superconscious Mind, paperback, 182 pp.; Studies of the Human Aura, paperback, 172 pp.; Corona Class Lessons...for those who would teach men the Way, paperback, 504 pp.)

Laggards, spiritual, 284
Lanello, 7; attainment in the power of invocation of, 278; Order of the Holy Child brought forth by, 96. See also Messenger(s).

(See *The Incarnations of the Magnanimous Heart of Lanello*, 2-audiocassette album series, including *Aesop* A8200, *Ikhnaton* A8243, *John Mark* A8255, *Longfellow* A83000, *Louis XIV* A82170, *Saint Bonaventure* A8220, and *Saladin* A8214)
"Lashback" (backlash), 19
Last Supper, 236, 237
Latticework, self as a, 219
Law: application of the, 160; individual responsibility to fulfill the, 181–83; training in, 313
Laxity, consciousness shifted into, 210
Leaders, 150–51
Leadership, of the nation, 205, 316
Lemuria: neutralization of misuses on, 67–68; restoration of, 273
Life: four stages of, 132n.4; those who pass from the screen of, 222–23
Light, 19; descends upon all, 57; effective increase of, 304–5; understanding of the, 160; your raising up of the, 137
Lightbearers, call to cut free, 277, 320–21
Limitation, self-limitation, 296–97
Living Flame of Love, 280
LORD, coming into the temple of the devotee, 301
Lord's Prayer, 248–49
"Lorica," 207
Los Angeles: Court of the Sacred Fire over, 119, 138; Four and Twenty Elders over, 112, 138, 316–17; interchange between New York and, 115; threefold flame fountain over, 112, 121n.16
Lost Years of Jesus, The, 34–36
Love, 31; intense, 303.
(See *Saint Germain On Alchemy: For the Adept in the Aquarian Age*, pp. 308–45)
Lucifer, 25, 34; one who determined to follow, 23; the one who turned aside, from his service, 32; rebellion of, 14; traduced by Peshu Alga, 25n.2.
(See *The Great White Brotherhood in the Culture, History and Religion of America*, pp. 231–37)

MacArthur, Gen. Douglas, 121n.1
Maharishi, 312
Mahasamadhi, 38; def., 44n.4
Maitreya, 63, 280; anti-Maitreya, 115; byword of initiates of, 203; coming of, 285; his clipper ship, 63; Mystery School of, 294n.4; name derived from Sanskrit, 58n; rebellion against, 92; ship of, 20.
(See 1975 *Pearls*, nos. 49–53, pp. 263–84; 1984 *Pearls*, nos. 6–22, pp. 53–166; nos.

37–46, pp. 327–86; no. 53, pp. 461–64; no. 54, pp. 465–70)
Mara, 44n.8
Marcos, President Ferdinand E., 139, 148n.14
Mary, Mother: Christmas Eve prayer to, 10–12 (See 1981 *Pearls*, pp. 3–4); mission to the nations called by, 133; presented as a child at the temple, 294n.3; at Summit University, 204.
(See *My Soul Doth Magnify the Lord!* paperback, 396 pp.)
Mass, prayer to Archangel Michael removed from, 247–48, 249
Master/disciple relationship, 89–90
Masters, face-to-face, 138. *See also* Ascended Masters
Mastery, in past ages, 281. *See also* Attainment
Media, 106; adverse, 143–44; bombardment through the, 20; media attack, 110, 121n.12, 127–28; misuse of the Word in the, 114; seraphim stand in the, 291
Meditation, which we have taught, 92
Melchizedek, 83
Mental quadrant, 19–20
Meru, God and Goddess, 40, 71
Meru, Mount, 18
Messenger(s): admonishments through the, 85; anointing of, 143, 221–22; astrology of, 311; the call to this, to come apart, 21–22; called upon the Karmic Board tens of thousands of times, 323; crown of victory upon the, 227; dependable for our purposes, 90; El Morya on, 124–25, 127–30, 125; in embodiment, 116; experienced the turning of worlds, 322; felt the momentum of Death and Hell, 266; had to surrender much, 236; have turned the tide in America, 140; having a, 3; history of, 215–16; initiations given to the, 284; Kuthumi's word from the, 82; learned to understand herself as a latticework, 219; as the lightning of our Brotherhood, 134; of the LORD, 230–31; with a mantle and an authority, 278–79; mantle of Guru upon the, 132n.3, 311; mantle of the office of, 142; mantle placed upon this, 133; must carry the flame of the Inner Retreat to the nations, 7; must personally and physically anoint souls, 142; necessity and protection

of the, 269; only difference between you and the, 211; our, 88; protection needed by those who wear the mantle of, 106; sending of the, 2–3; take not for granted our coming through the, 285; translation of the, 215; of Truth in this century, 93–94; victory of the sacred fire in the, 226; weight borne by the, 140–41; when the, leaves an area, 138–39; wherever the, places her feet, 117; will not stand between you and your transgressions, 144; witnesses the bottomless pit, 108. *See also* Lanello; Mother of the Flame.
(See *The Chela and the Path: Meeting the Challenge of Life in the Twentieth Century,* pp. 115–24; *Prayer and Meditation,* pp. 246–53)
Messenger's invocations, 10–11, 56, 66, 80, 120, 213, 241–42
Michael, Archangel, 121; Archangel Michael's Rosary, 243–64, 270; become chelas of, 110; call to, 277; chaplet to, 251–52; chelas enlisted in Archangel Michael's legions, 101; chelas enlisted in ranks of, 216; def., 121n.4; Electronic Presence of, 265; his decision in the hour of temptation, 245; Messenger's prayer to, 120; a most painful parting of, 23; perpetual vigil to, 268–69; Pope Leo XIII and the prayer to, 250; prayer to, removed from the Mass, 247–48, 249; qualifications for service with, 102–3, 106; stay very close to, 280–81; touch and Electronic Presence of, 24; at your side, 156–57. *See also* Archangels.
(See 1985 *Pearls,* no. 19, pp. 243–64; *Archangel Michael's Rosary for Armageddon,* 36-page booklet and single audiocassette B85108)
Middle East, 116, 216; laggard races in, 306; vengeance in the peoples of, 220–21
Ministering servants, 86.
(See 1985 *Pearls,* no. 42, pp. 501–20)
Money, laundered, 324n.8
Montessori, Maria, 74
Montessori Revolution, 73–74
Moodiness, 91
Morya. *See* El Morya
Mother: human and Divine, 83; Mother Flame, 68; World, 43, 46
Mother of the Flame, torch passed to, 44n.5

Motion-picture industry, 112–13
Mountain(s), 68; etheric plane in, 287
Mudra, earth-touching, 41
Murderous intent, 106
Music. *See* Rock music
Mystery school(s): coming of the, 285; held the flame, 102; of Maitreya, 294n.4; required, 93.
(*See* 1984 *Pearls,* no. 36, pp. 313–26)

Nazi, 33
Nephilim: gods called, 26n.14; as the people of the shem, 121n.2.
(See *Forbidden Mysteries of Enoch: The Untold Story of Men and Angels,* pp. 61–76, 265–303; *Planet Earth: The Future Is to the Gods,* 3-audiocassette album A8056)
Nevada, 275
New York: interchange between Los Angeles and, 115; third-eye chakra, 112
New Zealand, 139–40, 147n.5
Night, Dark, of the Spirit, 266
1984, year of the judgment of Peshu Alga, 25n.2
Nuclear holocaust, 34
Nuclear weapons, 136

Obedience, 95–96
Offering, acceptable, 90–91
One, Law of the, 168–69
Opportunity, today, 237
Order of Francis and Clare, 95–96, 97, 125, 168, 274
Order of the Brothers and Sisters of the Golden Robe, 96, 99; def., 99n.17
Order of the Child, 99n.16, 100
Order of the Golden Lily, 222–23
Order of the Holy Child, 96

Pallas Athena, 217
Parent(s), 72–73, 83–84
Passing, at the hour of, 26n.18. *See also* Transition
Passivity, 109
Pastors, judged, 298–99. *See also* Church(es)
Path, necessity of the, 277
Patrick, Saint: Archangel Jophiel called, 47; *Confession* of, 185–202; his letter to Corotick, 176–79, 180–81; life of, 169–75, 183–202; at Summit University, 204; take up his calling, 211–12; waged strategic warfare, 321
Patriotism, 140

Pearls of Wisdom: not read, 2; studying, 49. *See also* Teaching(s)
Persia, 215–16
Peshu Alga, 19, 25; final judgment and second death of, 14–15; judgment of, 17, 32–33, 42; original betrayal of God by, 25n.2; twin flame of, 33
Pestilence, 76
Philippines, 135, 139; casting down of the one called to, 313–14; events in, 148n.14; stump to, 116–18
Physical quadrant, 21
Pit, 234; bottomless, 107–8, 109, 117
Political parties, 137
Pope, defender of, 129–30
Pope Leo XIII, 250
Portia, 147
Poverty, 95–96
Prayer(s): hold the balance, 266–67; in public schools, 248–49; for vengeance, 162; which we have taught, 92
Preach(ing), the Word, 2, 209, 276–77
Preparedness, an hour for, 232
President, forces moving against your, 140
Problems, solution to, 137, 160
Prophecy: of darkness and destruction, 34; interpretation of, 71; which only you can fulfill, 161.
(See *Saint Germain On Prophecy: Coming World Changes*, paperback, 608 pp.; *Prophecy for the 1980s: The Handwriting on the Wall*, paperback, 184 pp.; "Saint Germain on Prophecy," 2 audiocassettes A87037; "Fátima Update," 4 audiocassettes K87033–K87036; "Halloween Prophecy 1987," 3 audiocassettes A87079 or 2 videocassettes GP87063; "Saint Germain On Prophecy from 1988 through the 1990s—the Astrology of World Karma," 3 audiocassettes A88024 or 2 videocassettes GP88019; "Saint Germain on Coming World Changes," videocassette V8606-1)
Prophets, who did not fail, 302
Psalms, 249
Psychology: healing of your, 82, 97; Kuthumi's promise to counsel you in personal, 217
Publishing: of the teaching, 52; of this activity, 275–76. *See also* Teaching(s)
Pyramid, upper levels of the, 31

Reaction, your, 98
Rebellion: against the Guru, 88–89; core, 91–92, 93; dweller of, 90; recognize, 286
Rebuke, responsibility for the, 181–82
Records, neutralization of, 67–68
Reincarnation, understanding of, 277
Religion(s): delivered to the people of Persia, 215–16; new world, 101–2. *See also* Theology
Religious institutions, 159–60
Religious movements, 34
Resurrection: meaning of, 287; to transcend the world, 305
Retreats, 103; travel to, 121n.4
Revolution, a spiritual, 269–70
Rhythm, 31
Rock music, 20, 107, 108–9; culture of, 17; those attacked by, 73–74.
(See 1987 *Pearls*, no. 36, pp. 327–68; "Rock and Roll in America," 4 audiocassettes B87069–B87072)
Roerich, Nicholas and Helena, 41, 44n.6.
(See *The Lost Years of Jesus*, pp. 239–80)
Rome, potentates of, 35
Royal Teton, retreat of the, 103
Royal Teton Ranch: has fulfilled Lanello's direction to this Messenger, 232; paying off of the, 78.
(See *Royal Teton Ranch News*, vols. 1, 2; "Starting a New Life: In a Self-Sufficient Spiritual Community in the Making," *The Coming Revolution: The Magazine for Higher Consciousness*, Summer 1986, pp. 26–31, 79–80)
Ruby fire, line of, 39
Ruby ray, science of, 287

Sabbath, 212
Saint Germain: accusation leveled against, 101–2; and his teaching, 226; was embodied as the Prophet Samuel, 148n.18.
(See *Lords of the Seven Rays: Mirror of Consciousness*, Book One, pp. 237–74, and Book Two, pp. 247–74; *Saint Germain On Alchemy: For the Adept in the Aquarian Age*, paperback, 544 pp.; *Saint Germain On Prophecy: Coming World Changes*, paperback, 608 pp.; 1977 *Pearls*, nos. 31–52, pp. 143–256; 1978 *Pearls*, nos. 1–7, pp. 1–38; *Saint Germain: Chohan of the Seventh Ray*, 2-audiocassette album A7648)
Saints: example of, 167–68; record of, 323
Samuel the Prophet, 148n.18
Sanat Kumara: call to, 277; his message concerning preaching of the Word, 209; legions who accompanied, to earth, 61; on Saint Patrick, 171–72, 175, 183–85; stands before

every lifestream, 61–62; volunteered to come to earth, 66n.2
Satan, in Pope Leo XIII's vision, 250
Saturday, penance on, 212
Scales, signifying balance, 63
School(s): of hard knocks, 82–83; prayer in public, 248–49. *See also* Education
Scorpio, 286
Scriptures, reincarnation taken from the, 277
Second death, 33
Second ray, of illumination, 41
Self: as a latticework, 219; lost identity and attainment of, 29; old, 4, 23; thy ascended, 59; True, 28, 206–7
Seraphim, 287; mark of a, 289; stand in the media, 291
Serapis Bey: at Luxor, 284–85; teaching on seraphim from, 291.
(See *Lords of the Seven Rays: Mirror of Consciousness*, Book One, pp. 149–81, and Book Two, pp. 135–68; *Dossier on the Ascension: The Story of the Soul's Acceleration into Higher Consciousness on the Path of Initiation*, paperback, 232 pp.; "Welcome to A Retreat on the Ascension" on *A Retreat on the Ascension*, 8-audiocassette album A7953)
Serpents: def., 291n; taking up of, 183–84. *See also* Fallen one(s)
Seventh ray: meaning of, 28; rituals of the, 31–32. *See also* Violet flame
Sheep, "feed my sheep," 300
Shepherds: to feed my sheep, 299–300; Shepherd's crook, 185
Shiva, in the Ascended Masters, 48
Silence, is consent, 179–80, 181
Sin(s): condition of, 210; confession of, 205, 239–40; consumed, 212; the will to, 206. *See also* Iniquities; Transgressions
Sirius, 311; God-government seated in, 310
Slavery, of personal karma, 171
Socialism, 'beast' of, 46
Solar plexus, 85
Son of God: commitment of one, 22; the lie of only one, 211; quickening and acceleration of the, 303. *See also* Christ
Soul: perfect the, 300; tender, 297–98
South Africa, 238.
(*See* Summit University Forum *Crossroads South Africa*, 2 audiocassettes A87061 or 2 videocassettes GP87029)
South America: Communism in, 78; corrupt ones in, 268

Soviet forces, 268
Soviet submarines, 115, 122n.18
Soviets, 116.
(See *Saint Germain On Prophecy: Coming World Changes*, Book Two, pp. 18–136, 190–99; 1987 *Pearls*, no. 3, pp. 39–72; Summit University Forums: *Tomas Schuman on Soviet Ideological Subversion*, 3-audiocassette album A84032 or 2 videocassettes 3304-01 and 3304-02; *Gen. Jan Sejna and Dr. Joseph Douglass, Jr.: Inside Soviet Military Strategy*, 3 audiocassettes B88016–B88018 or 3 videocassettes GP88001)
Spacecraft, 19.
(*See* "A Fantasia on the Duality of Good and Evil" on *Soul Liberation II*, 8-audiocassette album A7806; *Planet Earth: The Future Is to the Gods*, 3-audiocassette album A8056)
Spikenard, 284, 292
State of the Union message, 140
Story of the Irish Race, The, 169
Strategy, of Sirius, 315–16
Stubbornness, human, 284–85
Stump(ing): to Australia and the Philippines, 116–18, 147n.1; to the nations, 133–36, 138–39, 141–43, 145–46
Suicide: suicide entity, 228n.11; among teenagers, 223–24
Summit University: El Morya, Saint Patrick and Mother Mary at, 204–5; purpose of, 97, 168
Sword, of El Morya, 145–46
Synod of Laodicea, 247

Taurus, Dark Cycle in, 228n.4, 286
Teachers: becoming, 46–47, 49–50; false, 19, 54; of the Montessori revolution, 73–74; world, 51, 53. *See also* Educators
Teaching(s): of the Ascended Masters, 275–76; assimilation of the Ascended Masters', 1–3; exchange the, 51; false, 19; given because you need it, 285; know us through our, 88; necessity for this, 277; publishing the, 52; repeated in a mental manner, 50; surfeiting of, 235; those hungering and thirsting for this, 284; translated to ethnic groups, 272. *See also* Dictations; Pearls of Wisdom
Teenager(s), 186; suicide among, 223–24
Television sets, 73
Temple of the Sun, 70n.2
Temple of Victory, 216–17, 228n.5
Temptation, 236
Ten/four axis, clearing the, 286

Ten percent, judgment of the lowest, 317–20
Terrorism, 19; in Ireland, 185
Testing: by Maitreya, 39; to receive things permanent, 110–11. *See also* Initiation(s)
Tests, will increase, 237. *See also* Initiation(s)
Theology: of the Aquarian age, 211; liberation, 305. *See also* Religion(s)
Theosophical Society, 98n.1
Third ray, 275
Thoughtform, for 1985, 63–64
Threefold Flame Fountain, over Los Angeles, 112, 121n.16
Titicaca, Lake, 70n.2
Transgressions, of the Law, 144
Transition: in the hour of, 21; those making the, 50. *See also* Passing
Translation: Messenger's, 215; of Saint Germain's works into foreign languages, 226
Tree: of the knowledge of good and evil, 285; of Life, 29
Trial, 221, 231–32; fiery, 289
Tribes, twelve, of Israel, 148n.6
Truth: another name for the Universal Christ, 312; aura of the one who pursues, 322; in one individual, 313–14; power of, 217, 310
Turning point: a critical, 267; of life on earth, 61
Twin flames: to become gods of solar systems, 22; striving to meet one another, 27.
(*See* 1978 *Pearls,* nos. 34–47, pp. 177–246; *Twin Flames in Love I,* 8-audiocassette album A7856; *Twin Flames in Love II,* 3-audiocassette album A82155)
Two Witnesses, 71

Understanding, deeper, 53
United States, political parties in, 137. *See also* America
Uriel, Archangel, his report to the Lord of the World, 58–59. *See also* Archangels

Vatican Council II, 247
Vengeance, day of, 87–88
Venus, 274; souls of, 105–6
Venusians: rescue the fallen, 274–75; who have lost their way, 278
Vesta, 70, 70n.2
Victory: cannot be counted upon, 210; consecrated, 23; what has won every, 156
Victory, Mighty, Saint Patrick's vision of, 192
Vigil: for Ireland, 185, 204–5, 207; perpetual, 18, 268–69, 317; prayer, 117, 270
Violet flame: convert the nations by, 136–37; devours debris of the dweller on the threshold, 320; pave the way for, 135. *See also* Seventh ray. (*See The Science of the Spoken Word,* pp. 96–125; *Save the World with Violet Flame!* by Saint Germain, audiocassette B88019)
'Vipers', def., 48n. *See also* Fallen one(s)
Vision, year of, 65
Voice: of the living Word, 299; our gruff, 82–83

War, rumors of, 33. *See also* Battle
Warning, from Sanat Kumara, 62
Western Shamballa, 21, 39, 70n.2
Wicked, rebuke of the, 181–82. *See also* Fallen one(s)
Wisdom, flame of, 47
Woman: clothed with the Sun, 311, 318–19, 323; Divine, 271–72; laggard, 272; a little, 83; standing guard, 16
Women, an organization of and for, 273–74
Word: internalization of the, 28, 31; Law does require the spoken, 16; misuse of the, 114; nontransmission of the, 52; power of the spoken, 158–59; science of the spoken, 62; spoken and written, 313; voice of the living, 299; and Work as Alpha and Omega, 94; your attainment in the spoken, 114.
(*See The Liberating Power of the Word 1,* 6-audiocassette album A84035; *The Liberating Power of the Word 2,* 4-audiocassette album A84041)
World Teacher(s): def., 49n; keeping up with the, 75

Yogananda, Paramahansa, 41
Youth: judgment of conspirators against the Eternal, 59; as passive receivers of darkness, 108–9; the quest of, 35. *See also* Child; Children. (*See* "The Attack on Youth: Drugs, Alcohol, Nicotine, and Sugar" and "The Manipulation of Youth: Education and Family Life" on *Soul Liberation I,* 8-audiocassette album A7800)

Zarathustra, 228n.1